D1452765

THE
MEDIÆVAL
ARCHITECT

Frontispiece STRASSBURG CATHEDRAL. Detail of the west front begun in 1276 to the design of Erwin, master of the first German lodge of "freed masonry according to the English fashion" (see p. 138)

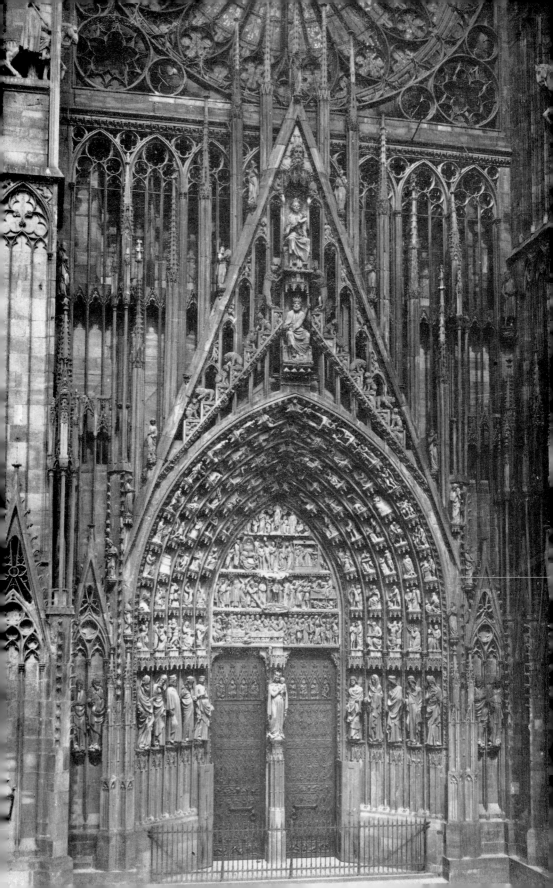

THE
MEDIÆVAL
ARCHITECT

John Harvey

ST. MARTIN'S PRESS NEW YORK

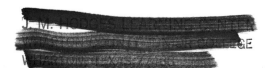

Other books by John Harvey

Henry Yeveley
Gothic England
The Plantagenets
Dublin
Tudor Architecture
The English Cathedrals
The Gothic World
English Mediaeval Architects
A Portrait of English Cathedrals
The Cathedrals of Spain
The Master Builders

Bibliographies
English Cathedrals—a Reader's Guide
Conservation of Old Buildings

Revised Muirhead's Blue Guides
Northern Spain
Southern Spain

Edited with translation
William Worcestre: Itineraries 1478-1480

Contents

SOURCES IN THE APPENDIX

Illustrations

Preface

IN spite of lip-service to Architecture as the Mistress Art, public interest in and knowledge of buildings and their designers has not been widespread in Britain. Yet it is as profoundly untrue and unfair to think of our country as a land without architecture as it was to describe it as a land without music. On the contrary, just as it was the Englishman John Dunstable who in the early fifteenth century led a new epoch in European music, so it was a small group of English master masons who, a century earlier, produced the elements of Late Gothic which were taken up by German and by French masters. Much earlier still there had been outstanding insular contributions to the development of Gothic architectural style in the twelfth and thirteenth centuries. All this was due to individual artists of genius, even though we may in many cases be ignorant of their names. It is a fallacy to regard the art and architecture of the Middle Ages as mysteriously different from the comparable products of other periods. This would hardly need emphasis outside the English-speaking world, yet since the mid-nineteenth century there has grown up, both in Britain and in the United States of America, a vastly misleading mythos. According to this, mediæval artists of western Christendom differed in kind from those of earlier and later times, and from those met with in the Islamic world and in the East. It has even become a fashionable article of faith to deny the title of "architect" to the designers of mediæval buildings, who at times are alleged to be non-existent on the fantastic grounds that mediæval men had an innate instinct for co-operative design. That such an instinct could conceivably have produced the multiplicity of varying designs of the highest complexity, for tracery and vaults, for towers and spires, for mouldings and details, is a fantastic absurdity. That it ever gained credence among the educated is testimony not merely to a strange lack of common sense, but to an almost total ignorance of the processes of design and building in architecture—whether ancient, mediæval or modern.

Whereas England in the period of Dallaway, Britton, Rickman and the brothers John Woody Papworth and Wyatt Papworth had led the way in the study of mediæval artistic personality, it was in France and

Germany that real progress was being made in the later nineteenth and early twentieth century. Sixty years ago Wilhelm Vöge could proclaim the vital fact that stylistic trends originate with important masters, to whose personalities the character of a period is due. Yet in England Lethaby was almost a lone voice, and even so authoritative a work as *The Architect in History* by Mr. Martin Shaw Briggs (Oxford: Clarendon Press, 1927) was persistently underrated. Briggs's notable book marked the turn of the tide, but it took a generation for it to be vindicated. Few would now dispute the fundamental unity of the practice of architecture, in all periods and places, but this is largely due to the impact of international scholarship upon the closed field of English-speaking art history. Continental scholars, aware of the great numbers of surviving mediæval drawings (see pages 101, 110) could never dismiss the architect as non-existent. French, Spanish, and Germanic and Central European students of architectural history were at all times aware of the true facts.

Although problems remain, it is now true to say that the picture which can be obtained of the mediæval architect, from study of his works and from the many documents now available, is a clear and full one. The evidence does not come all from one country or from one period, but covers the whole of western Europe and the five centuries after the millennial year, A.D. 1000, when minds freed from the expectation of an end to all worldly concerns were able to devote themselves to the expression of spiritual and æsthetic concepts in material form. A very great and continuing output of art was the result. It is the purpose of this book to show in some detail how this result was achieved in human terms, and in particular the origin, methods and organization of the men most responsible, namely the architects who acquired competence to design great buildings, to arrange for supplies of materials and labour with which to erect them, and to co-ordinate the specialists responsible for enrichment and decoration of various kinds.

It is not my intention to refute, step by step, the tedious arguments which have been brought forward in the attempt to show that architects did not exist in the Middle Ages. The literature of the controversy is already far too extensive, and much of it deserves to be forgotten. But there is one fundamental point, often made, that needs to be faced at the outset: the use, in the English language, of the word "Architect" to denote the designers of *mediæval* buildings. While linguistic usage down to the end of the nineteenth century is amply demonstrated by the *Oxford English Dictionary*, it has been argued that during the two generations or so of the present century the word has acquired a more precise signification, excluding the general and inclusive sense in which it has been understood since the sixteenth century. It must be said firmly that this argument has no sound basis and that it is contradicted by abundant actual usage. Since the matter is of fundamental importance a few extracts from leading authorities will here be given, in order of publication.

1906: Francis Bond, *Gothic Architecture in England* (page 2):

> When the Parthenon was built, or Santa Sophia, or Amiens Cathedral or Salisbury, even if the architect had gone through the "shops", as the British engineer still does, he would have too much to do with planning, design, drawings, and superintendence, to work at the buildings to any considerable extent with his own hands.

1918: G. G. Coulton, *Social Life in Britain* (page 476):

> Villard de Honnecourt . . . is the only medieval architect whose sketch-book has survived.

1924: M. R. James, Introduction to *Westminster Abbey* (R.C.H.M., page 5):

> There is a common belief that the architects of the great mediæval churches are nameless to us. As soon as records come to be examined the falsity of this notion is made plain.

1933: D. Knoop and G. P. Jones, *The Mediæval Mason* (pages 197 ff 200:

> Our study of mediæval building accounts corroborates what is now the received doctrine that the designer of a building was, as a rule, a master mason . . . In addition to skill with his tools, the mediæval mason-architect must have had [other qualifications] . . .
> The emergence of the type of architect represented by Webb and Wren, however, did not mean the disappearance of the other kind . . .

1947: R. Sencourt, *The Consecration of Genius* (page 140):

> The sculptors of Bourges, and the English workers in stained glass who, in their wish for freedom of design, forced on the architect the transom which led to the perpendicular style . . .

1951: D. M. Stenton, *English Society in the Early Middle Ages* (pages 266, 267):

> Anglo-Norman architects, while very generally preserving the ground-plan of the churches built in Normandy . . .
> Before the end of the twelfth century . . . English architects were moving towards the Early English forms.

1952 : L. F. Salzman, *Building in England down to 1540* (pages 4–5):

We must decide what we mean by an architect. An architect, then, is a man who is capable of envisaging a building, complete and in detail, before one stone is laid upon another and is also capable of so conveying his vision to the actual builders that they are able to translate it into actual reality.

In the concluding extract, Dr. Salzman has given what is probably the best definition of the term, and it is in this sense that the word Architect will be used throughout this book.

With the definition of the main subject there has to be coupled some precision of the qualifying term "mediæval". It will probably not be disputed that, in Western Europe, the Middle Ages came to an end about 1500, though many institutions and some features of artistic style survived later. In general, evidence quoted will be of earlier date than 1540 when, particularly in England where the dissolution of the monasteries was then complete, the main features of a way of life were rapidly giving place to something utterly different. It is far more difficult to set a precise date to the start of the Middle Ages. In Britain, the withdrawal of the Roman legions about 410, in the Roman Empire the division of 395, are dates commonly suggested; the collapse in the West of co-ordinated administration in the fifth century certainly led to the Dark Age—sometimes regarded as preceding the Middle Ages, sometimes as their opening phase. In any case, the amount of available evidence concerning western architects in the period 400–1000 is so slight that the question is academic. It is important to remember, however, that in the Eastern Empire, ruled from Constantinople, there was *an adjacent civilization* on a high level throughout these six centuries; and that during the last two of those centuries the Umayyad Caliphate of Cordova provided another higher civilization on European soil, ruling the greater part of the Iberian Peninsula. Both from Byzantine and from Moorish sources, directly and filtered through Italian channels, western Europe was always able to derive at least a reflection of culture and some few objects of art. The renewal of architecture after A.D. 1000 is an important part of the freshly re-inforced contacts between the West and these higher cultures on its frontiers.

Quite independently of the millennial hypothesis, there was a specific reason for the new relationships between Western Europe and the Eastern Mediterranean. For centuries, once the early fervour of the Muslims had died down, there had been an era of relatively peaceful co-existence, in which Christian pilgrims had no serious difficulties—beyond those of travel—to overcome, if they wished to visit the Holy Sites of Palestine. In the latter part of the tenth century conditions changed for the worse, and matters were brought to a head by the destruction of the Church of the Holy Sepulchre, on the orders of the Fatimid Caliph al-Hakim, in 1009. There followed a period of the gravest hardships for Christians, culminating in the indignities heaped upon the great pilgrimage of 1033 to commemorate the millenary of the Crucifixion. Though many other factors, including particularly the rise to supreme power in the Muslim world of Turkish dynasties, contributed to produce the conflict of the later eleventh century, it was the sense of outrage produced among western Christians by the events of 1009 and 1033 that led directly to the Crusades. It must be stressed that the "First Crusade" preached in 1095 was by no means the first of the crusades which, for primarily religious motives, had been in progress for nearly three generations. Thus the opening of the period of crusades coincides more or less exactly with the rise of the style of Western European art now known as "Romanesque" in the more limited sense.

Fundamental to an understanding of the emergence of mediæval art—in the sense of the architecture and the attendant decorative arts of the period 1000–1500—is the realization of the dominant part played by the movement of cultured and sophisticated human beings from the zones of higher civilization into the backward areas. This movement could be of two kinds: the first is represented by the missionary enterprise of bishops and priests from the Byzantine Empire—individuals of perhaps Syrian or Armenian origin—who came to the West to preach, or to rule dioceses. To men of higher culture such as these, the crude barbarism of most of north-western Europe must have been barely tolerable. To remedy this state of affairs they would at first have had to send overseas to regions of higher culture, and more advanced technical education, for artists able to improve the material conditions of their new homes, and to design and build cathedrals and churches not completely unworthy (see page 38). This importation of foreign artists produced a substantial change for the better by environmental means. To the extent that these artists may have brought their families with them, or founded new families in the West, they also raised the standards attainable in future generations by biological means. Nor must it be overlooked that the foreign priests had offspring of distinction, for there was no universal rule of clerical celibacy in force at the time in question.

The second type of movement was even more important, and was responsible for the flowering of mediæval culture upon the highest plane, putting it in the thirteenth and fourteenth centuries on a level with any of the most exquisite achievements of mankind. This was the arrival of biologically better blood in the families of the ruling dynasties of western Europe. Not at once, but spread over several centuries, there was a raising of the cultural level of crude and barbarous chieftains by successful matches with daughters of rulers a stage more cultured than themselves. In England we can catch a glimpse of the process in its early stages towards the end of the sixth century, when Æthelbert king of Kent married Bertha, daughter of the Merovingian king of Paris. The fact that this marriage led to the mission of Augustine in 597 and so to the implanting of Roman Christianity in England, has tended to obscure its even greater significance as a vital step in the biological progress of petty tribal chiefs towards brilliant cultural attainments and, much later, to world empire. Just as the importation of a few steeds of the best Arab blood made possible the modern European racehorse, so the bridal journeys of princesses given in marriage to western rulers provided the mainspring for the complex machine of mediæval European civilization. In this great and wonderful outburst of human culture the principal and most lasting adornment was architecture.

Something must be said of the plan of this book. It is meant mainly for those interested in the subject of historical architecture, rather than for specialist scholars; hence it is not in any sense a research thesis. It nevertheless incorporates a good deal of personal study of buildings and of documents in England and in other countries. Because of the need for limitation, the documentation is very largely drawn from French and English sources: there can be no doubt whatever as to the applicability of historical and literary material of the Gothic age in these two countries. Evidence from Spain, which had close architectural links with both France and England at various dates; and from Germany, which admittedly derived its Gothic architecture first from France, and its later developments from England, has been used, but more sparingly. Comparatively little reliance has been placed upon Italian sources since it can be argued that conditions in Rome and the lesser city states were utterly different from those in north-western Europe, while Gothic art in Sicily was inextricably mixed with its Saracenic inheritance, and Naples was under direct French and later, Spanish influence.

As far as possible, original documents are allowed to speak for themselves. This has necessitated translation in the case of Latin and foreign sources: the attempt has been made to produce versions which convey the sense in intelligible modern terms rather than to give precise literal equivalents; but crucial words from the original have been supplied. With one exception, all English texts have been modernized by re-spelling, even when this results in the use of obsolete—but still intelligible—phrasing. Words unintelligible to the modern reader have their equivalent supplied in parenthesis, but are surprisingly few. The single exception to the rule of modernization is formed by quotations from Chaucer, whose superb and witty verses must be read in the original.

References for all important facts strictly relevant to the subject are

given in a series of Notes printed at the end, with abbreviations combined
in the general Bibliography. Footnotes are employed mainly to give
necessary cross-references, or to mention points which interrupt the flow
of the argument. Attention should be drawn to what might otherwise
seem an inconsistency: the surname of the important fourteenth-century
architect is here spelt as "Yeveley" throughout. The spelling "Yevele",
used by the *Dictionary of National Biography* and accepted by me when
I wrote *Henry Yevele* (Batsford, 1944) is misleading phonetically; the
name should be pronounced exactly as the Derbyshire place-name from
which it is derived, now Yeaveley. It is regrettable that the lead given by
that great antiquary, John Gough Nichols, in his pioneer life of Yeveley
printed in 1864, was not consistently followed throughout.

My thanks are due to the authorities in charge of many buildings in
Britain, Ireland and abroad, and also to those of a large number of
libraries, record offices and museums. In particular I am greatly
indebted to the Warden and Fellows of Winchester College for the
opportunities given me to work on the buildings and documents in their
care. The book owes much to discussion over many years with a great
many persons, both among the dead and the living, too many for all to
be named individually. Outstanding among the former were the late
T. D. Atkinson, Herbert Chitty, Sir Alfred Clapham, R. P. Howgrave-
Graham, Douglas Knoop, E. A. Greening Lamborn and W. Douglas
Simpson. My personal thanks are addressed particularly to Messrs.
B. J. Ashwell and C. B. L. Barr, Professor Christopher Brooke, Messrs.
Ivor Bulmer-Thomas and L. S. Colchester, Professors K. J. Conant,
Sir Archibald Creswell, and Ralph H. C. Davis, Drs. A. B. Emden,
Leonard K. Elmhirst, Joan Evans, Eric A. Gee, Professor Kenneth P.
Harrison, Dr. Jacques Heyman, Mr. Arthur Oswald, Dr. L. R. Shelby,
Mr. L. E. Tanner, Dr. Arnold J. Taylor, Mr. and Mrs. W. J. Carpenter
Turner, and Professor George Zarnecki.

An even deeper debt is to my late father, William Harvey, who
inculcated a love for ancient buildings in me from early childhood
onwards, and with whom I visited, or worked on, many historic fabrics.
To my wife, who has likewise accompanied me in looking at and
discussing numberless buildings and historical problems, I express my
warmest gratitude.

To the Ancient Monuments Society I am indebted for permission to
reprint extensively from my article on 'Mediæval Design' first printed
in their *Transactions* (NS, vol. VI); to the Clarendon Press for the
extracts on pages 189–91 from M. R. James, *The Apocryphal New
Testament*; to Dr. Jacques Heyman for the quotations which he has
allowed me to use on pages 162–65; and to the Warden and Fellows
of Winchester College, who have allowed me to print the Form of
Holding Manorial Courts which appears on pages 257–61; as well as

for their copyright photographs Figs. 19 (by the late Sydney Pitcher), 20, 34 and 35 (by Mr. E. A. Sollars).

In connection with illustrations I would also express my gratitude to the Society of Antiquaries of London for permission to reproduce the drawings on pages 185–88 (from *The Antiquaries Journal*, vol XXVII); to Professor Robert Branner for his reconstructions from the Rheims Palimpsest on page 111 (*Journal of the Society of Architectural Historians*, Philadelphia, vol XVII); Professor Kenneth J. Conant for his plans on page 121 (*Speculum*, vol. XXXVIII); Mr. Arthur Gardner for the photographs Figs. 23, 24; Mrs. Howgrave-Graham for permission to reproduce Figs. 25, 48 from photographs by the late R. P. Howgrave-Graham; Mr. E. A. Sollars for Fig. 37, specially taken for this book; Mr. F. Hugh Thompson, M.C., for allowing the plan of Vale Royal Abbey on page 161 to be based on his survey (*The Antiquaries Journal*, vol. XLII); to the Dean and Chapter of Westminster for Figs. 18, 22 to the Dean and Canons of St. George's Chapel, Windsor, for their kind permission to reproduce Fig. 21; to the Friends of St. George's Chapel and Mr. Maurice F. Bond, O.B.E., for allowing me to reprint the drawing on page 117 (*Report*, 1961); and to the Friends of York Minster for permission to reproduce the plan on page 115 (40th *Report*) from a drawing by Mr. A. R. Whittaker. I am also grateful to Mrs. Robinson for her clear drawings of the maps and plans on pages 50, 134, 145 and 161.

To my publishers I owe thanks for their attention to all the details of production, and particularly to Mrs. Linda Rickard and Miss Brenda Parker for their work on the collection and arrangement of the illustrations.

18 January, 1971   JOHN H. HARVEY

Introduction

T HE study of architecture is beset with difficulty, not least because its precise nature is hard to define. We are not much helped by the dictionary: the *Concise Oxford Dictionary*, for instance, defines Architecture as "Science of building; thing built, structure; style of building; construction;" and adds that the derivation of the word is through French, from the Latin *architectura*. Following the word back, the *Petit Larousse* shows what the Frenchman understands: "*Art de construire et d'orner les édifices selon des règles determinés*"—the art of constructing and adorning buildings according to determined rules. The Latin *architectura*, "the art of building, architecture", is itself taken from *architectus*, "a master-builder, architect", with the important figurative sense "an inventor, deviser, author"; while the rare verb *architector*—"to build, construct, fabricate", is more important for its figurative sense "to devise, invent." To follow the word still further back to its Greek origins would be unprofitable, for their meaning changed in usage; but so far as the source of the Latin words is concerned, the elements are: *archie-*, chief or most excellent, the *tektón*, a carpenter, a builder, any craftsman, including a master of any art (*e.g.* poetry, as in Scots "maker"); and again having the figurative meaning of "planner, contriver, plotter or author".

Clearly the important senses of the group of words circle about the ideas of *invention* and *building*; and this at least gives us a hint suggesting where the line must be drawn between "architecture" and "building". Building, or any of its component crafts such as carpentry, masonry, and the like, is simply a technical skill, acquired and handed down. It is a method *already known* by which given practical problems can be solved. Architecture, on the contrary, deals with the solution of a fresh problem, and involves *creation**—or, as a mediæval thinker would have put it, the *imitation of the Creator*—that is to say,

---

*From the failure of creative inspiration in French Gothic after *c.* 1275 stems the decay of the style—see page 163.

invention of something that in the given context is new. The man who puts up a cottage, barn, or other vernacular building in a merely traditional style, the style or method in which he was trained, is not an architect, and his product is not architecture. On the contrary, any structure however small, if it is the result of creative design to fulfil a particular purpose or programme, is a work of architecture.

The essential faculty of an architect is then that of design. Whatever he may lack, he must have the capacity to plan, to devise, to invent. Obviously he must also have at least such knowledge of the technical processes of building as will enable him to design reasonably, taking advantage of the properties of materials, using them with economy, and producing structures that are durable and not likely to collapse in normal conditions unless seriously neglected. In quite modern times, during the last century or so, it has been common for the professional architect to learn the technical basis of his art only at second-hand; unlike the contemporary engineer, he is not obliged to "work in the shops" to complete his education. This may imply a serious adverse criticism of modern architectural training, but here the important thing to note is that it is a peculiarity of a recent period only, a divergence from the norm of the practice of architecture throughout history. Hence the misunderstanding of mediæval architects in the nineteenth and early twentieth centuries has been due, not to anything exceptional in the practice of the Middle Ages, but to a most unusual, even unnatural aspect of modern professionalism.

In order to design effectively an architect must not merely have a sound grasp of the technical aspects of the materials and craft skills involved; he must also have some framework of rules. As is notorious in all the arts, genius transcends strict rules, and at times all rules seem made merely to be broken; yet it is in fact only in response to the discipline enforced by, for example, grammar in the case of writing, prosody and rhyme in poetry, harmony and form in music, that higher art manifests itself. As Goethe put it in the concluding lines of his famous sonnet :

> In self-discipline is the Master first displayed,
> And Law alone can give us liberty.*

This brings us back to the French definition of architecture, which includes "determined rules" as necessary to the art. The essence of creation is the forming of order out of chaos, and this implies that the creative artist must necessarily observe some set of rules, even if they

---

* *Goethe's sämmtliche Werke,* "Epigrammatisch"; edition of 1840 in 40 volumes, Bd. 2, 229–30: "In der Beschränkung zeigt sich erst der Meister, Und das Gesetz nur kann uns Freiheit geben."

are rules which he has formulated for himself, or which he has observed—perhaps subconsciously—in nature.

During the last two thousand years there has been in the Western world only one complete set of rules for Architecture in written form, the ten books *De Architectura* of the Roman Vitruvius. Though almost completely devoid of literary merit, the work is a truly remarkable compendium of the actual techniques used in the building practice of ancient Greece and Rome, and deals adequately not only with architecture in the stricter sense, but with all the associated arts: fortification, town-planning, construction, styles and proportions, types of buildings, decoration, hydraulic engineering, astronomy with astrological influences and sundials, and machinery including mills, cranes and military engines. In spite of some obscurities due to the loss in transmission of diagrams intended to accompany the text, Vitruvius provides a complete, clear and reasonably intelligible picture of the practices of classical antiquity, and shows himself to have been a practising architect, engineer and builder. On technical subjects his views are still of value, for he undoubtedly had a thorough grounding in the fundamental skills, and an excellent grasp of the properties of materials. For the rules of building he is an admirable and trustworthy guide. It is his rules for design, drawn exclusively from Greek and Roman practice, that prove inadequate, in spite of the apparently simple form in which he presents them.

Architectural design in Greece and Rome was carried out within the framework of the Orders of Architecture, originally Doric, Ionic and Corinthian, with two more, Tuscan (a version of Doric) and Composite (based upon Ionic and Corinthian) added in Roman times. The proportions of columns with their capitals and bases, of mouldings, beams and parts of buildings in general, were laid down as a strict set of rules, though admitting of some minor degree of variation. It was only in later Roman times, especially in the oriental provinces of the Empire, that these rules came to be profoundly modified in practice. No written work embodying the later emancipation from the rules of Vitruvius, which belonged to the time of Augustus, has come down to us; possibly no such work was ever written. Throughout the periods of Early Christian, Byzantine, Carolingian, Romanesque and Gothic art there was no new treatise setting forth the rules governing proportion in design; nor was there any major written treatise of building technique other than that of Vitruvius. Only one fresh work of overlapping scope was produced, in the fourth century and probably under Theodosius the Great, the five books on military affairs by Vegetius (Flavius Vegetius Renatus). Because of its practical application to warfare, including siegecraft and naval affairs, the work of Vegetius continued to be copied,

translated and used throughout the Middle Ages. An English translation, made from a French version, was in existence before Western
printing, and was published by Caxton in 1489. The demand for
copies of Vegetius came largely from kings and their military com-
manders, (see pages 209, 215–16) and accounts for its continued popularity and uninterrupted success.

Vitruvius appealed, at least before the Renaissance of the fifteenth
and sixteenth centuries, to a public mainly of a different kind. His
was primarily a technical treatise for craftsmen involved in any of
the operations of building, engineering and surveying, for its
antiquated rules for design had become obsolete. Nevertheless the
work survived, and copies were widely distributed in Western Europe
during the Middle Ages. Within the last generation it has been
shown that the "rediscovery" of Vitruvius in the fifteenth century
was a misunderstanding of the real facts. It is not in dispute that the
early humanists Poggio Bracciolini and Cencio Rustici did find a
manuscript of Vitruvius at the monastery of St. Gall in 1416; but if
they supposed that what they had found was a lost classical work
they simply betrayed the limitations of their own knowledge. Not less
than eighty mediæval manuscripts of Vitruvius survive, though some
of these are of extracts only; but this number does not include copies
of the Vitruvian compilation of M. Cetius Faventinus, *De artis
architectonicæ liber*. Although the date of a good many of the
manuscripts is uncertain, it can be said that forty-one are later than
1400, leaving at least thirty-nine that must antedate the "rediscovery" of 1416. Disregarding the present situation of the copies,
and accepting the most probable provenance of each (where no
certain source is known), it can be said that eight are of unknown
origin, nine from Italy, six from France, six from Germany, seven
from England, two from the Netherlands and one possibly from
Poland. Further analysis shows that the earlier copies had quite a
different distribution, for all the Italian manuscripts are of relatively
late date.

Considering only those copies of Vitruvius which are likely to be
of the twelfth century or earlier, nineteen in all, and eliminating
three of uncertain provenance, we are left with sixteen manuscripts
probably written before 1200. Of these six belong to Germany, three
or four of them to Cologne, one possibly to Hildesheim and one to
Worms; five to France, two to the Netherlands, and three to
England. In the case of England, however, recent research has
provided additional facts concerning the former existence of copies
now lost. In addition to the seven surviving English copies or sets of
extracts, at least three other English versions existed before 1400:
one at Canterbury Cathedral priory, one at Bury St. Edmunds

abbey, and one at the Austin Friars at York. The surviving copies are two from the abbey of St. Augustine, Canterbury, both complete, with an additional set of extracts there (and furthermore St. Augustine's is the known source of extracts made by William of Malmesbury about 1130); and two other sets of extracts, one from Christ Church, Canterbury, and one from Winchester; as well as an almost complete version now at Tübingen and a complete manuscript probably from Durham.

Continental investigations have shown that copies of Vitruvius existed in the eleventh century in France, at Toul and either Rheims or Chartres, in the Low Countries, and at Gorze in the South Tyrol; and in the twelfth century at Rouen, Cluny and Montecassino. This is in addition to the early surviving manuscripts in Germany. When we consider the very great destruction of mediæval manuscripts, including the catalogues of mediæval libraries, the list is an impressive one. The invention of printing itself caused many manuscripts to be discarded, and the Reformation, the wars of religion and subsequent wars, and accidental fires, must have accounted for a substantial number of versions of which we know nothing. It is safe to assume that copies of Vitruvius, or of technical extracts from his work, existed at a sufficient number of major centres for effective use to be made of his precepts. In the case of one particular Vitruvian expedient, the acoustic jar, it has been shown lately by Professor Kenneth Harrison that this widespread, even if ineffectual, device was the direct outcome of the use of Vitruvius during the Middle Ages. Acquaintance with Vitruvius by men of learning, from Einhard and Alcuin to Hugh of St. Victor, Vincent of Beauvais, Albertus Magnus, Petrarch, Boccaccio and many others, is abundantly evidenced.

Vitruvius opens his work with a statement of first principles, and defines Architecture as consisting of six qualities: Order, Arrangement, Eurhythmy, Symmetry, Fitness and Economy. It is the two first, *ordinatio* and *dispositio*, which gave rise in mediæval times to the terms describing the *architectural* functions of the building masters, who "ordained" and "disposed" the work. The long continuance of this linguistic echo is itself a main proof of the continuity of Vitruvian tradition. Yet it is precisely here that Vitruvius was unable to give practical help to the mediæval architect who wanted rules by which he might produce a design. The Orders of Architecture had disappeared for all practical purposes, though their ghost still presides over the interior of Autun Cathedral, designed about 1120. As we shall see (pages 48-9) new canons of design, not from classical but from oriental sources, were in process of displacing what was left of classical forms after the Dark Age in the West and the rise, in the civilized East, of Byzantine, Armenian,

Georgian and Syrian styles. Before we can consider the new sources of mediæval design, however, we have to understand fully what is meant by "design" itself. Here again, as with architecture, the first step is to reach a satisfactory definition of the term.

The dictionary once more provides a framework of suggestions: design means a "mental plan", a "preliminary sketch for a picture, etc."; "delineation, pattern"; "artistic or literary groundwork, general idea, construction, plot, faculty of evolving these, invention". As a verb, to design is "to contrive, plan; to make a preliminary sketch of a picture; to draw a plan of a building etc. to be executed by others; to conceive a mental plan for, or construct the groundwork or plot of a book or work of art". These meanings are twofold: abstract, and concrete. There is the abstract sense of a *mental* plan, idea or invention; the concrete sense centres round a tangible sketch or drawing supplying the necessary information from which may be produced a finished work of art. That these two stages are implicit in the production of art was already a commonplace in the Middle Ages. Geoffrey de Vinsauf, discussing poetic composition soon after 1200, wrote in Latin to the following effect:

If a man has to lay the foundations of a house, he does not set rash hand to the work; the inward line of the heart measures forth the work in advance and the inner man prescribes a definite order of action; the hand of imagination designs the whole before that of the body does so: the pattern is first the prototype, then the tangible ... The inner compasses of the mind must encircle the whole quantity of material beforehand.

This was neatly paraphrased by Chaucer in his *Troilus*:

For every wight that hath an hous to founde
Ne renneth nought the werk for to biginne
With rakel hond, bot he wol byde a stounde,
And send his hertes lyne out fro with-inne
Alderfirst his purpos for to winne.

In the *Knightes Tale*, too, Chaucer gives a description of a major building project, the stone theatre a mile in circumference, a poetic exaggeration of Edward III's Round Table begun at Windsor and which in real life was 200 feet in diameter or over 600 feet round. Chaucer emphasizes the learning of contemporary architects:

For in the lond ther nas no crafty man,
That geometrie or ars-metrik can,
Ne purtreyour, ne kerver of images,
That Theseus ne yaf him mete and wages
The theatre for to maken and devyse.

There are other later references in literature to the subject of designers and design, but before returning to these there is a fundamental text of a different kind; it shows not merely that the process of design was understood by mediæval literary men, but that it was accepted as a fundamental truth by leaders of thought. Robert Grosseteste, later bishop of Lincoln and one of the greatest of mediæval philosophers and scientists, wrote about 1200 a letter to Master Adam Rufus in which he was primarily concerned to explain the neo-Platonic concept of God as the "form" of the creation. The whole passage, containing as it does specific reference to the architect, is of such importance that it must be set out at length. To make it readily intelligible in modern terms it has been necessary to use different words to represent the single Latin *forma* : design, form, mould, pattern, shape. Grosseteste wrote :

> To make clear how God is the form of his creatures . . . the meanings of this word "form" must be explained. It is said that the design is the model (*exemplar*) to which the craftsman looks to make (*formet*) his handiwork, in imitation of it and in its likeness. Thus the wooden last, to which the cobbler looks to form the sole accordingly, is called the pattern of the sole. Thus too the lives of good men, which we regard in order to form the manners of our life in their likeness, are called our pattern of living. That also is called a pattern, to which material to be shaped is applied and, by its application to it, receives the imitated shape of that to which it is applied. So we say of the silver seal that it is the pattern of the wax seal; and of the clay in which the statue is cast, that it is the mould of the statue. But when the artist (*artifex*) has in his mind the likeness of his work of art (*artificii*) and regards only that which he has in his mind, in order to shape his art in its likeness, that likeness of the work in the artist's mind is called the design of the work of art (*forma artificii*). Nor does this sense of design differ much from the sense of pattern first mentioned. So imagine in the artist's mind the design of the work to be made, as in the mind of the architect (*architecti*) the design and likeness of the house to be built; to this pattern and model (*exemplar*) he looks only that he may make the house in imitation of it.
>
> And imagine, even though it be impossible, that the will of the same architect wishing to build the house were so powerful that this will alone need be applied to shape the material into the house of the design in the architect's mind, so that by this application it will be fashioned into the house. Imagine also that the material of the house is fluid, and cannot retain the form

which it has received if it is separated from the design in the architect's mind, as water stamped with a silver seal, when the seal is removed, immediately loses the form which is received. So imagine the will of the craftsman (*artificis*) applying the material of the house to the form in the architect's mind, not only that by this application he may fashion it into the house, but also applying the material to the design that, as long as the house remains in being, the house may be kept in being in that form. In such a manner then in which its design, in the mind of such an architect, is the design of the house, so is art (*ars*), or wisdom (*sapientia*) or the word of Almighty God the pattern of all creatures. For it is at the same time both the model (*exemplar*) and the producer (*efficiens*), and what forms, and what keeps in the form given, while creatures are applied to it and removed from it.

While it might be argued that, coming from a distinguished philosopher, this reference to the architectural function was a mere echoed commonplace from classical times,* and had no direct reference to the architects of Grosseteste's own day, such an objection cannot possibly be sustained in face of the continued stream of literary references which prove that mediæval writers were perfectly well aware that the function of design was then performed by men who were members of the relevant building trades, masons, carpenters and the like. Thus Lydgate in his *Troy Book*, written in 1412–20, describes how King Priam, desiring to build a new Troy on a clear site, sent out to seek

> "For such workmen as were curious,
> Of wit inventive, of casting [mathematics] marvellous;
> Or such as could craft of geometry
> Or were subtle in their fantasy;
> And for everyone that was good deviser,
> Mason, hewer, or crafty quarrier;
> For every wright and passing [able] carpenter
> That may be found . . ."

The conjunction in this passage of the craft of geometry, mathematical knowledge, the function of "deviser", with such types of craftsmen as masons and carpenters is significant. The mention of skilled quarrymen is also of interest because there is a good deal of evidence that areas of stone quarrying were one of the main sources of the more highly trained types of mason.

The processes of architecture were briefly indicated in a few lines of Shakespeare's *Second Part of King Henry the Fourth* :

*Briggs pointed out the scriptural echo of I Corinthians iii.10 in the use of *sapiens architectus,* the Vulgate Latin for the σοφὸς ἀρχιτέκτων of the Greek text.

"When we mean to build
We first survey the plot, then draw the model;
And when we see the figure of the house,
Then must we rate the cost of the erection."

Here the practical operations of the architect on the plan, upon
details of material design ("the model"), and upon an estimate of
cost, are succinctly and accurately described. At any rate until the
opening of the seventeenth century there was a general understanding of the nature of architectural design, and this is clearly
demonstrated for England as well as on the continent. Yet later on
it is evident that the subject of artistic design has grown so
unfamiliar to the general public, and even to many historians, that
serious misconceptions have become commonplaces of controversy in
the literature of art.

It is because of this widespread misunderstanding that it is
necessary to begin the study of mediæval designers by asking what
is actually involved in the process of design itself. The human mind
does not work in a vacuum but requires raw material: a poem, a
novel, a painting, a work of music, a building, must have some
purpose or at least some subject matter. The conglomeration of
purpose, subject and materials forms the "conditions" of the work.
Even the most abstract of paintings has form and colour, and a
purely ornamental building has as its minimum purpose the need to
please or startle the eye. Such works divorced from any practical
end are relatively common in modern times; in the Middle Ages
they were very rare. For this reason the purposes of a mediæval
work of art, though frequently complex, are easy to grasp. A
church was the House of God, a shelter for worshippers, and a
picturebook of religious doctrine. Statuary, paintings and stained
glass told their stories in the manner of the strip-cartoon—we do
not have to assume this, for it is explicitly stated by Honorius of
Autun (about 1125) in his treatise *De gemma animae* (see page
226, chap. xxxii). The more distant detail of great windows and
wall-paintings may have been unintelligible to the naked eye, but it
was probably always expounded by vergers or guides to groups of
pilgrims and visitors.

In an age of faith the arts were largely in the service of religion,
and even objects for secular use might be decorated with subjects
from sacred history. The great architects of the Court Schools had
often trained as master masons concerned with the planning of
cathedrals and monasteries before they obtained their appointments
in the Royal Households of Europe. In these circumstances it is not
surprising that the *hieratic* or *iconographical* view of mediæval art

should have developed. What is not acceptable is the assumption that this meant that mediæval art became simply the inevitable outcome of a programme laid down by ecclesiastical patrons, thus excluding the element of design. There is of course a limited truth in this, to the extent that the plan of a church in outline, the subjects of paintings and stained glass, might be dictated by the needs and aims of those in control of the funds. This extends also to displays of such iconographical series as the History of Jesse, or the Types and Antitypes of the Old and New Testaments used as programme for the statuary on the west front of Wells Cathedral, a hoarding for the display of religious propaganda aimed at a largely illiterate populace.*

As examples of conditions limiting design we may consider a few texts. The patron might simply ask in general terms for an outstanding building, as did Abbot Gaucelin (1005–1029) at Fleury (St.-Benoit-sur-Loire): he "decided to build at the west end of the minster a tower of squared stones which he had brought by boat from the Nivernais. When the architect (*princeps artificum*) asked him for instructions on how he wished the work to be undertaken, he said most affably: 'Build it to be a model for the whole of France' ". More detailed instructions might suggest adherence to symbolism in features of the plan, as may be implied in the account of the rebuilding of Saint-Trond near Liège by Abbot Adelhard II (1055–1082):

> He pulled down the heavy pillars of the monastic church, though it was by no means ruinous, and instead set up handsome columns, completing the wall to the same height. In his time the fabric of this church was so much enlarged that one might say of it, as the learned doctors do of well fashioned churches, that it was formed after the image of the human body. For it had, as can still be seen, a chancel which, with the sanctuary, is like the head and neck; the choir with its stalls the chest; the transept projecting as two sleeves or wings on each side of the choir, the arms and hands; the crossing of the minster the belly; and the lower arm of the cross, displaying symmetrically two aisles on north and south, the thighs and shins.

A far more detailed analysis of symbolic relationships was provided at the onset of the Gothic period by Honorius of Autun, as already mentioned (see page 25). In a more practical way a sort of outline specification was laid down for castle-builders by Alexander Neckam in his encyclopædic treatment of terminology,

*William Worcestre in 1480 described the subjects.

written about 1190. As an exercise in the relationships of words to real life this is so interesting as to deserve extensive quotation :

> If a castle is to be properly built, let it be surrounded with a double ditch; let its site be protected by nature, that the motte may rise from a footing on the native rock or the defect of nature be helped out by the benefit of art and the mass of the walls, built of mortar and stones, grow out or rise as a lofty work. Upon this let a bristling hedge be well set with squared pales or stakes, and thorns. Afterwards see that the bailey is spacious; and let the wall have a foundation deep in the ground. Also let the lofty walls be buttressed with pillars placed outside and inside; but let the surface of the wall show a smoothness of mason's work as if trowelled. Let the crenellations stand in their due proportions; the brattices and turrets protect the summit of the tower; nor should hurdles be lacking, to carry stones for flinging down.
> Should the castle be besieged, let not the defenders of our fortress be driven to surrender; let them be provided with corn and wheat, wine, hams, bacon, pickled meat, black puddings, sausages, puddings, pork, mutton, beef, lamb and various vegetables. There is need of an ever-springing well; and of subtle posterns and underground ways through which help and succour may secretly be brought. Let there be also lances, catapults, bucklers, shields, arbalests, maces and mangonels.
> Let the body of the Hall be provided with a screens passage (*vestibulum*) next to which the porch may be rightly placed. It should also have a courtyard ... since the kitchens were wont to be made next the streets, that passers-by might perceive the smell and vapours of the kitchen. In the hall let there be posts set at the right distance apart. There is need of nails, posts, shingles, laths and beams, and rafters belonging to the roof of the house ...

An architect, then as now, could derive assistance from the limits set by the conditions, and from more precise schemes drawn up by the client (see page 241). Yet a clear distinction must be drawn between this influence of the programme, strong as it might be, and artistic design. This is seen clearly if we consider historically the requirements of Catholic liturgy as affecting churches. The essential conditions which must be fulfilled by every church remain unchanged and, within limits, it is a matter of indifference, liturgically speaking, in what style the church has been designed. The *æsthetic* intention remains entirely distinct from the set of conditions. All clients lay down certain requirements, for example the number and size of rooms in a house; some few clients may produce sketches to show what they want. But, save in the rarest instances, the client does not thus become the designer of the building.

Religious paintings and sculpture, of different periods but identical iconography, vary in treatment. Even where an artist was getting his iconography ready-made from a pattern-book or an illuminated manuscript, he seldom copied slavishly, but transformed the details into the mode of his own place and time. It is in fact the differences between a work and its prototype that are revealing, and this is most obviously exemplified in the iconography of the Crucifixion. This standard subject, produced at least once on a large scale for every church, and a myriad times for lesser fittings, varies so much in treatment that certain examples even possess an æsthetic appeal of such intense vitality that it transcends their iconographic significance for the onlooker.

Neither in the Middle Ages nor at any other time has design been identical with a particular doctrinal, philosophic or iconographical idea, or with any one set of conditions. Artistic design, however influenced, is a separate creative function of the artist's imagination, working upon the whole complex of factors, iconographical and material, which constitute the programme. To cite a modern instance : an architectural competition is based upon a set of requirements including the site and purpose of the building, its size and component parts, and possibly its materials. The natural characteristics of materials, the need for stability and legal regulations impose further restrictions upon the freedom of competitors. Yet in the entries submitted there is always a great variety of treatment.

There is an excellent example of this individuality operating in the Middle Ages. St. Bridget of Sweden (1302–73) received a series of revelations which laid down stringent conditions for the religious order which she was to found, and for the precise details of its buildings. The records of these revelations, of shortly before 1350, were accepted at Rome as having divine authority. They specified that each church of the order should have three aisles of equal width and height, each of five bays, a projecting choir at the west for the priests, to equal in width and height a bay of the central nave, but longer, and doorways in specified positions. In the north wall were to be five openings for the confession and communion of the nuns. Everything else was laid down in like detail. None the less, the actual houses of the order, built in Denmark, Finland, Estonia and Germany, show wide variations and their materials and *architectural* character are in every case of the region and not imported. This was so even at Gnadenburg in Bavaria, where the arrangements were most precisely copied from the mother-house of Vadstena in Sweden;

and at Pirita in Estonia where at least one of the masons, Stefan Liongasson, came from Vadstena.

It has been alleged that artistic individuality and personal style did not exist before the Renaissance, using that term in the specific sense of the revived interest in Roman art-forms in fifteenth-century Italy. Few if any facts have ever been adduced in support of this view, and such comparisons as are instituted are vague and misleading. Comparison and contrast must be confined to works truly comparable, for artistic personality in the fullest sense has been, at all periods and in all arts, the exception; most artists are relatively undistinguished. Even linguistically we may dwell on the etymological significance of this word : personal artistic style, the gift of genius, distinguishes its possessor from the common mean. The minor dramatists of Elizabethan England, the lesser contrapuntal composers of Bach's Germany, the musical common form of the later eighteenth century from which emerge the peaks of Mozart and Haydn; the general run of Dutch paintings, the architecture of most of Wren's contemporaries—in any of these the detection of personal idiom is difficult if not impossible. In any one art, at a given time, there will not be many artists of highly developed individuality; we shall not find a thirteenth-century parish church or a manorhouse of 1450 with the degree of personality displayed by St. Paul's Cathedral or Blenheim Palace. *But the converse is equally true* : it is rare indeed to find two mediæval villages with house fronts resembling one another in the stereotyped fashion of many Georgian streets. Every one of the important builds of different dates at cathedrals, palaces and castles is marked by its own character, flowing from the artistic personality of its designer.

It is now possible to return to a consideration of mediæval æsthetic canons and the bases of later mediæval—that is, Gothic— architecture. As we have seen, the famous work of Vitruvius did survive throughout the Middle Ages, and it was to some degree a basic source of technical knowledge and of ideas in planning; but it was certainly not used as a manual of design. There is probably some truth in the view that even the higher master craftsmen of the building trades had slight opportunities for direct study of books, even though many of them were certainly literate. Through their close relations with clerical patrons many of them had, however, plenty of opportunity to obtain Vitruvian precepts at second-hand, and actual technical practices do suggest that an initial study of Vitruvius underlay much of the traditional methods of building. The reason for the disuse of the Vitruvian principles of proportion was not just ignorance or neglect, but the supersession of these principles by another and more highly developed set of principles. It was pointed out by Enlart that there is a fundamental difference between classical and mediæval systems of proportion in architecture, in that the latter had constant reference to human scale. This is not merely evidenced by the dimensional system of statures, seen for example at Compostela at the end of the eleventh century (see page 232); it permeates the whole relationship of parts to the completed work. If one Greek or Roman temple was built to twice the length of another, every one of its parts was multiplied in the same ratio of two to one. This was not so in the Gothic period, where the designers' appreciation of natural fitness had taken a further step, possibly the result of observing that a large tree has leaves of the same size as those of a small tree of the same kind. Whatever the source, the Gothic architects certainly possessed an elaborate geometrical system which remained a secret of their own.

The most important source of information on this system of proportion is the album of Villard de Honnecourt, recording the practices of the first half of the thirteenth century. Far more explicit facts are derived from later sources which none the less indicate a long continued tradition. The best known is the account by Cesare Cesariano, in his 1521 edition of Vitruvius, of the rival systems of proportion discussed at the building of Milan Cathedral about 1385–1400. These differing systems were evidently national or regional. Secondly, there are several treatises by German masters, the earliest having been published in 1486 by Matthaeus Roritzer, ostensibly on the setting-out of pinnacles, but revealing a good deal of geometrical method of general application. Thirdly, and in some ways the most important because the most explicit, the mediæval matter incorporated in a Spanish treatise of 1681. What is preserved is the substance of a book which had existed in manuscript for over a century, embodying the practice of the famous architect Rodrigo Gil de Hontañón, who died in 1577, the last of a great dynasty of Spanish master masons who designed in Gothic style the final group of cathedrals in the Peninsula. Master Rodrigo Gil gives the geometrical methods for producing appropriately proportioned plans and sections for churches with a single nave, or with three or five aisles. These constructions apply to a number of the most important Gothic buildings of Spain, as was shown forty years ago by Lampérez.

Just as there had been several distinct Orders of classical architecture, each with its own rules, so there were several Gothic methods of proportion at first distinctive of particular regions but later carried abroad. Eventually the system, as applied in any one country or district, was of great complexity. It was never, so far as we know, committed to writing in its entirety, but had to be learned from a master by word of mouth and by practical demonstration. As time went on there was an increasing reliance upon recorded examples of plan, design and details, and in the fifteenth and sixteenth centuries a number of books bequeathed by master masons were probably of this nature. Such bequests included "patterns" left in 1417 and 1459 by the distinguished English architects Stephen Lote and John Clerke; the "books of portraitures" of Henry Smyth (1517), and the more extensive collection of portraitures, plates, books and other tools and instruments left in 1546 by Henry VIII's architect, John Molton, to an apprentice and two of his former assistants. Had some of these drawings and books survived they would provide English analogies for the late Gothic pattern-book bequeathed by Master Hans to the lodge of St. Theobald in Thann about 1470, and which is now in the National Library at Vienna.

Whether or not any of these collections amounted to a treatise upon the principles and methods of Gothic design is immaterial. It may be that chance discoveries will throw further light upon their precise nature. In the meantime it is certain from the evidence that has come down that there were geometrical and proportional rules and that they were highly complex. This makes it easy to understand why the study of the Vitruvian precepts became so popular after the Renaissance, and why this generalized study had so cataclysmic an effect upon European architecture. Only by years of apprenticeship or equivalent technical education could the older rules of Gothic be mastered; while the newly rediscovered classical rules of Vitruvius were easy enough for bishops to follow, and princes and the nobility and gentry could try their hand at design. This startling development had much to do with the subsequent depression of the master craftsmen and the rise of the professional architect to an established social position.*

Another major change was wrought in art by the introduction of the convention known as "linear perspective". This implied that in painting and sculpture there was a *scientific* link between the physiological function of the eye as a photographic lens, and the finished work. Just as the reintroduction of Vitruvian tenets proved a negation of the element of human scale, here too is the paradox that the discovery of perspective was not a liberation but a limitation. The eye as a lens can observe from one viewpoint only, but the mind is able to appreciate simultaneously not only the stereoscopic effect of an object seen with both eyes, but also successive appearances of the same object from different viewpoints. This faculty was exploited by artists of Ancient Egypt, of

*The uncertain status of the European artist, striving for acceptance, contrasts unfavourably wth the established rank and emolument of Chinese artists from remote antiquity.

Byzantium, and of Gothic Europe, and after a lapse of some four centuries is once again accepted orthodoxy.

What is in question is not the relative value of Gothic and Renaissance architecture, but the relative degree of freedom of the Gothic artist to express his personality. A major change had indeed taken place, in favour of greater individuality and originality, not at the end but at the beginning of the Gothic age. This change in the twelfth century has been termed a "Renaissance", but its character was different from that of the fifteenth and sixteenth centuries. The later revival was of Roman forms to the exclusion of national tradition, whereas the earlier revolution had been against the static dead hand of Rome and in favour of a dynamic art inspired by symbolism and expressing structural forces. At the very same time a similar artistic revolution occurred in the Near East. The round-arched and static architecture of Byzantium, conservatively fostered in Constantinople as late as the fifteenth century, was superseded in most of the Eastern Empire by the dynamic pointed-arched style brought out of Persia, Iraq and Syria by the Seljuk Turks as they pushed westwards in the eleventh and twelfth centuries.

The great change can be traced in all art forms: in handwriting, which preserved Roman characters down to 1100 and then rapidly broke away into Lombardic and Black Letter; in painting, where copying of earlier exemplars gave place to original designs based on natural models and on geometrical invention; in architecture, where the round arch and debased versions of the classic order yielded to the pointed arch. Fresh canons of proportion harmonized with a new, highly articulated construction, itself based on a sweeping improvement in technique. Lastly comes music, of special evidential value as a non-plastic art whose history has been worked out independently from surviving examples. All the early Christian hymns were scrupulously modelled on existing hymns, and Gregorian chant imposed uniformity on the Western Church to the exclusion of national variants. On the other hand the twelfth-century troubadours and trouvères attached great significance to originality. Music also demonstrates two further points: the words set often contain unorthodox doctrinal statements, proving that iconographical censorship was not omniscient, even regarding verbal error in doctrine; and the actual music of the time is far in advance of the theoretical treatises. The theoreticians were academic lecturers, frequently a century behind the practice of their own day. Yet were it not for the overwhelming amount of actually datable music now deciphered the notes of their lectures would be considered sound evidence of contemporary musical practice. Thus even

* *

in the field of church music, highly academic and ecclesiastical, the lead had passed from clerical theorists to experimental laymen before 1200.

In the highly technical field of the plastic arts, and especially in the complexities of large-scale architecture, the same holds true. Only men with a long training in the techniques of construction could possibly design great churches and castles that would stand up and adequately serve their purposes; and for reasons already given (see page 31) only long training would suffice for mastery of the geometrical systems underlying æsthetic design. The very rapid development of Gothic architecture shows that the masters were constantly experimenting and that they were keenly competitive.

Conditions of this kind naturally lead to the formation of individual styles among the competing artists; and we do in fact find highly individual personality in Gothic style if buildings of the same date and of related purpose are compared. This makes it all the more extraordinary that the claim should have been made that mediæval artists suffered from a psychological lack of personality so great as to merit the term "essential anonymity". No substantial evidence for this nonsensical hypothesis has ever been produced, yet several ingenious attempts to establish a case have been made within the last century. These largely contradict one another, and most of them have been clearly refuted; but because the literature of the subject has been profoundly contaminated it is necessary to enumerate the chief schemes of argument—for they cannot be described as bodies of evidence. There have been three main contentions :

1. That in the Middle Ages there were no individual artists; works of art were mere works made by spontaneous teams of craftsmen imbued with a common purpose and getting their results directly from the materials without any intervening stage of design, abstract or concrete. Mediæval man is consequently reduced to a purely instinctive gregarious creature comparable to the hive-bee. This, the most startling and interesting case, recommends itself to belief by its very impossibility. The hard facts of history completely refute this theory. Unlike the uniform cells of the honeybee, the products of mediæval craftsmen vary almost infinitely in size, shape, and every other characteristic. Not one single jot or tittle of evidence exists that mediæval—or indeed any other—men have ever set to work by mere spontaneous enthusiasm without either leadership or foresight. With much of the enormous body of positive evidence for mediæval design I have dealt elsewhere, and a good deal more will be recapitulated here.

2. The second argument is merely that we do not know the names

of mediæval artists; therefore they did not exist. Though this illogical view had a wide currency, it has been disposed of by the discovery of many thousands of names of artists of all kinds in all European countries. Incidentally, the great majority of these artists were laymen, not monastic or secular clerks.

3. The third scheme attempts to refine upon the second, by accepting the discovery of names linked to works, but alleging that in the Middle Ages men were not interested in them. Since so many names are found in impersonal sources of archival character, it is suggested that this implies a lack of interest and that this in turn must reflect a lack of personality in the artists themselves. This argument too is refuted by the many references which do occur in mediæval writings to outstanding artists and works of art. Further evidence of general esteem for the greater artists is supplied by the use of the title "Master" in referring to them, almost alone among non-academic laymen (see page 172, sec. 16). Furthermore, they were able to command relatively high fees which placed them on a level with the modern professional man, and were socially accepted as "esquires" and "gentlemen".

The literary records are impressive, and some of them are so extensive that they are here set out in full in the Appendices, as for example the account (see page 232) of the rebuilding of the cathedral of Santiago de Compostela. (Figs. 1a, 1b.) The work was undertaken in about 1071 by Bishop Diego Peláez, and two committees were set up. One was administrative and consisted of three clerics: Wicart, the treasurer Segered, and abbot Gundesund; the men in charge of the technical side of the works were the "marvellous master" Bernard, and Robert, in charge of the stonemasons, who numbered about fifty. Bernard was called "the Old", apparently to distinguish him from one of the canons, Bernardo Gutiérrez, who rather later took administrative charge. Not only are the names of these first architects preserved, but also those of their successors Esteban (in or before 1101) who also worked at Pamplona, and another Bernard (in 1109). Between them these masters account for the original works. Towards the end of the twelfth century the west front was added, with the Pórtico de la Gloria. (Fig. 1b.) Again the architect's name was placed on record, and a good deal is known about him. He was Master Mateo, a layman with a wife and family, in charge of bridge building in 1161, and in 1168 given a royal grant of the direction and mastership of the cathedral works. Twenty years later he had the special privilege of placing the great inscription on the lintel of the doors, recording that on 1st April, 1188 it had been set up by Master Mateo, who had directed the work from the start. Mateo was still alive in 1217, when he must have been over seventy-five, and his fame has never diminished. In Santiago his property in the Plaza de la Azabachería was still described in 1435 as the "Casas del maestro Mateo."

In the eleventh century the chronicler of St. Maxentius at Poitiers had thought it worthwhile to note that the architect Walter Coorland was sent about 1025 by Emma, Queen of England, to rebuild the monastery of St. Hilaire-le-Grand. At the end of that century Abbot Scotland's new church in the monastery of St. Augustine at Canterbury was built under the direction of Blithere, "a most distinguished master of the craftsmen". The St. Albans chronicle of the same period boasts that the architect of the Abbey, Master Robert, "excelled all the masons of his time"; while in the opening years of the twelfth century Croyland Abbey was built under the administrative charge of Prior Odo by Arnold "a lay-brother of the monastery but a most learned master of the art of masonry". Orderic Vital tells us that the Castle of Ivry was built by an architect (*architectus*) called Lanfred, "the praise of whose talents outdid all the craftsmen then in Gaul".

Towards 1200 Reginald of Durham referred to the Bishop's engineer Richard de Wolveston as a skilful craftsman and experienced architect (*artificiosus . . . opere et prudens architectus*), very well known by name and for his skill to all the inhabitants of the region, by which the whole of Durham and Northumberland was meant. Just across the English Channel, at the opening of the thirteenth century, a major defensive work was undertaken at the Castle of Ardres, near St. Omer, and full credit was given to the engineer, Master Simon. The whole account, by Lambert of Ardres, is so lively as to merit quotation at some length :

Arnold (II, count of Guines) . . . seeing that Ardres was at the centre of the county and had started to grow richer than the other castles and towns in the territory and so more coveted by his impatient enemies, decided to take greater precautions there. So he surrounded it with a great moat on the model of that at St. Omer, such as none had taken in hand, nor eye had seen, in the land of Guines. There were plenty of workmen available for making and digging this moat, hard pressed by the bitter season and the pangs of hunger rather than by the labour and heat of the day. On the job they could moderate their hunger by chatting to one another and lightening their labour with jokes. A great many people for various reasons gathered to watch the work on this vast ditch. There were poor—not among the workmen—who did not feel their poverty while they could enjoy the sight of the works; while rich men, knights, burgesses, and many priests and monks stood there not once a day but several times, for the pleasure of watching such a remarkable sight. Who, that was not listless and half dead of old age or troubles, would not have enjoyed seeing Master Simon, the dike engineer, (*fossarium*), so learned in geometrical work, proceeding in magistral manner with his rule (*virga*), and here and there setting out the work already conceived in his mind, not so much with his measuring-rod as with the yardstick (*pertica*) of his eyes; demolishing houses and barns, cutting down orchards and trees in flower and fruit; seeing to the ways prepared with the utmost care and labour for the accommodation of passers-by, not so much on holidays as on workdays; digging up the garths with their vegetables and plantations of flax, destroying and trampling down the sown plots to form paths, amid the indignation and groans of those cursing him under their breath.

The plinth of the south porch at Notre-Dame in Paris is inscribed as begun in 1258 by Jean de Chelles, then master mason; there are many other examples of the commemoration of artists in official inscriptions or records of their work. After the fall of part of the south nave of St. Albans Abbey in 1323 the rebuilding is stated to have been placed under the charge of Henry Wy, master mason, (Fig. 24) while the same chronicle of the abbots mentions Master Geoffrey the carpenter, the accomplished author of the choir stalls at the same period. Later in the fourteenth century the French poetess Christine de Pisan referred to the master mason of Charles V, Raymond du Temple, as "a learned artist who very well understood geometry, and who showed his knowledge in the designing of his buildings". Master Raymond was not only noted as a designer, but also as a constructional expert, for in 1401 he was asked to visit Troyes Cathedral to survey the fabric. He was too busy himself to undertake the journey of 100 miles in each direction, but recommended two other consultants (see page 218).

There was then a great deal of clearly expressed and intelligent interest in mediæval architects and their work, so much as to compare quite well with the infrequent mentions of Renaissance architects in purely literary and historical sources as late as the seventeenth and eighteenth centuries. In this respect mediæval architects were no better, and perhaps little worse off than their fellow practitioners of classical or modern times. Many artists of the present day meet with neglect, in spite of the existence of printing and other media of publicity and advertisement; in the Middle Ages, on the contrary, it is evident that a great many artists enjoyed widespread renown, being sent for from long distances. In 1153 the windows for the abbey of Braine-le-Comte in Hainault were made by English glass-painters; about 1220 Abbot David of Bristol wrote to the Dean of Wells to ask for the loan of his sculptor, "L.", to carve the pillars of the (Elder) Lady Chapel. A little later the album, or encyclopædia of building and art, of Villard d'Honnecourt proves the extensive travels of a Picard architect and engineer, who got as far as Hungary; it also demonstrates his knowledge of principles of proportion, and that he sketched details which he thought beautiful. In 1287 Etienne de Bonneuil went from Paris to Uppsala in northern Sweden to take charge of the work of the cathedral there; and in the same year Master John the mason son of Tyno went from St.-Dié in Alsace to repair the cathedral of Gyulafehérvár (Alba Iulia) in Transylvania, a distance of over 1,200 miles.

Even though journeys within England may seem relatively insignificant, there must have been compelling reasons for the employment at Winchester Cathedral in 1308 of a carpenter from Blofield in Norfolk, William Lyngwode. He worked for an architect, Thomas of Witney, who had probably come from that Oxfordshire town, a manor of the bishop of Winchester; Witney, as we shall see, was himself to be called as far as Exeter (see page 133). William Hunt, a London carver, was paid in 1467 for coming to Winchester College to design and draw out (*imaginando et excogitando*) a new roodloft for the Chapel. Instances could be multiplied, not only in Britain and in Europe, but also throughout the Islamic lands, where travel by artists was often over very long distances indeed. The claim that there was a lack of mediæval interest in artists, forming the third argument, falls to the ground.

4. The three fantasies rebutted above, though tenacious of life, may be considered extinct, but in recent years a fourth has emerged though, as far as I am aware, never enunciated as a clear-cut thesis. Emphasis is placed upon a supposed want of æsthetic *intention* in design, implying that the appearance of any mediæval work of art was a happy accident. Adherence to traditional style, sound manual training in a craft such as painting or stone cutting, and the adherence to iconographical schemes dictated by the clergy, are (it would seem) enough to make æsthetics superfluous. The rise of this strange proposition, fighting a rearguard action against the recognition of mediæval art, can only be regarded as the outcome of an intellectual snobbery. Architects and artists of the Middle Ages are considered, *ipso facto*, to be menial mechanics necessarily incapable of creative genius; credit for their wondrous works *must* be given exclusively to the clerical intelligentsia.

At a later stage we shall have to consider how far the idea of a dichotomy between creative intellect (on the part of the clerical order) and base manual skills is valid (see page 137; page 170, Sec. 3). Here it is necessary to reflect on the hieratic or iconographical approach to mediæval art. That the study of iconography provides a valuable clue to the workings of the mediæval mind is undoubted, but it is far less relevant to design in the æsthetic sense. As we have seen (see page 28), standard subjects such as the Crucifixion, or a set of Types and Antitypes, are irrelevant to *design* as such. The most rigidly controlled subject admits of varieties of treatment, and it is precisely in this variety that the creative faculty of the artist finds scope. If this were not the case, the interest of connoisseurs and critics in the primitives and old masters would be unintelligible. As in the first three cases, it is here again essential that we should appeal from mere assertions to the recorded facts. What were the æsthetic views and aims of the Middle Ages?

Abundant documentary evidence completely refutes any suggestion that Gothic people were not concerned with beauty. If we accept the famous definition of St. Thomas Aquinas, that "Beauty is that which pleases on sight", we can trace an interest in the beautiful back to a date long before the invention of Gothic style. Examples will follow, but it is as well to mention that beauty was in fact a major preoccupation of the philosophers of the thirteenth century. The discussions of the subject by Aquinas, by Adam de Belladonna, by Witelo, and by others, prove on the highest level that æsthetic interests existed. So voluminous is the evidence that a modern study takes up three volumes. It is true that this philosophic discussion of æsthetics was on a highly intellectual plane; we can learn far more of contemporary views on what constituted beauty by reference to works of art which drew forth expressions of esteem, or for which very high prices were paid.

The historian William of Malmesbury, writing about 1125, had a decided preoccupation with artistic questions and frequently made references to beauty. Even when referring to a period long past, in describing the work of St. Wilfrid at Hexham, built in 673–78, he records :

> Wonderful is the amount of building that he completed there, standing to an impressive height and surrounded with a number of spiral staircases. Much was built under his own direction (*arbitratu proprio*), but also by the architectural skill (*magisterio*) of masons (*cementariorum*), whom the hope of high pay had brought from Rome. It became notorious among the people at the time, and was even set down in writing, that there had never been such a building on this side of the Alps. Now visitors from Rome say the same, that those who see the work at Hexham would swear that it gave the impression of Roman pomp, so little damage has been done to the beauty (*venustatem*) of the building by time and warfare.

Malmesbury also refers to the beauty of his own abbey church at Malmesbury, and that of the finely carved altar brought by Aldhelm to Bruton in Somerset. The Ramsey Abbey chronicler tells us that the west front of the church built about 968 offered a beautiful sight from afar (see page 228). Eadmer, monk of Canterbury, says that Lanfranc's new buildings greatly excelled the old in beauty as well as size; the account by Gervase of the later rebuilding of the choir after the fire of 1174 is full of appreciation of the new design. Even in that unexpected source for æsthetic appreciation, Domesday Book, its sober compilers noted that the new church of Bermondsey, evidently just built by 1086, was "*pulchra*", fine, or handsome, or fair to look upon. In the course of the first half of the twelfth century occurred the great controversy as to the value or insignificance of material beauty, between Abbot Suger of St.-Denis and St. Bernard of Clairvaux (see pages 223-7), proving that the foremost minds of the age regarded æsthetics as a vital issue even if, in the case of Bernard, fiercely to deny their validity.

Not much later it was the merest common form to assume that architecture of importance must be beautiful as well as useful. A formula for a king to write to an abbot asking for a good architect was provided in a "Complete Letter-Writer" produced in 1178–87, and opens with a reference to nobility in art :

> There will never be a noble building if its architect (*architectus*) is ignoble. In the castle I have begun I require a tower (of such strength) that the innocent may not be in fear if I or my heirs are threatened. I have been delighted to hear that in your monastery you have builders (*positores*) of excellent works, and I trust in your kindness to let one of them come to me, so that his skill may give strength to the tower I desire. I pray you to send me a man that you know to be outstanding and out of the common run (*majorem pre ceteris*)."

The impression made by the building of stone vaults over the nave of Angers Cathedral (Fig. 3) about 1150 was emphasized by the chronicler who wrote of Normand de Doué, bishop of Angers 1150–53, that he "took down the timber beams of the nave of our church, threatening to fall from sheer old age, and began to build stone vaults of wondrous effect (*miro effectu*), spending £800 of his own money on the work".

A detailed account of the tower of Beverley Minster, built about 1050 but rebuilt after the fire of 1188, contains a number of reflections upon the possible antithesis between beauty and stability :

> There was then, over the crossing at the centre of the church, a very lofty tower of wonderful beauty and size, so that it was the boast of the excellence and fine quality of the mason's craft. The building of the tower had proceeded so far that its masonry was complete; all that remained to be done was to set upon it a stone spire (*tectum lapidei operis*) of proportionate height. The craftsmen in charge of the work were not as cautious as they should have been, nor as judicious as they were outstanding in their art; they were intent upon beauty rather than strength, on delighting the eye rather than ensuring stability (*magis invigilabant decori, quam fortitudini,*

magis delectationi quam commodo stabilitatis). For when they built
the four main piers as supports for the whole of the load to be placed
upon them, they set them in the old work elegantly rather than
firmly, in the way of those who sew a new patch into an old
garment. So it happened that neither the bases nor the shafts of the
piers were strong enough to hold up the enormous pile of such
astonishing and lofty height. Though their weakness could be seen
well enough in the course of the work by the cracks and the fall of
pieces (of stone), and by the splitting of marble shafts lengthwise
from base to cap; yet they did not consider leaving off the work once
begun. For it is certain that a building set upon a weak foundation is
bound to fall. Thus the more they added height to the stone spire the
more they hastened the downfall of the tower; and the more they
presumed to overload the piers and bases, the wider their cracks
opened.

That artists sought beauty in their works, and also strove to imitate
nature as best they could, is shown by the narrative of the crusade of
Richard Cœur-de-Lion, written about 1200. It refers to a degree of
beauty "the lineaments of which a painter working very hard could not
exactly imitate (*qualem nec pictor plurimum laborans linealiter imitar-
etur ad unguem*)." A very similar remark occurs a few years later in the
wonderful metrical life of St. Hugh of Lincoln, which includes what is
perhaps the finest literary description of architecture ever written in
England. Referring to reflections in the polished surface of marble
shafts, the poet writes: "If art by long persistence laboured to get the
likeness exact, it could hardly equal the reality (*ut si picturam similem
simulare laboret Ars conata diu, naturam vix imitetur*)." The architectural passage is too long to be inserted here (see page 236). Also from
the early years of the thirteenth century is a reference to the supersession of Romanesque work by the new Gothic style. The chronicle of the
Bishops of Auxerre in France refers to the decision, about 1215, to
demolish the old cathedral altogether that "it might grow young in a
more elegant style of novelty" (see page 230).

The fourteenth century, as the culmination of mediæval civilization,
naturally provides many references to beauty in art. From these only a
few can be quoted. In 1317 Archbishop Walter Reynolds wrote to the
Prior of Christchurch, Canterbury, bidding him admonish the painter
Jordan for having spread a report that the great reredos of the high
altar of the cathedral was to be sold. The rumour was false, "for Christ
the patron of our church knows that we have determined that that
painting should perpetually be kept there for the adornment of the altar
of His Church and ours, on account of its beauty (*propter eius
speciositatem*)". Three years later the Bishop of London was appealing

for contributions to carry out extensive and urgent repairs to the great steeple of St. Paul's Cathedral, described as "splendid and long famous" and "which used not only to delight the eyes of beholders with its beauty (*intuentibus sui decore venustare solebat aspectum*) but also offered increase of pious devotion to the contemplative". This latter point certainly refers to the theological and devotional reasons for the mediæval insistence upon tall pointed spires and pinnacles, prompting meditation and drawing it heavenwards. Three years later again, in 1323, two Irish Franciscans on their way to the Holy Land passed through England and France and recorded impressions of buildings they saw in Lichfield, London and Westminster (see page 239).

Even relatively ancient buildings were regarded as beautiful, as when a petition to the Pope in 1407 described the collapse of the thirteenth-century central tower of York Minster, a belfry which had been "lofty and delectable to see, to whose corners the aisles of the church seemed to cling". William Worcestre, visiting Exeter Cathedral (Fig. 7) in 1478, remarks that "the whole church is arched over in a most lovely way" (*pulcherimo modo*), and the register of St. Albans Abbey includes an even more definite piece of æsthetic criticism in describing the great altar-screen (Fig. 2) made for Abbot Walnyford about 1480–90 : "that most highly decorated, sumptuous and lofty face of the high altar, which greatly adorns the church and fills with pleasure the eyes of beholders; to all who gaze upon it, it is the most divine object in the whole kingdom". At the opening of the sixteenth century the brother architects Robert and William Vertue were boasting to Bishop Oliver King that the vault they had designed for the choir of his new abbey church at Bath (Fig. 5) would be so fine that "there shall be none so goodly, neither in England, nor in France" (see page 220).

We have now considered three main subjects in relation to mediæval art : what is meant by *architecture*; what constitutes *design*; and what were the reactions of the period to *beauty*. To conclude we may turn once more to the subject of artistic personality and its relation to authoritative tradition. In classical Greece and Rome such a tradition had grown up by stages of free evolution within the framework of the Orders. Freedom and further progress were largely excluded by the encyclopædic treatise of Vitruvius, but the move to Byzantium and the division of the Roman Empire were to lead to the rise of a new style with eastern antecedents, at first largely Syrian and later Armenian, that we know as Byzantine. Both Western and Eastern Roman art tended to become static : in the East work continued to be of high quality but was fossilized; in the West the barbarian invasions induced degradation. Improvements in the blood of western rulers, through marriages with princesses from further east, led much later to the resurgent art movements known as Carolingian, Ottonian and

Romanesque. Through the architecture of all these periods the Vitruvian Orders had a greater or less degreee of after-life, and the individual artist was dominated by the style. The onset of Gothic in the first half of the twelfth century for the first time reversed this dominance, and gave far greater scope for individual originality to the new masters of genius. If we regard the achievements of Ancient Greece as truly European, the advent of Gothic was the first notable era of creative action in Europe for fifteen hundred years; in the West, it is the only such inventive outburst of primarily æsthetic character.

The strength of Gothic architecture, as the mistress art in charge of the whole movement, lay in its direct relationship to human individuals: its methods were always taught personally and never by the medium of written texts. Hence its mystery to us, but hence also, while it lived, its superb vitality and regenerative power. For several centuries art remained in the hands of the experimental layman: neither royal nor ecclesiastical patrons had the knowledge of how it was done. The tragedy of the Renaissance lies in its recovery of the dead written code of Vitruvius as a method of design: architecture since 1500 has been as it were commentary and case-law on the Vitruvian Code. It has become the plaything of the highly literate and intellectual classes, and until the present century has been more and more divorced from technical reality. In spite of Brother Pugin's diatribes, the real weakness of the Renaissance was not fundamentally opposed by the Gothic Revival, which was based only upon a superficial study of the old monuments. Only the recovery of the governing code—which had never been reduced to writing—could possibly have justified the movement, and this was a point actually brought out by C. R. Cockerell in 1845.

In the present century there has been an architectural rebellion against all authority, whether of a written code or of a living tradition. Complete and absolute, not merely relative, freedom has been claimed as the right of the artist. Yet it is curious to note that one of the leaders of emancipated architecture, Le Corbusier, produced in Le Modulor a proportional system of neo-mediæval character. True genius and outstanding gifts will burst through all systems and transcend all codes, but as we have seen some form of law, of form, of rhythm, is vital at least for educational purposes. In the history of European architecture the conflict has not been between law and anarchy, but between the written Roman Code of Vitruvius and the customary common law of the Gothic building masters. Students of legal history will find a remarkable parallel in the twofold development of law in Western Europe, the written civil law of Rome and the traditional law of the northern peoples: precisely those

Franks, Burgundians, Lombards, Normans, Saxons and Goths amongst whom Gothic art came to light and flourished for half a millennium. In the ancient complexity of an unwritten customary law, accommodating itself to differences of experience from place to place, and in the governing principles of art, steadily developing and also regionally adapted, there is something consonant with the inner spirit of north-western Europe and especially of England. For England and her political and historical offshoots are still the living centre of the common law, vanquished almost everywhere else by the written code. So the material for discussion in this book will be largely drawn from English sources, which exemplify in the highest degree the natural development of Gothic design, where each generation produced organic growth in the body of tradition.

I

The Middle Ages and
Mediæval Architecture

"IF they went beyond taste by poking into barbarous ages when there was no taste one could forgive them," wrote Horace Walpole of the Society of Antiquaries in 1774; and he continued : "they catch at the first ugly thing they see, and take it for old because it is new to them, and then usher it pompously into the world as if they had made a discovery, though they have not yet cleared up a single point that is of the least importance or that tends to settle any obscure passage in history."

Behind the polemics of two centuries ago there is a hidden truth : that history is truly the story of taste, and that it is only those men, down the ages, who have possessed taste, that have created history. Among the ponderous burden of archæological finds of two hundred years there is a precious sprinkling of the salt of the earth : exhibits spread over some five millennia and over a great part of the habitable globe, showing to the percipient where the best taste has been exercised at any given moment. Often linked to the progress of urban civilization, but never identical with it, human culture has grown and had its being by the exercise of taste, that is of æsthetic discrimination. This discrimination is and has always been the possession of a minority of the human race, a relatively small number of men and women concerned with quality rather than quantity. All great art has been produced in response to the demands of this minority, and is the outward and visible sign of the presence—recognized or not—of a well-bred biological caste. It follows that the routes taken by this better blood can be traced by looking for those places and periods in which the most notable outbursts of art have occurred.

Several of the greatest periods of art are distant in time : in the early dynasties of Ancient Egypt; others distant in place, as the classical periods of China and Japan. Within what may be called the European theatre the whole of recorded history, together with all that has so far been added by archæological research, can show only two phases of the highest importance when judged by universal standards. The first of these, in Archaic and Periclean Greece, was geographically marginal, but has been of supreme value because it was accompanied by the organizing of scientific thought. It is this capacity for thought which has produced the modern world from the applied results of abstraction; and it is an odd reflection that the first European achievement of high art—in the temples of Greece, European, Asiatic and insular—was accomplished as a qualitative product of brains devoted primarily to mathematical quantity. The temples, and the rest of Greek art, display a taste based upon the geometrical expression of mathematics, as discovered and developed by leading minds from Pythagoras to Euclid. It is not for nothing that Pythagoras and Euclid have ever since remained uncanonized patrons of art.

The second, and far greater, artistic uprush was that of the Middle Ages. It belongs to the centuries from the eleventh to the sixteenth of the Christian era, and to Western Europe, and in its five hundred years of life it produced a greater bulk, in sheer quantity, of the highest art, than any other of recorded time. The union of exquisite quality with enormous productivity makes the study of mediæval art difficult, in spite of the losses brought by wars, revolutions, iconoclasm, pillage and mere accident. Yet it is this very difficulty which lends to the study of the Middle Ages much of its powerful attraction. We are intrigued by the fact that *here*, all around us, are the dozens of cathedrals, scores of abbeys and castles, hundreds of churches, thousands of minor works of art, which we know ourselves incapable of producing even with the help of modern advances in science and industry. Just to maintain them in sound condition often proves beyond our powers.

Among this impressive output the greatest achievements—not merely in size—are those of Architecture. As we have seen already (see pages 12, 18), architecture is a function, the creative imagination of structures in advance of their erection, destined to fulfil needs both practical and æsthetic. This flimsy dream fabric finds expression in the hard material reality of stone, timber, tiles and lead, through the medium of a series of techniques of craftsmanship in each of these materials. The same materials could be shaped, purely for practical purposes, in traditional ways handed down, and without the exercise of fresh and creative thought. This process yields vernacular structures, that is to say, folk-lore in the solid, evolving slowly in accordance with the availability of local materials, and the varying types of human craftsman. Regional appearance, varying as it does, is the outcome of this in the long run. Superimposed upon this web of traditional building methods and regional types is the inspired edifice of true architecture, responsive primarily to requirements imposed from above by the patron or client. Such requirements, including specifically æsthetic needs, came initially from the ruler: emperor, king, pope, doge, bishop, and provided the programme within which the architect—by whatever name he was known—had to produce a design and bring it to realization. Where, as in the case of churches and chapels, the buildings designed were to fulfil the purposes of religion, the programme included the evocation of the numinous, so that a design was filled with psychological overtones in accordance with symbols at least partly understood by a given public.

Architecture is, and always has been, the Mistress Art, all-embracing and setting the pace for the plastic and decorative arts. This is precisely because architecture is concerned with practical, æsthetic and psychological fulfilment at one and the same time. Sculpture, painting, and the host of minor arts are comprehended within architecture and owe to it their very existence. It is also in architecture that Man at times can come closest to success in his endeavours to imitate the Creator of the natural environment. The Middle Ages symbolized this clearly in representations of God the Father, as Creator of the Universe, measuring it out with the giant compasses of the architectural or speculative master mason.

Thus architecture can present, and in our period did present, a complete world-outlook. It is the physical extrusion of a state of mind, the clearest expression of a way of life. By observing the architecture of a given place produced in a given period we obtain the deepest insight into the motivation of the human society of which it forms the fossil shell. This remains true quite independently of whether that society consciously concerned itself with architecture as a means of expression, or discussed its symbolism and purpose. It is enough that the culture of that time and place simply expressed itself by that means: actions speak louder than words. Those societies which have consciously, and possibly self-consciously, considered and analysed architecture most fully are not necessarily the best equipped architecturally. Conversely, nothing is lacking to the totality of architectural expression from the mere fact that there may be no explicit or recorded signs of the appreciation of architecture as art. An Angkor Wat still buried in the jungle, even though exerting no influence whatever, is still as profoundly important for its own sake. Architecture is itself.

We are faced by a paradox: architecture in the Middle Ages is of supreme importance to Western Europe for its quality; yet its impact stems largely from its quantity. The great bulk of some individual buildings, not in itself, but when added to a superb quality of integrated design; and the enormous numbers of buildings preserved—not to mention the many totally lost—are certainly significant factors that have to be taken into account. Mere size cannot be of the essence of art; yet art obviously must be produced in some quantity to be adequately appreciated. To this extent it is legitimate to count heads, to reckon up the vast numbers of buildings in their various kinds. At all times, however, there must be present in each example numbered the character of high quality. Obviously there was a great deal of art of poor quality produced in the Middle Ages, as in any other period, and one must beware of the superstitious awe which regards all relics of early centuries as important simply because they are ancient. This is the folly of antiquarianism against which Horace Walpole protested vainly, but wisely (see page 45). Quality is best perceived and estimated by men of taste; but those criteria which a man of taste might invoke to substantiate his assessment of quality, after his lightning judgment had been made, can presumably be used as guides to the formulation of instructed answers. Quality can be present both in simple and in complex artefacts; but since the presence of "quality" implies remoteness from mere crudity, it must also indicate a certain degree of complexity of organization. The deceptively "simple" Paris model is really the outcome of untold and innumerable factors of subtle design. The qualification of art can thus be assimilated to the arrangement by natural scientists of the forms of biological life in ascending order from the simplest to the most complex, concluding in Man. It becomes evident that, within the orbit of Man himself, there is a hierarchy of artistic capacity: the highest art will be found where its internal organization was most nicely adapted to the faculty of æsthetic appreciation possessed by the very highest of human types.

It is not within the scope of this book to institute general comparisons between the great world cultures or the great periods of architecture. Yet it must be premised that there is some degree of consensus as to the relative, if not absolute, standing of a number of outstanding cultures. In Europe, as we have seen, such a consensus admits that the two great periods have been those of ancient Greece, and those of Western Christendom in the Middle Ages; to these, on the margins of Europe, we must add the output of the Byzantine epoch, and that of Islam. The close parallelism between artistic, and especially architectural, developments in Christendom and in Islam, from the eleventh century onwards, is not only of high significance, but is worthy of detailed study because of the fact that in both cultures there is a large body of surviving monuments coupled with extensive documentation. It is beyond hope that the fully detailed history of the ancient architecture of the Near East and of Egypt could ever be written: too great a proportion of the output has been lost, too many of the records. But in time it is well within the bounds of possibility that an adequate understanding of both Islamic and of Gothic architecture can be reached.

Emphasis is here laid upon Islamic art, because no single culture can be considered in absolute isolation; and the relations between

Christendom and Islam were intimate and prolonged, even if antagonistic. Furthermore, some of the vital factors of western mediæval art can be shown to derive from the Islamic area. The fundamental truth of the diffusion of culture has to be accepted, and with it the dependence of every period of art upon an antecedent period—whether that can be identified or not. Architectural historians in the West have for long concentrated upon one particular continuity of artistic doctrine : from Greece to Rome, to early and Byzantine Christendom, and thence through the Romanesque and Gothic periods to the Renaissance of interest in the forms of classical Rome and the Roman Empire. While there is some degree of truth in this pedigree of structural forms, it overlooks the existence of a fundamental distinction between two of its generations, the Romanesque and the Gothic. The deepest problem in architectural design is that of solids and voids and involves the structural methods of trabeation or arcuation—proper to timber and to stone respectively. In masonry buildings there is a primary distinction in the form of the arch. The arches of Roman antiquity and of the derivative styles down to Romanesque inclusive, and again in the Renaissance, are semicircular. To the round arch the basic contradiction is offered by the pointed arch, found in the Near East in early Islamic buildings, and later in Gothic work in the West. This change in the form of the arch marks a complete antithesis between the æsthetic of the Classical and Renaissance West on the one hand; and, on the other, the western Gothic and eastern Islamic forms of building. These, united in opposition, share a common basic symbolism, expressing the aspiring quality of verticality as against the static repose of the horizontal.

Superadded to this common foundation, the architectures of the Christian West and Muslim East came, early in the twelfth century, to share in a dependence upon the rediscovery and study of Euclidean geometry. This had been saved by its translation, first from the original Greek into Arabic in the ninth century A.D., then into Latin from the Arabic version early in the twelfth century. This common heritage resulted in an architecture which, both in East and West, was an exercise in the solid geometry of space and in the proportional arrangement of its parts. The concept, already referred to, of the Almighty acting as a Master Geometrician in the act of Creation, provided a theological model for imitation by the earthly architect. The skills involved in designing a complex preconceived pattern in the solid, and then by the operations of stereotomy—geometrical cutting of stones— bringing the design into material existence, far transcended the mere work of artisans and constituted an exemplified philosophy or religion made manifest.

Architecture, even though it was acknowledged as the mistress art, and its forms assiduously copied by minor artists, was not just that.

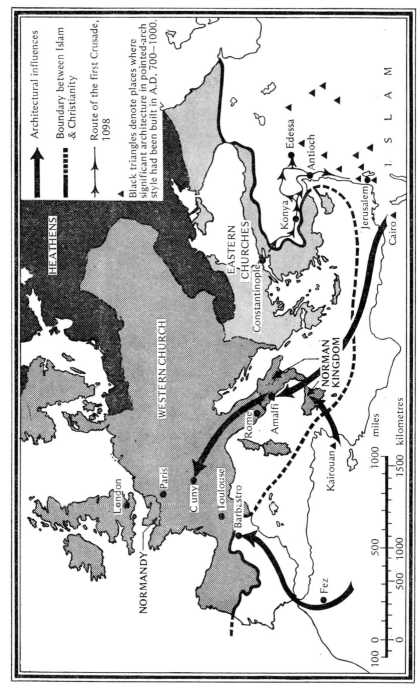

Europe and Mediterranean region: conditions relevant to the rise of the Gothic style.

During the mediæval period it provided a synthesis of Science and Art, of Reason and Emotion, of both the Numinous and the Practical; its æsthetic evaluation touched—as it ought always to touch—spirit, mind and body together. The architect was not simply a master craftsman of a traditional manual skill on the one hand, nor was he, on the other, an academic student of abstract science. Thus he escaped the lack of sophistication that is the inescapable penalty of the folk-artist, and at the same time avoided the practical incapacity of all too many modern architects, who are often unable to translate their ideas into effective material form through lack of an adequate practical training. It may be easier to grasp this point by thinking of the *mere* craftsman as one who has learned to play the piano by ear but knows nothing of musical theory or the great composers; and the architect, in the modern sense, as a professor of musical theory who cannot play the piano or any other musical instrument at all. It is this fantastic dichotomy of functions in the modern world that forces us to look back to the Middle Ages for the best example of the true architect, who combined in himself the whole of the knowledge and the skills required to produce effective and noble works. It must be admitted that comparatively few mediæval architects actually reached the topmost heights; yet the norm of their achievement was certainly on a higher plane than that of almost any other culture.

In dealing with the Middle Ages, as with any other extended period, it has to be remembered that constant internal development was taking place, and that constant external stimuli were being applied. The five centuries from A.D. 1000 to A.D. 1500 were not just a single undifferentiated phenomenon; but they do have a kind of coherence when contrasted with earlier and with later ages. In many ways they can more fitly be compared with early Chinese and Japanese civilization than with either Roman or Modern life. At the present day we can still obtain a first-hand impression of the kind of life involved by visiting the old cities of Fez or Tetuan in northern Morocco. In spite of the difference of official religion, there was very little in the fundamentals of everyday existence to distinguish between mediæval Europe on one side and the Near East or North Africa on the other. In the thirteenth century there was no single sharp transition, as from "white" to "black", on a journey between London and Fez by the stages Paris, Toulouse, Barcelona, Valencia, Granada, Tetuan; the transition from ruling Christendom to ruling Islam—both with important Jewish minorities—by way of cities and countries where the two great religions coexisted, was gradual. The two worlds were, for many purposes including major international trade, very nearly one. It is even probable that there would have been a much sharper sense of division between the western Christian and his Orthodox contemporary in Constantinople.

The common factor which united north-western and circum-Mediterranean cultures in our period was the climate of mental exploration and eagerness. Both in Islam and in Christendom men sought knowledge : from books, which were keenly sought and as keenly translated; and from repeated experiment by trial and error. Much modern literature, by its insistence on the obscurantism of some mediæval personalities,* has tended to conceal the fact that the foundations of modern empirical science were laid between the eleventh and the fourteenth centuries. It was, it is true, fashionable among many of the Schoolmen to accept without question the dicta, however mistaken, of Aristotle and other ancient authorities; yet at the same time truly enquiring free minds were at work. In the non-controversial field of architecture there were no hindrances to the formation of an empirical science comprehending both design and construction (see pages 162–65).

In discussing architectural education and methods at a later stage (see Chapter III, page 87) it will be necessary to consider what the relations were between mediæval architects and the intellectual life of their time. For the moment it is enough to say that their system was not exclusively based upon a combination of Euclidean geometry and practical experimentation. It acquired a substantial philosophical content drawn from the rediscovered Greek and Latin writers, some of them like Euclid transmitted to the West through Arabic versions, others surviving in the original to be recopied and studied afresh. A somewhat vague but none the less real architectural theory began to grow, based upon the two main theses of Proportion and Light. Proportion, as the basis of æsthetic system, depends upon the natural recognition of certain proportions as concordant, and thus as pleasing to the eye of the beholder. It is a matter of observation that certain simple geometrical relationships do yield proportions which are pleasing : such are the perfect square, the square-and-a-half, the double square. These extremely simple proportions undoubtedly lack subtlety, and it was found that a more sophisticated pleasure was experienced on seeing other proportions whose origins were less obvious. Notable among these are the relationship of the side to the height of an equilateral triangle (1 : 1.155), of the diagonal to the side of a square (1 : 1.414), and especially of the diagonal to the side of a regular pentagon (1 : 1.618), the so-called "Golden Cut". All of these proportions can be produced by simple geometry performed with a rule and a pair of compasses, and needed no calculation or knowledge of mathematical theory. Though understanding of the manipulations needed to perform each of these geometrical problems—and of course many others, starting with the

*The most famous instance of such obscurantism, the forced recantation of Galileo, did not occur until 1633!

setting-up of a right-angle—formed an important part of the skill required by a master mason, the methods did not constitute an *esoteric* secret. So far as secrecy was involved, and we shall see that there undoubtedly was a great deal of professional and industrial secrecy (see page 102), it was in straightforward defence of the privileges inseparable from specialized knowledge. It is misleading to talk of "The Secret" of the mediæval masons, as if it could be comprehended in a single arcane word, or at most in a compact statement of booklet length.

The "secrets" employed in mediæval architecture were largely matters of common plane and solid geometry solved entirely by practical methods learned by rote. To some extent there were other precepts derived from classical literature (*e.g.* the use of vinegar in splitting stone), and specifically from Vitruvius (the use of bond-timbers, of bond-stones through walls, of timber piles, of methods of levelling and of providing abutment). The sources of the various mediæval theories of proportionate design are complex, but they gave pleasure as an automatic result of their employment. Proportion occurs *as a natural phenomenon* in the harmonic series of musical progressions, and also in the relative frequencies of the wave-lengths of complementary colours. Thus the recognition of concordance in proportions has nothing esoteric about it; its foundation is in no sense metaphysical, but simply physical. It is important to stress this, as well as the simplicity of the geometrical and practical methods of setting out concordant proportions. The amazing results achieved by mediæval architects were not the outcome of divine revelation, nor did they require a highly academic education in the book-learning of their day.

It is a good deal less easy to express in any simple formula the attitude of the mediæval artist towards the other main pillar of his system : Light. In this case there was certainly a filtering down from the universities and the schoolmen of the contemporary philosophical theories of God as the Light of the World, illuminating the minds and spirits of men, and doing so through the intermediation of the works of men's hands. At the very opening of the Gothic age in the West this was already a commonplace for Abbot Suger at Saint-Denis, but at that time it was not mere physical illumination that was regarded as Light, but a quality of beauty informing the beholder. Later on in the architectural developments of the thirteenth century this became translated into physical terms, and during the fourteenth the implication of larger and ever larger windows becomes evident. The attenuation of solids and enlargement of voids, an important feature of Gothic economy of construction from the start, then became a major preoccupation of the mediæval architect as designer. It is a tribute to the soundness of Gothic structural experiments that such immense results were achieved in the direction of the piled-up enclosure of space, without there being any underlying basis of scientific technical theory. In spite of the fantastic achievements of a few great scientists at the end of the Middle Ages, notably Leonardo da Vinci, there was no mathematical Theory of Structures until the eighteenth century, and it was not put into effective use before 1800. As compared with the achievements of early and classical times, or those of the Far East, Gothic architecture must be ranked very highly for its attainment of great volume, complexity of articulation, extreme economy of materials, and capacity for the appropriate subordination of parts to a unified whole. The only other styles which can have any claim to serious comparison with Gothic in any of these respects are the Byzantine and the Saracenic.

Roman Imperial buildings had indeed been built on a vast scale, but few of them had any high degree of complex articulation, and what they achieved was done with lavish outlay of materials. The notable advance came when the Eastern Emperor Justinian in A.D. 532 entrusted the design of the new Santa Sophia in Constantinople to the two Greek architects Anthemius of Tralles and Isidorus of Miletus, both from Caria in south-west Asia Minor. Both were noted mathematicians, and Anthemius wrote on mirrors and burning-glasses—perhaps a significant preoccupation with the subject of Light. It is of importance for the study of mediæval architects that the historical accounts of the building of Santa Sophia include stories implying that Justinian himself claimed credit for aspects of the design, and even for structural devices. Whether these are true, or simply due to flattery of an all-powerful monarch, they provide a preview of the form common to so many statements in mediæval chronicles as to the responsibility of patrons and clients for the design of buildings. The utmost credit is indeed due to Justinian for his superb taste and for his evocation of the greatest single achievement in architecture up to his time. But it is hardly to be expected that he should contribute much that was specific to the designs and structural expedients of two of the most scientific architectural practitioners in history.

The fact is that for the production of all large-scale works of complex structure an architect is necessary—by no means a "professional" architect of the modern type, but none the less a highly specialized designer. This was always recognized by some patrons and, forming a favourable contrast to the reported vanity and self-satisfaction of Justinian, there stands the sympathetic figure of Ziyad ibn Abīhī, the Governor of Basra in A.D. 665. Having gathered together non-Muslim craftsmen to build the Kūfa mosque he gave credit to the master mason, saying: "That is what I desired, but I could not express it." Even for the relatively simple religious buildings of the earliest generations of Islam, it was necessary to find, generally among the unconverted Christian population, trained craftsmen and masters used to designing to a given programme. The fact that the Muslim programme was a new one presented no special problem; the "style" of the mosques would be no different from that of churches, or for that matter synagogues, designed by the same architects. Although characteristic fashions in Muslim or Jewish ornament might be used, the same architectural character was given to buildings of any of the three religions, or to contemporary secular buildings, such as the Jews' houses of Norman England. In a country where the three religions were able to form a satisfactory symbiosis it was even possible, as late as 1504, for collaborative architecture to be undertaken : in that year the municipality of Saragossa decided to erect a public clock tower and appointed an interdenominational board of five architects. Their names deserve commemoration, although the splendid tower built to their design was demolished in 1893 : Gabriel Gombao and Juan de Sariñena were Christians; Ezmed Ballabar and Monferiz, Muslims; and Juce Gali, a Jew.

The ready transference of ideas from one nation or community to another, even in the midst of war or through economic conflict, is proved again and again in the course of mediæval art. Examples of this will be given at a later stage. What is essential at the outset is to realize the vital role played by such transfers in giving to the West order for chaos, culture for crudity, and sophistication for savage outbursts of destruction. The mechanism of transfer might take several forms. Among these perhaps the most obvious is introducing foreign experts, as St. Wilfrid did in bringing architects from Rome itself to Hexham in the seventh century. At that same date Benedict Biscop brought stonemasons and glaziers into England from Rome and from Gaul. There is thus no doubt whatever that at the end of the Dark Age it was recognized that Rome, even in its barbarized state, could provide better building craftsmen than Britain, while Merovingian France was at least somewhat better off. The work carried out for St. Wilfrid at Hexham and at Ripon, however, suggests the possibility of a second form of influence. Both of his churches were provided with crypts that still survive, and these are not of simple plan. It is singular that these should have been constructed at the very time that the travelled bishop Arculf, on return from the Holy Land, was wrecked on the coast of Britain and reached Iona, there to relate his experiences and to set down sketch plans (copies of which still survive) of the holy places. It is not essential to believe that Wilfrid's crypts were planned in imitation of Arculf's sketches, but they could have been, and drawings brought back by pilgrims and travellers are certainly a major source of information throughout history.

That the plans of the Holy Places were imitated is, of course, notorious, and the round churches of the Templars and Hospitallers deliberately copied the plan of the Dome of the Rock, supposed to be the Temple of Solomon. As this had itself been based upon the great rotunda of the Church of the Holy Sepulchre, the latter was the true architectural origin. Other Western churches were directly imitated from the Holy Sepulchre, sometimes at the behest of returned pilgrims. As early as 1036 the priory of the Holy Sepulchre at Moutier-les-Jaligny (Allier) was founded by Hictor, a nobleman who had just returned from a pilgrimage to Jerusalem. A few years later this example was followed at Neuvy-Saint-Sépulcre (Indre), where Geoffrey, vicomte of Bourges, had the church built "on the model (*ad formam*) of the Holy Sepulchre at Jerusalem". The possibility of some degree of imitation of oriental models had been present even a generation earlier, when Fulk III, count of Anjou, immediately after returning from Jerusalem, in 1020, had founded the monastery of St. Nicholas at Angers.

Intentional copying of remote models, whether by means of careful measurement, rough sketching, or from memory, was thus in vogue in the eleventh century, and took its place in the great movement of church building vividly described by Raoul Glaber :

> Just after the millennium, about the third year following, there happened through almost all the lands of the (Christian) world, but especially in Italy and France, a great rebuilding of church fabrics. For notwithstanding that many of them were already in a fit state and had very little need of improvement, yet every community of Christendom vied with another to possess one still better. It looked as though the very globe had shaken itself, throwing off its old age, immediately to put on a white robe of churches. The faithful everywhere changed almost all the cathedrals, and other minsters of many saints as well as the lesser churches of the towns, into a better form.

The general account of Glaber is given specific confirmation by the detailed story of the rebuilding of the abbey church of St.-Rémi at Rheims (Fig. 6). This is of particular interest for two reasons : that the church was deliberately intended to be larger and more elaborate than any other in France—which implies some compiled information regarding the size and character of other major churches; and because the employment of skilled architects is thought worthy of mention :

> In the year A.D. 1005 abbot Airard, considering that a number of pastors of the Lord's flock in his time had shone throughout France by their care for putting their aged churches into better condition, decided to set to work on the renewal of what had been entrusted to his care. For this purpose he brought together men regarded as

skilled in architecture (*qui architecturæ periti ferebantur*), and began to build the new church from its foundations with squared stones. It was much more elaborate and ambitious than those already rebuilt in France, as above mentioned, so that it was beyond the capacity of himself and the men of his time to complete it ... Thierry (abbot 1034–45), on succeeding Airard, resolved to complete the rebuilding of his church, which his predecessor had started. But what was begun was far too large to be finished, so that—had he determined to continue the work—it could not have been brought to completion. So, after taking counsel of those who were, among themselves, regarded as the most skilful, and of the elders of the province of Rheims [possibly an early architectural congress; see pp. 142–43] he undertook with some difficulty the demolition of the work already begun. No sooner was it pulled down, leaving in place some foundations which the architects considered necessary (*quae architectis visa sunt necessaria*) for the future buildings, he began to build the divine house with a form of structure easier to complete, yet by no means inferior, as can easily be seen by those who look at it.

Several things in this detailed statement are worth noting. The reference to the ambitious scale of the church planned in 1005 can be justified by the actual dimensions of the reduced successor dedicated in 1049. The central span of its aisled nave is about 43 feet in width, about the same as at Speyer Cathedral (about 1030) and wider than any other clear span of its time except for the 52 feet of the aisleless nave at Angers Cathedral. Considerably later in the century St. Ambrogio at Milan, one of the grandest churches of the epoch, was content with a slightly smaller span (about $42\frac{1}{2}$ feet). Finally, within the last quarter of the century, there came the still wider spans of the aisleless nave of York Minster, shown by recent excavation to have been about 45 feet across, and the central span at the metropolitan cathedral of Tarragona in Spain, of some 46 feet. Secondly it is revealing that the chronicler in the same breath refers to skilled architects as responsible for the design, and to the abbot as the "builder". Throughout the Middle Ages the same formula was adopted, to the confusion of historians who have repeatedly sought to take such statements literally, and to credit distinguished churchmen, not merely with being their own architects, but also as being do-it-yourself builders. In a few cases, it is true, ecclesiastics of noted sanctity, like St. Hugh of Lincoln, did carry stones and mortar, but it was as a work of humility, not one of technical skill. Finally we may notice that both the earlier and the later works were in the charge of a plurality of architects, certainly comparable to the Saragossa council of faiths of 1504, and quite probably to many genuinely collaborative architectural partnerships of modern times.

The great rebuilding after the millennium was certainly on a larger scale, and also in a new style, more definitely under remote foreign influences than that of the seventh to the tenth centuries. Yet it was to all appearances simply the fact that the churches were new and white, and larger than the old fabrics, that struck reporters. Recognition of stylistic change as such was soon to come. The break of style, from Anglo-Saxon to Norman in England, occurred at the direct inspiration of King Edward the Confessor, whose new buildings for the abbey at Westminster (1050–65) were in the continental Romanesque style which has ever since been known as Norman. William of Malmesbury, the greatest English historian of the early twelfth century, writing about 1120, tells of the opening of the year 1066 :

> So, full of years and of glory, he (King Edward) yielded up his innocent spirit to the heavenly kingdom, and was buried on the feast of the Epiphany (6th January) in that same church which he himself had built, the first in England of that style of design (*illo compositionis genere*) which now almost all are copying at enormous expense.

Once again we may correct the literal sense of the phrase : "which he himself had built". The names of the Confessor's building staff are on record, and present a curious problem, since all are clearly Saxon and not Norman. The master mason was Godwin Gretsyd, with a wife Wendelburh and a son Ælfwin, owning substantial property at Southampton and a benefactor of Hyde Abbey at Winchester. Teinfrith, the king's "church-wright", must have been the master carpenter, and was rewarded with a grant of land at Shepperton, Middlesex. Thirdly there was Leofsi Duddeson, fitz Dudda, or "Leofsi of London", who "had charge of the masons of the church" (*qui preerat illius ecclesiæ cementariis*). He was a very substantial landowner at Wormley in Hertfordshire, where he had at least the 2½ hides (about 300 acres) of land which he eventually gave to Westminster Abbey. Leofsi may have been in administrative control of the building works, though the phrase "*preerat cementariis*" is sometimes used to describe the warden or master's deputy who acted as foreman.

Edward the Confessor, though a king of Anglo-Saxon England, deliberately chose the Norman style of architecture for his great monastery, and at least three of his native subjects were sufficiently competent to produce in this foreign style a church and monastic buildings of considerable importance for the period. Although at first sight curious, the king's choice was not really surprising. In the first place, Edward's mother Emma was herself a Norman, daughter of duke Richard. Secondly, owing to the successful Danish invasion which put Sweyn on the throne of England in 1013, Edward's whole youth and early manhood was spent in exile in Normandy. He was in fact a Norman by domicile for over twenty-five years, and on his return to England he must have seen that the future lay with his maternal and adoptive rather than with his paternal inheritance.

During the lifetime of the Confessor the Normans became the leading power in Europe and exercised their dynamic talents over an immense area. Their outstanding exploit, among many minor crusades and expeditions against the Saracens, was the conquest of Sicily and of most of southern Italy—what was later to become the Kingdom of the Two Sicilies, or of Naples. Through their victories in the Mediterranean region the Normans, led by Robert Guiscard and other members of his family, came into intimate contact with the cultured and highly civilized world of Islam. A softer and more elegant way of life lay before them, and they were quick to adopt a great deal of its sophistication. The effect at home in Normandy was not long delayed, as we learn from a detailed history of the bishops of Coutances :

> Geoffrey I de Montbray, bishop of Coutances in Normandy (1049–93), by night and day strove with all his might and main towards the building and improvement of his church. So that he might render it renowned and glorious he set out (c. 1050–60) on pilgrimage to Apulia and Calabria to visit Robert Guiscard, who came from his own diocese, as well as other barons related to him and his pupils and acquaintance there. He brought back much gold, silver, precious stones, and various rich stuffs by way of offerings ... Since he did not have any possessions of the church, either in the city of Coutances or in the suburbs, a place where the bishop could reside or even stable his horse, not even a house of his own save a certain humble outshot which projected from the walls of the cathedral, he ... bought for £300 from William the most victorious duke of the Normans, afterwards also the glorious king of the English, the better half of the city suburbs, with the tolls and dues, the mills, and many houses of one Grimold. Afterwards he built the bishop's hall and other offices, and planted a considerable coppice and vineyard ... At Coutances he also made two pools with mills; he won part of the site of the park from the Count of Mortain and surrounded the park with a double ditch and a palisade. Within he sowed acorns and took pains to grow oaks and beeches and other forest trees, filling the park with deer from England ... he built a stone bridge over the Vire ... For the church he appointed a precentor and succentor, a schoolmaster, keepers of the church, clerks and prebendaries, goldsmiths, blacksmiths, carpenters and a master mason (*magistrum cœmentarium*).

A new pattern, to become extremely familiar in course of time, had appeared, on Norman soil, but very shortly to be carried into England with the victorious troops of 1066. Bishops reformed their cathedral establishments, put the clerical and lay staff upon a proper permanent footing, built palaces for themselves, and began that habit of creating parks and woods which was to have such an impact upon the historical landscapes of northern France and of England. The enclosed park, or "paradise", with pools of water and shady trees, had been typical of the Near East from time immemorial. It was introduced by the Muslims to Sicily, and was now brought at a single leap to the far north-west of Europe. Normandy and England might not have palms, figs or olives; but they did have a plentiful rainfall, noble species of indigenous forest trees, and a climate in which vineyards could flourish. Even if the wine were not of the best, it was plentiful; and experiment with other fruits, better acclimatized, yielded cider and perry. The Normans, like the latterday army of Napoleon, learned rapidly to march on their stomachs, and carried on with them to their new conquests not only their *batterie de cuisine* but an extensive vocabulary of foodstuffs which supplanted for ever almost every English word for eatables.

Turning again to William of Malmesbury, who sums up the Norman character in their first half-century as masters of England:

> As I have said, they wished to have huge buildings, but modest expenses; to envy their equals, to surpass their betters; to defend their subjects from outsiders while robbing them themselves. Upon their arrival (1066) they raised the standard of religion which in England had died down; you may see everywhere churches in the cities, monasteries in the villages and towns, rising in a new style of building (*novo ædificandi genere*); the country flourishing after a modern manner (*recenti ritu*).

That the Normans desired, and obtained, huge buildings was no exaggeration: for the first time England came to have buildings large by any standard in history. It was precisely the problems set by the enormous scale of the new works that challenged the resources of men with architectural skills; and in producing an organization capable of assembling the materials and work force, laid the foundations of English industrialism.

Although there were some large churches in Normandy, it was in England that the Norman style approached megalomania. Perhaps not quite as large as the great church of Cluny III, those of Winchester Cathedral and of Bury St. Edmunds abbey were nevertheless in the same class, and Winchester at least was very considerably longer than Cluny. The Norman York Minster, after extensions in the first thirty years of the twelfth century, and Old St. Paul's in London, formed a class of runners-up to the Cluny category. In a second class Durham was a little larger than Santiago de Compostela, substantially bigger than St. Sernin at Toulouse or St. Martin at Tours, the largest of the French pilgrimage churches. Churches of this magnitude were only possible—and most of them were built within one or two generations—because of the enthusiasm for religion which went hand in hand with the Norman warriors. It may be that their consciences were uneasy; it is certain that their generosity in church endowments was fantastic in relation to the maximum national budgets of their period.

The love of huge buildings was not limited to churches. The second of the Norman kings, William Rufus, built for his palace at Westminster the largest hall north of the Alps, and one that was to remain the largest for some 150 years, until it was surpassed by the royal Salle des Pas Perdus in Paris. To give some comparative idea of scale, the central space of the Basilica of Maxentius and Constantine in Rome measured 265 feet by 83 feet and was 120 feet high (built A.D. 312); in the Near East the Throne Room of Chosroes I (the Great Arch) at Ctesiphon had the same span, 83 feet, but was only 160 feet long (built A.D. 550). In Europe north of the Alps in the middle of the eleventh century (about 1040–50) the Imperial Hall at Goslar (Fig. 8) was only 145 feet in length by a span of 45 feet. The new Westminster Hall of William II covered two and a half times this area, being 238 feet long and 68 feet in span, although it was divided into three aisles by ranges of posts supporting the roof trusses.

Few of the architects of the great Norman churches are known to us by name. Robert, the master of St. Albans, we have already met as a man celebrated in his own day. Hugh the mason, probably the designer of Winchester Cathedral, held two ploughlands under Bishop Walchelin in 1086. Master Andrew was in charge at St. Paul's in London in the 1130s and later, while the great nave was rising. A certain Ælric, who had undoubtedly had a share in the building of the nave of Durham (1099–1128), went to Scotland and was master at the building of the royal abbey of Dunfermline in the second quarter of the century; the estate granted to him took from him the name of Masterton, and he was certainly the first great architect to work in Scotland. The name of the Westminster Hall master was not recorded, but it may be deduced from Sir Charles Clay's detailed study of the hereditary keepership of the Old Palace of Westminster. In Henry II's reign the keeper was Nathanael de Leveland, whose duties were performed by deputy by Ailnoth, the king's "engineer" (chief architect); but Nathanael's father, Geoffrey de Leveland, had himself been the royal engineer to Henry I in 1130, and derived his office from his father, Wimund de Leveland, who was already keeper of the Palace before 1100. Since the great hall of Rufus is known to have been built in 1097–99, it is a reasonable conclusion that Wimund de Leveland, royal engineer, was its designer. He and his descendants held a knight's fee of land of the Archbishop of Canterbury at Leaveland, near Faversham in Kent; Wimund was contemporary with Archbishop Anselm, for whom he may have worked at Canterbury, but this is mere conjecture. What we know is that the Norman church of the rival abbey of St. Augustine's, Canterbury, was built under one Blithere between 1070 and 1091, when he was described as "the most distinguished master of the craftsmen and director of the admirable church (*præstantissimus artificum magister, templique spectabilis dictator*)".

Before going on to consider the mediæval architect himself something more must be said on certain aspects of the mediæval background to architecture. We have already seen Bishop Geoffrey de Montbray of Coutances, visiting his relatives in the South of Italy and coming back to sow acorns and beechmast, forming a park beside his new episcopal palace. This was not an isolated phenomenon; from it arises a never-ending stream of consequences, in France and in England. Particularly in England, the end-product is the landscape style and the cult of the picturesque, developed by way of a keen observation of nature and living things (in the Middle Ages, notably birds, so often portrayed in the margins of illuminated manuscripts). Evidence for keen interest in landscape and topography can be carried back to Norman times, and because it provides such clear evidence of a certain coupling of sophistication with naivety it is an important corrective to the more solid facts of the history of state and the history of art.

Here is the little seaside town of Fécamp (Fig. 9) in Normandy, seen about 1110 in the reign of King Henry I by an early clerical tourist, Baudri, archbishop of the Breton province of Dol (1107–30):

> At length I saw Fécamp, of which I had heard much from pilgrims . . . I was received into the cloister, I saw the length of the church, the noble size of the house of God, its plenitude of fine ornaments. There was one thing in that church which pleased me not a little, that for the praise and worship of God is mentioned by David in his Psalms (CL.4): *Praise God*, he says, *on the strings and organ*. There I saw such a musical instrument, made of air-pipes which, when blown by means of bellows, render for the players a soft melody; by its joined compass and symphonic sound it united deep, middle and high voices, so that one might think it a choir of clerks singing together: boys, old men and youths meeting and harmonizing in praise. They call this the organs, and play it at certain times. . . .
>
> Not to pass over the site of Fécamp, I shall acquit myself in a few words on the place. It is like a garden of Paradise, set in a lovely

enclosed valley, between two hills, surrounded by farmland on one side and a charming little wood on the other. This seems to be of such even growth that it might be thought to have grown on a single day or to have been cropped back in height. The summits of its boughs and leaves and twigs are so thick that by their shade and strength they favour both the earth and the view: they keep off the heat of the sun and repel the onset of the rains. The trees stand up somewhat from their stocks, not very tall, but pleasant to stroll under. The sea is close to Fécamp, for it lies not a mile off, abounding in fish, with daily tides; there is a sheltered harbour where the pleasant clean water laps the quayside. There are springs of fresh water and it is a place fit for orchards, growing good apple trees. The stream flowing by the castle has windings both pleasant and serviceable (presumably for defence), and the splendid castle is surrounded by very strong walls. The Seine, the river of the country, is some fifteen miles from Fécamp; it has plentiful fisheries and provides Fécamp with this food. The abbey stands on the cliff, surrounded with very fine high walls; it is in great part covered with lead. Its church is called the gate of heaven and the palace of God himself, and is likened to the heavenly Jerusalem. It shines with gold and silver, is honoured with silken vestments and relics of the saints, glories in the special invocation of the Holy Trinity ... pilgrims throng to it in solemn crowds.

Archbishop Baudri was exceptionally articulate for his time, but he was not altogether different from the general run of cultured observers. Among the vast throngs of solemn pilgrims to Fécamp and to many other shrines there were clearly many who, like Spanish holidaymakers at the present day, could combine pleasure with instruction and holy contemplation. Strolling under the shade of the trees suggests the alamedas of the Peninsula and the institution of the *paseo*, the saunter with friends in the gardens and avenues around the city, so common also in Turkey and as far away as the Lowlands of Scotland. Mediæval bishops and abbots and their chroniclers through the twelfth and thirteenth centuries revert to this theme, and from what we know of royal and noble households there can be no doubt that parks, gardens and landscape often did form a frame to architecture, not by accident but of intent. In each development there is a probability amounting to a moral certainty that the inspiration came from Sicily by way of the comings and goings of its Norman lords, or from the Crusader states in the Near East.

William the Conqueror was notoriously fond of hunting and it was through the same addiction that his son Rufus came to his mysterious death. Both hunting and hawking, the open-air sports of the ancient world, owe much of their charm to the pleasure of contacts with the landscape in all weathers and, as is evident from the surviving treatises, to the opportunities afforded for serious observation of the habits of animals and birds. These pleasures in themselves might be enjoyed in the wild, but royal and episcopal taste demanded improvement also. By 1110 the park at Woodstock was being enclosed within a stone wall, and Henry I was stocking it as a zoological gardens with lions, lynxes, leopards, camels and a porcupine sent from Montpelier and compared by the historian William of Malmesbury with the scientific account of it given by Pliny the Younger in the eighth book of his Natural History, and by Isidore in his Etymologies. The king's manorhouse and garden, known as Kingsbury, beside his new borough of Dunstable, covered nine acres. The way in which such country estates were deliberately designed for pleasure appears from the detailed description of the works done in 1145–58 for Bishop Guillaume de Passavant of Le Mans:

> At Le Mans, near the church of St. Ouen, he built a stone manorhouse of considerable size and roofed it with stone. Near this he made the chamber where he himself lay, brilliantly lit by a range of windows along each side. Though the materials were good, the craftsmanship was even better, for the quality of these works and the design of the chamber did great credit to the genius of the architect (*ingenium artificis*) which there displayed both beauty and fine taste (*pulcrius et subtilius relucebat*). He set the chapel adjoining the chamber; notwithstanding that its beauty was greater when it came first from the craftsman's hand, it was painted with figures exactly depicting different kinds of animals with wonderful skill, captivating not just the eyes but the minds of beholders. Their attention was so held that they stopped to take pleasure in them, forgetful of their work. Those for whom business waited seemed quite unconcerned, carried away by these pictures.
>
> Thirdly, next the chapel he laid out a hall, whose whole design (*compositio*) and particularly that of its windows, was of such beauty that it seemed to be by the same hand as the other two buildings, or by one yet more skilful; so that there the architect might be thought to have outdone himself. Lower down, on the sites of the houses he bought, he had a garden (*viridarium*) planted with many sorts of trees for grafting foreign fruits (*per insertionem fructus alienos*), equally lovely; for those leaning out of the hall windows to admire the beauty of the trees, and others in the garden looking at the fair show of the windows, could both delight in what they saw.

Rather later the bishop of Auxerre, Hugh de Noyers, was having similar improvements carried out in the grounds of his manor at Charbuy (Yonne), between 1183 and 1206:

At Charbuy, a town belonging to the see (five miles west of Auxerre), he provided every pleasure and improvement that the industry of man could accomplish. The woods, beset with briars and undergrowth and thus of little value, he cleared and brought into cultivation. There he made gardens and planted trees of different sorts so that, apart from deriving pleasure from them, he also got great quantities of fruit. He surrounded a large part of the woods with a ring fence carried from the gate at the near end to the dam of the third pool, and enclosed within a pretty quantity of wild beasts. These might be seen grazing in their herds by those in the palace, a pleasing sight.

This last remark indicates the growth of spectatorship as a pastime. Among the favourite recreations of the courtiers of Europe was the watching of tournaments, joustings and, later on, tilting. It was usual for temporary staging to be erected, but at the Cheapside Tournament of 1331 the royal box collapsed, precipitating Queen Phillippa and her ladies and seriously injuring distinguished spectators beneath. The carpenters responsible were saved from punishment through the intercession of the Queen on her knees before Edward III; but the king then had "a fair building of stone", a gallery of two storeys, built along the north front of St. Mary-le-Bow church as a permanent grandstand. It continued to be used by royalty for watching great shows until the time of Henry VIII*, and though it did not, apparently, set a fashion, it had at least one architectural descendant. Jousting was the sport of Richard II's half-brother John Holand, earl of Huntingdon and later duke of Exeter. Building the first great English country-house at Dartington in South Devon, between 1388 and 1400, Holand had his private apartments ranged around a courtyard so placed that a two-storied gallery looked down upon an arena formed out of a natural combe beneath. The quantity of jousting equipment found at Dartington Hall after Holand's death confirms his reputation and for once proves the truth of the local tradition that has long described the place as the "tournament ground" or (anachronistically) "the tiltyard".

After the introduction of tilting in the fifteenth century the "Tiltyard Walls" were built at Kenilworth Castle in 1464, and Kenilworth was undoubtedly another instance of the noble residence where provision was made for recreational shows. A survey taken about 1545 for Henry VIII described the "strong tower" of John of Gaunt's state apartments as having "large windows opening towards the park and the great mere current (flowing) under the same, very commodiously to see the deer coursed and to see the fish taken." John of Gaunt, as titular king of

---

*"The tradition was so strong that, when Bow Church was rebuilt by Wren, a royal gallery overlooking the street was provided."

Castile, had in the late fourteenth century turned Kenilworth into a royal palace of the highest class, and after his time it was still further improved by Henry V, who about 1414 had a summer pavilion built within a separate moat beyond the far end of the great lake. This was known as "Le plesans en marys" and was doubtless inspired by Everswell ("Rosamond's Bower") in the park at Woodstock. The model of Everswell must indeed have spread far and wide, even to quite minor imitations, for within the first few years after Wykeham's fellows had settled into Winchester College they had in their mainly utilitarian garden a hedged and railed pleasance of walks and arbours, entered through a gate, and called "Rosemoundes Bowre".

The fashion for emparking and gardening had descended in the social scale more than 150 years before the first mention in 1403, of the Winchester College bower. Matthew Paris provides a potted biography in somewhat scurrilous vein of one of the new rich of the first half of the thirteenth century:

> A certain lettered knight or knightly clerk, Paulin Peyvre by name, died at London on 5th June (1251). He was steward to King Henry III and one of his principal councillors. When he first came into touch with the Court he owned hardly enough land for two ploughs, but soon he had got hold of so many lands and rents by fair means or foul that he had more than fifty carucates (*i.e.* hides, each of about 120 acres) of good land and could be seen to have risen to the wealth and luxury of earls. He was an insatiable buyer-up of estates and an unrivalled builder of manorhouses. To say nothing of the rest he so beset one, named Toddington (in Bedfordshire) with a palisade, chapel, chambers (*thalamis*) and other houses of stone, roofed with lead, and with orchards and pools, that it became the wonder of beholders. For during many years the workmen on his buildings were said to be paid as much as £5 a week or frequently 10 marks (£6 13s. 4d.) for their wages.* (Paulin died and was buried at London, but his heart at Toddington; his widow remarried Sir John de Gray of Wilton), a man endowed with good taste as well as manly (*elegans et strenuus*)... and so as an unexpected heir dwelt in the noble buildings, as yet hardly finished.

The reference to the luxury of earls suggests that by about 1200 there must have been a number of the higher nobility in England with enough taste to have, not merely large and comfortable living apartments, but also the amenities of parks and gardens. Monastic houses had always had gardens and orchards, partly for economic reasons but

---

*At the time an ordinary labourer might take 3d. a day or 1s. 6d. a week; a skilled craftsman 4d. to 6d. a day; the suggestion is that Peyvre had a labour force of at least fifty men constantly at work.

also to fulfil obligations of their rule. Infirmary gardens grew a wide range of herbs needed for medicine, but even in Norman times they were regarded also as flower gardens for pleasure, for about 1092 William Rufus and his courtiers demanded admission to the nunnery gardens at Romsey "as if to look at the roses and other flowering herbs". The king really wished to see the heiress of the Saxon line, Edith Matilda of Scotland, who was boarding in the convent school and then aged twelve; but the cautious mother abbess quickly disguised her in a nun's veil and put her among the procession of nuns to walk through the garden before the king, who did not seek further information.

By the later thirteenth century the cult of gardening was spreading, and not only abbeys, but also the country manorhouses of the abbots were being provided with new gardens. One of the great formers of such gardens was William de Colerne, abbot of Malmesbury (1260–92), who made new gardens at Crudwell and at Purton, both in Wiltshire, the latter garden having two pools, as well as a mill with millpond close by. At Malmesbury Abbey itself :

> next to the abbot's garden he built a great and noble hall and another lesser hall at its gable end, roofed with stone tile; and had the building which had formerly been the hall converted into a chamber ... When he had bought the houses and plots of Ralph de Porta and the widow of Thurstan le Brasur beside the abbot's garden, he had a vineyard planted there and surrounded with a stone wall on all sides. He also made a herb-garden [or arbour?] next to that vineyard, alongside the King's Wall, and caused vines and fruit trees to be planted all over the abbot's garden.

The relationship between mediæval architecture and gardening has been dwelt upon at some length because it has in the past been seriously underrated; and also because it shows so clearly that the æsthetic interests of cultured men in the Middle Ages did not differ in kind from those of other times. The twelfth-century bishops of Le Mans and Auxerre were in no way concerned with theology or iconography in arranging the layout of their palace grounds; still less were laymen, from kings and earls down to the newly rich bourgeoisie. Mediæval people, in spite of differences of emphasis, were not fundamentally unlike those of the present day or of any other age. The pleasures of watching sports, or the activity of others on building sites; of strolling under shady trees and in flower gardens; of contemplating notable works of architecture in fine surroundings, are all common factors which make the mediæval scene intelligible. It is above all necessary to avoid picturing the whole Gothic epoch as fossilized into fixed hieratic attitudes, or as mysteriously singled out by Providence for special treatment.

Within the wide field of this mediæval scene as a whole we have now to concentrate attention upon the figure of the architect. Often unknown to us by name, he was all the same in charge of all that required the exercise of his supreme function of design : not only of individual buildings, but of their layout and surroundings. It is true that some town-plans "just growed" by haphazard; but other new boroughs, such as Dunstable in the time of Henry I, the bastides of France, Winchelsea and Hull in the thirteenth century, were planned. When an opportunity offered, as in the planning of the new Salisbury Cathedral on a fresh site in 1220, the frame of a great building was considered as an integral part of the unit of design. This is not to say that the chief architect of any major building was necessarily personally responsible for all these aspects, any more than the appointment of an architect in modern times precludes the consultation also of town planners, landscape designers, sculptors, painters, or makers of furniture and fittings. Yet at all times, when some great scheme is being planned, and involves this multitude of varying but related functions, that of co-ordinator and commander-in-chief belongs to the architect.

II

The Mediæval
Architect

THE term architect has been limited by modern professionalism and even by law; in the attempt to raise their professional and social status to an equality with the ancient callings of physic and the law, practitioners of the nineteenth and twentieth centuries have paradoxically tended to overlook one of the greatest qualities of their predecessors. It is customary in our day to think of artists as vainglorious and individualistic, and this stems not merely from observation, but from reading highly exceptional autobiographies such as that of Benvenuto Cellini. Such freakish "show-offs" do produce entertaining reading at times—though the self-centred vanity of Wordsworth might even tend to take away from the pleasure of his poetry—but they are not typical. Much of the modern misconception of the mediæval architect is due to the fact that he was more often than not filled with a spirit of genuine humility, yet mixed with a proper and self-respecting pride in his work. It was rather the patrons who boasted of the genius which was in fact that of their architects. This theme was touched in the relationship between Justinian and his architects (see page 54), and in a different way found expression in the anticipatory boast of the chapter of Seville (Fig. 10) in 1401, when they recorded their decision to "build such and so great a church that those who see it finished may think us mad".*

It was well remarked by Coleridge that those who "have tried their talents . . . and have failed" for that reason turn critics. There is also much truth in the complementary fact, that successful artists seldom turn their hands to criticism or to producing theories of art. The dynamic force of inner genius gives them no leisure for such inessential activities. So the immense scale and quality of mediæval architecture kept its exponents fully occupied, and for that reason we do not get from them detailed written treatises. In this context it is

---

*"Fagamos una iglesia tal e tan grande, que los que la vieren acabada nos tengan por locos."

noteworthy that the one outstanding book on the whole field of architecture was written by the highly competent mediocrity, Vitruvius. "Do as I say, not as I do" is the mark of the preacher; the mediæval architect, like all the greatest artists, was content to let his actions speak louder than words and to leave behind him for emulation the best that—as he saw it—God could produce by using him as a vehicle.

The more or less total lack of literary exposition of the art of architecture within our period, natural as it is, means that the history of the art has be to written externally. We must deduce the correct answers, primarily from the works themselves, but also from surviving records of many different kinds. On the whole, the evidence of factual archives: contracts, accounts, lawsuits, is preferable to that of descriptive historians. Just occasionally a letter or some other fragment of personalia will brighten the scene with a gleam of human interest; a few of the best historians will display their capacity for entering into the underlying motives and characteristics of artistic activity. But these glimpses must be accepted as a bonus, and when they are absent great caution must be exercised before any stress is laid on the "negative evidence" of absence. Before going further, two documentary instances will be given of the dangers of relying on the apparent absence of evidence. A great deal depends upon mere chance survival, and perhaps even more on the good or bad luck of the modern scholar in coming across the survivals.

The first example is concerned with the rise of apprenticeship as a formal means of providing education in craft skills. It is not in dispute that the word *apprenticius*, one who apprehends or learns (French *apprendre*), appears first only in the thirteenth century, and probably first in the specifically legal sense of students of law. Simultaneously or almost immediately afterwards the word began to be applied to learners who were bound to masters by a special form of legal contract. Again, it is not in dispute that thoughout the ages there must have been learners in every skill, though they were not bound by specific contract, and were not known as apprentices. What concerns us here is the tendency in modern scholarship to seek special reasons for the (apparently) late development of the apprentice system in the building trades which included the main body of mediæval architects. In particular it has been suggested that masons' apprentices did not exist until near the end of the fourteenth century, because—so it was thought—they were not mentioned in any document. They may indeed have been uncommon, but they did exist, for a few instances have come to light proving that masons took apprentices throughout the fourteenth century. The earliest document to appear so far, of 1307, is important because it goes further and proves that at that time the method was already a commonplace. Its evidential value is strengthened by the fact that it refers to the remoter parts of the north of England.

In 1292 the little town of Stamfordham, Northumberland, was shaken by the murder of a local freeholder, Adam fitzJoseph. His widow Alice accused one Robert de Horsley of the crime. Fifteen years later the murdered man's son, John, decided to train as a mason :

> This is an agreement made between John fitzAdam fitzJoseph of Stamfordham and William the mason (*cementarium*) of the same, namely that the foresaid John has leased and granted to the foresaid William a messuage and four acres of land with their appurtenances in Stamfordham for the term of nine years, the term to begin at the feast of Whitsun (14th May) in the year 1307, in exchange for his keep in board and clothing and for his training (*erudicione*) through the whole of the foresaid term to learn his craft (*ad misterium suum adiscendum*). And the foresaid William shall do the due and accustomed services to the chief lord of the fee and the external services and aids to our lord the King. And if the foresaid John should die within the said term without completing his service to the foresaid William, then the said William shall keep the whole of the said land to the end of the said term and shall maintain it in as good condition as he received it. And if the foresaid William shall refuse to maintain or to teach the foresaid John in manner of an apprentice (*more apprenticii*) and according to the custom of his craft (*misterii sui*) through the whole of the said term, the foresaid John may (take back) the land for himself (*some words lost*) ... shall pay his costs assessed by the view of lawful men at the end of the term or shall hold the said land beyond the said term until his costs have been recovered from the foresaid land. And if the said William should die within the said term and Margaret his wife survive him, the foresaid Margaret shall have the foresaid building repaired anew, for her dower ... And if it should exceed the third part of her dower the foresaid Margaret shall restore to the foresaid John as much as a true valuation shall adjudge. With these witnesses : William of Hawkwell, John of Matfen, William of Eachwick, Thomas of Hawkwell, Duncan of Stamfordham.

The impression made by this agreement, of a highly organized provincial society including a mason prepared to educate the boy for nine years, has to be set against the all-too-common picture of barbarous and completely isolated rural communities. As we shall see in connection with the long journeys made by architects, communications were quite adequate and did not form any bar to the diffusion of ideas. The second document which helps to put a different emphasis on received doctrine concerns the use of chimneys, more especially chimneys built of brick. It is quite well known that some wall-chimneys of stone were being built in the twelfth century, but the insertion of brick chimneys into houses of moderate size is commonly regarded as a phenomenon of the middle and latter part of the sixteenth century. This is mainly because William Harrison (1534–1593), in his *Description of England* published in 1577, put "the multitude of chimneys lately erected" first of the things "marvellously altered in England" within the recollection of "old men yet dwelling in the village". This was, of course, a merely local statement from a rural area; but it has been made the foundation-stone of a mighty edifice of deductions. Just as there had been substantial making and usage of brick for walling, at least in some parts of England, for centuries before then, so in the case of chimneys there had been use of brick. A lease of 14th August, 1481, from Westminster Abbey to Richard Blandford of the city of Westminster, "Fremason", and his wife Elizabeth, specified that Blandford was to build or have built on each of the two tenements demised for thirty years "a kitchen of good oak timber and a chimney of brick and mortar (*breke et semento*)" within the two first years of the tenancy.

Both of these documents bring up the great disparity that may, and often does, exist between general statistics and the specific facts of given cases. In the history of invention and of the great developments in human culture it is not relevant that a particular phenomenon such as apprenticeship or brick chimneys should have been relatively rare before a certain date. The significant date is that at which the invention was first made and when it was first put into effective practice. Sheer superstition vitiates a great deal of otherwise well informed writings which should have real authority. An example of this is the extremely widely spread belief, supported by books, articles, and word of mouth, that timber was not sawn in the Middle Ages, but trimmed with an adze; and that a great tree would consequently yield only a single broad plank by means of a vast amount of hard work. This is sheer nonsense, as can be demonstrated from the many references in documents to saws and to sawyers, including pairs of pit-sawyers who produced boards and planks by conversion of larger scantlings. What is of even greater interest and significance is that the intensely practical and realistic album of Villard de Honnecourt includes a diagram of a mechanical saw driven by water power. From this we know that there were already saw-mills in the north of France early in the thirteenth century.

The surviving documents, some of which will be quoted to show the status and development of architecture during the period, are significant *for themselves* and not as parts of a statistical whole. What the records show is that, from the eleventh century at any rate, there was a considerable number of adequately skilled craftsmen, although it was not until early in the following century, after the First Crusade, that higher skills and precision made their appearance. At all times the master craftsmen were treated as worthy of consideration, and by no means as the low menials that have been pictured so often. About 1073 the abbey of Lérins began a tower of refuge on the Ile St.-Honorat off the coast of Provence, opposite Cannes, and their contract with the builders survived to be brought into a historical compilation by one of the monks at the end of the sixteenth century:

> The abbot should pay 500 *sous* to the masters, and they should perform five feet of work, and so on until completion. It must be built as aforesaid five feet in height and of the thickness of a cane's length (about 6½ English feet)* at the thinnest. For the foundation the arrangement shall be thus: if they have to dig down three feet below ground, the masters must complete the whole; but if four, then the abbot shall perform one foot and the masters three. The abbot shall lend a yoke of oxen for drawing stone; the monastery must cut down timber and carry it to the kiln; the masters must do everything else. The monastery shall also give food in the refectory, as is given to every monk, to each of the masters.

The final provision for the masters' boarding with the monks is significant as to their high status.

On Christmas Eve 1091 there was a severe tornado in Flanders, causing the belfry of the church of St.-Pierre at Oudenbourg near Bruges to lean dangerously to the east from the tower on which it stood. The inhabitants "summoned master craftsmen (*architectos*) with all speed and promised rewards (*statutis praemiis*) if they could set it back. They gave hopeful undertakings, brought ropes, set up engines (*balistas*) and straps for binding, giving much evidence of their skill." At midnight on New Year's Eve a sudden flash of lightning miraculously put the belfry firmly back on its seatings, before the engineers could put their devices into operation.

Here is further evidence to add to that for the building of St. Rémi at Rheims in the campaigns of 1005 and 1040 (see pages 56–57), that it was common in the earlier Romanesque period (using that term in its stricter modern sense) to employ a plurality of masters. It is not to be inferred that "the architect" as a single individual did not then exist, but the records and the surviving works both indicate that works

*The *canna* used in Provence contained eight palms each of about nine inches, or threequarters of the French *pied-du-roi*.

of a high degree of originality were less common than they were later. Even the amazing design of Justinian's Santa Sophia is attributed to a pair of architects working together, so that there was respectable precedent for collaboration. But it does seem to mark a stage in development in the West, when about the period of the Norman Conquest single names of designers start to appear in a stream at first intermittent but soon developing into a steady flood. Some of these names have already been mentioned and in general—apart from a few Italian masters—this emergence of individuals can be associated with the new style of more highly competent design which we think of as Norman.

Something has already been said of the Normans and of their direct contacts with the Islamic world in Sicily, even before they took part in the so-called First Crusade (see pages 59–60). Another important aspect of the Norman achievement consisted in their major participation in crusades in Spain, where contingents from the French-speaking world fought alongside the Aragonese and Castilians in the eleventh-century phases of the Reconquest of the Peninsula from the Moors. One specific event, the capture of Barbastro from the Beni Hud princes of Saragossa in 1064, must have been responsible for extensive repercussions throughout western Europe. Many thousands of Saracen prisoners were taken and sent into France and to Rome and Constantinople. Among them were singers and musicians of the highest quality, and it is indicative of the impact made by this artistic import upon the Aquitaine of Duke William VIII, leader of the expedition, that his son and heir, born in 1071, became famous in history as the earliest of the troubadours. In music and poetry, which included Arabic forms of stanza characteristic of Moorish Spain, there is no doubt of the immediate responsibility of this southern raid for the transfer of major art forms from the Islamic world to western Christendom. It must be supposed that among the prisoners there were other artists, presumably including the military engineers concerned with the defence of Barbastro. The many hundreds of female captives must have brought into northern Europe a substantial influx of the more cultured blood of the south.

At this point we approach two of the main problems regarding the mediæval architect: taken as a sector of society, who were architects; and what were the sources of their intellectual equipment? The second of these questions can more conveniently be dealt with later as a function of the architect's education. Here we must consider the more fundamental issue of the social category occupied by architects within a decidedly hierarchical structure of classes. Two serious misconceptions have ruled in this field. One is that the mediæval scene was entirely dominated by the clerical order, including both academical clerks with university degrees, and monks and friars; and that no kind of intellectual activity or higher art was imaginable outside the clerical ranks. The other is that the theoretical distinction laid down between a "noble" art such as Music, which was a subject of the academic Quadrivium, and a "base or menial" craft such as the skill of a mason or a carpenter, had a real and tangible sense in sorting out the sheep from the goats. In both of these views there may be some modicum of truth, but neither of them had substantial validity when it came to dealing with the actual cases of distinguished artists.

What tends to be overlooked in the climate of modern opinion is the supreme importance of breeding in mediæval civilization. This applies not just to noble breeding, or royal and gentle families, but also through society at large. It was to be expected that sons would follow their father's trade or craft as a rule, abandon it for some other livelihood only by exception. Study of the published rolls of Freemen of various cities, showing the trades taken up by patrimony, provides an excellent demonstration of this. In the building trades, as with others, this is borne out by finding many members of the same family engaged in the craft, sometimes as members of a family firm, but also independently. Training in the family shop or at the bench by father or uncle certainly played a great part in education before apprenticeship. In a much wider field the fundamental fact of the hereditary character of many crafts has very recently been demonstrated by Professor C. D. Darlington, who refers, for instance, to the surprise of Roman travellers when they were "told that a court architect's family in Alexandria claimed to have followed their profession through several dynasties without interruption", and to the setting up at Kiti-Kamakura in Japan in the thirteenth century A.D., by Buddhist refugees from China, of "a monastery whose family of hereditary carpenters was still in its service in the twentieth century". That such long continued exercise of the arts in families is in Japan the rule rather than the exception has long been known, but we do not have to go to the Far East or to Ancient Egypt to find examples: in Scotland the family of Mylne were Master Masons to the Crown from 1481 for seven generations, and have been architects continuously from the fifteenth century to the present day.

Hitherto little attention has been paid to the explicit claim of the mediæval masons to descent from lords' sons, but the scriptural and legendary elements in the "history" supplied by the *Constitutions* (see page 191 ff.) should not imply complete rejection of the rest. It is clear that a great deal of the history of mediæval masoncraft is contained in these authentic documents, and they should be regarded as providing genuine clues for further research. It is historically true, for example, that only men of free status could enter the craft guilds, and the Articles of the English Masons (in the *Constitutions*) insist that masters should not in any circumstances take apprentices of bond blood, not only because this might lead to conflict with their masters, but because the craft had originated among "great lords' children freely begotten". There is an immense amount of conclusive documentary evidence that masons and carpenters normally were freemen and that, in their higher ranks at any rate, they were generally also freeholders of substantial properties.

Without necessarily accepting the view that mediæval architects could actually trace descent from families in the peerage, there is a good deal of evidence proving that many of them did come from families of good standing. A number of them used coat-armour and many were termed either "gentlemen" or "esquires" at a time when these distinctions implied gentle blood or else a degree of personal distinction that was accepted as giving equal status with the gentry. John Russell, who had been Usher in Chamber and Marshal in Hall to "Good Duke Humphrey" of Gloucester (1391–1447) gave in his *Book of Nurture* the official table of precedence which must have had far earlier origins : it concludes with the ranks of "Worshipful merchants and rich artificers, Gentlemen well nurtured and of good manners" as sitting together "at a table of good squires". Another list of the same period, not limited by the requirements of verse, sets forth the order as "a parson of church (*i.e.* a rector), a secular priest, a merchant, a gentleman, an Artificer, a yeoman of good name"; it being understood that everyone, down to the yeoman of good reputation, sat at the table of esquires, and not with servants or those of menial position. Whether an artificer ranked immediately above or below a gentleman is immaterial; the official table of Court precedence is incontrovertible proof of his being a person of condition and by no means a labourer. We may strongly suspect, even if not prove so definitely, that this standing was due to the importance accorded to the creative faculty of design displayed by master craftsmen and artists (see page 173, sec, 17).

The very application of the term "Master", in Latin *Magister*, is of itself highly significant. As a mark of status it begins to be used in the first half of the twelfth century,* and almost simultaneously for the academic Master who had taken a university degree, and for a Master who was a distinguished artist or craftsman. The history of the origins of universities in western Europe indicates that if one of the two usages was in imitation of the other, it was the academic bodies which took over the traditional organisation of material crafts which taught the skill of a trade. The inculcation of craft methods had, inevitably,

---

*The Lombard Laws of A.D. 643 refer to *magistri* in charge of building (see p. 144), and this probably was a mark of status.

continued within families from remote antiquity, whereas the idea of a university was certainly new in the West in the eleventh century, even though it may have owed much to the imitation of already well established teaching bodies in the Islamic world.

It is no exaggeration to say that artisans in general took a place in mediæval society very close to that of gentlemen of coat-armour, and that masters of individual distinction could reach a position of renown which tended in fact to put them above the general run of the gentry. This was true of well-to-do painters and sculptors, and applied with greater force to architects and military engineers, who had particular opportunities for moving among their distinguished patrons, ecclesiastical or noble. The masters in the royal service in each of the kingdoms of mediæval Europe had pre-eminence except in the Germanic region, which was covered by the territorial organization of the cathedral lodges, headed by that of Strassburg Cathedral and with subordinate jurisdictions at Bern, Cologne and Vienna.

The naming of individual architects, never altogether absent, becomes more frequent in texts from about the period of the Norman Conquest, while in the twelfth century chroniclers often dwell upon the skill of designers. Important accounts are those of the building of the pilgrimage church of Santiago de Compostela under Bernard "the Old", *mirabilis magister* (see page 232), of the planning of a complex residence in the Castle of Ardres by Louis de Bourbourg (see page 207), and the full details given by Gervase of Canterbury about the successive architects William of Sens and William the Englishman (see page 210). Rather later in date is the letter written between 1192 and 1203 by Étienne de Tournai, asking the abbot of St. Bavo at Ghent to receive into his monastery the son of one Master G., an artist well known in Tournai, "whose merits are in high repute, not only here but also in many other places and churches, for his magnificent works and outstanding examples of his skill," and going on to praise his honourable and gentle character.

The fame of mediæval architects must have been widespread, since they were sent for from great distances. The renown of Robert, the designer of the Norman abbey at St. Albans, was placed on record, as was that of Richard de Wolveston, the architect and engineer to the bishop of Durham some generations later. In a less personal way other records show that the reputation of the designer travelled far and wide even in an age without printing or even any public postal service. When Richard Poore, bishop of Sarum 1217–1228, decided to move his cathedral "from its waterless hill (Old Sarum), cramped by the earl's castle (to the site of new Salisbury), he laid out spacious foundations by the advice of famous architects (*nobilium artificum*) whom he had invited from distant parts, and himself laid the first stone", He received help from Henry III and from the nobility, and Henry of Avranches, the king's poet, produced ingenious Latin verses to the effect that: "The King gives treasures (*opes*), the bishop his aid (*opem*), the stonecutters provide the workmanship (*lapicidæ dant operam*); of all three there is need (*opus*) for the work (*opus*) to stand."

The problem of plurality of designers, acting in collaboration, has already been mentioned (see pages 73–4). Though it was to occur throughout the Middle Ages (as it has done through modern times to the present day) it became less common in the thirteenth century, when the classical picture of the typical architect (Fig. 11) was presented by a Dominican preacher, Nicholas de Biard, railing against lazy bishops whose material rewards were very high. In 1261 a sermon included:

> "Masters of the masons (*magistri cementariorum*), carrying a yard-stick and with gloves on their hands, say to others: "Cut it for me this way", and do no work; yet they receive higher pay, as do many present-day bishops." In another of his sermons, Biard asked his congregation to note that: "Some work by word alone, for in those great buildings there is wont to be one chief master who ordains by word alone, rarely or never setting hand to the work, and yet gets higher pay than the rest. So there are many in the Church who have fat livings, and God knows what good they do. They labour with the tongue alone saying, 'Thus you should do', while they themselves do none of these things."

The mention of the high pay received by chief architects, a rate which certainly put them into the class of "rich artificers" mentioned by John Russell (see page 76), leads to consideration of the very extensive evidence provided by accounts and other records for the rewards of mediæval architecture. Without considering the difficult question of the changing value of money, it is possible to reckon the importance of the designer by taking the relative factor by which his salary or fees exceeded the wages of the fully skilled stonemason actually employed full time in cutting or laying stones. The difference in rate varied greatly, but it was usual for a master of architectural status to be paid twice as much as a working mason, and designers of distinction took three or four times the craftsman's rate. The ratio rose to a multiplier of six in the case of top men such as Hugh Herland the carpenter at the end of his career under Richard II, and Edward I's foreign expert, the Savoyard military engineer James of St. George, was paid about ten times the amount that working masons or carpenters took in wages. Even in Scotland, a poor country, the master mason of Roslin Chapel was paid fees of 40*l*. Scots a year, as against the stonecutter's rate of 10*l*.

For the reasons already given we may suppose that a considerable number of architects belonged to families of substantial position and even to the minor gentry. Their individual achievements enabled them still further to better their status and to emerge from the general level of the population quite as much as has been possible for architects in modern times. Master Walter of Hereford, outstanding in the service of Edward I, and master of the works at Caernarvon Castle (Fig. 12) from 1295, was actually granted a right of jurisdiction over the workmen, described in 1305 as his "free court", from which he took as perquisites the fines assessed upon contractors and others who did not keep to their undertakings. In 1347 Master Richard de Felstede, carpenter, a citizen of London, who had undertaken to make the timberwork of a great roof at Kenilworth for the Earl of Lancaster, was to have a robe of the suit of the earl's "gentlemen" (*gentils hommes*). In 1391 John Sampson, an Oxford mason accused of breaking the Statute of Labourers by taking more than the standard rate of pay, was acquitted. The justices found that: "inasmuch as he is a master mason of freestone and highly knowledgeable (*sapiens*) and subtle in that craft and in carving (*entaille*) and because the payments to such masons cannot be assessed with the payments of other masons of a different degree and station owing to the depth of his discretion and knowledge of that craft, he is dismissed at discretion (see page 144)."

In some cases it is possible to identify a triple division of skill and of social status. The Hall-Book of New College, Oxford, preserves the record of the guests who dined on 25th March, 1389: the triumvirate of the King's architects, namely Henry Yeveley and William Wynford, the master masons, and Hugh Herland the chief carpenter, all of whom sat at the high table; with the fellows there sat an assistant brought by Yeveley, perhaps his warden or deputy Walter Walton; while three servants, one of each of the three masters, took their meal with the College household. In 1436 the abbey of Bury St. Edmunds engaged a master to rebuild their steeple, John Wood of Colchester. Wood was to have board in the refectory for himself and his man, he as a gentleman and his servant as a yeoman, and whenever the convent issued liveries, Wood was to have a robe of gentleman's livery, and his servant one of yeoman's livery. The ordinary working masons and carpenters would not get robes or livery, and if they received board it would be with the other menial servants of the monastery.

In one or two cases there is some evidence of relationship to families of the country squirearchy. Possibly the most interesting of these concerns Master Ivo the mason, in charge of work at York in 1331 for Archbishop Melton. He can be identified with Ivo de Raghton, mason, who had taken up the freedom of York in 1317 and who was in 1327 assessed to the lay subsidy at £3 15*s.* 5*d.* in the parish of Holy Trinity,

Goodramgate, where he was the third richest man in the parish. Other masons and carpenters were assessed at between 10s. and 30s., except for two of the carpenters, John Hardyng, rated on £1 17s. 6d., and Robert de Lincoln, probably the Minister's master carpenter, residing in the parish of St. Michael-le-Belfrey, assessed at £2 5s. In the whole of England only one source can be found for the surname Raghton, the place Raughton in the parish of Dalston, in Cumberland. In Raughton lived the family of de Raghton who held their lands of the Crown by Grand Serjeanty of keeping the King's hawks in the Forest of Carlisle; they bore arms: *Sable a chevron argent between three quatrefoils pierced argent.* Furthermore, in the recorded pedigree of this family the rare name Ivo occurs in three generations, down to an Ivo de Raughton dead by 1328, who could well have been the father of the mason. This evidence of relationship would by itself be strong, but it is further confirmed by the strength of the stylistic association between the east front of Carlisle Cathedral (Fig. 15) designed between 1318 and 1322, and the upper part of the west front at York (Fig. 14) built between 1322 and 1339. This highly individual style of rich Curvilinear also appears in other works patronized by Archbishop Melton : the nave, and the reredos behind the high altar at Beverley Minster, in progress in 1324–34, the great cast window of Selby Abbey, begun about 1330, and the shrine of St. William at York, of which substantial fragments survive. The same influence is felt in the Southwell pulpitum and the south rose at Lincoln.

In the fifteenth century there were two notable masons named Stowell : John, who in 1458 took up the freedom of Wells, Somerset, worked at the Cathedral, and in 1470 for the parish church of St. Cuthbert. The other, Robert Stowell, received a Crown appointment as master of stonemasons at Windsor Castle in 1452; later worked at Westminster Abbey and at St. Margaret's Church, had a private practice, and died in 1505. He had been granted the office of King's Master Mason by Richard III in 1483, but the grant never became effective; all the same, he was an architect of distinguished career, and is referred to in documents as "gentleman alias esquire". It is reasonable to suppose that he and John Stowell both belonged to the Somerset family of Stowell of Stowell, some four miles south-west of Wincanton, who bore the arms : *Gules a cross lozengy argent.*

In view of the great emphasis placed upon the importance of the literate cleric in the Middle Ages, it is somewhat paradoxical that a very high proportion of clerks and monks should have come from relatively undistinguished families. The reason is a very simple one : that in an age mainly dominated by men of breeding, having family links with one another, with the higher nobility and with the royal families of Europe, the Church provided the only avenue for advancement to boys of humble birth. This is a powerful argument against the idea that any large number of clerks or monks would have had the necessary skills to act as architects. At the same time the clerical architect did exist, and something must be said to indicate the part he played in mediæval design. It is first necessary to distinguish between the secular clergy and members of monastic orders, and further to separate lay-brothers from choir-monks, and both from Augustinian Canons Regular. It may be premised that, out of a total of some 1200 English architects or surmised architects of the five centuries from 1050 to 1550, only about eighteen, or one and a half per cent, can be accepted as possibly or certainly clerical architects. Of these only two were secular priests; three were Austin Canons; five were monks; six lay-brothers (of whom three were Benedictine and three Cistercian); one was a member of the house of St. Robert of Knaresborough; and one was a Knight Templar.

The number of reasonably certain architects among these clerics amounts only to some five or six: all three of the Cistercian lay-brothers, the mason John of Waverley, and two carpenters, Henry of Corfe and Robert of Holmcultram; the early twelfth-century lay-brother of Croyland, Arnold; the Austin Canon Edmund of St. Andrew, a master carver and carpenter for Edward III; and Thomas Northwich, Benedictine monk of Evesham. Northwich is said to have been responsible for building the great tower of the abbey church; it collapsed soon after his death, no tribute to his technical skill. Ralph of Northampton, an Austin Canon sent by Henry III in 1227 to make a fishpond at Woodstock, may have had technical ability, but this is not evidenced. Rather stronger is the case for another Augustinian, Brother John Gowselle of Torksey Priory, Lincs., who was said in 1440 to be "learned in the art of stonemasonry", yet disobedient in not taking heed to the works of the church and priory. At another visitation, in 1442, it was stated that Robert Man, prior of the Benedictine Priory of Daventry, Northamptonshire, was "of no account in matters temporal . . . albeit he has some degree of experience in the craft of stonemason and carpenter (*licet aliqualem habeat experienciam in artificio cementario et carpentario*)".

Brother William of Knaresborough simply cut stones as a working mason; John of Flanders, or of St. Omer, who seems to be the same man as John of St. Albans, was an expert sculptor, but not necessarily an architect; William Corvehill, Cluniac monk of Wenlock (died 1546) was a bit of everything: "excellently and singularly experte in dyverse of the VII liberal sciences and especially in geometre, not greatly by speculacion, but by experience; and few or non of handye crafte but that he had a very gud insight in them, as the making of organs, of a clocke an chimes, an in kerving, in masonrie, and weving of silke, an in peynting . . . a gud Bell founder and a maker of the frame for bells".

We are left with two monks and two priests as seriously debatable clerical artists: Walter of Colchester (died 1248), sacrist of St. Albans, an unrivalled painter and carver (*pictor et sculptor incomparabilis*) and his secular colleague Elias of Dereham (died 1245), Canon of Salisbury and Wells, makers of the shrine for Thomas Becket set up in 1220; with Peter of Colechurch, the priest said to have designed—or built—a wooden bridge over the Thames in 1163, and to have begun the first stone London Bridge in 1176, dying in 1205; and with Alan Walsingham, sacrist of Ely and goldsmith, credited with the design of the octagon of Ely Cathedral.

Colechurch very probably was an architect, or a structural engineer, in as strict a sense as the terms need be used. There is no reason to rob him of the credit of bridging London's river, and the evidence and tradition in his favour are strong. The same cannot be said of any of the other three cases in this category. Walter Colchester may be dismissed as an artist other than an architect; there is not a scrap of evidence in favour of his having ever designed any building. Controversy over Elias of Dereham and Alan of Walsingham will probably continue to the end of time, and it is impossible to re-examine either case briefly. But it must be said that no clear case for the architectural status, either of the priest Dereham or the monk Walsingham, has ever been made out. Both were undoubtedly enlightened patrons of building works; both were manual artists of high skill in goldsmith's work and the like; both must have contributed considerably more in the way of æsthetic understanding than do most clients. The fame of Elias of Dereham depends mainly upon the assessment formed by Horace Walpole two centuries ago; and it is probable that Walpole would have viewed his own case differently had he known that identity with Elias the Engineer was chronologically impossible and suggested only because of misreading of a record in the printed sources then available.

While admitting that there were a few clerical architects, it must be emphasized that, at any rate after the period of the Norman Conquest, they were a rarity not only in England, but in Europe as a whole. The ideas of the monks as builders and of canons and bishops working on drawing boards are myths. Few would now assert that William of Wykeham was an architect; the claim was fully disposed of long ago. Yet Wykeham was once the star claimant as a typical mediæval architect; whereas he was in reality a great administrator and civil servant; a loyal if not distinguished prime minister; and one of the most enlightened educationalists and art patrons this country has ever seen. A recent book by Sir William Hayter has demonstrated the magnitude of Wykeham's achievement *as a patron*, firmly rejecting hypothetical claims to status as an architect. The fact that Wykeham's "tame" architect was the royal master mason William Wynford (Figs. 19, 20) has always been on record in Wykeham's own will, and the passage relating to his rebuilding of the nave of Winchester Cathedral has so wide a relevance as to deserve quotation at length.

Wykeham executed his will, a very long document to which he must have given extended thought, on 24th July, 1403. After asking to be buried "in the middle of a certain chapel by me newly built on the south side of the nave of" Winchester Cathedral, he devoted a long section to the arrangements for rebuilding the nave, a work already begun in 1394.

Since God has loved the splendour of his House and the place of his habitation, to the honour and praise of the same God and our Lord Jesus Christ and St. Mary his mother, and of his Apostles Peter and Paul, and of the patrons of my aforesaid church, and of Saints Birinus, Swithun, Edda and Ethelwold, whose bodies and relics are contained in the said church, I will and ordain that my Executors shall cause to be remade and duly repaired the body or middle of the aforesaid church between the south and north aisles, from the west door of the choir of the same church down to the west end, in walls, windows and vault (*valto*), honestly and honourably, conformably and decently according to the requirements and design (*formam*) and manner of the new work of the aforesaid aisles now begun, as well as the same aisles for the same length, up to the sum of Two Thousand Five Hundred Marks, if it should be needful to spend so much on the work abovesaid for the completion and finishing of the same, according to the manner and design above laid down. With the following conditions kept : that the Prior and Convent of the abovesaid church shall find all the scaffold necessary or suitable (*opportunum*) for the foresaid work; and that they shall freely and without charge permit lime and sand to be dug from their lands and quarries wherever my Executors shall think fit to obtain it from their men and tenants in the best and most useful way for the speedier and happier expedition of the said work, and to be carried and led away by the workmen of the same new work of the said church deputed for the purpose by me or my Executors, until the work of the same as thus set forth be totally completed; and so that the stones, lead, ironwork, timber, glass and other material whatsoever of the old work of the same church shall altogether yield, remain and be converted to the use, help and utility of the abovesaid new work. I will and ordain also that the disposition and ordinance of the same new work shall be performed by Master William Wynford and others sufficient, discreet and approved in that art, deputed by my Executors, if need be; and that dom Simon Membury, now Surveyor and also Paymaster of the said work shall also be Paymaster and Surveyor in future during the

abovesaid work, by survey, testimony and control of Brother John
Wayte, monk of my said church, and now Controller of the
abovesaid work on behalf of the said Prior and Convent, so long as
he shall be whole and unharmed and able to work thereat : but
otherwise, if he should be lacking, or unable to work, then by the
survey, testimony and control of another monk of the said church,
discreet, sufficient and suitable in this matter, to be chosen in
Chapter by the said Prior and Convent during the work mentioned.
And that payment for the said works shall be made from time to
time by the ordinance, disposition and discretion of all my Executors,
or at the least five of them, sworn faithfully to administer my
testament . . .

Also I bequeath for the windows both upper and lower of the
south side of the foresaid church repaired by me, to be glazed well,
honestly and decently according to the ordinance and disposition of
my Executors, Five Hundred Marks. And I will that these glass
windows be made beginning at the west end of the foresaid church in
the new work by me made in series and in order until the completion
and finishing of all the windows of the said new work of the south
side. And if anything then remain of the said sum not expended, I
will that it be fully expended on the windows of the north aisle,
beginning at the west end at the first window of the new work made
by me, and so continuing to the east end, as I have ordained above
for the south side.

Wykeham died on 25th September 1404 and was followed less than
a year later, on 26th July 1405, by his architect William Wynford.
Wynford had for six years enjoyed generous provision made for him by
the Prior and Convent of St. Swithun's Cathedral who :

have given granted and by this our present writing have confirmed to
William Wyneford, for his good service to us and to our church by
him done and to be done in future, that every day as long as he shall
live he may be at dinner and at supper in the Prior's hall of the
church aforesaid at the table of the same Prior, unless great numbers
there or the presence of important or distinguished magnates of the
country should prevent it, with his servant (*valecto*) at the servants'
table in the same hall, if the foresaid William pleases; and if he shall
wish to keep his chamber he shall have liberty to take in his chamber,
from the kitchen of the foresaid Prior as one of the esquires of the
same Prior takes in his hall, both at dinner and at supper, two loaves
of bread called "payndemayn" and two other loaves called
"Wytechuynes" and a black loaf called "blacchynum", with a gallon
and a half of the best ale as the convent takes, for himself and for his
servant, once a day. We grant also for us and our successors to the

foresaid William that he shall have the chamber in which he now dwells in the hospice of the Master of the Work of our church aforesaid for his whole life, with a robe each year of the suit of the esquires of the said prior with lamb's fur and with a robe for his servant as one of the servants of the said Prior takes, if it shall happen that the foresaid Prior is giving livery. And every day that the foresaid William eats in the hall of the said Prior he shall have half a gallon of the best ale of the convent for his repast, and every night from the feast of All Saints (1st November) to the feast of Purification of the Blessed Mary (2nd February) he shall have two candles which are given to the esquires at the same time for their livery. And if the foresaid William shall wish to ride he shall have a horse for himself and another for his servant by order of the said Prior, and every year he shall have two cartloads of fuel for the winter season. To have to receive and to hold all things in the abovesaid manner and form as has been noted and to the foresaid William for his whole life from us and our successors quietly well and in peace, without diminution hindrance or any contradiction of us or of our successors. We also grant by these presents that the foresaid William be received as a special brother of our chapter and that there be done for him (*i.e.* by way of masses and prayers) in life and after death as for one of the brothers of our congregation is wont to be done. In witness of all which things we have caused our common seal to be appended to these. Given at Winchester in our chapter house, the 1st day of the month of April in the year of the Lord 1399.

There can be no doubt that "that art" in which Wynford was sufficient and discreet was Architecture. Abundant records exist to show that master masons holding comparable positions and responsible for the "disposition and ordinance" of works were carrying out the function of design. In the same period Master Robert Lesyngham, apparently from Gloucester, visited Exeter Cathedral (Fig. 7) to "survey and ordain the work of the new cloister" for a period of seventeen weeks; a sheet of parchment was bought for him "to show the design (*formam*) of the work", as well as a cord to measure the cloister. Wynford's contemporary in the royal service, Henry Yeveley, held for forty years from 1360 until his death in 1400 the office of King's Master Mason, but different documents give him a variety of descriptions meaning the same thing: "Disposer of the King's Works pertaining to the art of masonry", "Director of the works", and, most pertinent, "Deviser of masonry". A century later the ordinances of the royal household in the time of Edward IV refer to the chief carpenter, plumber, joiner and glazier, but do not mention the chief mason: he appears as the

"Devisor of buildings". To devise, to dispose and ordain, to design; these are the functions—variant nomenclatures for one and the same function—of the men responsible for the amazing works of the Middle Ages. Even though the results attained may differ, these same functions are the duty of the architect of today. They had, through the development of centuries and under various names, been performed by those master craftsmen, adequately trained in technical skills and endowed with some degree of creative genius, whom we here term collectively the mediæval architect.

III

Education of the Architect

BEFORE tackling the problem of how the mediæval architect was educated, we are once again confronted with the difficulty of definitions. A widespread superstition of this century identifies education with literacy; but this is not supported by standard dictionaries. Education is firstly, the bringing up of the young; secondly, systematic instruction; thirdly, the development of character *or* mental powers. Although a large part in many systems of education has been played by learning to read, to write, and to cast accounts, these are no essential part of instruction or the development of character. Even though it is usual to find literacy associated with high mental powers, this is not inevitable: the Emperor Akbar was undoubtedly a man of very high mental powers, and also in every sense of the word a very well educated man; yet by deliberate choice he refrained from learning to read and write.

It is essential that a practising architect should be able to draw, and to use rule, square and compasses; reading and writing are not necessary, though this is not to say that many architects have been totally illiterate. What it does mean is that there is no need to prove that mediæval master craftsmen could read and write in order to show that they could have functioned as architects. To the fallacy that regards literacy as education there is added another; that a statistic of literacy expressed as a percentage of, for example, an adequate body of attestations comprising both marks and personal signatures, is relevant for some other purpose. As with most forms of statistics, such figures presuppose that curious figure, the "average man", or "average master mason", and lead to such absurdities as the "average family of" say 2.157 children. Averages of this kind sometimes have meaning where the individuals composing the total body examined have a real homogeneity; but where, as in the case of craftsmen and artists, they have grossly varying personal skills, they tend to be misleading. They have little relevance to the mediæval architect for, even were it possible to obtain a large statistical sample evidencing literacy of master masons and master carpenters—the two main bodies of men who normally provided the architects of the Middle Ages—the precise standing of each master, *architecturally speaking,* would have to be known before the figures could be analysed meaningfully. In a recent study Dr. L. R. Shelby has shown that in the period 1544–72 an average of 43 per cent of the carpenters who authenticated the court records of the London Carpenters Company signed their own names. Since it has never been suggested that *every* master carpenter, or master mason, functioned as an architect (for many must have been concerned with the production of purely traditional building or with the manufacture of components made to measure), these figures have no relationship which can be measured to the question of how far mediæval *architects* were literate.

There are very strong reasons for supposing that, at any rate from the thirteenth century, a high proportion of the significant architects were literate. The evidence has been discussed more than once, and here it is enough to say that the album of Honnecourt shows that Villard and two of his successors who added to the book were literate both in Latin and French; that a number of masters held appointments as keepers of the works or as controllers of the accounts, and that there is more explicit evidence in a few cases of the despatch and receipt of letters by craftsmen. Among the documents preserved at Westminster Abbey concerning the works of the eastern nave is a letter of about 20th July, 1259, from William de Engelby, Sheriff of Lincoln, to "his friend Magister John Le Mazun," informing him that on St. Margaret's day (20th July) he sent from St. Botulf (*i.e.* Boston, Lincs) to London by the king's order 387 pieces of lead containing 43 carrats ... etc. etc., as testified by two tallies sent by the bearer of the letter. In about 1261 another letter arrived, for Master John's successor Master Robert de Beverley, from Richard Le Wyte of the Purbeck quarry concerning the purchase and shipping of stones for the Abbey works.

At a later date we have at least one letter actually written by the master mason of the works at Calais in 1421, John Pinkhill, to King Henry V :

> Sovereign lord, in as humble wise as any true liege man can think or deem, I recommend me unto your noble grace; having in mine heart continually imprinted, amongst your other high commandments, given to me at your departing for Calais, that special commandment by which ye charged me that I should algates [always] write unto your Highness, from time to time, of

all matters that me seemed necessary or expedient to signify unto your highness.

In performing of the which your commandment, like it your Highness to conceive that the fundament of your Chapel, within your Castle of Calais, and the walls over—height above the ground in the lowest place eight feet—whereof I send you the pattern by John Makyn, servant to Thomas de la Crosse, bringer of this. And as touching the stone of this country that should be for the jambs of your doors and windows of your said chapel, I dare not take upon me to set no more thereof upon your works, it fretteth and fareth so foul with itself that, had I not ordained linseed oil to bed it with, it would not have endured nor pleased your Highness. Wherefore I have purveyed thirteen tons tight of Caen stone for to speed your works withal, and more I shall purvey in all the haste possible, for I cannot see that none other stone will be so profitable for your said works.

And, for God's sake, sovereign lord, like you of your benign grace to have me excused now and at all times of my rude and uncunning writing to your Highness, the which abassheth me full much, to write unto your high estate of any matter, saving your will and commandment aforesaid, the which I shall ever obey and perform to the uttermost that is possible unto me whilst my life endureth. Sovereign lord, I beseech Almighty God keep you in continual prosperity, to his pleasance and your heart's desire, and send you victory of all your enemies for his much mercy.

After about 1400 letters were mostly written in English and so were contracts and many other business documents. French rapidly went out of use at Court and throughout the country, as the rather delayed result of the change of language of instruction in petty schools from French to English in 1350. Everyone who had learned the "three Rs" before the Black Death would have been literate in French at least, and those who proceeded to grammar and cathedral schools would have obtained a smattering of the sort of Latin used for keeping accounts and writing contracts. Since the phenomenon of the lettered layman was well known by the early thirteenth century, as we know for instance from the case of Paulin Peyvre (see page 66), we should accept that most architects of standing, from 1200 onwards at any rate, were likely to be literate in three languages, though after 1400 this was reduced to two.

The education that was essential to the future architect was that of methods of planning and design, besides the craft skill of masonry, carpentry, or quite often of both trades. The basic knowledge of arithmetic acquired at school would need to be expanded by experience in mensuration, for one of the most important professional functions of the architect consisted of the checking of quantities for payment, as Henry Yeveley did at Cowling Castle in 1381 (see page 247). In the earlier period, before about 1300, budding masons and carpenters must mainly have trained with their fathers or other elder relatives, and this ensured the handing down of specific family traditions in the forming of details, planning, proportions and the like. On the continent the case of the great fourteenth-century family of Parler is notorious, but there are many examples in all countries of Europe of sons succeeding fathers in architectural offices. In England, for example, there was the dynasty of de Canterbury, the royal masters from the time of Edward I to nearly the middle of the fourteenth century; at York Minster in 1351 William Hoton senior was succeeded by his namesake; at Chester in 1433 John Asser the son took the office which had belonged to his father of the same name; in 1516 Henry Redman became master mason to Westminster Abbey in succession to his father Thomas Redman. The evidence can be indefinitely multiplied by study of the principal families of craftsmen of all trades, so that there is practical certainty as to the usual method of imparting craft information.

From the late thirteenth century apprenticeship began, as we have already seen, to provide an alternative method of entering one of the building crafts. What was taught by a master to his apprentice is not likely to have differed in any way from the teaching of father to son, and to this extent the question of apprenticeship is immaterial. The existence of apprenticeship, as a means of learning a craft from someone other than a blood relative must, however, have tended to loosen the boundaries of the trade "castes". Since hereditary influences played a very considerable part in the later Middle Ages, they probably were even stronger in the early part of the period. We have seen that the inheritance of an office relevant to the practice of architecture, though not actually architectural, that of keepership of the Old Palace of Westminster, probably reveals the name of the architect to William Rufus. (See pages 61–62). At a time when, before the rule of strict clerical celibacy had been introduced, even a hereditary living was normal, it would not be surprising if architecture in its higher ranks was quite largely a matter of inheritance by blood or marriage.

In mediæval times and down to the present day, the usual term of apprenticeship has been for seven years, and this has applied to all crafts. So far as the manual side of stonemasonry is concerned, master masons of the twentieth century regard seven years as an essential minimum, and the working apprenticeship even then has to be supplemented by evening classes in draughtsmanship and building construction. Both the traditional usage of times still within living memory, and the documents of the last few centuries, show that training usually began at the age of thirteen or fourteen, allowing apprenticeship to end at twenty or twenty-one. This was not, however, the end of the period of education in the building crafts, for after being out of his indentures of apprenticeship the young craftsman had then to spend three years working as an "improver" before being regarded as fully trained. It was these years, roughly between the ages of twenty-one and twenty-four, that included the wanderyears normal for masons. During these three years the young mason was expected to move from job to job, gaining practical experience of different types of work, for example on houses, churches or castles. His wanderings were not necessarily into foreign lands, but it is likely that the first-hand knowledge of foreign details by at any rate some of the Gothic architects was acquired through the practice of crossing the Channel and finding work overseas.

The boast of Robert and William Vertue (Fig. 21) in 1502 that the vault they had designed for Bath Abbey would excel all in England and in France implies that they were aware of the latest developments in vaulting abroad (see page 220). In the case of Robert Vertue we can suggest when he may have travelled. His father, Adam Vertue, worked at Westminster Abbey as an ordinary mason from January to December 1475 at the standard wage of 3s. 4d. a week. In May Robert appeared and was paid only 1s. 8d. a week; this was increased to 2s. at the end of a year and he worked on until July 1478, and was then absent for two months. In the years 1476–77 and 1477–78 he was given livery worth 8s. besides his wages. From September 1479 until February 1480 he was paid at 2s. 4d. a week, and for the two years 1478–79 and 1479–80 he had livery worth 9s. each year. For three full years he was absent, but returned in March, 1483, and took the normal rate of 3s. 4d. as a working mason up to 24th April, 1490. He was one of the higher ranking masons in that he took an extra 4d. a week for setting on one occasion, and in 1484 was sent to the Reigate quarries for four weeks. It can be safely assumed that the three years which intervened between his leaving the Abbey works as a junior early in 1480, and his return as a fully paid mason exactly three years afterwards to the month, were the wanderyears that constituted his improvership. He may have gone abroad then, or later, for nothing is known for certain of his career after he left the Abbey in 1490, until he appears in October 1499, as a master in charge of works at Greenwich Palace for Henry VII. His brother William must have trained elsewhere, for nothing is known of his career before the start of the new church at Bath.

On the continent it was usual for graduation, in any craft, to follow the presentation of a "masterwork" made to demonstrate competence. There is no really clear evidence for this in England; likewise there is a good deal of uncertainty as to the means by which a fully trained journeyman might become a master. The title "journeyman" has given rise to much misunderstanding, as it has been supposed to derive from the wanderyears or from journeys in search of work. In fact it means a hired man who works for a daily rate of pay (old French *jornee*), and by far the greater number of mediæval stonemasons and carpenters never rose to be anything more than journeymen. In one sense at least, a master in any craft was a fully trained man who ceased to work as a journeyman upon setting up his own shop. This might occur if he inherited money or married a woman of property, regardless of his status as a more or less highly skilled craftsman. Where detailed registers of individual craft guilds survive in addition to the rolls of entry to the freedom of a city, it is possible to show that in many crafts it was normal to take up the freedom of the guild or company at about the same time—but sometimes a year or more before or after—as the freedom of the city was taken; and also that this was often done at or about the age of twenty-one. In such cases it is to be presumed that the apprentice out of his indentures had sufficient capital behind him to set up in business without passing through any intermediate stages as a servant.

In the Middle Ages, at any rate in the building trades, it is probable that there was much less chance of becoming a "little master", employing journeymen. The capital required to be able to take on jobs "at task", that is for an inclusive price as in work by contract, would have been greater than in many crafts, and there must always have been a demand for substantial numbers of hired men. On the contrary, the supply of architecturally trained masons and carpenters was always small, and consequently offered a good avenue for advancement. We can but surmise that it was the hope of becoming an architect that induced John fitzAdam in 1307 to arrange for so long a training as nine years (see page 71). He must already have been more than fourteen years old, so that his agreement with William the mason of Stamfordham would not expire until he was twenty-three or twenty-four. The resumption of his property at the end of the term would mean that he had enough capital to start up in practice as a master of architectural status, or else as a building contractor in a fair way.

Even though we cannot be quite sure of the precise steps taken, there was certainly a threefold division in the mediæval skilled crafts, into the ranks of apprentice, journeyman, and master; these corresponded both in origin and in character to the academic scholar, bachelor and master. In the case of masons in particular there was, as we have just seen, the possibility of becoming a contractor, carrying out specified works at a fixed price for profit, and this also applied to woodworkers such as carpenters and joiners. On the margin of all these three crafts was that of the sculptor, carving details or figures in either wood or stone. It is certainly significant that a number of mediæval masters of undoubtedly architectural status were also carvers, or carried on business as makers of effigies, tombs and monuments. There was in a good many cases also a clear connection between the practice of contracting, sometimes on a large scale, and employment as an architect in work for other employers. The case of Henry Yeveley, whose work as a building contractor brought him great wealth, is outstanding in this sense, for during most of his recorded career he was certainly also a designer. Earlier in the fourteenth century the case of Simon of Canterbury, a London carpenter, is also instructive. For a period of forty-two years (1299–1341), he can be traced as a man of some standing in the City. He was never described as "Master" before 1316, but was usually so described after that year; in 1308 and 1313 he took on contracts of substantial size. Facts such as these imply that the trained craftsman with enough capital would undertake tasks, supplying cut or carved stones, or timber framing; would later be able to take on bigger contracts; and might eventually launch out with his own shop and yard, by which time (either with or without some form of graduation ceremony) he was known as Master.

There was obviously a marked gulf between the mason or carpenter whose training merely comprised the essentials of the trade, as needed by a working journeyman, and his fellow who was to act as architect for churches, castles or royal palaces. The designer required a great deal of specialized knowledge that was useless to the hired stonecutter; even the setter, taking a higher rate for the correct use of level and plumb, did not require any extensive acquaintance with geometry. It was undoubtedly practical knowledge of geometry that differentiated the architect from the mere mason or carpenter. Later on, in discussing the organization of the mediæval architects, something will be said concerning the statements on this subject in the Constitutions of masonry (see pages 130, 170 sec. 3, 173–4 sec. 20). Here it is noted that the study of practical geometry was indeed of the essence of architectural design. The traditional history attributed the rise of masonry to Euclid, and this betrays at least second-hand knowledge of one of the main sources of Gothic architectural skills. This was not a mere boast by the masons themselves; precisely the same theme was touched upon by the poet John Lydgate, who was a Benedictine monk of Bury, an architectural centre of the first magnitude. In the *Falls of Princes* he described Nimrod "making his masons For to compass and cast their devises Geometricians in their divisions", and elsewhere he wrote: "By craft of Euclid mason doth his cure, To sue his mould's rule, and his plumbline." The connection between the Father of Geometry and the practice of architecture was not only recognized in the West: a hundred years later the great Turkish architect Sinan was acclaimed as "the Euclid of his century".

The arrival of Euclidean geometry in western Europe can be dated with close accuracy to 1120 or within the next few years. The first version, from the Arabic translation of the Greek text, was made by a Saxon Englishman, Adelard of Bath, between about 1116 and 1120. Adelard had travelled for seven years, taking in Salerno, Sicily and the Near East, between about 1107 and 1115, and he had either visited Spain or had close contacts with groups of translators in Spain, possibly through the converted Jew Petrus Alphonsi who settled in England and became physician to Henry I. Adelard, whose earlier career had been largely spent in France, studying at Tours and then teaching at Laon, moved in court circles and by 1130 was again living in Bath and in receipt of a Crown pension from King Henry, a patron of learning and art. Adelard lived to complete a second and greatly improved translation of Euclid, which became the favourite edition used in the universities for long after. He also, about 1145, composed a treatise on the astrolabe which was, among many other purposes, used as a surveying instrument. This treatise he dedicated, from Bath, to the young prince Henry (later Henry II) who was then studying not far off, at Bristol.

The arrival in western Europe of a complete version of Euclid's *Elements* coincided with the adoption of the improvements introduced by Arabic astronomy in 1120. It can be no mere accident that this placing of the world of thought within a strictly scientific framework parallels the sudden rise of the new Gothic art and architecture. Contacts of a close kind there must have been between the very first generation of western scientists and the building masters who were within a few years able to apply exact science to the setting-out of plans and details, the production of drawings to scale, and the design of structures according to new canons of proportion. The transmission of the essential facts from the learned clerks of Laon, Paris, Oxford or Chartres to the actual architects is sometimes seen as a difficulty. This is mainly because the whole trend of western civilization since the Industrial Revolution of the late eighteenth century has been in the direction of snobbery, class exclusiveness, and class war. Before 1700, not in spite of but really because of the genuinely hierarchical bases of society, such compartmentation was unthinkable, as it is today, for example, in Spain. To understand the possibility, in fact the certainty, of discussion of new ideas taking place between clerics and laymen we have only to bear in mind two things: the first is the hospitality of monastic houses and colleges, where lay visitors—notably *including master masons, master carpenters, and other distinguished artists*—were entertained at the high table. The second point, perhaps of less general application, but of even greater force in relation to the highest levels of art production, is the part played by the king and his immediate councillors in deliberately seeking out the best talents and employing them. Within the circle of the royal household, the Court, and the legal and administrative offices which accompanied the king on his almost constant journeys, clerks and laymen were in immediate day-to-day relationships with each other.

All the greater building works were under administrative control of clerks or monks: as we saw (see page 34), the construction of Santiago Cathedral was administered by a committee of three churchmen, one architect, and his assistant in direct charge of the masons. The king of the model letter composed about 1180 wrote to an abbot, knowing that the monastery had a permanent building staff, and asked for an architect of distinction (see page 39). The monks of Canterbury, after their Norman choir had been burned down, must have sent to great distances to ask for masters of special skill, to have found among the applicants one with experience of the new Gothic works at Sens. It is obvious that the church establishments large enough to maintain a works department, like Coutances after the reforms of Bishop Geoffrey (see page 59), were proud of their architectural experts and must have kept them up-to-date with relevant matter from new scientific or technical manuscripts reaching the library. It would, after all, be the natural reaction of the librarian who had just acquired a copy of Vitruvius to consult the nearest architect as to the meaning of its technical matter, especially as he was likely to meet that architect at dinner and supper every day. Even though we know that some mediæval architects had a competent knowledge of Latin, this was by no means an essential prerequisite before they could get the parts of the new learning useful for their art.

The interpenetration of clerical and lay society in this way, notably at the Royal Court and in the greater monastic and cathedral establishments, accounts for a very large part of the knowledge acquired by the architects. Whether it was acquired during the years of their formal education or not, is hardly material. But it is probable that there was at least one other source of such geometrical and technical knowledge:

actual personal contact with Saracen architects. This must have happened in two ways, either when a western master on crusade or pilgrimage was taking notes of methods employed in the Near East; or when a prisoner-of-war, perhaps a Syrian military engineer, was attached to his labour force in England or France by his captor on return home. In the nature of things we have little information about such contacts, but the Syrian knight Usamah Ibn-Munkidh tells a revealing story of the son of a Frankish woman captured by his father, who lived from 1068 to 1137. The boy, named Raoul, accepted Islam and "learned the art of working marble from a stonecutter who had paved the home of my father"; then married a Muslim woman who bore him two sons. When these children were five or six years old the family left and joined the Franks at Afamiyah, the ancient Apamea and modern Qal'ah-al-Mudiq, and the father and both sons went over to Christianity. In the other direction we have the story of the Saracen mason "Lalys" who is said to have built Neath Abbey, founded in 1130, and to have became an architect to Henry I. Vague and unsatisfying as are the meagre details of this statement, the further declaration that Lalys "taught the art to many of the Welsh and English" could not have been fabricated, as it agrees with the fundamental probabilities of the case.

The background to the story of Lalys is that he had been brought from Palestine by Richard de Granville, a near relative of Robert fitzHamon, who had conquered Glamorgan with his Norman knights by about 1090. FitzHamon left no son, but his daughter Mabel was the ward of Henry I and about 1120 was married to the eldest of the King's bastard sons, Robert, who was then created Earl of Gloucester. The close links with the court of Henry I implied by the wardship of the heiress of Glamorgan, and her relationship to Richard de Granville, fully account for the suggestion that his captive Lalys went on to become the king's own architect. De Granville had the first castle at Neath built by Lalys as a bulwark against the Welsh, at a date certainly earlier than 1130, since the castle chapel is referred to in the charter of foundation of the abbey, granted by Granville and his wife Constance. Lalys is also said to have been the architect of "the most celebrated monasteries, castles and churches in the country", presumably referring to the land of Glamorgan. However much the tale may have been improved by legendary embroidery, it provides exactly the right conditions at just the right time.

There is at least one technical device found in a number of English buildings of the twelfth century which certainly has a direct derivation from Saracenic sources: the flat arch with joggled jointing, found used as a means of spanning large fireplaces at Fountains Abbey warming-house and Conisbrough Castle, to give two examples. The copy of oriental workmanship is so precise that it can only have been made by a

Saracenic mason working in England, or by an English mason who had been in the Near East and learned the method there at first-hand. That there were other possible sources of information of a more general kind is shown by the presence of three distinguished Greeks, thought to have been merchants from Byzantium, at the consecration in 1133 of the priory church of St. Bartholomew the Great, Smithfield, in London. The church had been begun in 1123 as part of the foundation by Rahere, the king's jester and minstrel. Again we are led back to the immediate court circle of Henry I.

The uses of geometry in setting up right angles and performing other necessary functions in drawing and marking out the plan of a building; and its use in drawing to a determined scale, are obvious. The greatly improved accuracy of setting out in the later eleventh, and more especially in the twelfth century, is explained by the reflex action of the rediscovery of Euclidean geometry. In regard to survey and drawing to scale there is an important record in the chronicle of Lambert of Ardres, referring to events of about 1139. One Aymar had rebelled against the Count of Guines and had raised a bulwark and built a keep to the north of Audruicq. Later his rebellion was put down and the warlike engines he had set above his bulwark destroyed; the place was called Aumerval, *i.e.* Aymer's ditch. Later on Henry, castellan of Bourbourg, in his turn decided to make aggressive use of the old earthworks:

[He] sent surveyors (*geometricos*) and carpenters to Aumerval to go about the site with measuring rods (*geometricalibus perticis*) and take the dimensions of the bulwark to scale (*proportionaliter*). According to the size of the site they were to prepare secretly at Bourbourg, without the knowledge of Arnold [the Count of Guines] and those of Guines, a tower and warlike defences and other engines, and set them up at Aumerval in the silent watches of the night, with a strong force of soldiers. So said Henry, and lo and behold! everything was prepared and set up on top of the bulwark . . . When Arnold, rising early, saw the tower and its defences and other warlike array built upon Aumerval so suddenly and unexpectedly, he raised the whole district (*patriam*) to arms.

With the evidence of surviving drawings we shall deal later (see page 110), but the fact of surveys and drawings showing architectural designs has so vital a connection with the education of mediæval architects that the subject must be mentioned. From the remote antiquity of XVIIIth dynasty Egypt (about 1570–1320 B.C.) there is a *continuous* chain of evidence for architectural scale drawing, throughout all the higher cultures of the Near and Middle East, and in classical and mediæval Europe. The evidence has best been brought together by Sir Archibald

Creswell, in connection with the Islamic side of the tradition. Examples are given at different dates of taking plans and drawings of existing buildings, for emulation; and of producing drawings of new designs, from which estimates of cost could be prepared; and later setting out the buildings on the site from the drawn plan. Of particular interest are the case of the the Abbasid Caliph Al-Mansur, who in A.D. 774 decided to transfer the markets of Bagdad to a new site: "He then had a large garment brought, traced on it the plan of the markets, *etc.*, allotted each craft its respective place;" and that of the architect of the mosque of Ibn Tulun in Cairo, begun in A.D. 876, to whom skins were given on which to draw the plan. Improved draughtsmanship, like the pointed arch, technical devices in stonecutting, the refinements of civilization and pleasure gardens, was doubtless borrowed from the Saracens.

In discussing the whole question of geometrical proportions used in the design of mediæval buildings, Professor Kenneth Conant has remarked that "the practical working systems which produce a building are more important than literary-minded critics suspect". This is a wise *caveat* against becoming entangled in the lengthy tables of mathematical formulæ, bristling with square and cube roots, that clutter much recent literature on this subject. So far as there is direct surviving evidence for systems of mediæval proportion, it indicates that they were the result of direct use of geometrical methods, and never involved calculation. Arithmetical and algebraic functions are there, but they went unrecognized by the craftsmen who reached their objective by a different road. The kind of training in proportional geometry that a young Gothic architect would have received consisted of specific problems, learned by rote, and to be solved with rule and compasses. Until quite late in the period they probably did not come out of books or collections of diagrams, but were passed down from generation to generation. Here and there, as in some of the diagrams added by Honnecourt's successors to his album, a cryptic jotting may have served as a reminder.

The use, not merely of drawing boards fitted with tee-squares and set-squares, but of specially shaped squares able to yield given proportions such as the Golden Cut, was doubtless part of the more advanced technical education given. Trestle drawing boards are shown on a late Roman grave slab from the Catacombs, in a miniature of the early fourteenth century in the so-called "Queen Mary's Psalter", and are mentioned in accounts. They were used for preparing small scale drawings. Really large drawings and details to full size were commonly drawn out upon a plaster floor specially laid for the purpose. Measurements were taken with perch-rods of customary lengths such as $16\frac{1}{2}$, 18 or 20 feet; with yard-sticks or "canes" of two yards—the ancestors of the modern six-foot rod; and with long cords. At least some measuring rods were graduated in feet and inches, or in feet and half- and quarter-feet, as survey dimensions of plots of ground were recorded in both forms.

So far as generalization is possible, we may thus summarize the education of mediæval architects of the higher grade, able to design major works at castles and cathedrals. It is notable that design by the same man of different classes of building was normal, specialization relatively rare. The boy was taught at home or in the petty school, probably kept by the parish priest in the church or its porch, between the ages of five and nine or ten, by which time he would have a competent knowledge of reading and writing in English and in French; perhaps also a little Latin. By ten he probably moved on to the grammar school or possibly some other school held in the precincts of a cathedral or monastery; there he stayed until aged thirteen or fourteen, learning in school hours little but Latin. Alternatively he would have been attached as a page to the household circle of a knightly family, where he would learn deportment and etiquette, together with book-learning; the last would be more French than Latin, as evidenced by the building contracts and leases drawn up for the governing class, so often in French until about 1400. If his schooling were, as in many cases it probably was, on a day-boy basis, the boy would have begun picking up at home and in his father's shop a good deal of the rudiments of one of the crafts, masonry or carpentry, or perhaps carving. From about fourteen he became an apprentice or the equivalent as a private trainee, spending about the next three years on the basic skills of the handicraft: the choosing, hewing and squaring of the material, the standard methods of finishing, jointing and working to different shapes. These three years corresponded to the Trivium in academic studies. Afterwards, from about seventeen to twenty-one, his main concern was to master and to memorize the very many problems in practical geometry involved in setting-out arch and vault voussoirs, tracery, and proportional design. In some cases training might be prolonged to nine years in all, but this may have included two years of intensive practical work as a substitute for three wanderyears after the end of his training. During the wanderyears he gained actual experience as a journeyman on jobs of various kinds, and at times went overseas. Then or later he might also join a pilgrimage, to Rome, to Santiago or to Jerusalem; or one of the smaller inland pilgrimages such as those to Walsingham or Canterbury. Like most young artists at all periods, he would have had a sketch book of some kind with him, and in it would have noted details and devices that he saw. In general such sketch books were, as they usually are now, of quite ephemeral and personal interest. In the case of the more methodical they may have given rise to notable albums such as that of Honnecourt, or books of portraitures filled with collections of details used and filed for reference.

At the end of his training the aspirant had, at least in some cases, to make and present a masterwork in response to a set problem in craftsmanship or design—or in both. His graduation may have been accompanied by formalities; it was pretty certainly beset with horse play. In the special case of the stonemason, the fully trained man was allotted his personal mark by the lodge, or was allowed to use a family mark which had been that of his father before him, possibly differenced on the same principle as in heraldry. Although no registers of marks dating from mediæval times survive, so far as is known, it is reasonably certain that in the later Middle Ages some kind of registration must have been employed. In Germany and central Europe there were separate "*Meisterzeichen*", signs used by masters of architectural status, as distinct from a personal mark to identify output from the banker. So far this usage has not been discovered in England. With or without it, the budding master was ready for work.

IV

Methods: Drawings, Models and Moulds

HOW did the mediæval architect achieve his works, often large in scale, complex in organization, and exquisitely proportioned in detail? The full answer to this question is itself necessarily complex, but the short answer is: by drawing. To those trained in any of the structural arts or crafts, this answer will look like the stale repetition of a commonplace; yet armchair students have frequently denied that drawings were made for, or were necessary to, the production of cathedrals and castles, churches, chapels and monuments. Drawings, in some form, are as essential a means of transmission of ideas between designer and workmen as is some method of musical notation essential to the performance of all complex harmonized and contrapuntal music.

It is first essential to put aside preconceptions as to what constitutes a drawing. Someone who wishes to erect a shed in his garden can buy materials and make it himself; but his design must come from one of two sources. Either he obtains a set of blueprints showing to scale the construction of the sort of shed he has in mind; or he thinks it out for himself and makes sketches at least. In the latter case he acts as his own architect; and the sketches, however simple, with the addition of the lines he draws in marking out the wood for cutting, are the drawings. Even reduced to such simple terms, every structural task demands drawing before tools can be taken to the material. It is not necessary that every drawing should be on a separate sheet of paper, parchment or linen, nor need it have permanence beyond the end of its immediate utility for the job in hand.

This last point is overlooked by those who argue, entirely from negative evidence, that if many working drawings had been needed, at least a substantial number of them would have survived. There are two quite distinct answers to this, of which the final and conclusive one is that many working drawings from the Middle Ages have survived, covering the three centuries from 1200 to 1500. All the same it is worth giving some consideration to the reasons for the lack of such drawings in England during the earlier part of this period, and their general rarity. Since the invention of printing it is notorious that, of many works licensed to be printed—and which apparently actually were printed and published—not a single copy is known to survive. This is most commonly due to the ephemeral interest of the items: once used they were thrown away, and may survive in fragments used for bookbinding, as lining papers, or for wrapping. Exactly this fate has befallen a number of those mediæval architectural drawings which do survive. They have been cut up, for re-use as valuable sheets of parchment or strong paper, used to strengthen bookbindings (as with the Stuttgart fragments) or even to form covers for paper account books (as with the Winchester plan of about 1390). Many parchment drawings, probably including collections which had been preserved as of current importance up to the time of the Reformation, must have been melted down for glue. But at all times the majority of drawings on paper, parchment or linen were used on the building site until they were dirty and torn, and were discarded as of no further use. In this fate they were not singular: most of the many thousands of individual receipts forming vouchers to accounts, and preserved until the audit of the current year, have always been destroyed. It is only with the slow growth of antiquarianism from the end of the Middle Ages onwards, that more than stray items of this kind have been deliberately preserved. Drawings, maps and plans have also been particularly liable to destruction on account of their large size; they cannot be accommodated normally in a drawer or pigeon-hole, but must be rolled up and so made relatively inaccessible and difficult to consult.

It is, therefore, not at all surprising, but quite predictable, that few working drawings of the Middle Ages should have survived. Two further reasons have contributed to the holocaust. Of these one is the habit of mediæval, and more recent traditional, craftsmen of drawing to a large scale or full-size on boards, boarded floors, or on specially made slabs of hard plaster. In these cases the drawings, once used, were smeared over, and the surface used again for a fresh job. The drawings of any one job are automatically obscured or obliterated by the repeated process. The other reason goes much deeper: it is that of craft secrecy. This has nothing to do with the esoteric secrecy of mystical cults, though the two forms of secret may coexist, as in Freemasonry. It is secrecy of exactly the same kind that is practised in industry today, and can be traced back as far as Assyria in the seventeenth century B.C. The late Sir Leonard Woolley told the fantastic story of the secret formula for manufacturing glazed earthenware, set down as a cuneiform cryptogram *one thousand years* before the formula was published in intelligible language, but interpreted by the modern Assyriologists C. J. Gadd and R. Campbell Thompson so accurately that the "precise instructions and observations, both as regards quantities and methods, could be followed out some 3600 years later and brought to an immediately successful issue" when a practical test was made.

Every one of the ancient craft skills has secrets of this kind which are not disclosed to non-members of the craft. For this reason a great deal about the refinements of technical processes in many trades has never been published and is closely guarded even now. In spite of the popularity, since the sixteenth century, of pattern-books and technical manuals on design and building techniques, it is noticeable again and again that the *precise* methods formerly used are left vague, to the mystification of modern scholars. That a rigorous secrecy regarding the skills of the building trades was actively practised is shown by the remarkable account of the murder of Conrad, bishop of Utrecht, in 1099. Bishop Conrad, who had caused the church of St. Mary to be built at great expense, obtained the secret of how the water was to be kept out of the foundations from the son of the master mason, Plebeus. The master, on discovering that the bishop had learned this important secret, stabbed him with a knife after mass. This story is important not only for the evidence of the existence of craft secrecy, but for the fact that this secrecy had to be preserved even against the client, the patron or "lord" of the work, at whose expense it was being carried out; and that the master regarded the murder of his client as the lesser of two evils.

The fact of rigorous secrecy through the mediæval centuries is fully confirmed by the strict wording of the relevant article of the Ordinances of the German Lodge Masons ratified at their famous Congress at Regensburg in 1459 :

> No craftsman, whether Master or Warden or Fellow (journeyman) shall teach by means of any extract (*us keinem uszuge*) how to set up from the ground-plan (*us dem Grunde zu nemen*) to anyone whomsoever who is not of our handicraft, who has not employed his days on stonemasonry.

Within a generation or so this rule had been abrogated in practice by the publication of a booklet by Matthew Roritzer, himself the cathedral architect at Regensburg (1486) (see page 125). In his preface to the bishop of Eichstett, Roritzer declares that he has undertaken to expound somewhat of the art of geometry, "not for private glory but altogether for general benefit". Whatever the reason may have been, the sudden reversal of the rule of secrecy led, in the Germanic region, to the publication and compilation of a number of other late instruction books of Gothic. It may also account for the survival of the great "plan-chests" of Strassburg and Vienna.

In England the Constitutions were less explicit, but the Third Point

in both the early versions enjoins secrecy upon the whole craft, starting
with the apprentice :

> "The third point must be several
> With the apprentice, know it well;
> His master's counsel he keep and close,
> And his fellows', by his good purpose.
> The privities of the chamber tell he no man,
> Nor in the lodge whatsoever they done.
> Whatsoever thou hearest or seest them do,
> Tell it no man, wheresoever thou go.
> The counsel of the hall and eke of bower
> Keep it well to great honour,
> Lest it would turn thyself to blame
> And bring the craft into great shame."

(for the full text of the Constitutions from the prose version, see page
191 ff.).

Here then we have the main reason for two separate phenomena of
mediæval architecture : the extreme rarity of *working* drawings; and
the fact that mediæval architects were members of the building crafts.
The extremely few exceptions to the latter rule are largely accounted
for, as we have seen, by men who had already trained as building
craftsmen taking up holy orders or joining a monastic order as lay-
brothers. The rarest exceptions apart, architectural design according to
the rules of the accepted proportions and methods *could only be done*
by a master of one of the building trades—usually stonemasonry; and
only these masters, whose careers had begun by patrimony or by
pupilage, possessed the special skills in geometrical setting-up which
enabled the essential working drawings to be made. Conversely, we
have the reason why the literary sources for that period, compiled
almost entirely by clerics, are so uninformative as to architectural
methods, however much detail they may give as to the history of
particular building works and architects; the clerks could not tell us the
answers because they did not know them themselves.

Piecing together what evidence there is, in England and abroad, it is
possible to give at least a general account of methods used. These
methods were inculcated orally and were not usually explained in
written words, though sometimes (as in Honnecourt's album) cryptic
diagrams might be set down. As there was no dependence on text
books, the body of tradition was fluid, constantly in process of adaptation by individuals and by the response of each generation to new
fashions received from abroad or produced in response to particular
programmes set by the highest classes of patron. There was in this
progress a deliberate attempt to reach perfection in design, to refine

both proportioned details and the techniques of construction. The imitation of existing buildings is quite commonly mentioned in contracts, (see page 251), usually with the proviso that the new work shall be like the model "or better"; and in other cases masters were sent long distances to view existing buildings. William Humberville, master mason in 1369–79 for the building of the library of Merton College, Oxford, journeyed to Sherborne, Salisbury, Winchester and London, "with the purpose of viewing the library of the Preaching Friars", to get ideas; Pedro Balaguer, architect of the famous belfry or Miguelete of Valencia, was sent as far afield as Lérida and Narbonne—some 400 miles each way—to examine towers in 1414; in 1450 Roger Growdon was instructed to view the steeples of Callington in Cornwall, Buckland, Tavistock, and Ashburton, and to use the best of them as a pattern for the tower of Totnes parish church. In this last case it is evident that Ashburton provided the pattern, but that Growdon greatly enriched the new design. The combined effects of imitation of this sort on the one hand, and on the other emulation of a rival city or monastery, account for a great deal of the progress made. That this process had started even before Gothic style had replaced Romanesque is proved by the fully dimensioned description of the monastery of Cluny (Cluny II) made about 1032 (see page 241); and by the record that the Cistercian abbot of Aduard in the Dutch diocese of Groningen about 1124 sent a lay-brother to Clairvaux to take the plan of the abbey so that it might be copied at Aduard. The long-term process involved amounted to a steady downward percolation of design, beginning with royal palaces and chapels, cathedrals and greater monasteries, and passing through lesser churches, priories and manorhouses, to end in small houses and chapels in areas remote from the source of each wave of inspiration.

The attempt to improve upon an admired model took two main forms: greater refinement of proportions and detail in design; and economy in the use of materials made possible by developing new techniques of construction. To take examples from the Norman period in England, the heavy crudity of St. John's Chapel in the White Tower of the Tower of London (c. 1097) and of the crypt of Worcester Cathedral (c. 1084–92) must be contrasted with the progressive effects attained in the series: Norwich Cathedral ambulatory (1096–1120), Durham nave (1099–1133), Peterborough south transept (1117–1155), and the towers of Castor Church, Northamptonshire (c. 1124) and of the great gateway of Bury St. Edmunds (c. 1130). A main factor in improvement was the attenuation of supports made possible by advances in hewing and laying ashlar masonry soon after 1100 (see page 229); Professor Conant has commented that the cross-sectional area of supports at Compostela is only one quarter of that at St.-Bénigne, Dijon. The amazing reduction in size of piers during the century after the building of Durham was shown by a series of plans, all to the same scale, published by E. S. Prior in 1900.

As time went on, and mastery of the improved techniques became more assured, architects strove increasingly to attain a unity of aesthetic composition. This is especially seen in the design of individual bays, where the sharp horizontal divisions of early work into stories were later modified (in the first half of the thirteenth century) to form an overall integrated pattern. Later still this, together with the enlargement of windows to provide greater illumination, culminated in the "glasshouse church". Increasing complexity required a higher degree of organization in subordinating parts to the whole; more light, which made the large expanses of plain masonry look bare, led to the development of pattern in relief. This, especially in England, became in effect the spreading of window-tracery in a "blind" form over the solid walls, and contributed to the national Perpendicular style.

Reference has already been made to the introduction of certain special skills from the Muslim world, notably the flat arch with joggled joints. It is virtually certain that a good deal of the improved precision in late Romanesque work, after 1100, and still more the geometrical methods involved in setting out the highly articulated Gothic vaults, came from the same eastern sources. Better hoisting engines with blocks and tackle made it possible to raise much heavier stones, and this also led to improved appearance. The existence of water-driven saw mills early in the thirteenth century implies a degree of sophistication in mechanics borne out by the excellent cutting of seal matrices and of moulds for such manufactured products as pilgrim badges and patterned ventilators of lead.

By the side of new methods certain old and tried devices seem to have stayed in use for a very long time. One of these was the method of building a vault upon a mound of earth. This was seen in Rome when the vault of the cellar of the English Hospice was under construction in 1450. John Capgrave, who comments on the fact in his book *Ye Solace of Pilgrimes*, states that the same method was given by tradition for the building of the enormous dome of the Pantheon. Capgrave's interest implies that the method was not familiar in the England of his time (1393–1464); but it would not be applicable or necessary, to the setting of the fan vaults of the fifteenth century, as these formed a jigsaw puzzle of specially shaped blocks, on which the apparent ribs were left in relief but had no independent structural existence. (Page 164). At an earlier date, when wide spans of vault-web had to be filled in between simple cross-arches and diagonal ribs, the earthen mound in a modified form seems indeed to have been the solution of the problem. The word "mound" leads to a misconception : that a *solid* heap of earth, 100 feet high or more, is meant, which is ridiculous. On the contrary, a clue is provided by the rough-and-ready method still in use in the Near East, of building a rough centering, or in the case of a cellar or single-storey house merely a piled-up heap of brushwood, and then with earth or clay forming a "mound" of the required shape on top. The building accounts of Troyes Cathedral in the second half of the fourteenth century show that earth was being used for the building of arches and vaults : "5 tumbrils of earth for making the small arch behind the great arch on the side of the treasury" ... "7 tumbrils of earth for making the small vaults damaged (*delaceratas*) by the fall of the great tower" (account of 1366/67). "For taking out of the church the cleanings done in the course of a year and the old earth of the vaults of Our Lady ..." (account of 1380). Considerable numbers of woven hurdles were bought, at Troyes and many other mediæval buildings; many of them are clearly stated to have been for the gangways of scaffolding, and illuminations depict this usage. But hurdles have also been found, in a fragmentary condition, adhering to the inner surface of vaults, in Ireland, and in the North of England (at Lancaster Castle and Helmsley Castle, Yorkshire); hurdles bent to shape, with or without the addition on the outer surface of earth to provide a smooth surface, were therefore one method of centering for vaults, but probably an early and provincial one. The building of the late vaults of the nave of Westminster Abbey involved a great deal of timberwork by carpenters, suggesting that the normal modern method had by that time been adopted.

While the techniques of construction belong essentially to the function of the builder, those of survey and setting-out are so closely linked to drawing and design that they must be dealt with as part of the methods of the architect. The secret survey of Aumerval already mentioned (see page 97), and the construction elsewhere of timberwork made to fit the site, indicate a high degree of skill in surveying by 1139 in the county of Flanders. Much earlier still, in 969, St. Oswald, bishop of Worcester 961–92, is described as arranging for the foundation of Ramsey Abbey :

He sought most keenly for masons (*cementarios*) who would know how to set out the foundations of the monastery in a proper way, with the straight line of the rule, the threefold triangle and the compasses (*qui recta rectitudine regulae et triangulo ternario atque circino scirent honorifice monasterii fundamenta exordiri*).

This account implies direct observation of the operations of marking out a base line and setting-up a right-angle by means of a triangle of correct proportions, for example with sides as 3, 4 and 5, the appropriate dimensions being marked out with the compasses from the ends of the straight base line. Without quite such precision as to the methods used, Gerald the Welshman in the 1180s described his dream of Henry II's son John "in a green plain . . . after the fashion of surveyors . . . marking the turf, making lines on all sides over the surface of the earth, clearly drawing the plan of a building".

There is not much information as to levelling, but in the Low Countries artificial cuts and dykes were formed and sluices made, which led to the formation of an empirical knowledge of waterwork. When Edward I wished to maintain water constantly in the moat of the Tower of London, he sent to Flanders and obtained the services of an expert, Master Walter le Fleming, who came over and spent nine weeks arranging the channel and sluices, getting £9 in all for his fees and expenses. But earlier than this some levelling device was probably used since, as the late Sidney Toy pointed out, the upper floors of the towers of Skenfrith Castle, Monmouthshire, built in 1201–05, are all on exactly the same level. Skenfrith Castle was at the time in the custody of Hubert de Burgh, as was Colchester Castle, where works were carried out under an engineer bearing the unusual name of Forcinus or Fortinus. It is possible that he was another foreign expert.

Surveying and drawing involve the use of units of measurement, and thus of rods or cords marked with the standard units employed. In general the surviving Gothic drawings of technical character are not provided with figured scales, but sometimes these can be worked out and indicate the use of feet of twelve inches, and inches divided into such normal sub-units as eighths, tenths or twelfths. The original drawings for Segovia Cathedral in Spain, preserved in the cathedral library, are of about 1522, and exceptionally are provided with figured scales: these represent the design of Juan Gil de Hontañón, father of that Rodrigo Gil whose treatise in part survives. About 1220 Leonardo of Pisa stated that "fields and the dimensions of houses are measured with poles and linear feet and inches", and survey dimensions are even given in half inches on a "platte" of a London Bridge property made in 1470 by the Bridge Warden and Robert Wheteley, master carpenter. Rods, poles or perches were of different values, not only in different countries but in regions according to local custom. The normal English perch was and is of $16\frac{1}{2}$ feet, but there were local perches of 18, 20 or 24 feet also in use. The values of the foot across Europe varied greatly from $10\frac{1}{8}$ inches (257 mm) in Aragon up to 14 inches (356.4 mm) at Bordeaux. In England there may have been some use of the Roman foot ($11\frac{5}{8}''$; 295 mm), and there certainly was of the Norman foot of $11\frac{3}{4}$ inches (297.77 mm), but from the time of Henry I the foot became standardized at the length it still retains (304.8 mm). In France the foot which ultimately became the standard was likewise laid down by royal authority, the *pied-du-roi* of Paris of $12\frac{3}{4}$ inches English measure (324.84 mm).

It can be seen that the employment of different standards at original and subsequent builds could easily produce misinterpretations of the design; still more misunderstanding on the part of modern students of the intentions of the architect. Professor Conant has shown that at Cluny there was a modular unit of 5 Roman feet (1.475 metres or 4 feet $10\frac{1}{16}$ inches), but that earlier work there had used a longer foot of $13\frac{3}{8}$ inches (340 mm). So far as the design of plans and bays was concerned, these minor differences in unit would not affect the proportionate geometry involved. Except that the absolute size, and thus the proportion to human scale, would differ within certain limits, a building could be made from the drawings by the use of any recognized standard.

The drawings themselves, as we have seen, might be on wood, or plaster, or on sheets of parchment and, later, paper; or on lengths of cloth (see pages 97–9, 101). Apart from modifications in the technique of drawing, the nature of the surface was immaterial so long as it was sufficiently smooth, and allowed the lines to be clearly seen. The fundamental techniques of technical drawing do not seem to have changed very greatly from Ancient Egyptian times, though the drawing materials—lead, charcoal, graphite, ink—have varied. Much mediæval drawing was done with a pointed metal stylus similar to those still used by masons for marking setting-out lines on stone. A variant of the stylus, with rounded point, was also used for "blind" drawing on parchment. The lines ruled or struck in (with compasses or rather dividers) blind could be used for rough construction; the final lines later inked in, freehand in some cases. In other examples the appearance of the lines on the surface of the parchment indicates the use of some form of ruling pen with a pair of metal blades adjusted with screws. This is presumably what is meant by the payment of 8s. in 1531 recorded in the accounts for Henry VIII's works at Westminster, for "two payre skrewis for tracerye roddis provided for the maister mason to drawe with in his tracery house".

The drawings were made on a wooden tracing board of the same kind as an architect's drawing board of the late nineteenth or early twentieth century, laid upon a pair of trestles. Master William Hurley, the king's master carpenter, was in 1324 paid 18d. for making such a board and its trestles, for drawing out tabernacles (*pro tabernaculis supertractand.*) and a week later 10d. was paid for an empty barrel, probably of well-seasoned timber, for making thereof rules and squares for the masons (*pro regulis et scuyris inde faciendis ad cement'*). It was perhaps for making squares of some special form that Henry Redman, the master mason, was allowed "glewe and sprigg nale to make his tools and other necessaries" in the accounts of 1515 for Wolsey's works at York Place, Westminster. Until near the end of the Middle Ages most small scale drawings were on parchment (see page 252). Skins were bought for the masters to draw out their designs, as in the case of the Exeter cloisters in 1377–8, or at Eton College in 1457 when a calf-skin was bought in London "to make upon it a certain portraiture of the site and building of the College". By the early years of the sixteenth century large sheets of paper, "Royal" size (25 inches × 20 inches), were bought, as for John Lebons, one of Henry VIII's architects at Hampton Court, to draw "platts" upon in 1537.

The surviving technical drawings have been much discussed over a long period, and only a brief summary will be attempted here. So far as England is concerned, there are very few indeed dating from before 1500, and those belong either to the stages of design (page 118, Fig. 33) or consultation with the client. (Fig. 49). Several designs for traceriede windows, found as graffiti on stone or plaster surfaces, could have been used as "shorthand" working drawings; the real working detail would have been set out, with precision and with the joint lines, on floors or cartoons now lost. The earliest of those so far noted belong to the thirteenth century. No general ground plan for a projected building survives, no plan for a chapel or separate build, or for a monument, no elevation for a building or for a single bay, no structural cross-section. On the other hand, competent plans showing the arrangements of water-supply systems survive, from the mid-twelfth century for Canterbury Cathedral Priory, from the early thirteenth century of springs supplying Waltham Abbey, of the mid-fifteenth century for the London Charterhouse. These, and some of the graffiti, prove that a high standard of draughtsmanship did exist, at any rate from the twelfth century onwards, and this quite independently of what may be deduced from the accurate cutting of materials, which necessarily betrays prior marking out amounting to technical drawing.

Fortunately the continental material is more abundant, though its distribution is very uneven. The album of Villard de Honnecourt remains the earliest survivor, but that a most important one, in the class of strictly technical drawing. It records plans, both of existing and projected buildings, design of structural details, of sculpture, and of many technical devices. In part it is the personal record of a much travelled Picard architect, sketching details which pleased or interested him, though it is almost certainly not the actual sketch book which he carried with him, but a fair copy intended for study. Honnecourt himself must have intended the album we have, together with parts of it cut out and now lost, as a kind of reference handbook; and two of his successors within the next few generations made additions to it. There is thus a strong presumption that it owes its preservation to its having been kept as a precious manual for consultation in one of the great building lodges of north-eastern France, probably the collegiate church

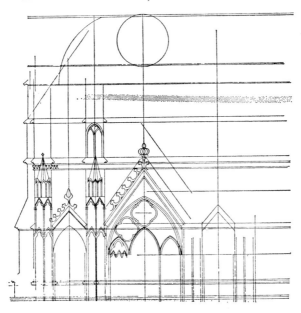

Two designs for fronts of aisled churches, *c.* 1240–50, by the Master of the Rheims Palimpsest, possibly Hugh Libergiers; from the reconstructions by Dr Robert Branner.

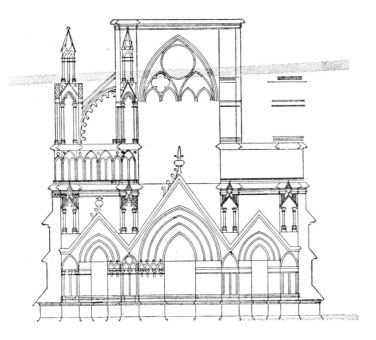

of St. Quentin. Slightly later than the famous album are the drawings of the Rheims palimpsest, belonging almost certainly to the period *c.* 1240–60 and related to the church of St. Nicaise and possibly to its architect Hugh Libergiers. Rather later still are the first of the great elevational drawings for Strassburg Cathedral, (Frontispiece), which fortunately preserves a large number of working drawings covering the whole mediæval period from 1275.

In the course of recent studies of these earliest surviving drawings of strictly technical character and in some form of orthographic projection, different views have been expressed as to their place in architectural development. On the one hand it has been held that the excellent quality of the draughtsmanship displayed by Honnecourt and by the Rheims and Strassburg masters throughout the middle of the thirteenth century argues strongly that there must have been a long tradition of earlier drawings of the same kind, now lost. Recently there has been a swing to the opposite extreme by Dr. Robert Branner, whose detailed study of the drawings themselves has marked a great advance in knowledge. Dr. Branner argues that project-drawings on a small scale were probably first used about 1220, very likely at Cambrai Cathedral, and that they had not been used when Rheims Cathedral was begun in 1210. It may, of course, be true that small-scale drawings on parchment were indeed an innovation of the early thirteenth century, but the extensive use of drawing by the architects of Gothic from the start seems inescapable. In this context one remark by Dr. Branner himself is highly significant. Referring to the fact that the instruments first used for drawing on parchment appear to have been those used for tracing profiles, the small compass and the small ruler, he adds: "Between 1100 and 1200 these were refined considerably, if the development of profiles of ribs and imposts is a criterion." This independently confirms the very marked improvement in techniques which occurred well back in the twelfth century, concurrently with the replacement of Romanesque architectural style by Gothic. There was an influx into western Europe of technical draughtsmanship hitherto unknown, but it came fairly soon after 1100 and can only have been due to direct contacts with the Near East, where there had been a continuous tradition of architectural drawing going back to the early dynasties of Egypt.

For the three centuries of High and Late Gothic architecture in Central Europe there is luckily abundant graphic evidence. It comprises the architectural archives of two of the greatest cathedrals, Strassburg (Fig. 44) and Vienna (Figs. 46, 51), while important drawings survive from the works of Cologne Cathedral (Fig. 45), Ulm (Figs. 30–32, 42, 47, 52), Prague, and a number of major churches in Switzerland, Germany, and Bohemia. There are a few drawings from France

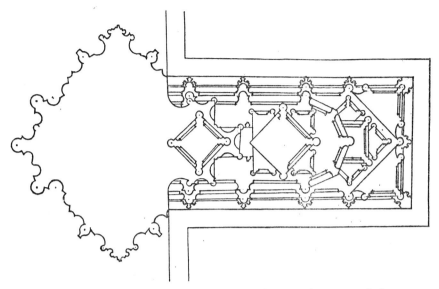

Vienna: St Stephen's Cathedral: drawing for one buttress of the nave, showing superimposed plans of nichework and pinnacles at different levels.

(Strassburg is here regarded as historically German in its architecture) and some from Spain, as well as a good many in Italy. Many of these drawings, and the complementary references in documents, have been discussed over the past generation or so by a number of scholars, Hahnloser and Kletzl in particular, while Bruno Grimschitz has produced a most notable pioneer study of the fifteenth-century architect Hanns Puchspaum, the first biography of a mediæval architect to be illustrated with reproductions of his own drawings as well as photographs of his surviving works. Most of these studies have been in German, but more recently American scholars have produced a substantial literature in English. A major synthesis has now been undertaken by Mr. François Bucher, whose preliminary assessment refers to the at least relative "neglect of over 2,200 mediæval plans and designs as well as theoretical treatises and working drawings" by historians of art.*

From Mr. Bucher's analysis it emerges (1) that design procedures changed little until the end of the sixteenth century; (2) that the general statement of Vitruvius as to the status and essential equipment of an architect remained valid for Gothic; (3) that the design technique of geometric development was used as "a utilitarian approach to design . . . without a theoretical geometrical basis". Furthermore, the

*Mention should be made of the compact but important study of Gothic methods made by the Hungarian scholar József Csemegi.

historical implications of the evidence suggest that this body of practical geometry can be considered independently of the study in mediæval universities, of actual texts of Euclid. Thus at a single stroke one of the most formidable objections of the armchair theorists has been removed : it was not in any way necessary for the architects to be men with a "higher education" in the sense of academic book-learning, for they already possessed, through different channels, a corpus of traditional geometrical methods, handed down, adequate for their purposes. It can be added that not only master craftsmen, but also architects, of the present day, without being highly trained mathematicians, make use of analogous though not identical processes of manipulative geometry in the course of design and of setting out of masonry.

Although the few survivals of the English output of mediæval drawings are a disappointment after the riches preserved abroad, we must not lose sight of the fact that much of the initial impetus behind the Germanic flowering of *Sondergotik* came from England. The documentary evidence in England is rich in proofs of the use and former existence of drawings, and of the making of lodges and tracing-houses for the masons and masters. Most of this evidence has been published and discussed in detail but a few instances may be considered here. It will be seen that very early in the twelfth century a derivation of "lodge" was being offered in connection with the remarkable house designed for the Castle of Ardres by Master Louis de Bourbourg (see page 207) : that a lodge was a place for conversation, that is a parlour. On building sites it included the banker or covered shed wherein the cutting masons hewed stones on the bench. It must be carefully distinguished from the tracing-house, which might be but was not necessarily adjacent. The lodge with the banker must generally if not invariably have been at ground level for convenience of handling the stones. The two surviving tracing-houses in England are at an upper-floor level, and it is doubtless to this that they owe their preservation. It must be emphasized that the tracing-house was the preserve of the master, his assistants and pupils, and formed the architectural drawing office expressive of the function of design; whereas the lodge was accessible to all the working masons. This is made clear by a York Minster ordinance of 1409, mentioning the site for building the new lodge for at least twelve masons to work on "the fourth pier", in addition to the old lodge in which at least twenty masons were to work. The tracing-house (page 115), though in the same region on plan as the site for the new lodge, was some sixty feet up a spiral staircase and provided with its own permanent wall fireplace and with a garderobe. At Wells the tracing-house was the room above the North Porch to the nave.

There were many lodges that had nothing to do with building

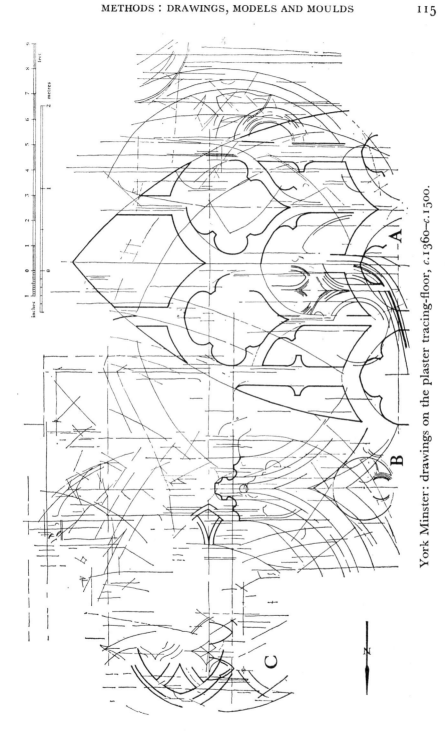

York Minster: drawings on the plaster tracing-floor, *c.*1360–*c.*1500.

operations: the word was used for many types of shed or hut; but the tracing-house existed solely for architectural purposes and its presence indicates the site of major works of design. The most detailed references are to the tracing-houses at St. Stephen's Chapel, Westminster, in 1325 and later. There was a large tracing-house of the Master Mason, and at least one other, allocated to the master carpenter. References, generally implying the pre-existence rather than the new making of a tracing house, occur at Windsor Castle from 1350, Westminster Abbey from 1372, Exeter Cathedral in 1375, St. Paul's London from 1381 (where the drawing office was that of the Dean and Chapter), Ely Cathedral from 1360, which is about the date when the surviving York tracing-floor must have been brought into use. There is presumptive evidence for a tracing-house in the Tower of London by 1274 and one existed there in 1547, along with more than one in the Palace of Westminster. At Knaresborough Castle in 1307 there is a mention of the "*domus tracer*", and at Scarborough Castle on 2nd January 1429/30 an inventory shows that in the "logge" there were three stone axes, six irons, two setting chisels, one "kevell", one hammer axe and two trowels; while in the "Trasynghous" were two pairs of iron compasses, one the length of a yard, "another lesse", and four planes. The planes were doubtless for smoothing wainscots for making moulds. In 1359 Master William de Helpeston was to make a tracing-house for his new work at Vale Royal Abbey (see pages 216–18).

In 1366 and again in 1396 Master Hugh Herland, (Fig 20), the king's chief carpenter, was granted in Westminster Palace a little house for keeping his instruments, and for making *formulas* and moulds (templates) for his carpentry works. The word *formulas* has been translated as "models" and this may well be correct, but evidence as to the use of models of any kind in north-west Europe during the Middle Ages is unsatisfactory. From the sixteenth century onwards in all parts, and considerably before that date in Italy at least, it was normal practice to produce a wooden scale model of an intended building. This served two main purposes: to show to the client and obtain an informed approval which the exhibition of two-dimensional drawings could not win; and as a basis for taking off the quantities of materials to produce a detailed estimate of cost. Many of these models survive, among them that of Sir Christopher Wren for St. Paul's Cathedral in London. At the end of the Gothic period models of parts were certainly made; the paper cutout showing patterns of vaulting ribs, intended to be bent to demonstrate the appearance in three-dimensional space, is a simple device which may have an ancestry going back long before the earliest surviving examples. In some cases there is strong presumptive evidence that models of supports, buttressing masses and arches may have been made for structural testing (see page 163). It is hard to believe that the architects

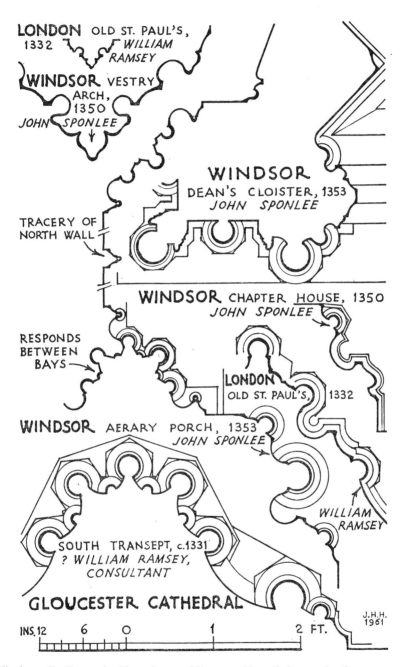

LONDON OLD ST. PAUL'S, 1332 WILLIAM RAMSEY

WINDSOR VESTRY ARCH, 1350 JOHN SPONLEE

WINDSOR DEAN'S CLOISTER, 1353 JOHN SPONLEE

TRACERY OF NORTH WALL

WINDSOR CHAPTER HOUSE, 1350 JOHN SPONLEE

RESPONDS BETWEEN BAYS

LONDON OLD ST. PAUL'S, 1332

WINDSOR AERARY PORCH, 1353 JOHN SPONLEE

WILLIAM RAMSEY

SOUTH TRANSEPT, c.1331 ? WILLIAM RAMSEY, CONSULTANT

GLOUCESTER CATHEDRAL

INS. 12   6   O   1   2 FT.

J.H.H. 1961

Windsor, St George's Chapel: moulding profiles of the work of 1350–1353 compared with the earliest Perpendicular details of the previous twenty years.

of the great towers of the fourteenth and fifteenth centuries were content to risk immense sums of money and many lives without some empirical knowledge gained by direct experiment.

Design, at first a concept in the brain of the architect, was sketched out in general terms and the plan determined upon a basis of squares or other repeated units. From this, by traditional methods of modular geometry, the elevation and section were set up, and the overall sizes of all main members worked out, again by manipulative geometry. For each member: a vault-rib, moulded pier, window-jamb or mullion, a suitable series of mouldings had to be designed and then transferred to a thin but rigid sheet to be cut out as a template. In modern times such templates are usually of zinc; in a rather earlier period they were of thin iron plate; still earlier some may have been of lead. But the documents leave no doubt that by far the greatest number in the Middle Ages were made out of thin panels of wainscot oak. These were planed thin and smooth, the profile of the block and its mouldings carefully drawn on, and then cut out exactly to the line. Throughout

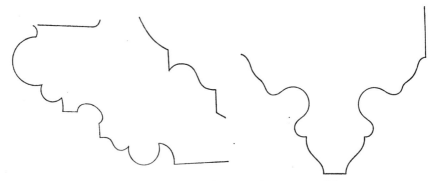

Moulding profiles drawn on parchment sheets, English, *c.* 1350–1375 (Pepysian Sketchbook).

the period it was the master in person who drew the profiles, and they are therefore comparable to a painter's brush strokes as the signature of individual style. The templates or moulds were delivered to the working masons, apparently with some formality, and in some contracts they are specified either as having been delivered, or to be delivered.

A good example of this is the famous contract for making the new masonry details for Westminster Hall (Fig. 36) to the designs of Henry Yeveley in 1395 (see page 250). The relevant account survives and shows that the provisions of the contract were carried out:

Task— Richard Washbourne and John Swalwe masons for making the masonry of the whole stone table [i.e. the cornice] with Reigate stone hewn on both sides of the walls of the aforesaid Hall of the height of two feet of assize above the old wall of the same Hall and also for the setting of Marr stone for strengthening the aforesaid table according to the effect of designs and templates (*formarum et moldarum*) made by the counsel and advice of Master Henry Yeveley and delivered to the same masons by Walter Walton deputy of the same Henry . . .

Throughout the whole of the Gothic period this fundamental method remained constant, however much or however little use of sketches and small-scale drawings the master may have made at different periods or in any given case. The statement that Master William of Sens at Canterbury in 1175 handed templates to the carvers who were to cut detail for the new work (see page 211), could be repeated for every work of architecture. The function of architect was expressed by the master in every case by his drawing of his exactly profiled design for the mouldings and details of every part of the building; copies of his designs or other drawings, such as position plans (of which late Gothic examples exist at Strassburg and Vienna), might be added and in 1395 this happened at Westminster Hall, though we do not know exactly what other drawings were made and delivered on Yeveley's behalf. What is certain is that Washbourne and Swalwe had nothing to do but to hew to the line; they were not in any sense sharers in the architectural credit for the job. As definitely as in the cases of Wren or Adam or Lutyens, it was Master Henry Yeveley who was the architect.

V

Planning: Proportional Theories and Techniques

A S might be expected, the plans of earlier buildings tend to be relatively simple, while at a later date there was increasing complexity and sophistication. In the Romanesque period, that is to say during the phases which lasted in England from the late tenth century to the opening of the twelfth, the key to planning was essentially the use of squared paper for design sketches. A grid of lines, crossing one another at right angles and at even distances apart, was laid down and the plan composed of groups of squares. The earliest Ancient Egyptian drawings preserved show this system already in use, with the design in black ink on a sheet of papyrus squared in red. Exactly the same method was used through classical times, and applied to pattern as well as to architectural planning. The standard pattern-books of the mosaicists who laid floors have been reconstructed from surviving examples, and repeats of the design shown, for example, to have been squares of sides that could be expressed in Roman feet, and usually subdivided into a squaring of 10 to each side of the unit. Thus the modular unit for the mosaic floors of Constantine's fourth-century church of the Nativity at Bethlehem was $2\frac{1}{2}$ Roman feet, so that each small square was $\frac{1}{4}$ R. ft, and each of these small squares was composed of 100 (10 × 10) of the standard *tesseræ*.

We have seen that Professor Conant's detailed excavation and analysis at Cluny have demonstrated the existence in the plan of a modular unit of 5 R. ft (see page 109), and he has further indicated the extent to which the plan, designed on this basis, exemplified theories of mathematical "perfection" in numbers as set forth by Isidore of Seville: "nave span 35 feet = 1 + 6 + 28; divisioning of the axis of the rectangular part of the church, 531 feet = 6 + 1 + 28 + 496. The apse was based on the symbolic number 7. Plato's 'succession by squares' (1, 3, 9, 27) determined the lines of the main portal. More important was the use of the Pythagorean series of 'musical numbers' (2, 3, 4, 6, 8, 9, 12), recognized by mediæval philosophers as fundamental to the order and stability of the Universe, and to beauty in

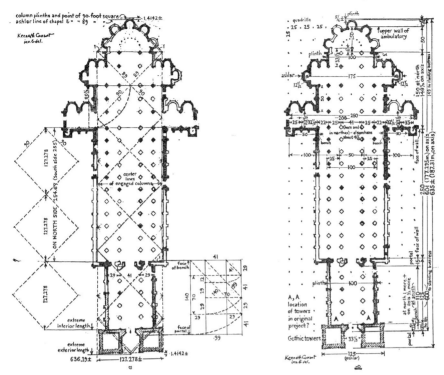

Cluny Abbey church: the plan of *c.*1080 and later related to proportional systems set out in Roman feet of 295 mm., from drawings by Professor Kenneth John Conant.

the arts. A phrase of Boëthius, dependent on Plato and Augustine, implies that *Geometry makes visual the musical consonances.* This was true of Gunzo's Cluny: *a list of all its important dimensions is the result* when the modules are multiplied, respectively, by the series of 'musical numbers'."

Cluny III was exceptional, not only in its size, but in the fact that its great wealth enabled it to obtain the most distinguished help. The monk Gunzo, who declared that St. Peter and St. Paul had appeared to him in a vision, stretching cords to mark the limits of the plan, was a musician of distinction (*psalmista precipuus*). he other reputed author of the scheme, Hezelo (or Hesello, or Zehlon), was a canon of Liège who later became a monk of Cluny, dying in 1123 after spending much of his life on the building works there. He is said to have been a mathematician. Though described as "architects" of the church it is difficult, for reasons already given (see pages 80–3, 104), to accept that this was their real function. It is much more likely that they were the leading members of the building committee (exactly like Wicart,

Segered and Gundesund at the contemporary work of Santiago), (see pages 235–36), who dictated a programme in unusual detail, with dimensions laid down after theoretical work by the mathematician Hezelo (on the supposition that he had spent some forty years on the works, and was thus concerned from the start).

The plan of Cluny unquestionably demonstrates that, whatever theoretical systems of number may have been incorporated by sheer ingenuity, the essential basis was a squared mesh of major units of 25 Roman feet. The internal lengths of both nave and transept were exactly ten of these units, or 250 R. ft; from the east end of the nave to the line of springing of the great apse was six units, or 150 R. ft; the radius of the apse was two units or 50 R. ft. The setting-out lines for the arcades were placed touching the outside of the piers of the nave and aisles, not on their axes, at spans of 50 and 25 Roman feet. An interesting comparison is provided by the Norman York Minister recently excavated, where the major unit again seems to have been 25 feet, but almost certainly Norman rather than Roman feet (100 Norman feet make 97 feet 8 inches statute measure; 100 Roman feet only 96 feet 8 inches). The York plan, formulated about 1080 and thus exactly contemporary with the formation of the Cluny programme, has a length of six units (150 feet) for the nave and for the transept giving a crossing of two units or 50 feet, with an eastern arm of five units to the springing line of the apse.

Planning is not merely a question of finding suitable overall proportions for a building and for its respective parts. It also involves, as every architect knows, ingenuity of a certain common-sense kind. Houses, which involve the interrelationships of the various aspects of daily life, exemplify this to a much greater extent than churches. It is true that monasteries were a special instance of the house, but since each Order had a more or less fixed programme, the opportunities for the exercise of individuality in solutions were relatively small. For this reason the details of the house built in the Castle of Ardres by Louis de Bourbourg about 1120 (see page 207) provide an example of outstanding value, proving that even before the opening of the Gothic age there was a degree of sophistication in residential accommodation. Houses were not just pieces of traditional vernacular building: they might have entries cunningly planned for defence (surely a detail derived from Crusading experience?), passages and partitions, rooms with individual fires, and private bedrooms. It is true that such fine houses were at that time for the select few, but the main fact is that they existed at all.

At the same time that Arnold of Ardres was having one of the first of modern residences built in western Europe, a Benedictine monk of forty was elected abbot of St.-Denis, the royal monastery six miles to the north of Paris. Suger (1081–1151) was the master-patron of the whole

Gothic age, and although he was not himself an architect, his career and personality had the greatest significance for mediæval architecture. As a notable diplomat and statesman, Suger moved in the highest circles. He had been educated at St.-Denis with his exact contemporary the French prince who was in 1108 to become Louis VI, and until the king's death in 1137, Suger was his most devoted and loyal supporter. He travelled a good deal on royal business, and while provost of the abbey of Berneval-le-Grand (Seine Inferieure) in Normandy, came to have also a high admiration for the administration of Henry I, whose friend he became in spite of the rivalry between the two kings, of France and England. Suger also lived, for the two years before he became abbot of St.-Denis, with the Burgundian pope Calixtus II in Rome.* He was thus in immediate contact with all the main directors of western society at the vital period, including both the sovereigns who, between them, controlled the fate of western Christendom, and with the Cluniac movement in the person of a pope of noble Burgundian family who had been chosen at Cluny itself as a candidate to heal schism in the Church. Below these exalted circles Suger, immediately upon his election as abbot of St.-Denis in 1122, took his place as in some sense the arbiter of western Christendom.

Suger had excellent, if colourful taste, and one of his first actions as abbot was, in his own words: "to have removed from the midst of the church a dark blocking wall which cut across it, lest the beauty of the church's size should be obscured by such a barrier." Some will reprehend Suger in this, blaming him as the author of the "theory of the vista"; but in the course of time his name was to find itself in good company when, in 1920, Sir Ronald Storrs as military governor of Jerusalem had a similarly disfiguring wall removed from an even more famous early basilica, the Church of the Nativity at Bethelehem. Suger was by no means a vandal as regarded ancient works of art, and did much to restore the Carolingian church.

Suger took a strong and positive line as an æsthetic philosopher, against the embittered asceticism of St. Bernard (see page 223). He sincerely believed in the glorification of God by means of every form of material art. Keenly interested in art and craftsmanship, he was certainly one of the greatest and most effective patrons, but was not an architect. Suger tells us himself that he "summoned the best painters I could find from different regions" for the wall-paintings of the old church, and that he caused new windows of stained glass "to be painted by the exquisite hands of many masters from different regions", so that there can be no doubt of his eclecticism. Regrettably he tells us nothing of his chief architect, but he lets slip an important sign of his skill in

*Thus immediately after the visit of Pope Calixtus to Autun, probably related to the founding of St. Lazarus's cathedral there.

saying that the plan of the new work was "cunningly provided (*provisum est . . . sagaciter*)" to be aligned with the old "by means of geometrical and arithmetical instruments (*geometricis et aritmeticis instrumentis*)." Whoever he was, the architect was a man of genius, not merely provided with this up-to-date knowledge of scientific method, but an innovator in design who took the fullest advantage of the latest available techniques. In the new work of the east end, built precisely between 14th July, 1140, and 11th June, 1144, he broke completely with the old Romanesque tradition of thick walls of poor quality. As Dr. Peter Kidson has put it, "the delicacy of the masonry in the new choir ran counter to the trend of almost every great building in northern Europe of the previous half-century."

So far as plans are concerned, we have seen that their principal subdivisions and proportions were based upon squaring, and this could be laid out upon the ground with cords once a base line and a right-angle had been determined geometrically. The proportionate determination of all other details of the building—even though in reality irregularities might creep in—was a matter of development with rule and compasses according to certain systems. To some extent the various systems in use, each of which gave a proportionately different height to a building of the same plan, tended to be regional or national. So far they have not been traced back in detail to their origins. Discussion has been obscured rather than clarified by a vast literature concerned with possible symbolism, numerology (a little of which probably was intentional), and arithmetical and algebraic analysis. Almost the whole of this literature must be disregarded in seeking for the empirical means by which the architects reached their remarkable results. Apart from the curious attempt to justify designs for Milan Cathedral, late in the fourteenth century, by bringing in a theoretical mathematician, the whole of the processes of rendering the ideal design specific in all its parts were steps in applied geometry carried out as a "construction" of lines

Professor Creswell has shown how the design of the Dome of the Rock at Jerusalem (A.D. 684–91) follows a simple geometrical procedure, with very ancient roots in the Near East. Furthermore, the main dimensions of the rotunda are virtually identical with those—both span and height, which equal one another—of the rotunda of the Anastasis at the Church of the Holy Sepulchre. Although the dimensions must certainly have been copied by direct measurement, the rest of the setting-out at the Dome of the Rock was done afresh, but according to the same principles which had been used throughout the region, long before Muslim times. The construction lines for the plan of the Dome of the Rock are essentially those of two squares crossed at 45 degrees; since the height of the masonry walls supporting the dome is equal to the internal span, the building is designed on the square, or Ad Quadratum. This was later to become one of the main systems of proportion used in the Gothic period, especially in Northern Europe. In Italy the normal proportion was based upon the equilateral triangle; the geometrical development of this system, Ad Triangulum or A Trigono, applied to many Gothic buildings of lesser relative height. In applying any of these ideal systems it must be kept in mind that artists, however much they may use aids to design, tend to make adjustments by eye; this is one of the main reasons why many attempts to find the "secret" of mediæval design fail abysmally. The dimensions found, modified by the placing of walls inside, outside, or centred upon lines of the theoretical mesh, simply will not yield results that are mathematically convincing.

This is by no means to say that there was not adherence to system : the facts of the controversy regarding the system to be employed at Milan Cathedral, recorded and published in 1521 by Cesare Cesariano in his commentary upon Vitruvius, are enough to prove that systems existed. In the last twenty-five years there has been much to-do over Cesariano, but as Chaucer put it:

> . . . out of olde feldes, as men seith,
> Cometh al this newe corn fro yeer to yere;
> And out of olde bokes, in good feith,
> Cometh al this newe science that men lere.

In this case the old books are those written, largely in England, in the first half of the nineteenth century, and to which adequate modern acknowledgement is long overdue. The rediscoverer of Cesariano, in a relevant sense, was John Sidney Hawkins (1758–1842), son of Sir John Hawkins the historian of music; but Hawkins' history of Gothic (1813) failed to fulfil the promise of his researches. It was left for Charles Robert Cockerell (1788–1863), first in his lectures at the Royal Academy in 1841, later in his valuable paper on "William of Wykeham" published in the Winchester volume (1846) of the Archæological Institute, to do something like justice to the principles of design revealed by Cesariano. Serious modern research in this field, though still based upon the (regrettably partly frustrated) publication by Cesariano, is in debt to Cockerell.

Cockerell did not attempt to reduce all mediæval buildings to a single system, and wisely remarked that in France and Germany "another rule of distribution (not yet discovered) is more frequent." As Cockerell was writing—in fact before 10th September, 1845, when he read this paper at Winchester—the other rule, "of the Square", was being republished in the form of a translation into modern German by Reichensperger of Roritzer's booklet of 1486 on the geometrical construction of pinnacles (Trier, 1845) (see page 103); the original, in scarcely intelligible dialect, had already been reprinted by Carl Heideloff in 1844. The subject was taken up in England by John Woody Papworth, who in the *Archæological Journal* for 1847 published a condensed version with diagrams, and in 1848, as an essay for the great *Dictionary of Architecture* undertaken by the Architectural Publication Society, a complete edition in English, with Reichensperger's observations and his own notes. Until fully illustrated editions of all the late German instruction booklets appear, Papworth's version—too long to reprint here—remains the standard consideration of the subject. The *Dictionary*, in its article "Proportion", gives a general discussion of historical methods of geometrical design with a very full bibliography of the subject down to 1877.

Although it is impossible at present to anticipate the solutions which may become available when all the surviving drawings and all of the albums and instruction booklets have been fully studied, certain lines of investigation may be suggested. One of the most fruitful would seem to be the search for reasons, within the techniques of different geometrical systems of design, for major differences in types of plan and form. For instance, the square east end of early northern churches, including many in England, a form rejected almost everywhere else but adopted for the early Cistercian monastic churches; the dome, a normal form throughout the Near East and in Italy, spreading across France, yet rejected almost entirely by the north-west (apart from a few structural exceptions such as the internally domed keep of Pembroke Castle); the cult of the central tower in Normandy and England and its neglect elsewhere. Similarly the opposition between the oblong and the polygonal chapter house poses special problems, notably because as a plan-form this runs contrary to the English resistance to the dome, polygonal chapters being practically restricted to England. In the use of polygons, where the octagon is usual, an "Ad Quadratum" feature, why is it that there should have been, early in the fourteenth century, a wave of interest in the "Ad Triangulum" hexagon and its derivatives? To some extent the answer to this last problem seems to lie in direct importation, around 1300, of Saracenic patterns based on interlaced circles, but this may well be only a part of the story.

Before leaving the subject of methods of design a word must be added on the use of instruments. In discussing mediæval architectural education we found that, as distinct from the tools of the stoneworkers found in the lodge, the master's tracing-house contained large and small compasses. The York Minster lodge in 1399 had an iron compass, but on the whole there are few references to this instrument, almost certainly, as Dr. Salzman suggests, because it was a personal possession of the master. The building employer commonly paid for axes, hammers, and various sorts of cold chisel, but most other instruments were, more often than not, the responsibility of the individual craftsmen, as indeed they generally are to this day. The working stonemason had to employ rule, square and at times compasses to mark out his work on the stone; the setters used level and plumb-bob. For putting a fine surface on to stone of different types the later mediæval usage was to make parallel lines scored with a claw-chisel, or later still with a broken saw-blade; the latter could, of course, be used only on fairly soft stones, as it was dragged by hand, not struck with a hammer. The master, for his designs and for his setting-out, needed pairs of compasses and dividers of different sizes—the very large for full-size works, the smaller for scale drawing, and bow-compasses for detailed work on sheets of parchment or paper. The date when compasses provided with a pen attachment were first used has not been established, and in England it was still common at least as late as about 1540 for curves to be struck in with dividers, "blind", and then inked over freehand; whereas the use of some form of ruling pen for straight lines had, as mentioned before (see page 109), come in much earlier.

The forms of square used by the masters present an intriguing problem. Normal squares, such as have been in use at all periods, existed; but beside them there is evidence for the employment of squares having one curved arm, or both arms tapering. A strong case for the latter as equivalent to "adjusted" setsquares for the automatic production of the Golden Cut proportion by manipulation has recently been made by Mr. B. G. Morgan, and this appears to be convincing. It is certain that special proportions, including the Golden Cut, were much favoured by mediæval designers, and were achieved with sufficient accuracy to prove intention. As certainly, the methods used were fundamentally simple and geometrical, and in the earlier part of the period the operation was doubtless carried out with compasses or strings. Later on, however, a master must have invented the short cut of devising special squares, similar in principle to the specially cut set-squares employed in the offices of some modern architects for the same purpose. It has been objected by Dr. Shelby that such a square could not have been used to set out construction lines hundreds of feet in length, and with sufficient accuracy. The answer to this would seem to be that these tapered squares were for use *only* in design, not in setting-out. If they were used to produce small-scale drawings, the relevant diagonals could then be measured off to scale, and marked off by using long cords, at full-size on the site. The square with tapered arms would then be one of the special symbols of the architect in his function as designer. This appears to be borne out by the surviving illustrations of this form of square (Fig. 11).

Planning and design were not solely based upon geometrical systems and symbolic numbers. As time went on the architects developed by means of imitation and progressive improvement a body of ideas which presented a sophisticated approach to all the problems set by their clients and also satisfied their æsthetic sense. In England this development took place largely during the fourteenth century. Whereas earlier vaults, for instance, had been set out with "true" curves struck from a centre, they began after 1300 to be "fudged" by hand-drawn curves in order to present a more suave appearance at the springing. Instead of lurching off into space awkwardly, as seen from below, the diagonal ribs were smoothed upwards to set them back into a single sheaf with the cross-arches and wall-ribs. A marked example of this is seen in the contrast between the management of the earlier choir and later nave vaults in Exeter Cathedral, the change being introduced in the course of the first half of the fourteenth century (see page 135). It is likely that the impression of loveliness received by William Worcestre in 1478 was derived from his first sight on entering the nave. A still later development of this idea was to lead to the fan-vault, peculiar to English design, where all the ribs had the same curve and were equally spaced out on plan.

In plan there was, also during the fourteenth century, a growth of standardization or rationalization. The ancient quadrangular scheme of monastic cloisters was applied elsewhere, perhaps first to "prestige" cloisters at secular cathedrals, such as the magnificent addition of c.1263–84 at Salisbury. Another secular cloister, of two storeys, and enclosing an octagonal chapter house, was begun at St. Paul's, London, in 1332; the plan of the regular quadrangle, with or without cloister walks, was applied to university colleges, to castles, to schools and hospitals. The first of these non-monastic claustral plans surrounded by offices or dwellings seems to have been the Dean's Cloister at Windsor, built within the royal castle in 1350–56 to house the canons of St. George's. Architecturally it may have been suggested by William Ramsey, the king's master mason, before his death in 1349, and the further development of this idea is closely associated with a succession of architects to the Crown. Henry Yeveley's little college for chantry priests at Cobham in Kent, begun about 1370, his immense quadrangle of the London Charterhouse started in the next year; and his colleague William Wynford's plans for New College, Oxford, Winchester College and, probably, Bodiam Castle, begun in 1385, continue this theme. New College, though not built until 1380–86, may have been designed some years earlier. At any rate, several marked improvements in planning and design were made by Wynford before the start at Winchester in 1387, as has recently been remarked by Sir William Hayter.

The closely integrated quadrangular plan for castles was exploited from about 1378 in the North of England by John Lewyn, chief mason to the Bishop of Durham. Bolton Castle was certainly by Lewyn, and stylistic resemblances and links with his known patrons—for besides his official post he had a widespread practice for the Crown and among the northern lords—indicate that the castles of Sheriff Hutton, Wressle and Lumley may well be by him. Another aspect of the integration of planning is exemplified by the low western or Galilee porch. This, as an extrusion on the west fronts of churches, had a distinguished ancestry going back to early Gothic times. It appeared in major form at the Sainte-Chapelle in Paris, built in 1243–48, and incorporated into an important west front, in the build at St. Albans Abbey of c. 1195–1214. The chapel of St. George in Windsor Castle, built in 1240–43, had a western narthex or porch, and it may have been Wynford's acquaintance with this chapel during his period of work in Windsor Castle that suggested to him the ingenious plan which he adopted at Winchester College. There, one long range comprises chapel, hall (on first floor level over the original schoolroom), and offices. To give a handsome entrance to the chapel it is provided with a western porch, low enough to be fitted under the dais of the hall above, which runs eastward to the west wall of the chapel proper, rising on the east side of the porch. Such ingenuity in "vertical planning" marks a new epoch. Similarly, Wynford must have pressed his patron Wykeham to pay for the "corrections" made to the north and south elevations of the Middle Gate tower. There a horizontal stringcourse cut across the tower above the gateway in the ground storey, but as a part of the original work this section of the continuous string has been cut out and returned upwards at each side before crossing the tower, thus giving an æsthetically more satisfying upthrust instead of lopping the tower off from its base (Fig. 35).

It must not be thought that the sophisticated planning of the fourteenth century by any means implies an antecedent barbarism in the earlier Gothic. As we have seen, there was indeed crudity and poor constructional skill in Anglo-Saxon times, giving way to a first wave of improvement and a capacity to design on a grand scale in the Norman period. Soon after 1100 this was overtaken by the greater wave of higher civilization and better appreciation of art and refinement that invaded Europe, and gave rise to the first Gothic architecture. The speed with which the new way of life and the new art were adopted in different regions depended largely on political conditions. In the case of England there is no doubt that, as a conquered kingdom (and therefore of greater prestige value than the duchy of Normandy), the country enjoyed preferential treatment after 1066. For this reason the new cathedrals here were on a grander scale, and architecture of all kinds had a greater degree of elaboration than was usual in Normandy itself.

Already noticeable under the Conqueror, this phase of grandeur and relative complexity became more marked under William Rufus. There is at least a quality of metaphorical truth in the story that Rufus, on being asked why he was building so large a hall at Westminster, answered that in fact it was merely the chamber for the immense hall that he meant to have built next.

The accession of Henry I, his marriage to the well educated Edith Matilda, and his long reign, conspired to favour England still more after 1100. Henry is not for nothing nicknamed "Beauclerc": perhaps not himself as deeply learned as the name implies, he was at any rate a patron of scholarship and science in an age of rapid advances in many fields. With the long start given by Norman construction over that of the French Royal Domain, the first Gothic architecture might well have centred upon London rather than upon Paris if Henry I had left a stable succession. As it was, he died in 1135, at the very time that Abbot Suger was taking the first steps towards the new west front of St.-Denis, built in 1137–40 and prelude to the advanced and more definitely "Gothic" choir. The political stability of France, where a line of able kings succeeded one another, made Paris for the time being the capital of western Europe. The next turn of Fortune's wheel, bringing Henry II to the throne of England in 1154, for a time favoured insular development, but the internecine warfare of the Angevin family and the quarrel with Becket again caused a setback. In spite of this, and as some compensation for the fact that the metropolitan cathedral had to bring in a French architect in 1174, England was able to develop the first styles of pure Gothic, freed from the round arch and from the remains of the classic Order, at Wells from 1175 and at Lincoln from 1192. It is unnecessary to follow in detail the ding-dong battle for priority which continued for the next century, still following the political fortunes of the two royal houses, but there is marked significance in the opening of the phase of Curvilinear Gothic in England about 1290. This was the first of the national styles to arise out of the international spread, from the Ile-de-France, in the first 150 years of Gothic.

English architecture by the latter part of the thirteenth century, though to a certain degree subordinated to stylistic influences from France, was in part inspired by a completely independent stream of native æsthetics derived from the linear quality of Celtic pattern and of Anglo-Saxon draughtsmanship. There is no French precedent for the enormously long English cathedrals and greater churches nor, apart from Cluny, for the gigantic area covered by Winchester, Bury St. Edmunds, York Minster and Old St. Paul's. As we have seen, the Westminster Hall of Rufus was unrivalled among post-Roman halls in the West for 150 years (see pages 61, 129). In certain arts, notably embroidery, England led the western world; in stained glass she equalled even if she did not excel the French schools, and by the middle of the twelfth century had been sending expert glaziers abroad (see page 36). The great towers of England, from that of St. Albans in the eleventh century, through those of Norwich and Ely to the thirteenth century work at Lincoln and Old St. Paul's, to Wells, Hereford, Salisbury, Worcester—without mentioning the galaxy of later belfries —form a series without rival as works of brilliant design by architects of genius. In size they are indeed outdone by the greatest German steeples, but not in æsthetic quality.

The reason for England's new artistic independence towards the end of the thirteenth century was the dominance of Edward I, by sheer force of character, over the western scene. He had also, as a Crusader, acquired first-hand knowledge of the Near East and was not limited, as most of his predecessors had been, by any petty western parochialism of outlook. Diplomatic relations were far-reaching, and in reply to a visit to London by envoys of the Mongol Ilkhan of Persia in 1289, a mission was despatched two years later under Sir Geoffrey Langley, Edward's old companion in arms from the crusade of 1270–74. By way of Genoa, Constantinople, and Trebizond the English envoys reached Anatolia, then passing overland to Erzerum, to the Mongol Court in summer quarters near Mount Ararat, on to Tabriz, and then back, stopping at various "towns of the Saracens and Armenians". The contacts made by such an embassy could obviously have great significance for art, and in this case it is suggestive to find that one member of the party was Robert "Sculptor". Architectural fruits of a journey by the Italian Austinfriar Giovanni, a few years later, were said to include "plans and drawings of all the buildings which he had seen, amongst others the drawing of the roof of a great palace in India beyond the sea." The people of Padua, on his return, were so taken with this drawing that they asked Fra Giovanni to roof their great civic hall in the same way. The Palazzo della Ragione (Fig. 38), an enormous structure 240 feet long by 84 feet in span, was built about 1306 and still exists; its roof is of surprisingly little intrinsic interest, being simply a gigantic timber barrel vault, held together with many iron tie-rods.

Within a few years of Langley's embassy diaper patterns appear in English art, notably at Canterbury Cathedral, suggesting directly Saracenic inspiration in their geometry. Interlacing circles, forming hexagons, and uses of the hexagon as a plan form, continue through the first half of the fourteenth century, and are accompanied by exotic motives such as those of the famous north porch at St. Mary Redcliffe, Bristol. The great octagon of Ely was set out in 1323 by someone who came from London for the purpose, and its plan is so extraordinary as to indicate direct information concerning the domed mausoleum of the Ilkhan Uljaitu at Sultanieh, built in 1307–13. Within a few years the introduction to England of the four-centred arch within a square frame again implies direct borrowing from Persia of a noticeable feature which did not take root in France or anywhere in Europe. Other motives immediately suggestive of features adopted in the English Perpendicular style of about 1330 and later are found in Cairo in the hundred years from 1211 to 1319; they include the curious straightened "wire-netting" reticulation which was so soon to contradict the flowing lines of the previous generation as exemplified particularly in the work of Master Ivo de Raghton. It cannot be mere coincidence that all the suggestions of Oriental influence upon English Gothic fall within the period, c. 1290–1335, when the Mongol dynasty of Ilkhans, cultivating relations with the West, were the great power of the Middle East.

With the flowering of the richest Curvilinear in the North between 1315 and 1340 we have already dealt in considering the career of Ivo de Raghton (see pages 79–80), but this was only one among a number of "regional" (but in fact probably personal) schools that flourished in the first half of the fourteenth century. The fountain head of style throughout the period lay at Canterbury, which provided a dynasty of architects who moved to London and served as king's master masons in three reigns. At Canterbury there developed an unusual, so-called Kentish style, highly idiosyncratic and directly influenced by the arrival of exotic patterns based upon interlacing circles and hexagons. Master Michael of Canterbury (see page 245) was chief mason at the Cathedral from 1275 to 1290, but was also active in London on the building of the house of the Prior of Canterbury in Cheapside. He attracted the notice of Edward I, who commissioned him to design the memorial cross in Cheapside after the death of Queen Eleanour of Castile in 1290. By 1292 Master Michael had begun the building of St. Stephen's Chapel in the Palace of Westminster, and in spite of long periods of suspension of the works he was still in charge in 1321 but died soon after, when he was succeeded by Thomas of Canterbury, probably his son. Under the Canterburys, the building lodge of St. Stephen's employed a large number of masons from many districts, and these men later moved away from Westminster, carrying with them elements of the Court Style, and the latest ideas in construction, to various regions of provincial England.

Structural expedients of the time included the extensive use of iron bars, for example the pair, each fifteen feet long, used to support the central mullion of the east window of St. Stephen's Chapel in 1332. Similar bars, but used as concealed reinforcement, were laid in the stone transom of the great south window of Gloucester Cathedral, c. 1335, and within the next few years bars of hidden reinforcement were used by Richard Farleigh, architect for the great central tower added to Salisbury Cathedral (Fig. 39). Farleigh was already architect to the abbeys of Reading and Bath when he was appointed at Salisbury in 1334, and he was probably also the designer of the central tower of Pershore Abbey, in Worcestershire. In 1352–53 he was master at Exeter Cathedral, but his home was at Keynsham, near Bath; he was still living there in 1363. Farleigh, who may well have been the Master Richard of Reading paid for carving images for the gable of St. Stephen's Chapel in 1332, was typical of the period in his wide practice. Even in the thirteenth century outstanding masters were running several jobs at once, and were acting in many ways like the modern professional architect; they did not at all conform to the idea that a single master controlled one job at a time and had to be resident upon it.

Among the many English architects of the Curvilinear period (page 134) it is possible within limited space to follow the career only of one: Thomas of Witney. A few months after the start of the works on St. Stephen's Chapel in 1292 one Thomas de Witteneye appears among the masons, and worked continuously for a year; then after an absence of nine months he worked there again from July to September, 1294. He was paid at first $5\frac{1}{2}d$. a day, and later 2s 9d. a week, indicating at that period a fully trained but junior craftsman. He was probably born about 1270, and in the town of Witney, Oxfordshire, an important manor belonging to the bishops of Winchester: this was to have its effect upon his later career. It is also not without significance that the splendid central tower of Witney Church was built in the thirteenth century under the influence of the central tower of Old St. Paul's. We lose sight of Thomas Witney for some fifteen years, until he appears (the identity is proved by later documents) as "Master T. of W., mason", in charge of the rebuilding of the presbytery of Winchester Cathedral at the joint expense of the bishop and the priory about 1315. From 1316 until 1340, or possibly 1342, he was master mason to Exeter Cathedral, completing the crossing and building the nave and the west front. He also designed the pulpitum, a work with detail of great stylistic significance, built in 1317–25, the reredos, and the sedilia of 1316–22. There can be little doubt that he was the master Thomas of Winchester who had earlier been brought to Exeter in connection with the making of the Bishop's Throne in 1312–13 and who was paid 3s. a week and given 5s. on his departure for his home (*versus patriam suam*). At Exeter Witney resided until 1324 continually, in a house in the Close for which the Chapter paid rent of £1 12s. 0d., as well as the fees of £6 13s. 4d. yearly which they granted him. In 1329 John Grandisson, the bishop of Exeter, wrote to the Prior and convent of St. Swithun, Winchester, urging them to pay arrears of a daily corrody and

England: journeys of architects, 1292–1353

yearly pension which they owed to Witney, "a dearly loved member of our household and a valuable and willing servant to us and to our church of Exeter". Soon afterwards Grandisson wrote to the abbot and convent of Sherborne, Dorset, recommending J. de Sparkeforde, son of Master Thomas de Wytteneye, "whose industry is of special value for the repair and in part new building of the fabric of our church of Exeter by his skill". The son's name rather suggests that he had been born at Sparkford (St. Cross), close to Winchester. Thomas "cementarius" had livery of the prior of St. Swithun, Winchester, in 1334–35.

So far we are on certain ground, but considerations of style suggest a good deal more. In 1323 one Thomas the Mason witnessed a document at Wells along with members of the Chapter there, and was presumably the master in charge of the works; around this period these included the Lady Chapel, the retrochoir, and the central tower. The bases of the piers in the retrochoir have most unusual mouldings which closely resemble those of the clustered shafts of the Exeter pulpitum; the tower, in its original state before drastic alterations in the fifteenth century, was extremely like that at Witney but on a larger scale; and the Wells Lady Chapel has window tracery of cusped spherical triangles, employed by Thomas Witney in the north transept and nave of Exeter. This unusual tracery also fills the clerestory windows of the nave of Malmesbury Abbey, Wilts. Finally there is the possibility that the crossing of the chapel at Merton College, Oxford, in progress under Master Thomas the Mason in 1330–32, may also have been to his design, for the clustered shafts and the bases and caps of the piers once again resemble the nave piers at Exeter. In or soon after 1340 Witney must have died, aged a little over seventy.

Witney's Exeter pulpitum contains what may be the earliest of four-centred arches in England, though this is slightly disguised by the fact that it is also an ogee arch. The wooden Bishop's Throne, the design of which is here attributed to him, contains the same design of cusped spherical triangles in its tracery work that is found in stone in his windows. These and other details mark a highly individual style, and as has been mentioned Witney was also responsible for the adjustment made to the true curves of the ribs of the Exeter nave vault (see page 128). If he designed the Exeter throne, as seems virtually certain, he provides an instance of a mason who was responsible for carpentry, and this raises another interesting possibility. One of the most remarkable of structural inventions was the hammer-beam truss, whereby a system of triangulation made it possible for principal rafters, thus stiffened, to bridge large spans without intermediate supports. A sketch in Honnecourt's album shows that he understood the principle, but it was never developed in France, and the earliest known example is the roof of the Pilgrims' Hall of Winchester Cathedral priory (Fig. 37).

Dated to 1325 by the purchase of slates, this remarkable structure belongs to the period of Witney's architectural responsibility. Whether or not it constituted a pioneer experiment, this roof goes far to explain the unexpected south-western distribution of the few early roofs of hammerbeam type (Winchester, Salisbury, Dartington and Exeter Law Library).

Undoubtedly Witney was in some ways an unusual figure, yet not abnormal in the ferment of his time. He certainly carried new ideas in art to regions beyond the direct influence of the Court architects and played a leading part in the development of "south-western Decorated", at the same time that his contemporary Ivo de Raghton was creating the "northern Curvilinear" so much prized abroad (see page 151). These products of English genius gave to Germany the inspiration for *Sondergotik* and to France the Flamboyant. Within the same orbit, of designers trained by or in touch with the chief masters of the royal works, a counter-current was beginning to move firmly away from exuberance towards Perpendicular, a style so sturdily insular as to have no external appeal whatever. This rational and economical fashion was adopted as the culmination of national stylistic development, but like the fantasy and extravagance of the Curvilinear which it displaced, its qualities displayed cultural riches out of all proportion to England's meagre financial resources. These architectural fireworks of the fourteenth century are one of the greatest of all triumphs of mind over matter.

VI

Organization and Professionalism

THE modern divorce between the architect and the building craftsman, who are now never the same person, makes it difficult to
grasp the form of organization to which mediæval architects belonged.
The very fact that the leading practitioners of the crafts of stonemasonry and carpentry were creative artists, and not just highly trained
artisans, involves a difference of kind between the ordinary craft guild
and the lodges and congresses of the masons. On the level of technical
skills it was indeed akin to the guilds; but so far as the designing
masters were concerned it had much of the character of a professional
body. We have no precise word to describe this sort of society or
assembly; the representative of the mediæval word "mistery" leads us
into a confused tangle of ambiguities and mistaken etymologies. Commonly supposed to bear relation to the Greek word which gives our
language "mystery", with religious and numinous overtones, the mistery
of the Middle Ages was really a *ministerium*, a ministry or service done
in a particular art. But a third root also enters, in the Romance
corruptions of *magisterium*, mastery, or the state of being a master. For
example, in Spanish, *mæstría* (derived from *magister*) means skill or
ability, and was confused in sense with *mester*, "mistery", a craft, skill
or occupation. The same confusions occur in Italian and French forms.

Appropriately enough, the earliest documents we have that give full
details of organization and rules are those governing the *mestier*
(modern French *métier*) of the Paris masons, stonecutters, plasterers and
mortar-makers. Promulgated in 1268, these statutes probably represent
a codification of a much earlier state of affairs. They are concerned
quite largely with the regulation of apprenticeship, which was to be for
at least six years. A master could take only one apprentice at a time,
until the first had been in training for five years, when a second might
be started. The King had granted the mastery of the Masons to
Guillaume de Saint-Patu, and he and his successors were to have the
lesser justice and the fines of the masons, plasterers and others; this was
in other words a similar jurisdiction to that which Walter of Hereford

had rather later at Caernarvon. This fact of autonomy of the masons is of the utmost importance, showing that they were a self-governing body without being a corporation having a common seal. Like other mediæval courts of regulation, theirs were not courts of record, so that the lack of documents has no implications. It is worth noting one of the very few such courts to survive in Europe, the Tribunal de las Aguas which meets every Thursday at noon in the north doorway of Valencia Cathedral to regulate the irrigation of the huerta; the Tribunal has never kept written records, but is known to have met continuously since before the Reconquest of 1238 and, it is believed, since foundation by the caliph Hakam II (961–76).

The Paris statutes refer to ancient tradition in stating that the chief master of the mistery, all stonecutters, and the mortar-makers, had been quit of guard duty since the time of Charles Martel, "as the elders (or aldermen, *preudome*) have heard said from father to son". Charles Martel (689–741), grandfather of Charlemagne and victor at Poitiers over the invading Moors in 732, received his name of Martel, "the Hammer", from his military prowess, but it served to endear him to artisan hammermen in search of a patron. The rule of secrecy was invoked by the statutes in a rather unusual way: "The masons, mortar-makers and plasterers may have as many helpers and servants (*tant aides et vallés*) in their craft (*mestier*) as they wish, so long as they do not show to any of them any point of their craft." This means that instruction must never be given to any pupil other than an apprentice, except for the master's own sons born in lawful wedlock, as provided by another article.

Only seven years after the promulgation of the Paris statutes a lodge of masons with autonomous jurisdiction was founded at Strassburg under Master Erwin "von Steinbach" who, in the following year 1276, was to begin the west front of the cathedral (Frontispiece). This lodge is said to have been confirmed in its rights by the Habsburg Emperor Rudolf I in 1275, and to have been made the master lodge for Germany (the whole German-speaking area of Europe) in 1277. What is of even greater interest is that the lodge was said to be one of "freed masonry" (*i.e.* of masons with their own jurisdiction) "according to the English fashion". This carries back to the opening of the reign of Edward I the English custom of a free jurisdiction of masons and gives independent support to the main features of the account given of themselves by the English documents (the Constitutions, see page 191, for the full text) which, in their surviving form, are rather more than a century later. It also demonstrates the direct international links subsisting between architects in the thirteenth century, and shows how it was that English style could later be carried into Germany and there be accepted as the basis for further experiments in design.

The English Constitutions themselves provide the best evidence of organization and are besides of extraordinary interest in their own right. In the versions that survive, one in prose and one in verse, they represent the state of affairs in the second half of the fourteenth century, the age of Yeveley and Wynford. But reference is made to earlier books in Latin and in French, with the implication that at least part of the Constitutions as we have them are a re-translation into English. Setting aside the "Regius Poem", which seems to have been composed by a cleric—though standing in some very close relationship, probably brother, to a master mason—the prose version consists of two parts; these are a "New Long History" of the craft, written about 1350–90, and the "Old Charges" incorporating the "Old Short History" which are earlier and must have existed by 1360. The Old Charges, intended to be read aloud to open every meeting of the lodge, are in somewhat antiquated but reasonably clear English, far from uneducated. The New Long History is literature on a much higher plane, deserving to be read for its own fluent and forceful, even if largely legendary account of the story of Geometry in practice, i.e. Masonry, from the Creation downwards.

The Constitutions, shorn of matter which is or may well be unhistorical, tell us a good deal which is not to be doubted when it is taken along with external evidence, both English and foreign. The body of Masons was ruled by Masters, who were those of the greatest skill, but they were a free association of free men, known to one another as "fellow" in that they all regarded themselves as of true, albeit far away, noble birth. This concept, not now very readily intelligible in England, still burns with a bright flame in Spain; every Castilian sincerely holds that he, and every other Castilian, is a *caballero*—that is a knight, with all the implications of gentle blood and what is still familiar to us as "chivalry". The Spanish attitude has nothing specially to do with architects or any category of society, affecting society as a whole; but its psychology remains closely akin to that which informs the Constitutions of Geometry. The mediæval master masons, who were also the architects of the period, rightly or wrongly believed that their special skill was the most notable on earth because it had the "most part of this science of Geometry"; and Geometry in turn, being the Science used by God Himself to create the world, was "the science that all reasonable men live by".

The pseudo-historical information given by the Constitutions starts to become interesting and suggestive when it reaches the "worthy king in France that was clept ... Charles the second". As it stands this statement is mysterious, since it appears to mean Charles the Bald (840–77) —Charlemagne being notionally Charles I—but a number of the later manuscripts of the Old Charges read "Charles Martel" in this passage;

and in view of the tradition handed down in the Paris statutes of 1268 this must certainly be what the compiler intended. His ideas of the sequence of historical chronology were extremely hazy in any case, for he jumps back to St. Amphibalus and St. Alban immediately after the section on King Charles of France. What was in his mind was that this was an early king of France *other than* Charlemagne; and it is only Charles Martel, anomalous in that he was ruler but never king, of whom it would be possible to imagine that he had been a mason (hence "Martel") before he was king. The confused statement that he was king by election is also explained. We need not necessarily believe in the historicity of the account, but it is evident that masons in the thirteenth and fourteenth centuries, both in France and in England, had a tradition that their craft owed special privileges to Charles Martel, who ruled from 715 to 743.

The privileges mentioned in France were such as it was practical to claim as factual exemptions. In England, however, they were concerned with organization : (1) "charges and manners of his (Charles's) device, of the which some be yet used in France"; (2) an assembly once a year; (3) a jurisdiction residing in the assembly ("to be ruled by masters and fellows of all things amiss"). The "history" continues, after interpolating the first charges in England given by St. Alban, with a statement that the "youngest son" of King Athelstan was a master of "speculative" Geometry and thus loved masons, becoming a mason himself, giving them "charges and manners as it is now used in England and in other countries". This seems to refer to the known adoption of English customs at Strassburg in 1275, and to their further spread on the continent. The son of Athelstan (who, historically, had no legitimate sons) is in some later manuscripts called Edwin, holding an assembly at York. This is certainly intended to bring into the story the historical Edwin, king of Northumbria 616–32, who was responsible for the building of the first stone church at York under Paulinus, soon after his baptism in a timber church on 12th April, 627. Incidentally, it is this feature of the legend, along with the very great and continuing importance of the York Minster building lodge, that accounts for the prominence of York in the history of modern Freemasonry. Athelstan's "son" in the New Long History purchased a patent of his father King Athelstan confirming the right of the masons to hold their assembly, and himself "ordained that they should have reasonable pay". In the incorporated Old Charges the story is slightly different, in that there is no mention of the "son" and Athelstan himself is credited with ordaining the arrangements for holding the assembly. In this version Athelstan (924–39), by common assent of his council and great lords, provided that the assembly should be held once a year or once in three years "as need were", in the form of congregations of all master masons and fellows held "from province to province and from country to country".

In mediaeval documents it is common to find the word "country" used in the sense of a county or shire, or at least of an administrative area, and this is to be understood here. The concluding statements on the assemblies or congregations provide that to give added support "if need be" to the Master of the Congregation "against rebels and upbearing the right of the realm", the Sheriff of the country (*i.e.* county) or the Mayor of the city or Alderman of the town in which the congregation is held should be "fellow and associate" to the Master. This would mean that the Master and the Sheriff (or other chief magistrate of the official local administration) would sit together on the bench of the court in which the congregation was held. The congregations were thus not secret, since they were formally associated with the local government of mediæval England; among the first charges to all of the craft was that "they shall be true to the King of England and to the realm". The nature of the court held, as described in the Old Charges, is closely paralleled by the usage of the customary manorial courts held all over England until within living memory but now (in spite of their prolific written records) fast becoming forgotten and misunderstood. Since the perpetuation of customary usage is strictly stereotyped, the precise methods used to hold manorial courts in the first quarter of the twentieth century have high relevance and are included for comparison (see page 257).

Before returning to the historical problems raised by the statements on Charles Martel, on Edwin, and on Athelstan, it may be as well to look at the confirmatory external evidence proving that, certainly in the fourteenth century, and by very strong presumption in the thirteenth, congregations of the masons actually were held. The question of how often assemblies were held—annually or triennially—is of little importance, since this was to be determined "as need were". What is of great practical concern, however, is the rule that congregations were to be held in provinces *and* in counties. This hints at not less than two levels on which meetings were held; the lower level of a single English shire, with corresponding local meetings in cities and corporate towns legally outside the jurisdiction of the sheriffs of counties; and larger meetings covering a region comprising several counties. One might expect that there would also be, on rare occasions, a national assembly including delegates from all parts of England, on the same lines as the general congresses of the German Lodge Masons held at Regensburg in 1459 and later, and possibly earlier too. The distance which had to be travelled, in each direction, to Regensburg in 1459 was up to about 300 miles, in the case of Bern. An assembly held in London would demand about the same from a Carlisle delegate; but any fairly central place chosen would be easier to attend than the German congress. It is then reasonable to conclude that there may, at intervals of perhaps as much as twenty years or more, have been national assemblies; the point is worth making, since this would explain more easily than any other means, the diffusion of style and customs to the remotest parts.

Taking only the facts for which the Constitutions vouch, it seems likely that there were both county congregations and also assemblies from larger provinces or regions. It may be that the county meetings were held yearly, and those in the larger regions once in three years. The early evidence indicating that the organization of assemblies may already have existed in the thirteenth century is imprecise but suggestive. On 13th March, 1244–45, King Henry III sent his master mason Henry de Reyns and his master carpenter Simon de Norhampton to York to advise upon York Castle after conference "with other masters expert in the like skills" (*aliis magistris in consimilibus scienciis expertis*). On 14th January, 1256–57, the king appointed the next chief mason, Master John of Gloucester, and the carpenter Master Alexander, to be chief masters of the royal works touching their respective crafts "this side (*i.e.* South) the Trent and Humber", specifically because the works had suffered damage through being carried out by sheriffs on the king's behalf. This may imply only the formation of a primitive Office of Works, but it could also have much wider implications.

In 1320 Pope John XXII granted a Bull to Hereford Cathedral in aid of works which the petitioners wished to carry out "upon the ancient foundation which is thought to be firm and solid in the judgment of masons or architects regarded as skilled in their art (*judicio cementariorum seu architectorum qui in arte sua reputabantur periti*)". Here again there may have been a privately convened consultation with individual masters, but such a verdict could be reached much more easily when the county or regional assembly was in session. Information gathered from a far wider area, in fact from the whole country, is referred to by Thomas Rudborne, the fifteenth-century chronicler of Winchester Cathedral. In giving an account of the fall of the original Norman central tower in 1107 and its subsequent rebuilding in the form which even now survives, he states that it was in his time "according to masons the firmest of all towers of its kind in the realm of England (*et adhuc extat secundum latomos firmissima inter omnes hujusmodi turres in regno Angliæ*)". This clearly implies that masons were in a position to be well informed as to the great church towers of the whole country. Again such information could most easily be obtained through a system of regular assemblies at different spots, held periodically. It is commonly objected that communications in the Middle Ages were too bad to have allowed of any general inland travel; but this is manifestly untrue. Mediæval roads, not yet used by any large number of wheeled vehicles, were in a far better state, for riding, than were the roads described in the seventeenth century, for example. There is an immense body of evidence, both general and specifically relating to building operations, which proves conclusively the long journeys made quite frequently by architects and craftsmen.

In the contract for the building of the eastern chapels of Vale Royal Abbey in Cheshire in 1359 (see page 216), provision was made for assessment in case of disputes by "good men of the country and masons", indicating a body of masons with some recognized standing. This is even more clearly suggested by two clauses in the contract of 1434 for building the nave of Fotheringhay Church, Northants. The foundations were to be set out "by oversight of masters of the same craft"; and possible disputes over the competence of mason setters appointed by the Duke of York's masters of the works were to be settled "by oversight of master-masons of the country." Again "county", of Northamptonshire, is to be understood, and some organizational means of readily summoning a group of masters of recognized reputation is implied.

Finally we have the explicit evidence of an Act of Parliament of 1425 (3 Henry VI, c. 1). This was passed because of complaint that "by the yearly congregations and confederacies made by the masons in their general chapters assembled" the Statutes of Labourers as to wage rates were being broken. The Act forbade the holding of such chapters and congregations on pain that those responsible for holding them should be guilty of felony, while other masons attending them should be liable to imprisonment and fines. The law may have been impossible to enforce, for no evidence of any prosecutions under it has ever been discovered. It has been doubted that the yearly congregations mentioned in this Act can be the same as those described in the Constitutions, partly because the earlier Act of 1360 (34 Edward III, c. 9), which laid down that congregations and chapters of masons and carpenters should be void and wholly annulled, is seen as directed against new and illegal conspiracies due to the inflation which followed the Black Death. Furthermore, it has been argued that assemblies which included the sheriff of a county or mayor of a city could not have engaged in defiance of the law. This last point has no real force; the presence of the sheriff or mayor was not mandatory, but merely permissive.

Another question is raised by Wycliffe's views expressed in *The Grete Sentens of Curs*, written towards the end of Edward III's reign. He argued that "all false conspirators be cursed of God and man... Also all new fraternities or guilds made of men seem openly to run in (*i.e.* incur) this curse ... also men of subtle craft, as free masons and others, seem openly cursed by this sentence. For they conspire together that no man of their craft shall take less on a day than they set ..." If Wycliffe's two separate remarks are taken together, they could mean that the free masons had formed a *new* fraternity or guild to maintain high wage rates on trades union principles, against the Common Good expressed in the Statutes of Labourers. Now it does seem likely, seeing that the versions of the Constitutions that we have are later than the Statutes of Labourers, that the reference to King Athelstan having ordained that the mason should have reasonable pay was a piece of propaganda directed against the official attempt to pin wages down. If this were the case, and the reference to pay inserted after the Black Death, it would mean that the congregations regularly held for normal purposes of the craft from time immemorial were taken over by a militant body of journeymen who saw their chance to use the assembly for their own ends. In this case the Statutes of 1360 and 1425 directed against the chapters of masons and carpenters applied only to this improper use of the assemblies. The case of John Sampson, acquitted at Oxford in 1391 of a breach of the Statute of Labourers on the ground of his special skill (see page 79), shows that even when prosecution did occur, the law was tempered in respect of the architect or building master of outstanding gifts.

It is now possible to go back to the problem of the historicity of the references in the Constitutions to Charles Martel, Edwin and Athelstan; or rather to consider what is likely to have been the real origin of the organization of masons in the Middle Ages. This takes us once more to foreign sources. There had in Roman times been guilds (*collegia*) of architects, but no certain continuity can be proved between these classical guilds and the masons' guild in Lombardy mentioned in 643 in the laws of King Rotharis (636–52). The two laws (Articles 143 and 145) which refer to masons describe the building master as a *Magister Comacinus*, and are concerned only with his liability for fatal accidents. Absolutely nothing else of this Lombard organization of the seventh century is known, yet whole books of fantasy and controversy have been published about the "Comacine Masters" under a misapprehension, that the word *comacinus* had something to do with the place Como. This is linguistically impossible, and it has been proved conclusively that the word means exactly what it says: a mason associated with others. So that in the middle of the Dark Ages, in Lombardy, there was a recognized organization of masons who were linked ("*co-*") with one another. This has considerable significance in the light of the important later developments in Lombard architecture. As late as 1175 building work in the north-east of Spain was entrusted to Lombard masons (see page 243), and the word *Lambardus* was being used as a synonym for mason. Together with the structural remains of Lombardic architecture, the slight documentary references to Lombard masters—which include also a price scale of 714 for architectural and building work issued by the authority of King Liutprand—give a glimpse of organization probably continuous from the early seventh century until the twelfth—from "sub-Roman" times right on to the opening of the Gothic period. Seeing that the masters themselves, in and before 643, must have been Roman rather than Lombard, as Sir Thomas Graham Jackson long ago pointed out, it is not altogether far-fetched to regard this organization as responsible throughout the Dark Ages for continuing the traditions of Vitruvius in living form.

This gives real sense to the term Romanesque, which is a style originating in that spread by the Lombard masters. Though demonstrative historical proof is lacking, it is at least more likely than not that the architectural masters brought from Rome to Hexham in 673 belonged to the same widespread guild system (see page 38). It is not entirely fanciful to suppose that this could have led to some form of organization among builders in England thereafter. Nor must it be forgotten that Paulinus, who baptized King Edwin at York in 627, had himself come from Rome, and that his stone church was very probably built by imported masons half a century before Wilfrid's works in the North. In spite of the confused details of the History as recorded in the Constitutions it is therefore at least possible that the story is not wholly fabricated, but does contain elements of reflected truth. The nature of masons' work, very different in kind from that of all shop crafts, lends

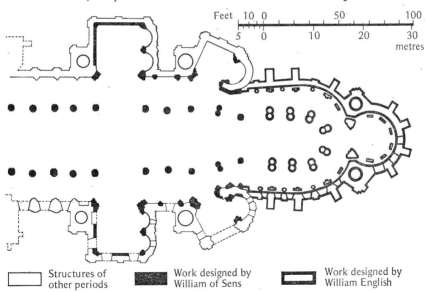

Feet 10 0 — 50 — 100

5 0 — 10 — 20 — 30
metres

Structures of other periods Work designed by William of Sens Work designed by William English

Canterbury Cathedral: plan of the choir to show the new works designed by William of Sens, 1174–1178, and William English, 1179–1184.

itself to the rather loose form of guild indicated by the evidence, and there is no inherent reason why there should not have been some form of association between masons in Anglo-Saxon England. The invocation of King Athelstan may be due simply to his name ("Noble Stone"), but he was reputed to have made many grants of liberties and privileges, notably to the great northern churches and, for example, to the guild of Minstrels of Beverley.

When we come to the name of Charles Martel it is obvious that an element of French masonic tradition has entered the picture. It seems likely that this association with the privileges claimed in Paris in the thirteenth century is due to the arrival of French masons after the Norman Conquest, but how long after we cannot say. The very close architectural links across the Channel from the time of the Confessor to that of Henry III, a space of 200 years, make constant interchanges between the masons of the two countries not merely probable but certain. Whether English masters ever attended international congresses held in France is highly problematical, but the convocation of distant masters of Canterbury (Figs. 40, 41) in 1174, which included Master William of Sens, proves that during the twelfth century there was enough communication in the architectural field for masters to be drawn long distances across national frontiers. Likewise the London Assizes of Building of 1189 and 1212, though promulgated by civic authority, not by any guild of craftsmen, betray highly sophisticated technical knowledge of urban housing and amenities. The 1189 document is particularly interesting for its historical appendix on the rebuilding of the City after the Great Fire of the first year of King Stephen (1136):

> Memorandum, that in ancient times the greater part of the city was built (*hospitata*) of wood, and the houses covered with straw and thatch and the like forms of roofing; so that when any house had caught fire most of the City was burnt in that same fire, as happened in the first year of the reign of King Stephen. . . . . Afterwards many citizens, to avoid such risks as far as they could, built on their sites a stone house roofed with thick tiles . . .

In the year after the Fire of London, 1137, there was a series of destructive fires in York, destroying not only the Minster, St. Mary's Abbey and the Great Hospital, but also thirty-nine churches and Holy Trinity Priory. Even in the troubled reign of Stephen much rebuilding must have gone on after fires such as these, and for the reasons assigned by the 1189 London Assize a great deal of the walling will have been of stone. The sudden great demand for masons—for there were serious fires at several other cities besides London and York within the same few years—may have had far-reaching secondary effects; the beginning of the transition from Romanesque to Gothic style would have added another important factor tending towards closer organization. Whatever may have been the case in Saxon and Norman times, it is probable that the middle of the twelfth century saw some form of regional or national association among masons, and that from this within the next hundred years there developed the arrangements described as existing in the second half of the fourteenth century, in the earliest surviving versions of the Constitutions. It must in any case be remembered that the textual history of the mediæval Constitutions is highly complex, indicating a considerable period of written development before any of the surviving versions were made; that the reference to older books in Latin and French puts back still further the date of the earliest written compilation on the subject; and that the organization itself may have existed for a very long time without producing any written records at all.

The whole subject of the German Lodges and Guilds of masons was described in such detail by the late Paul Frankl in *The Gothic* that only a brief summary will be attempted here. On the Continent, or at least in the Germanic region, there was a strict division between local guilds of masons, comparable to the London Mason's Company, and the great organization of Lodge masons which stretched across the whole Empire and beyond it through Hungary and Switzerland. This system of Lodge masons also stretched into Imperial Italy, for an ordinance of the Siena Cathedral lodge, quoted by Frankl, is of 1292 and was then stated to have been turned into Italian from the Latin, to avoid misunderstandings. So there was an earlier written ordinance in Latin, at any rate as far back as the period of the setting up of the Strassburg Lodge in 1275. The fact that Strassburg and Siena were both within the Empire, yet Strassburg chose to go abroad to England for the "fashion" of masonic association proves the overwhelming importance, by 1275, of pure Gothic style. Germans, still in the process of adopting Gothic from abroad, both from French and from English sources, could already reject the Italian contemporary style exemplified at Siena, and prefer England to France as their model.

The first of the German ordinances to survive dates from 1397 and relates to the guild stonemasons of the city of Trier. It is thus comparable to the Paris regulations of 1268 and to the London regulations for the trade of masons of 1356. Although there were many points of resemblance between the arrangements of the guild masons and the lodge masons, Frankl emphasizes the difference implied by the determination of the lodges to maintain their own autonomous jurisdiction, while the guilds of local masons were quite content to accept the verdicts of the municipal courts. Another ordinance of a city guild of masons survives for Erfurt and dates from 1423, while there is a 1441 ordinance of the lodge of Siena Cathedral. Soon after the middle of the fifteenth century comes the great group of Lodge ordinances associated primarily with the Regensburg congress of 1459. Shortly before there had been meetings of masons at Speyer and at Strassburg, but their proceedings do not seem to have survived. On the other hand, the Saxon masons held their own congress in 1462, and have left a record, as have those of the Tirol, who held two meetings, at Sterzing and later at Hall near Innsbruck, in February 1460. In the long run the Tirolese and the Saxon masons, though with some reservations, joined the centralized organization at least nominally controlled by the Chief Master at Strassburg. So far as is known, this fifteenth-century co-ordination of the craft throughout the Germanic area had no parallel elsewhere.

The very detailed information set out in the Regensburg ordinances of 1459 shows that the German lodge masons had six categories instead of the usual three : apprentice, journeyman and master. The additional grades were foreman (*Parlier*), the English warden, between the journeyman and the master; the workmaster (*Werkmeister*), a higher grade than the simple master ; and "servant of art" (*Kunstdiener*), journeyman who served the master for an extra time in order to get special training. As in the English Constitutions, stress was laid on the personal morality of the mason : no workman or master working on stone was to live in concubinage. Every apprentice had to produce testimony from his father as to his legitimate birth, a point which bears out at least a part of the English insistence upon the masons as well born. It was not imperative for the journeyman to wander after he had completed his apprenticeship, but if he wished to proceed to the rank of *Parlier* he had to wander for at least a year. Apprenticeship had been cut down to five years.

Frankl gives an account, from the various sources of evidence, of the German system of education for stonemasons. He concludes that all of them had to be able to read and write, and that they had attended monastic schools, where instruction was given chiefly in Latin, until they were fourteen, when they began their apprenticeship. As in England, the evidence for the strictly architectural side of their training is very scanty, but in addition to the strict facts there is the useful hypothesis that the grade of "servants of art" was the means by which a journeyman who had already thoroughly learned the manual trade of a stonemason could by serving the workmaster learn in addition the architectural methods of design as an art. Even though the documentary evidence falls short of absolute proof of this, the conclusion seems almost certainly right. A corollary is that whereas the ordinary master was what we still in the twentieth century understand by a master mason, the workmaster was an architect. This again is not certain, but extremely likely.

The later German ordinances are valuable for the detailed light they throw upon the subject of graduation and the making of masterworks. A Regensburg ordinance of the guild of stonemasons made in 1514 provides that a journeyman must make six masterworks in order to graduate:

1. a simple quadripartite vault
2. a stone doorway of pieces
3. a simple gateway
4. a projection or profile (*i.e.* a cornice)
5. foundation walls for a house, and where a wall or corner has become damaged to repair the wall and know how to mend it
6. to know from the height of any wall its proper thickness and how to make an adequate foundation for it.

What is of outstanding interest is that, in case it was not feasible for him to execute a masterwork (such as no. 5 above), he was to demonstrate with a model of clay. This at least proves the making of models early in the sixteenth century; and if they were used for training, they must *a fortiori* have been used seriously by the workmaster for discovering solutions to new problems (see page 163). One other question is answered by a late ordinance of 1563: the mason's mark, described as a mark of honour (*Ehren zeichen*) was given to the apprentice when he was promoted to journeyman.

The German lodge masons, in contrast to the local guild masons, were undoubtedly what we should term a professional body. Starting from the basis of English masons' customs as they were in the middle of the thirteenth century, the immensely large and long continued works of Strassburg Cathedral gave impetus to a highly complex development and to successful empire-building on the part of the chief architects of Strassburg. With some difficulty they were able to bring into a vast territorial organization lesser provincial groups of masons in particular districts, so that by the end of the fifteenth century they exercised at least a nominal control over all the German-speaking lands within the Empire, and some beyond it. There does not seem ever to have been any directly comparable solution, or even an attempt at one, elsewhere. Not even France, with its strong historical trend towards centralization, produced anything like it. But in England there was a later development of a different kind when the conversation in the lodge moved on from stonemasonry to architecture, from architecture to the subject of the supreme Architect and His Geometry. The quasi-historical introduction to the Constitutions took on renewed life, with its ingenious dovetailing of Scripture and classical and archæological material. We cannot follow the fantastic course taken by old stonemasonry as it met, after 1603, with the different traditions of Scots masons, and a century later was metamorphosed into the Speculative Freemasonry that became totally divorced from the earlier organization of operative lodges of the technical kind.

The English assemblies and congregations may not have been so completely separate as their German counterparts from the guilds of masons in the towns, but a very large part of their work was done at the great churches. In spite of the refoundation of cathedrals by Henry VIII, the Dissolution of the monasteries and the Reformation together put an end for a very long time to all major structural works on the English minsters. Nowhere is there a real continuity of work or staff; even at York Minster, which comes closer to having a continuous record than any other of the great cathedrals, there is a gap in the series of recorded master masons from the death of John Forman in 1558 to the appointment of Thomas Beane in 1597, simply as a mason in charge of maintenance. The end of the Middle Ages made a real break with the past; the saddest of all losses was the human pride and artistic autonomy of the great workmasters who had been the architects of the noblest outpouring of buildings ever seen. The rise of modern professionalism three centuries later was a most inadequate restitution.

VII

National and
International Art

ALL arts and sciences are derivative: each period of activity is based upon something that has gone before. The process of such derivation is not regular and moves both at different speeds and by unexpected jumps—mutations in the language of biology. In the history of art there are both major mutations, giving rise to a whole new epoch such as the Byzantine, the Gothic—and minor changes which quite suddenly form the starting point of a new fashion in style. We have seen that in mediæval England two such new styles: Curvilinear, based upon the flowing "ogee" curve, and Perpendicular, derived from straight and often vertical lines, followed one another within only a little more than one generation (see page 136). This instance is of peculiar interest in that, while Curvilinear turned the tables upon France and became the most evocative and formative of all the particular Gothic styles, and thus had a very wide effect internationally; Perpendicular on the contrary, as if by subconscious prophetic foresight of England's loss, a hundred years later, of the French war and her foothold on the Continent, took a more highly individualist and specifically national turn than any other fashion.

The fundamental reasons for such changes are to be sought in the personalities of the leading figures of any period: the interplay of character among the monarchs, prelates and statesmen of public and diplomatic life. As they were—and this was a biological quality decided by their ancestry—so would their taste be; and according to their taste, so the artists of the time would produce their works, for he who pays the piper calls the tune. Few artists can afford to indulge their personality to the extent of working against the taste of the leading patrons available at a given time. In some rare instances outstanding personality, or force of external circumstances, pushes an artist out of his own orbit so that he becomes an exile in some distant country. In such cases foreign skills are carried by the refugee, and if they meet with appreciation from the rulers of his adopted home, may give rise to startling changes and fresh departures.

In the whole history of Europe the most extraordinary instance of this dependence of art and fashion upon personalities and good luck was that of Ziryāb (Abu 'l-Hasān "Alī ibn Nāfi", A.D. 789–857), the Iraqi court singer and Beau Brummel. Ziryāb's fantastic story, discovered by E. Levi-Provençal in an unpublished Arabic chronicle, but confirmed by other well-known sources, reads like a fairy tale. Trained as a musician at the Bagdad Court of Hārūn ar-Rashīd, Ziryāb incurred the jealousy of his master, the musician Ishák al-Mawsilī and had to flee the country. He reached Kairouan in Tunisia whence he was invited to Cordova by the Umayyad emir al-Hakam I. On landing at Algeciras, Ziryāb learned that his new patron was dead; but luck stepped in, and the new monarch 'Abd ar-Rahmān II honoured his father's intentions. This was in 822, and for the next thirty-five years the Iraqi artist played a leading part, not merely in musical life, but in introducing all the niceties of oriental refinement to the West, including not only fashions in dress and new recipes in cookery, but also the standard order of courses served at table for over a thousand years since, from soup to dessert, and the use of toothpaste.

An enormous part has been played at all times by fortuitous events such as this; but these events are themselves carried on the great waves of political rise and fall. The overwhelming debt owed by modern Europe to the East has never yet been fully admitted. Not just fashionable behaviour brought from Bagdad to Cordova, but inventions of outstanding importance such as the making of paper and of glazed earthenware, have moved northward from Moorish Spain. At a later date the route of importation tended to be through Sicily after the Normans; later still it was from Palestine, Syria and Anatolia with returning Crusaders. It is a strange survival of *odium theologicum* into the age of modern scepticism, that, while there is a substantial agreement about the inventions derived from China by the West, suggestions of Muslim influence are commonly met by denial and by minimization, and this negative reaction is intensified in regard to Turkish sources. In spite of the fundamental change from paganism to Christianity, it is quite usual to think of a "classical continuum" from ancient Greece through Rome to the Eastern and Byzantine Empire; but this stops short at 1453. Yet the cleavage between the culture of antiquity and later times was quite as much in the devastations and resettlements of the Iconoclastic period, and the Latin occupation from 1204 as it was in the Turkish Conquest of the fifteenth century.

Mehmet II saw himself as Roman Emperor and as the first of a new Byzantine, albeit Muslim, dynasty : the Roman Empire did not come to an end on 29th May, 1453, but on 10th November, 1922. In fact the Turkish revitalization of Byzantium led directly, among many other things, to the great outburst of Western gardening in the sixteenth century, when again the happy accident of Ogier de Busbecq, an ambassador who was a botanical herbalist, led not only to the introduction of hyacinths, lilac, lilies, ranunculus, tulips and much else, but to the saving of the *Codex Vindobonensis*. Most of our certain knowledge of the Greek nomenclature of plants is due to this extraordinary and beautiful survival, a copy of the *Materia Medica* of Dioscorides illuminated about 512 with recognizable versions of much earlier originals. Far later still another lucky accident brought back with Lady Mary Wortley Montagu in 1718 the practice of inoculation for smallpox normal in the Ottoman Empire.

Though remote from the practice of architecture, such borrowings are not irrelevant. They show how the transmission of information, possibly of an importance that cannot be exaggerated, may depend upon a single individual and upon a fortunate set of circumstances. We are warned against disbelief in diffusion, including the derivation of artistic detail from places very far off. It was no coincidence that the window tracery used in the crypt of St. Stephen's Chapel at Westminster about 1320 included the ogee-quatrefoil in exactly the form that had been so favourite a motive in pre-Han and Han China (fourth century B.C. to second century A.D.); undoubtedly it was part of the "package deal" which had brought a variety of Oriental ideas to England from or through Persia in the preceding generation. Decorative patternwork of interlaced circles and hexagons, as already mentioned (see page 131), was another introduction from the same region about 1300. More definitely architectural was the four-centred arch within a square surround, a distinctively Persian motive, which appears suddenly in England (and generally not elsewhere in Europe) in the first half of the fourteenth century; furthermore, the early examples are often acutely pointed, with the upper arcs straight or nearly straight, as in Persian usage. Akin to this detail, but with a two-centred arch, is a version found in the doorways to the York Chapter House of *c.* 1290–1310; the triangular spandrels between the arch and the surround were soon to become a typical motive of Perpendicular.

Architectural transmission took different forms and might be direct or indirect. Indirect information, by means of a word-of-mouth description or a rough sketch, might be acquired from almost any traveller; or it could take the form of a written account sent in a letter. Depending upon the amount of detail given, and whether specific dimensions were included, even such indirect sources were capable of transmitting certain general forms from a distance, however great. For example, it is possible that the earliest pointed arches in Europe might have been built simply from description of this unusual form by someone who had been to the Near East—even though this is probably not the actual method by which the pointed arch did reach the West. Any visual detail, if it were not too complicated, could be acquired in this way, if it had made a sufficient impression on the traveller. The use of polychrome masonry too might simply be the result of casual observation and admiration for its effect, and this would apply also to simple forms of decoration such as the cusped arch. In fact the early distribution of this in south-western France indicates direct contacts with Moorish Spain.

An improvement upon the description or casual sketch by a layman would be the more careful drawing made by a traveller with artistic talents or training, or even by a technical draughtsman who had taken the trouble to measure and draw out a detail he admired. Such copying, but with deliberate intent, was one of the chief ways in which Gothic details, and even major structural designs, found their way from one part of Europe to another, and from end to end of England. In Germany and Austria this method can be demonstrated by the survival of copies and versions of the plans, elevations and sections of one building among the contents of the plan chest of another. Even before the start of Gothic we have seen that a lay-brother might be sent a return journey of 800 miles, to bring a measured plan of Clairvaux Abbey to be copied in the north of Friesland (see page 105). Hence, although local and regional styles did exist, there was no reason at all why buildings of importance should not be designed in accordance with a remote style. The patron might expressly order that a building, or a given feature, should be copied from one that already existed, and this is exemplified over and over again in the contracts and in documents such as the order by Henry III in 1243 that his new chapel in Windsor Castle was to have a high wooden roof painted to look like stonework "in the manner of the roof of the new work of Lichfield". Suggestions such as this derived from the constant travelling of mediæval kings with their courts, and of noblemen and bishops who moved from one of their manors to another, eating up the available provisions, since it was easier and cheaper to move oneself to supplies than to pay heavy expenses for slow transport of goods liable to spoil on the way. This meant that the mediæval client, above a certain level, was likely to have a considerably wider personal knowledge of recent developments in style than would the relatively sedentary clients of today.

Travel by the architects took place on a considerable scale. In the course of, or after training there were the wanderyears; there were journeys on behalf of clients whose buildings lay spread out at different manors, appropriated churches or the like; and there were the journeys to attend the congregations of the craft, whether annually or occasionally. Rather more exceptional were the cases of masters being sent long distances, as Henry de Reyns was to York, on official business. Some of these journeys might be long indeed, as when the French master Eudes de Montreuil accompanied St. Louis on crusade, and designed military works at Jaffa. Edward I found a Savoyard engineer, James of St. George, whom he rewarded highly as the expert in charge of his castles in North Wales. Even though the names of individual architects may not be known, it is reasonable to suspect that many of the leading crusaders were accompanied by their master mason or engineer. The family of the Angevins were noted patrons of architecture, military, ecclesiastical and civil, as well as being outstanding crusaders. It would be surprising if there were no connection between these two facets of their character. Fulk V, Count of Anjou (1090–1143) actually became King of Jerusalem in 1131, but he had already been in Palestine in 1120. His son Geoffrey Plantagenet (1113–1151) was rather more than a dabbler in military engineering himself, and was deeply versed in Vegetius (see page 208). In 1190 William, an English mason, went on crusade with Richard Cœur-de-Lion and built a church at Acre. At an earlier date, when it has considerably greater significance, one John the mason (*cementarius*) was a monk of La Trinité at Vendôme who was borrowed by the bishop of Le Mans as architect for the nave of the Romanesque cathedral, rebuilt between 1099 and 1120. Letters from John's abbot to bishop Hildebert de Lavardin, referring to his excommunication of John for bad behaviour, mention that John had "returned to Jerusalem". This implies that he had been there earlier, and presumably before his work at Le Mans.

With the case of Saracen prisoners of war we have dealt earlier (see pages 74, 96). This must have been one of the ways in which not merely surface pattern, but structural techniques unknown in the West, such as the joggled flat arch, were introduced. The very marked improvement in masonry and jointing soon after 1100 may reflect the coming of a number of Muslim stonecutters able to demonstrate their traditional methods, which at the time were certainly better than those of the Franks and Normans. The arrival of well trained foreign craftsmen on their wanderyears or otherwise, and their taking up work, must have been another way in which ideas in design and construction crossed mediæval frontiers. The cases of William of Sens at Canterbury in 1174, of Raymond the Lombard at La Seo de Urgel the following year, and of the Rouen mason Durandus, who crossed the Channel to take charge at Beaulieu Abbey in 1224, are examples.

Embittered discussion has taken place over the question whether inventions in military architecture at the time of the First Crusade were moving from West to East or *vice versa*. In spite of the literary fame of T. E. Lawrence's study, admittedly an early if not juvenile work—in favour of Crusader influence upon the Saracens—there is now no doubt whatever that it was the Franks who were at the receiving end. The production of conclusive evidence is very largely due to the penetrating and exhaustive studies made over the last fifty years by Sir Archibald Creswell. The crucial devices can be shown in every case—as with the pointed arch—to have originated in the Near or Middle East even centuries before the time of the First Crusade. To take one instance, the earliest use of the machicolation for defensive purposes is at Dār Qītā in Syria, in a watch-tower dated to A.D. 551! This priority is not exclusively in military works, for the famous rose window of the south transept of Lausanne Cathedral, so inaccurately drawn by Villard de Honnecourt, designed in the first third of the thirteenth century, seems to be based on a grille in the Al-Azhar mosque in Cairo of almost a century earlier (between 1130 and 1149). The "straight reticulations" of early Perpendicular tracery can, as has been seen, be derived from Cairene windows of the thirteenth century (see page 132).

There has been a tendency in recent years to exaggerate the debt of English Gothic to France. The priority of the Ile-de-France in the first period of Gothic design at St.-Denis and at Chartres, between 1130 and 1160, is admitted; but even so the structural aspects of the new style owed much to the Norman exploitation, at a decidedly earlier date, of both the ribbed vault and the flying buttress, even if in a concealed form. The sources of Gothic were by no means exclusively French, nor was its development. French, or at least Frankish, architecture was indeed regarded as the new fashion in Germany through most of the thirteenth century (see page 230), and Cologne Cathedral, founded in 1248, was in its early stages entirely French in inspiration. Yet by 1275 we have seen that it was to the organization of the English masons that Strassburg looked for a model (see page 138), and this almost certainly implies a cultural and perhaps political revulsion against French influence in the Rhineland. The interesting thing here is that the chance to copy English organization is only likely to have arisen because of æsthetic interest in the specifically English developments of Gothic style during the reign of Henry III. This might at first sight seem improbable : when has there been a period more distinctly under direct French influences than was the mid-thirteenth century under Henry III. A king of England who wished, after a visit to Paris, that he could carry away the Sainte-Chapelle on a cart; a king who caused his royal abbey of Westminster to be rebuilt on immediately French models between 1245 and 1269, and who employed as his chief architect a master who, though probably of English birth, was known by a name which seems to mean Henry of Rheims.

The new factor that had loomed up between 1269 and 1275 was the four years of crusade by the lord Edward starting in 1270, and ending in 1274 with his triumphant return to England as a king who had been proclaimed in his absence. On Edward's return journey he was, in later language, the toast of Europe, and English prestige stood at the highest peak it has ever reached. Crowned heads and pretenders jostled each other to lay their disputes before Edward for his impartial arbitration. We must therefore accept that it was not English Gothic style of 1275 that was admired, but the English "thing" personified in the king who was himself England.* Yet within a few years the artistic scene had changed for the better and before the end of the century a new and thoroughly English Gothic was arising, owing much to France but even more to the combination of native and oriental motives. As we have already seen, the riches of the English Curvilinear style in its various regional forms seemed almost inexhaustible (see pages 131–36).

English Gothic style, as a native product owing relatively little to direct borrowings from France, took a fresh start about 1290, though one great work, the nave of York Minster begun in 1291, has markedly French relationships. Its bay design, a pioneer in unifying triforium and clerestory, is none the less derived from a series of English models of which the most recent was the choir of the suffragan cathedral at Southwell (1234–50). The rather close likeness in general impression to Troyes Cathedral, however, is one of a number of factors which point towards specific interchanges with Champagne due to the marriage of Edmund, younger brother of Edward I, Earl of Lancaster and titular King of Sicily, to the widow of Count Henry III of Navarre and Champagne in 1275, and to his continued association with Champagne until his death in 1296.

The campaigns and castle building of Edward I gave great scope to engineers during his reign. But there was work of other kinds, too, and several of the great churches of the Friars, now destroyed, belonged to the period. Outstanding among them was the London Grey Friars at Newgate, endowed by Queen Margaret, and for whose works Master Walter of Hereford brought masons in 1306. A new type of church planning, with slender piers and large windows admitting floods of light, was being produced for the orders of friars and had repercussions on the design of large parish churches for new towns, such as those of Winchelsea and Hull. The association of Master Walter of Hereford with this style is interesting, as he had been master of the works at Winchcombe Abbey and was later architect for Edward I's Vale Royal Abbey in Cheshire, though most of his later work was at Caernarvon Castle and in connection with the royal campaigns in Scotland. He is an outstanding example of the versatility of the mediæval architect, in disproof of the old myth that masters were tied for life to monastic, collegiate, military or civil works respectively.

In reality versatility was the rule, and in this respect there is no difference between the mediæval and the modern architect. Just as at

---

*Paradoxically, Edward himself patronized military engineers brought from Savoy; but their style had little permanent effect on English Gothic.

the present day some designers will specialize on schools or housing, so in the Middle Ages there were masters constantly occupied within some limited field. But in both cases general practice and the acceptance of work as it comes in is normal. There is another implication behind the many cases where an architect was occupied on some local work and then was called into a more distinguished position by the king or some magnate. It is that the master in question had already, in spite of the absence of newspapers and other modern media of publicity, achieved fame and a wide reputation. The peripatetic routine of the Court and of the patrons as a class goes far to explain this, but it is the fact itself which needs to be kept in mind. A ponderous weight of ill-informed literature, suggesting the isolation of mediæval communities in conditions not far removed from savagery, has to be resisted and thrown off.

The transmission of elements of design over a long period and across the Channel can be shown in one instance that played a part in the formation of the English Perpendicular style. In 1248 the Sainte Chapelle in the royal palace at Paris was dedicated, and was certainly then complete. It marked the end of a period which corresponded with the epoch in which all the great Gothic cathedrals of northern France were designed. The French "cathedral style" in its latest form was, in that same year, taken to Cologne on the Rhine to provide Germany with an "export Gothic" minster able to rival Beauvais in immense scale, and to incorporate beauties of detail from the conspectus of style available to the architect, Master Gerard. In some sense the laying out of the plan of Cologne can be regarded as the full-stop placed at the end of an age. But the chapter was reopened for a curious reason: the grave difficulties which were being experienced throughout southern France in stamping out the Albigensian heresy. The cruel civil war of 1220–29 had not succeeded in quelling the hatred for the North and the deep attachment of Languedoc to its own ways, including its religion. Finally in 1245 the heretical cathedral of Montségur was occupied by royal troops and the Inquisition. At this period someone had the brilliant idea that what was needed in the South was a campaign of building of new cathedrals of the magnificent type already built, or in process of completion, in the North of France.

The carrying out of this scheme was gradual, and the first step was to carry the classic French cathedral as far as the Massif Central. By 1248 an outline plan had been formulated for the building of such a new cathedral at Clermont Ferrand; bishop Hugh de la Tour had promised land to enlarge the site before his death in the next year. The project was slow to get under way, and Dr. Robert Branner regards the most probable date for the real start of works as 1262. From then onwards for the next twenty-five years the architect, Jean Des Champs, was in charge of Clermont Cathedral and of a whole wave of successors pushing on to the extremities of Languedoc : Narbonne and Toulouse, both begun in 1272, Limoges in 1273, and Rodez in 1277. The case of Narbonne Cathedral demonstrates the ecclesiastical scheme behind the spread of these northern churches, for it was supported by a Bull granted in 1268 by Clement IV for a cathedral "to imitate the noble and magnificently worked churches which are built in the kingdom of France".

The background of Jean Des Champs lay in Paris and to the north of Paris, so that his first step, to Clermont, took him well over 200 miles; his move onwards to Narbonne was nearly as much again. Once more the conquest of space by the combination of high directing power (royal and papal policy) and personality (Des Champs as architect) is demonstrated. Several of these great schemes never were finished, and all of them went on slowly over a long period. What concerns us here is that at Clermont Ferrand the direction was carried on by Pierre Des Champs, the son of Jean, from 1287 to 1325, and that about 1310 he had reached the stage of detailed design for the doorway of the south transept. The mouldings of the bases of this doorway, though following by a natural sequence from his father's earlier profiles, show that Pierre had produced a new kind of base moulding. At the foot of the shaft the new base verged upon the form of a double-ogee or "bracket" mould-ing; and lower down a sub-base or plinth was formed with a flared out skirt-like profile like the section of one side of a bell. Whereas the overall design of Clermont and the rest of the new southern cathedrals in northern style had been produced by Jean in a relatively conservative fashion, rather than in the new type of the "glasshouse", the develop-ment of detail under his son Pierre was an innovation in the suave and exquisitely regulated taste of the opening fourteenth century.

Either by mere chance or, far more probably, by the spread of reputation among international circles of master masons, this radically new style in profiles attracted the English architect William Ramsey. Perhaps actual full-size profiles were brought from Clermont to England by some intermediary. What is much more likely is that Ramsey, who was probably born in the last years of the thirteenth century and was working as a fully trained mason on St. Stephen's Chapel by 1325, had been to Clermont during his wanderyears about 1315, and had seen at first hand the fresh details and the drawings being prepared for other new work in the cathedral tracing-house. The new type of base, not as a direct copy, but transformed by Ramsey's personal idiom, appears in England in his Chapter House at St. Paul's, London, begun in 1332, and in his presbytery of Lichfield Cathedral, whither he was called in May 1337. The association of this type of base with the St. Paul's work, the first to have the essential detail of

Perpendicular tracery, resulted in Ramsey's bases becoming the prototype for the stock Perpendicular base mouldings of the final two centuries of English Gothic (see page 184).

English Perpendicular style, initiated by Ramsey, was brought to fruition in the second half of the fourteenth century by the codifying work of the two great architects in royal service, Henry Yeveley and William Wynford. It was carried to the extremities of the country by a generation of younger designers, trained on the king's works of the thirty years after the Black Death of 1348–49 in which William Ramsey had died. By this time, the latter part of the reign of Edward III, mediæval culture in England was reaching its culmination, and material civilization was becoming amazingly subtle and sophisticated. The five centuries that had elapsed since the heyday of the Umayyad Court at Cordova had at last taught northern Europe its lesson. Monarchs now belonged to an international caste of high breeding, distinguished from most of their subjects by the far greater amount of Byzantine, Oriental and Moorish blood in their veins. As if by stealth the best features of the ancient Asiatic reservoir of human advancement had taken over control of the energy and determination supplied by the successful warriors and traders of north-western Europe. Owing to the extinction of the main line of the Capetian royal house of France in 1328 at the death of Charles IV, the political initiative passed into the energetic hands of the young Edward III of England. During the next generation he made his country the dominant power in the West.

The political and economic fortunes of England had perhaps just passed their apogee by the time that Edward III's grandson Richard II came to the throne in 1377; but the period of his personal rule from 1389 to 1399 marked the highest peak ever reached by cultural refinement in this country. This was achieved by far-reaching artistic relationships with the Low Countries and with the Rhineland area of Germany, as well as with France and Spain. Within the orbit of this new internationalism English painting produced its supreme triumph in the Wilton Diptych of about 1395, glass-painting the windows of New College, Oxford, Winchester College (from 1393) and the east window of York Minster (1405–08), masonry and carpentry the noblest work in English architecture, the transformation of Westminster Hall for the king in 1394–99. The two architects, Henry Yeveley (died 1400) and Hugh Herland (died 1405), along with their colleague William Wynford (died 1405), who had begun to transform the nave of Winchester Cathedral into Perpendicular in 1394, were responsible for the full consolidation of a peculiarly and exclusively national style.

Though Perpendicular became a national style in a sense and to a degree that no previous Gothic style had been exclusively the hallmark of a single political unit, it did not completely exclude influences from

1a. SANTIAGO DE COMPOSTELA. Nave of the cathedral, built in 1088–1128 under Esteban and his son Bernardo, following the design of 1075 by Bernardo the elder, called "the marvellous master" (see p. 34)

1b. SANTIAGO DE COMPOSTELA. The added Pórtico de la Gloria of 1168–1211, designed by Mateo and signed by him in the inscription above the doorways (see pp. 34–5)

2. ST. ALBANS CATHEDRAL. The altar-screen made for Abbot Walynford about 1480, described at the time as "the most divine object in the whole kingdom" (see p. 41)

3. ANGERS CATHEDRAL. Interior of the nave with the vault "of wondrous effect" built about 1150 (see pp. 39)

4. WIMPFEN-IM-THAL. St. Peter's collegiate church, built in 1268–78 by a mason "straight from Paris", in the French style (see p. 156, 230)

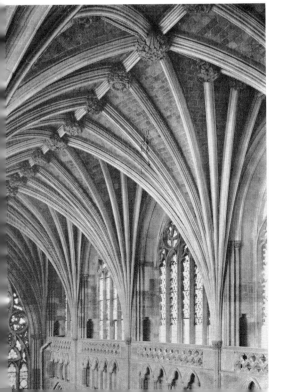

5. BATH ABBEY. The vaults designed by the brothers Robert and William Vertue in 1502 were to be unequalled, "neither in England nor in France" (see p. 41)

6. ST. RÉMI, RHEIMS, begun in 1005 as the largest church in France, and completed in 1034–45; the west front and vault are Gothic additions (see p. 56)

7. EXETER CATHEDRAL. The nave vault, a refinement of design by Thomas Witney (see p. 128). A century-and-a-half later, in 1478, William Worcestre was moved to remark that the church was "arched over in a most lovely way" (see p. 41)

8. GOSLAR. The Imperial Hall, built about 1040–50 (see p. 61)

9. FÉCAMP. The Norman abbey in Gothic guise (see p. 62)

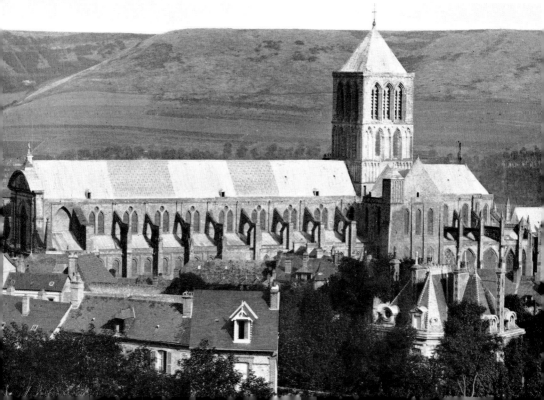

10. SEVILLE CATHEDRAL, intended by the Chapter to be "such that those
who see it finished may think us mad." The nave of 1402–32, probably
designed by a Norman, Charles Galter of Rouen (see p. 69)

sic collato: memoria donacons indelebi
liter perpetuetur. Et hoc eali largitate og
ramme z condicebue: ut de regno Anglie uiss

Willego dum. q mterpretat volent
Yere eni vir bone fuit uoluntaris
sturpe regia omum. regiq offe of

11. KING AND ARCHITECT. A lively impression, about 1250, by Matthew Paris, showing the master mason, with his square and compass, receiving instructions, with craftsmen at work (see p. 78)

12. CAERNARVON CASTLE. Designed for Edward I by a Savoyard military engineer, James of St. George, and built under Walter of Hereford (see p. 79)

13. LICHFIELD CATHEDRAL. The west front and towers, whose niceties of design (see p. 165) are probably due to Nicholas of Eyton. The "beautiful church . . . with most lofty stone towers" was noted by the pilgrim Simon Simeon in 1323 (see p. 239)

14. YORK MINSTER. West window, 1322–39

15. CARLISLE CATHEDRAL. East window, designed in 1318–22, though completed later in the century

CURVILINEAR DESIGN, seen in two great windows here attributed (see p. 80) to Ivo de Raghton

ARCHITECTS OF PRAGUE CATHEDRAL:
16. Peter Parler, the great German architect who, until his death in 1399, continued the works begun by 17. the Frenchman, Matthieu d'Arras, in 1344–52

18. WESTMINSTER ABBEY. Probably the first architect, Henry of Reyns

19. WINCHESTER COLLEGE. William Wynford (died 1405), designer of Wykeham's architectural works (see (pp. 83–5). Note headgear and reflective posture of both these masters

20. WINCHESTER COLLEGE. The building masters in the stained glass (1393, copied 1821) of the east window of the Chapel: the Carpenter (Hugh Herland, died 1405); William Wynford, mason (see also plate 19), the principal architect; and Simon Membury, a priest, the clerk of the works in charge of administration and accountancy

21. ST. GEORGE'S CHAPEL, WINDSOR. William Vertue (died 1527), architect of the nave and vaults (see also plate 48), in the stained glass of the west window

22. WESTMINSTER ABBEY. Probably Master John of Gloucester, in charge 1253–60 (see p. 88)

24. ST. ALBANS CATHEDRAL. Henry Wy, architect in 1324 for rebuilding the fallen bays of the nave (see p. 36); his bust is given equal prominence with those of King, Queen and Abbot

23. EXETER CATHEDRAL. The architect of the choir, either William Luve or, more probably, Thomas Witney (see p. 135)

25. BRISTOL CATHEDRAL. Unknown architect

26, 27. VIENNA, ST. STEPHEN'S CATHEDRAL. Two portraits of Anton Pilgram
(died 1515), designer of the organ-gallery and the nave pulpit (see also plate 29)

28. LANDSHUT, ST. MARTIN. The architect Hans Stethaimer (died 1432)

29 (*opposite*). VIENNA, ST. STEPHEN'S CATHEDRAL. The nave pulpit, designed about 1512 by Anton Pilgram, the great architect whose portrait appears below it (see also plate 27)

30, 31 (*above*). ULM CATHEDRAL. Details from the design for a tabernacle, a drawing on seven sheets of paper now in the Victoria and Albert Museum, London. The design is probably that which Hans Niesenberger was invited to supply in 1462

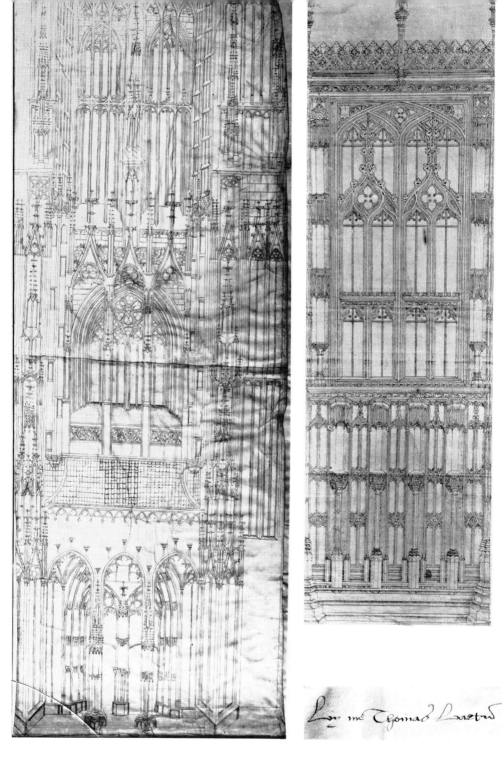

32. ULM CATHEDRAL. Design for the west front and tower, now in the
Victoria and Albert Museum, London

33. WINCHESTER CATHEDRAL. Design for Bishop Fox's Chantry made about
1525 by Thomas Bertie or Bartu (died 1555), ancestor of the Earls of
Abingdon and Lindsey and of other noblemen

34. The architect's signature, "by me Thomas Bartu", on a deed of 1544
at Winchester College

35. WINCHESTER COLLEGE. The south side of Middle Gate, showing alteration of the design in course of erection, about 1390. The level courses of black flints above the central archway, here and on the north side, indicate that the moulded string-course at first ran horizontally across, the vertical "thrust" being an æsthetic afterthought by the architect William Wynford (see p. 129)

36. WESTMINSTER HALL. The great hall of the principal palace of the kings of England was planned on a gigantic scale for William Rufus and built in 1097–9. Three centuries later an open timber roof, designed by Hugh Herland on the hammer-beam principle, was substituted for ranges of posts in 1393–1400 at the instance of Richard II. New windows, cornices and other details were supplied to the design of Herland's colleague Henry Yeveley (see p. 118)

37. WINCHESTER, PILGRIMS' HALL. An early experiment in the hammer-beam truss, probably built in 1325 while Thomas Witney (see plates 7, 23) was architect to the Cathedral priory (see p. 135)

38. PADUA, PALAZZO DELLA RAGIONE. The enormous roof, of timber held together with iron tie-rods, was built about 1306 to the design of Giovanni, an Austin friar and traveller to the Orient, who is said to have based it on "the roof of a great palace in India" (see p. 131)

39. SALISBURY CATHEDRAL. The central tower and spire, added to the earlier church after 1334 by Richard Farleigh, were provided with reinforcements of wrought iron buried in the thickness of the masonry (see p. 133)

41. CANTERBURY CATHEDRAL. The choir, designed by the French architect, William of Sens, and largely built under

40. A detail of the Corona at the east end, built to the design of William English in 1183–4 (see pp. 77, 146,

42. ULM CATHEDRAL. Detail from a design for the second storey of the tower, showing the advanced technique of draughtsmanship in the fifteenth century. The drawing is now in the Victoria and Albert Museum, London

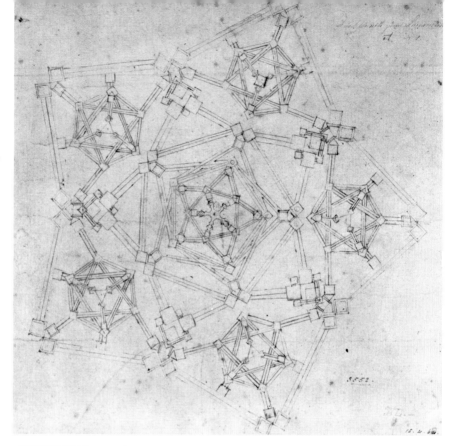

43. A design based on the regular pentagon, possibly for a canopy of *c.* 1470 at Ulm Cathedral

44 (*below*). Detail from a design for the spire of Strassburg Cathedral, made about 1420 by Johann Hültz

COLOGNE CATHEDRAL. The
rchment drawings for the
st front and spires, long lost
t rediscovered early in the
eteenth century, and used
the completion of the build-
; in 1842–80

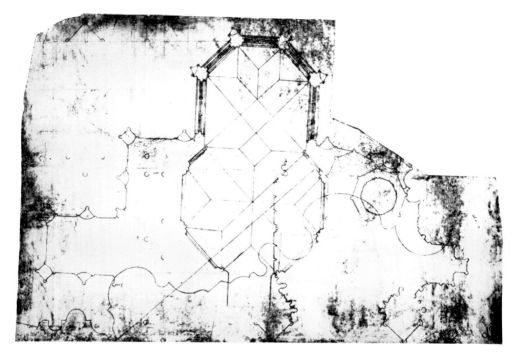

46.　VIENNA, ST. STEPHEN'S CATHEDRAL. Plan of Chapel of St. Barbara showing scheme of vaulting and, superimposed, the profile of a series of mouldings

47.　ULM CATHEDRAL. Plan of the central porch of the west front, showing different levels superimposed on the same drawing

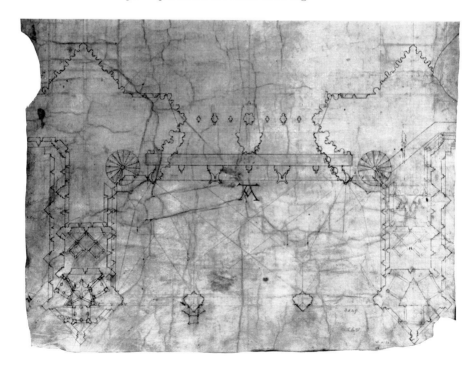

48. WESTMINSTER ABBEY. A detail of the fan and pendant vault designed
for Henry VII's Chapel of William Vertue (see also plates 5, 21) about 1515,
described later in the sixteenth century as "the only rare work in the world"
(see p. 165)

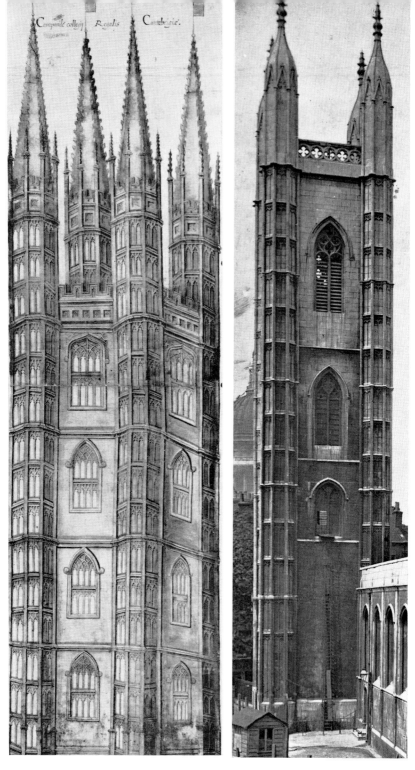

49. CAMBRIDGE. Design for the great tower of King's College, about 1450, perhaps by Reginald Ely

50. LONDON. Tower of the church of St. Mary Aldermary, begun in 1510 (see p. 170); the upper part was rebuilt under Wren after the Fire of 1666

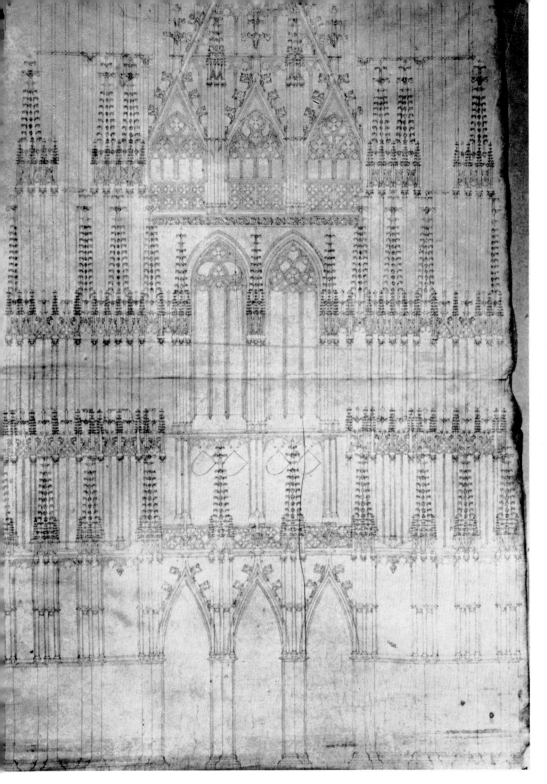

51. VIENNA, ST. STEPHEN'S CATHEDRAL. Elevation of North Tower (see also plate 52). The first design drawn by Hanns Puchspaum.

52.   VIENNA, ST. STEPHEN'S CATHEDRAL. Detail of design for North Tower
(see also plate 51). Note that this is a different scheme

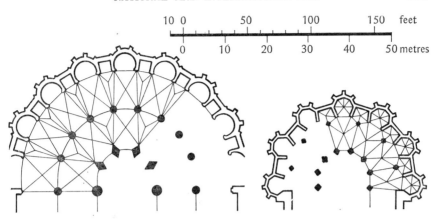

Comparative plans of Toledo Cathedral: chevet designed by Master Martin, *c*.1225; and Vale Royal Abbey, chevet designed by William Helpston, 1359.

overseas. In 1359 English architecture had taken the unusual form of chevet with radiating polygonal and square chapels from Toledo (see page 216), another instance of the direct link between political and diplomatic activity and the channels for the transmission of artistic style (see above). But there was surprisingly little apparent reaction in insular design to the reconquest of Normandy and northern France under Henry V, and the period of union of the two Crowns under Henry VI from 1422 until the loss of Paris in 1436. On the contrary, there is a certain amount of evidence for a superiority complex on the part of English architects of the late Gothic period. This was not simply due to patriotic euphoria at the victories of Henry V at Agincourt and elsewhere. It was rather due to the opportunity to study at first-hand the actual state of architecture in France and to compare it with the English achievement.

It has long been evident that in the field of carpentry the English designers of the fourteenth century far outstripped all rivals, and in the structural and æsthetic aspects alike of the form of hammerbeam truss devised by Herland for Westminster Hall reached a peak that has never been equalled elsewhere at any time. This extraordinary development of timber framing and trussing was exactly what might have been expected of the linear genius of English artists. It was in the mutual interplay of posts, beams and braces that English love of pattern for its own sake could best find expression. The whole concept of the stone vault as necessarily the ideal of roofing to space was abandoned, and for all great halls and for most churches the timber roof intended for display, exquisitely embellished with angels, bosses, shields and cusping, was regarded as the best of all possible solutions. Even where an appearance of vaulting was æsthetically desirable it was commonly achieved by means of an imitation vault carried out in wood, and itself supported by a hidden construction of great ingenuity above it.

This vogue for timber vaults had a long ancestry in England. We have seen that Henry III so admired an example at Lichfield Cathedral that in 1243 he gave orders for it to be imitated in his new chapel at Windsor (see page 154), though its small span of twenty-eight feet would have been easy to vault in stone. In the middle of the same century the great transept of York Minster was vaulted in wood from the start, and the nave and choir were similarly vaulted later on account of their great span. Very remarkable timber vaults were built over the Chapter House at York and over the choir of St. Albans Abbey in the fourteenth century, and towards its end the Chapel of Winchester College and the choir of Arundel collegiate church. Other timber vaults of first-class scale were built at Winchester Cathedral and at Chester Abbey. Unique as a roof-form is the wooden vaulting of the octagon at Ely, devised by the king's chief carpenter William Hurley (died 1354) and built in 1328–40. Only the great influence of the psychotic view of Ruskin, that such imitations of masonry form were insincere to the point of immorality, could have prevented these ingenious and beautiful works from receiving the modern praise that is their due.

In the meantime, very recent studies of mediæval buildings from the structural and engineering viewpoint by Dr. Jacques Heyman have thrown a flood of welcome light upon the scene. Both for stone and timber structures we now have, what before was notably lacking, an objective value-judgment on Gothic constructional science based upon quantitative analysis. It is now possible to pronounce with authority, not upon the æsthetic factors alone, for assessment of these must always be personal and subjective, but on the relative value of mediæval designs considered solely for their practical effectiveness and structural stability. It is no exaggeration to say that Dr. Heyman's work forms one of the most valuable contributions ever made to the field of mediæval studies. The essence of his conclusions can best be expressed in his own words. Referring to the fact that mediæval science did not permit of the mathematical calculation of thrusts, and that "advances must have been made by trial and error, by experiments with the actual structure as well as with models" he goes on "looking at . . . the complete glass curtain-walls of the Sainte-Chapelle in Paris, one is tempted to sense a mastery of building technique greater than any that can be ascribed to mere trial and error". Dr. Heyman continues, giving conclusions of remarkable impact upon history: "This mastery was maintained with complete authority for only a very short period, in a very limited region: for about 144 years in France. In 1140 work started on the new choir of the abbey church of St.-Denis . . . The collapse of Beauvais in 1284 signalled the end of the greatest period of cathedral building . . . It is true that Gothic continued to develop . . . and that isolated peaks were reached, not only æsthetically, but also structurally (*e.g.* fan vaults in England)."

Going further into the problems raised by the collapse of Beauvais, Heyman remarks that "the decay sensed by the eye after about 1250 stems from a slow relaxation of the firm structural grasp that had been acquired during the preceding hundred years". This he amplifies by pointing out the muddled approach of the architects of the late fourteenth century when faced with the problem of the design of Milan Cathedral. "The Italians, at least, did not know how to build a cathedral;" but what in a way was worse, the Parisian architect, Jean Mignot, showed by his criticisms that his views were limited by a set of rules; but this "did not mean that he himself *understood* the rules to which he worked . . . rules were, to Mignot, something out of a book . . . whose meanings and, indeed, whose very reasons for existence, were becoming more and more dim with the passage of time." Again, "the rules, formulated and tested, lay guarded in the lodges, dead". The Gothic architect had, by trial and error in the twelfth and thirteenth centuries, reached a series of numerical rules of proportion satisfactory for masonry construction. By adherence to these rules, in point of fact, few buildings collapsed (whereas many collapses had occurred of Romanesque towers and other works). The rules were so good, and had so adequate a factor of safety, that "structural elements could be assembled almost at random and yet result in a safe structure"; but once this conclusion is believed "to be true for *any* cathedral, then the slide has started from Gothic into Renaissance". In a detailed study of the behaviour of vaults Heyman makes two more points of great importance : one is that the large scale models actually made during the Middle Ages, notably that of San Petronio, Bologna of 1390, "can be used with complete confidence to check the stability of the whole or of any part of the real structure". Secondly, reverting to the records of Mignot's intervention at Milan, and his now famous assertion : "*Ars sine scientia nihil est*", Heyman shows that, far from being "the initiation of a new age of architecture, when practical experience would be firmly reinforced by theory" it "implies in reality that, in future, any quarrel between practice and theory would be resolved in favour of theory; and by theory he means that *scientia,* that pedantry of the written word, contained in the mysteries of the Lodges, whose significance, however empirical, eluded more and more Mignot and his successors. Villard's manuscript . . . would come in time to have an almost Biblical authority (or the authority, equally stultifying of a

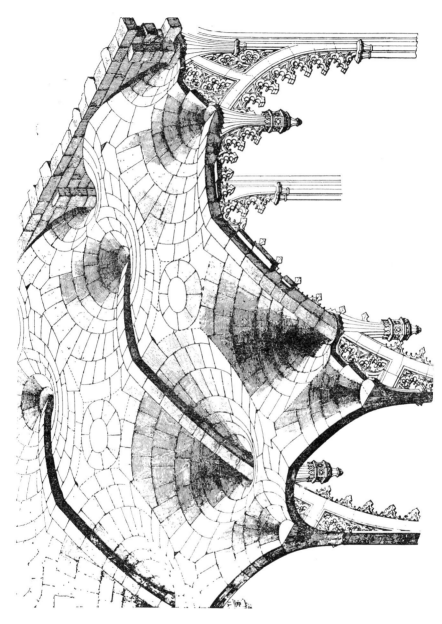

Westminster Abbey, Henry VII's Chapel: diagram showing elaborate arrangement of stones in the fan vault, designed by William Vertue, *c.*1510. (Willis 1842)

modern Code of Practice), and is, perhaps, a symbol of that internal decay which ensured the death of Gothic at the Renaissance".

It is highly significant that a modern engineer can find the later experiments of the English architects, culminating in fan vaulting, a satisfactory continuation of the early experimentation which made Gothic so vital for 150 years. In England this was not a limit, and it is possible to find, for example, special approaches to perfection in the niceties of design of Lichfield Cathedral (Fig. 13), regarded purely from a structural viewpoint. It is certain that English master masons and master carpenters never did abdicate in favour of a code of practice; rather they continued until they were swept away by the stoppage of major church works and by the Renaissance pattern-books, to seek fresh worlds to conquer. Among the last and most wonderful of these triumphs of structural geometry was Henry VII's Chapel with its pendant and fan vaulting (Fig. 48, page 164) accurately formed of interlocking pieces. Later on, when the Renaissance was firmly in the saddle and Gothic work in general deemed barbaric, John Norden (1548–1625) could write of the chapel: "whoso beholdeth . . . the body and internal glory he shall find it so admirable both in the vaulting on the roof in regard of the curiosity of work as also in the proportion. And the walls, windows and the rest so exquisitely performed that he will deem them to be the only rare work in the world and as Leland says the wonder of the worlds. This mirror of art and architect is not only in itself beautiful, but it is also beautified with many rare and glorious monuments. . . ."

Epilogue and Conclusions

THE real decadence of Gothic at the heart of its homeland, Paris, after the third quarter of the thirteenth century is now an established fact; the French architects, though still displaying ingenuity and producing beautiful detail, had succumbed to the perfections of their own code. This statement has a reminiscent ring, as if it were an echo: and so it is. The architectural code in France had become as it were a reflection of the encyclopædic code of religion and life produced by the philosophized theology of the Schoolmen. France, which at the turn of the eleventh and twelfth centuries had been bubbling over with the eager desire to learn, had at the highest intellectual levels become self-satisfied that it had learned all that there was to know. The magnificent tree of true science: the objective search for truth, concealed a hidden disease and was dead at the core, smitten by the virus of *hubris,* a smug Pharisaism of the mind: the great original *trahison des clercs.*

What saved England and Germany from the same fate was their continued insistence upon free enquiry and a refusal to set limits to knowledge and to exploration. At the very time—the mid-thirteenth century—when the centres of European thought were stifled, the two great figures of Roger Bacon (*c.* 1214–92) in England and Albert of Cologne (Albertus Magnus, *c.* 1205–80) in Germany continued to bear aloft the banner of experiment; Bacon even stood out against dogmatic suffocation and suffered for his principles. Later another Englishman, William of Ockham, withstood papal tyranny and laid sound philosophical foundations for the stand made by royal authority against papal encroachments and which found expression in England in the Statutes of Provisors of 1306 and 1351 and of Præmunire in 1353 and 1393. Ockham spent the last twenty years of his life (*c.* 1285–1349) in Germany, and likewise gave his support to the thesis of imperial supremacy.

The continuance of a climate of opinion favourable to honest doubt prevented the onset of that kind of deadening certainty which put an end to the original growth of French Gothic. The later growths in

England and Germany may not have had the fine bouquet of the *premier cru*, but they were still alive. This can be seen in Germany in the long survival of a great deal of Gothic after the Middle Ages, so that even at the end of the eighteenth century Goethe could penetrate to the mediæval spirit to a degree impossible elsewhere; and also in the continuity of the structural forms of architecture in spite of the invasion by Renaissance detail. It was in Germany that there was the strongest tradition of Gothic survival, and the preservation of the great collections of drawings at Strassburg and Vienna is certainly in part at least due to this conservatism. In England affairs did not go so well, and in spite of a few unexpected survivals on a rather crude level even into the first half of the eighteenth century, the story of Gothic architecture really ends with the reign of Henry VIII.

The end of English Gothic was a tragedy in the real sense, in that what was killed was a living organism still full of sap, and that it was deliberately destroyed to leave room for an artificial revival of a long-dead style both climatically and traditionally unsuitable; and whose manifestations at the time were mostly lacking in taste and refinement. This is not to say that there were no weaknesses in late Gothic in England; but they were not irremediable, and much had already been done to recover lost ground in the course of the fifteenth century. We saw that English architects at the time of Henry V's victories were able to feel superior to the then state of design in France; but the state of English architecture in the first half of the fifteenth century was disappointingly stagnant after the glories of the reign of Richard II.

Whereas the architecture of Yeveley and Wynford had been, as Lethaby so well put it, "big and bare", an uncertainty of purpose crept into design after 1400 and attempted to cover lack of inspiration by repetitive patternwork and by a growing complexity of mouldings on a smaller scale. This happened as a result of the deaths of the great designers of Yeveley's generation, leaving no completely adequate replacements—the same phenomenon occurred in poetry at the death of Chaucer—and on a more basic plane because of the usurpation of the throne in 1399 which had led to a breakdown in government and society. A few sound architects who had been in some sense pupils of Yeveley: William Colchester and Stephen Lote; or of Wynford: Richard Winchcombe, Robert Hulle, continued to do good work, but it lacked inspiration. This somewhat despondent art, singularly enough, was reproved by the taste of leading noblemen, at Oxford in 1440, and by the personal views of Henry VI in 1447 when he came to formulate the detailed programme for King's College, Cambridge (see pages 252–256). It is possible that the "magnates" who disliked Winchcombe's elaborate detail in the Divinity Schools merely wished to simplify in order to save money, or it is possible that their leader was "Good Duke Humphrey" of Gloucester (1391–1447), whose interest in Renaissance humanism led him to give the University Library (to be housed above the Schools) a manuscript of Vitruvius. It is quite possible, though not proven, that the duke's taste had been sufficiently formed by humanism to make him reject the rather small-scale and fussy detail of the first work on the Schools.

The king's attitude is perhaps easier to explain. Henry VI based his plan of education, at Eton and Cambridge, directly on the working model of Wykeham's two colleges, at Winchester and Oxford. He spent substantial periods staying at Winchester to study Wynford's buildings, as well as the collegiate arrangements and the education, at first hand. He had a plan of the buildings there made for study, and his sentiment went so far that he even brought soil from Winchester to mingle with the foundations of his own college. There is a mellow loveliness in Wynford's style in the courts at Winchester that recalls the best of Ancient Greek architecture. Henry VI's sojourn must have convinced him that this combination of grand scale with simplicity enriched by few but exquisite embellishments was the ideal home for the proper training of youth. His own foundations were to be vastly bigger, but he was determined that their character should be the same. It was an irony of fate that his political misfortune should have left his buildings unaccomplished for so long that, when Henry VII instructed John Wastell to proceed to completion at Cambridge, the stylistic outlook in Court circles had changed so radically that the intentions of the royal saint were superseded.

How did this happen? Through much of the fifteenth century the spark of genius had been noticeably lacking in England, not in architecture alone. The one English artist of the very highest gifts, the composer John Dunstable, achieved his fame first on the Continent. In spite of a few outstanding works such as the Perpendicular transformation of the choir of Sherborne Abbey, Dorset, and the building of the Beauchamp Chapel at St. Mary's, Warwick, English design in general lacked interest. It is beyond coincidence that this negative aspect lasted only through the Lancastrian period (1400–60) and the first ten years of the reign of Edward IV, when he was deeply committed to a policy of financial retrenchment, and the country was only slowly recovering from trade depression and the political chaos of the Wars of the Roses. But after the few months of Henry VI's tragic "readeption" of the throne in 1470–71 Edward IV returned, fresh from his exile in Flanders, filled with the determination to live splendidly. Almost at once a richer note was struck in decoration, in furnishing; the plain and even bald "gridiron" middle phase of Perpendicular suddenly gave place to an interweaving of renewed Curvilinear details and ogee curves. The bread cast upon the waters by the English architects of the fourteenth century, whose style had been so eagerly seized by Germany and the Low Countries, had indeed returned after many days. In the last two generations of the Middle Ages, from about 1475 until the actual Dissolution of the monasteries in 1536–40, the architectural harvest in England was immensely rich, not merely in quantity and scale, but in superb quality. Hardly ever had such towers risen on all sides; never had such timber roofs and screens been hewn and carved; and in the exploitation of ingenuity and sheer delight in overcoming difficulties the designers of vaults outdid all their predecessors.

This last fling of English Gothic owed a good deal to foreign artists and craftsmen : Netherlandish names start with a trickle in the 1470s and become a minor flood in the reign of Henry VIII. In this respect England felt the impact of the Burgundian age of greatness, as did Spain. Like Spain, England was strong enough in her own school of design to digest the foreign elements and make them her own. Strange as are the polygonal transepts of St. George's Chapel, Windsor, we are not conscious of them as in any sense out of place; with masterly skill both apses and turrets are integrated into the great south front of the Chapel, a pioneer exercise in near-symmetry. While this importation of the polygonal transept came from the Low countries, the star-polygon employed in Henry VII's Tower at Windsor, for the windows of his Chapel at Westminster, and later by Wolsey for the turrets of the great gate at Oxford that became Tom Tower, were drawn from the Mudéjar style as practised in Saragossa at the time that the envoys of Ferdinand the Catholic left for London to arrange the marriage of Catherine of Aragon with the Tudor Prince Arthur. As we know, that was the same time that the last triumph of religious toleration in Spain, the Torre Nueva, was being designed by a committee of architects drawn from each of the faiths of Aragon.

The close of the Middle Ages was marked by strange paradox: that the moment of Spain's triumph in the Reconquest of the Peninsula, to lead all too soon to bitter persecutions, should have been celebrated by a brilliant architectural design emerging from designers of three religions in collaboration. That again at the same time, the discovery of the riches of America should have caused the depreciation of all currencies due to the flood of silver and gold, and have thus led to the inflation spiral which has been the greatest curse of the last four centuries. That in England, the victim of Henry IV's usurpation, the greatest of educational foundations should be due to the usurper's saintly grandson. That a new usurpation, by Henry VII, should have been the means of bringing to completion at least great part of the designs made for Henry VI; and that the final triumphs of the English Gothic—not merely at Eton and Cambridge, but at Windsor and

Westminster, all of an incomparable richness of detail—should all have been associated with the Royal Saint, whose will had been that his architecture should "proceed in large form, clean and substantial". The final irony concerns the minimal fulfilment of one of his most grandiose plans, for a great tower in his Cambridge college. The show-drawing produced for his approval, rolled up in some official pigeon-hole for generations, at last reached the British Museum, and there survives. Between 1450 and 1510 a copy of it must have become available and have been studied, for when the parishioners of St. Mary Aldermary in the city of London built a new tower to their church, it took the form of a reduced version of this campanile that never was (Figs. 49, 50).

CONCLUSIONS

We have followed long and winding trails from the Dark Ages to the close of mediæval civilization soon after 1500. It may be of use to recapitulate some of the main conclusions reached.

1. The period studied, for which reasonably adequate materials survive, runs from shortly before A.D. 1000 until just after 1500.

2. Within that period the leading art, setting the pace for the rest of the plastic and minor arts, was Architecture.

3. The practice of Architecture, and the capacity to design in the architectural sense, was in the hands of laymen who had enjoyed first a general education up to the "thirteen-plus" level; had then for from five to seven years acquired the manual skills of one of the building crafts: stonemasonry or carpentry in most cases; and who had, from their Master, learned the traditional methods of design by geometrical manipulation of rule, square and compass, and numerical formulæ which had been derived from trial and error, to ensure stability.

4. These Architects, and all full members of the crafts to which they belonged, were of free status and of legitimate birth. They laid great stress upon morality and honesty in their dealings; and upon the strictest secrecy in regard to the technical methods of the craft. There is no evidence that any secrets of esoteric doctrine were included.

5. In the earlier part of the period, before the rise of many, sharply differentiated, craft guilds, it was usual for the fully trained builder to have knowledge of all building materials, and also to have a sufficient acquaintance with the related arts of sculpture, painting, stained glass and furnishings to be able to maintain control over all the artists employed on the job for which they were responsible designers and supervisors.

6. The craft of masons had a high degree of organization and, at an

uncertain date well before the middle of the thirteenth century, had acquired autonomy from the mediæval system of local government, on account of their largely migratory work. The body of the craft constituted an assembly or congregation, ruled by its own masters and constituting a customary Court, analogous to the local courts of hundreds and manors.

7. This craft organization derived at least some part of its traditions from the association of Lombard building craftsmen which had been responsible for the rise of the Romanesque style, and which had a continuous history in North Italy back to the early part of the seventh century. Since, at that date, the associated craftsmen were in some sense Romans under Lombard rule, it is more likely than not that they in turn derived from the building *collegia* of classical Rome, and thus kept alive parts of the technical tradition of Vitruvius, and the ghost of his system of design.

8. The Lombard organization, so far as it had taken root in north-west Europe, was in a state of degeneracy by the eleventh century, and many of its exponents were ignorant of the means to ensure the structural stability of large buildings. The revitalization of the craft derived entirely from Oriental sources : to some degree from Moorish Spain; so far as affects the first large-scale Romanesque buildings of the eleventh century, probably from Sicily through Amalfi; in the phases which produced, first the improved techniques of stone-cutting and jointing just after 1100, and secondly the Gothic style after 1137–1140 (at St.-Denis), from Palestine, Syria and south-eastern Anatolia as a result of the First Crusade and the direct contacts then produced between Saracens and Franks.

9. The introduction of the pointed arch in the last two phases of the penetration of the western crafts by Saracenic influences produced an entirely new æsthetic, together with an incentive to fresh experiments in structure and technique. Gothic art and architecture were the outcome.

10. A very large part in the formation of late Romanesque and early Gothic architecture, and the accompanying civilization, was played by the Normans. Their share in the early crusades in Spain, their conquests of southern Italy, Sicily and England, and their participation in the First Crusade all gave them outstanding opportunities to profit from the contact between Saracenic impulses and their own energetic ambition.

11. At the relevant period the Normans had become French-speaking, and it was this, rather than any political pre-eminence of Paris at the time, that produced the universal association of the new art with the "French" or "Franks". The architecture which was adopted by lands which did not speak French, notably the Germanic region and the Peninsula, was French or Frankish architecture.

12. The successful rise of Gothic was due primarily to the lead given

by outstanding royal patrons : Henry I of England, Louis VI and Louis VII of France. Their initiative and taste were derived from their relatively high breeding in a biological sense.

13. Probably during the twelfth century, and associated with the rise of Gothic style, the craft organization will have become fixed in France and England, with frequent intercourse between the two countries; and then carried into Germany *via* the Rhineland and into Spain. National and regional assemblies and congregations will slowly have emerged.

14. In the early days of the reorganization of the craft, during the twelfth century and in places where the common language was French, there must have been confusion between the root-words "mason" (French *maçon, machon, masson, etc.*) meaning a hewer of stone (of unknown derivation) and *"maison"* (Latin *mansio*), meaning dwelling-house (Classical Latin, from *maneo*, a stay, place of abode). This is demonstrated by the utter confusion of the early forms of the French derivatives *maisoner* (*massoner, mesoner, etc.*) meaning to build, and *maisonage* (*masonage, mesonage, etc.*), the action of building, or a house; or the materials of construction, "masonry". Whatever may be the true etymology of "mason", to the twelfth-century members of the associated crafts it meant a builder. Hence, before the strict differentiation of the craft guilds, the mason included the carpenter and all other trades concerned in actual building.

15. In regard to the later epithet "free mason", later still "free-mason" as one word, or *"franc maçon"*, with equivalent literal meaning *or* the alternative sense of "Frank mason", it is impossible to accept the usual derivation from free *stone* as an exclusive and straightforward etymology. Again it has to be taken as certain that mental confusion existed with the freedom claimed, and achieved, by the craft in its autonomous jurisdiction. This is not to say that every mediæval reference to a "free mason" means a mason belonging to the lodge organization as opposed to one who was a member of a local guild; mediæval nomenclature was not strict and explicit in matters of everyday life, and clear-cut definitions that will work regardless of context are impossible.

16. The craft organization, going back as it did to Lombard times, is far earlier than the first universities in the mediæval sense. While we know nothing of the methods used to educate masons by the Lombard craft, it is on record that their graduates were masters (*Magistri*), and there is no escape from the conclusion that in so far as the new universities of about 1100 were organized in the grades of scholar, bachelor and master, this was in direct imitation of pre-existing craft organization. For the specific new craft of logical argument, the general methods of handing down the old technical skills were adopted. It was the Master of craft who had priority, and this is why not even the most

arrogant of academic intellectuals was ever able to deny to the master craftsman his right to the title *Magister*.

17. By yet another philological confusion between the two words *ministerium* and *magisterium*, or rather their eroded Romance derivatives, the craft "mistery" was thought of as "mastery". The fact that the members of the craft were freemen and undoubtedly bound together many times over by blood relationships gave them a special sense of corporate pride reinforced by pride of family and "race". The overwhelming importance of the technical ability of craftsmen in early civilization is shown in folk-lore by the famous passage in the ancient Welsh romance of Kilhwch and Olwen, where the porter refuses to open the gate because "there is revelry in Arthur's hall, and none may enter therein but the son of a king of a privileged country, or a craftsman bringing his craft".

18. During the whole of the early period of the international formation of Gothic, all masters would have been able to communicate with one another in French. Whatever may have been the case with the rank-and-file craftsmen, those masters who were capable of design and were thus architects in function, were literate; their education, up to the age of thirteen or fourteen, had been in schools where the language of instruction was French. In England this was still the case until 1350, and French remained the language of pleading in the courts of law until 1362. There is evidence that many mediæval architects also had an adequate knowledge of Latin.

19. The attainment of each grade in the craft system was almost certainly marked by (*a*) some form of examination; (*b*) a ceremony. The little evidence that exists on the subject, mostly of rather late date, suggests that the ordinary level attained in the craft was that of journeyman, implying only fully trained *manual* skill; that a journeyman might later be able to become a master if he came into money; or otherwise by getting further instruction from a master with a view to advancing to the rank of warden, where he had to learn to act with the impartiality of a professional man as "true mean between his master and his fellows". At a late date in Germany there was a differentiation of title between a master, who might be an independent building contractor, and a workmaster, who was certainly an architect in the full sense. Some such distinction, but without an express nomenclature, probably existed very much earlier.

20. The master who was an architect (*a*) knew the traditional rules of proportion and geometrical methods of setting out a building in all its parts and details, from a single basic unit. In a limited sense this was, as Frankl claimed, the "Secret" of the masons; but in fact it comprehended a great many different propositions based upon Euclidean geometry. In this sense the knowledge of the craft was

revolutionized soon after 1120 by the arrival in the West of a full text (in Latin) of Euclid's *Elements*. This contact with Euclid both gave to the craft its special pride in geometry as a practical science; and provided a sure foundation for the body of empirical knowledge built up in the next 150 years. (*b*) The master transmitted the details of his design to the working craftsmen by means of templates cut precisely to shape on the profiles which he had drawn of every moulding or detail to full size. In all analysis of mediæval architecture, notably in attribution to known or unknown architects, the profiles of the mouldings are the essential clue to personality (pages 117, 118, 177–87). It cannot be too strongly emphasized that the comparison of visual detail (which can be done from photographs or accurate small scale drawings), as indulged in by nearly all architectural historians, is secondary to the study of profiles, and very frequently misleading. (*c*) The master was usually a highly competent geometrical draughtsman, and prepared plans and other drawings at various scales and/or at full size. From early in the thirteenth century it is certain that both sketches and drawings in orthographic projection were made on sheets of parchment; but not to the exclusion of other materials where the drawing might be scrubbed off or smeared out of existence.

21. The Masters in the earlier Gothic period dealt with every aspect of architecture, the building crafts, machinery and the invention of devices. In this they followed the precepts of Vitruvius, and quite consciously. Considerable use was made of technical methods derived from Vitruvius, and there was a wide distribution in the major art centres of (*a*) complete copies of Vitruvius; (*b*) extracts from Vitruvius; (*c*) the compilation of M. Cetius Faventinus. On the other hand, Vitruvius was *not* used as a sacrosanct building code, or as a manual of design.

22. A large part of the progress made in mediæval architecture was due to direct competition and to emulation of admired buildings as models. Great skill was employed in adaptation. Mediæval law was not generally concerned with problems of copyright or of plagiarism, but this was largely because drawings tended to be a closely guarded secret. Apart from the accidental survival of the album of Villard de Honnecourt, there are extremely few *portable* drawings of the period before 1275; *i.e.* the period of active progress in the development of a living Gothic architecture. Late evidence from Germany indicates a growing appreciation of the importance and value of the drawings to building owners.

23. Architectural design in the period from 1100 to 1550 was almost exclusively a function of master craftsmen, who were normally freemen of married status and literate, but not clerks. The apparent exceptions to this rule are extremely few and mostly unimportant; even of these few

quite half are instances of the craftsman who, after completing his technical training, entered holy orders or became a monk or a lay-brother in a monastic order.

24. Mediæval patrons provided programmes to be fulfilled, just as clients of all other periods. Many of these programmes were concerned with liturgical needs or symbolism, but the fulfilment of these requirements did not in any way affect the freedom of the architect to give the building its stylistic and individual form. The details and particularly the profiles of all mouldings, which gave to the form of the building its plasticity and light-and-shade, were entirely at the master's will.

25. Mediæval architects generally were not so insistently individualistic or self-conscious as the more eccentric artists of the Renaissance and of recent times. On the other hand their styles have as much originality and can be differentiated as clearly as those of architects of any other place or time.

26. In their own view, and according to a specific tradition, mediæval masons regarded themselves as of gentle blood. They were not menials and the masters were, so far as records are available, treated socially as "gentlemen" and as "esquires of minor degree". Master craftsmen who acquired wealth might even rank in precedence above gentlemen or along with them. Wardens and other assistants to masters ranked as yeomen. In a few cases the relationship of mediæval architects to families of accepted gentle blood can be regarded as proven.

27. In conclusion we have to consider how far the study of mediæval architects and their work has meaning for us now. In a general way this opens the question of the validity of historical studies and of antiquarian æsthetics. Presumably there will always be some for whom the past has no positive significance; but it is unlikely that any of them will read this book. The problem then may be reframed: among the historical styles of architecture some will have greater relevance to us, others less; in comparison with the styles of antiquity, of the Far East, of Ancient America, of the Renaissance and early modern times, has mediæval architecture a particular message that cannot be had from the rest? The answer is that it has, for two main reasons. Firstly, as has been said already, it is the one truly great architectural style of Western Europe, including Britain. It has the immediate relevance of being an architecture that grew up in our own climate, fashioned with our native materials, and to a large extent by the brains and hands of our own ancestors. In this way it is inescapable that the mediæval buildings of this region must have a deeper meaning to us than any others.

The second reason goes deeper, for it does not depend upon the accident of position, but on fundamentals. It is that the fully developed architecture of the period: the later Romanesque of large scale and the

Gothic, so long as in any given area it remained a living style, represent the most highly developed and completely sophisticated system in art, at any rate in the plastic arts. The cathedral—including, architecturally considered, all greater churches designed for choir services—corresponds in architecture to the place of the symphony in music; and one might even add that bay design is an equivalent to sonata form. The proportionate relationships, which at their best are of exquisite nicety, are actually concerned with the same numerical progressions as those of harmony, and are founded on the same natural laws. We may not judge the mediæval masons, in their account of the origins of their craft, to have been accurate historians or particularly well informed, but they did well to mention Pythagoras and to attribute the development of their science to the "worthy clerk Euclid". For architecture is a solid counterpart of music, and both arts rest firmly upon the same mathematical basis. Geometry, like music, is a universal language with meaning to all; and of all those who have ever used it, the mediæval architects spoke it most eloquently.

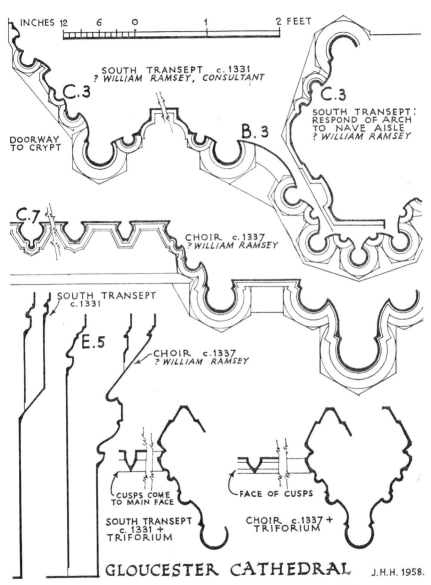

INCHES 12 6 0 1 2 FEET

C.3

SOUTH TRANSEPT c.1331
? WILLIAM RAMSEY, CONSULTANT

DOORWAY
TO CRYPT

B.3

C.3

SOUTH TRANSEPT:
RESPOND OF ARCH
TO NAVE AISLE
? WILLIAM RAMSEY

C.7

CHOIR c.1337
? WILLIAM RAMSEY

SOUTH TRANSEPT
c.1331

E.5

CHOIR c.1337
? WILLIAM RAMSEY

CUSPS COME
TO MAIN FACE

FACE OF CUSPS

SOUTH TRANSEPT
c.1331 +
TRIFORIUM

CHOIR c.1337 +
TRIFORIUM

GLOUCESTER CATHEDRAL J.H.H. 1958.

Origin of the Perpendicular style: profiles of mouldings.

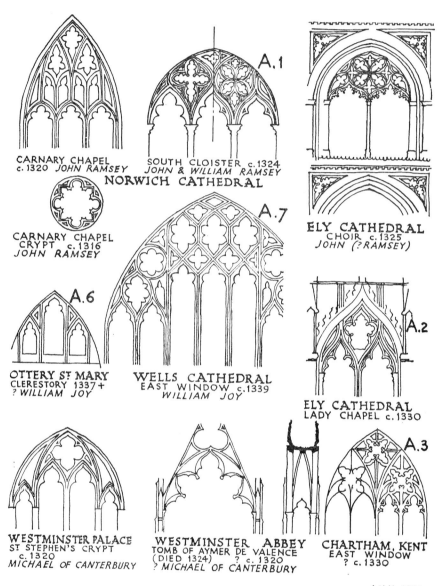

CARNARY CHAPEL
c.1320 *JOHN RAMSEY*

SOUTH CLOISTER c.1324
JOHN & WILLIAM RAMSEY

NORWICH CATHEDRAL

A.1

CARNARY CHAPEL
CRYPT c.1316
JOHN RAMSEY

ELY CATHEDRAL
CHOIR c.1325
JOHN (?RAMSEY)

A.7

A.6

OTTERY S? MARY
CLERESTORY 1337+
? WILLIAM JOY

WELLS CATHEDRAL
EAST WINDOW c.1339
WILLIAM JOY

A.2

ELY CATHEDRAL
LADY CHAPEL c.1330

WESTMINSTER PALACE
S? STEPHEN'S CRYPT
c.1320
MICHAEL OF CANTERBURY

WESTMINSTER ABBEY
TOMB OF AYMER DE VALENCE
(DIED 1324)   ? c.1320
? MICHAEL OF CANTERBURY

CHARTHAM, KENT
EAST WINDOW
? c.1330

A.3

J.H.H. 1958.

Origin of the Perpendicular style: window tracery.

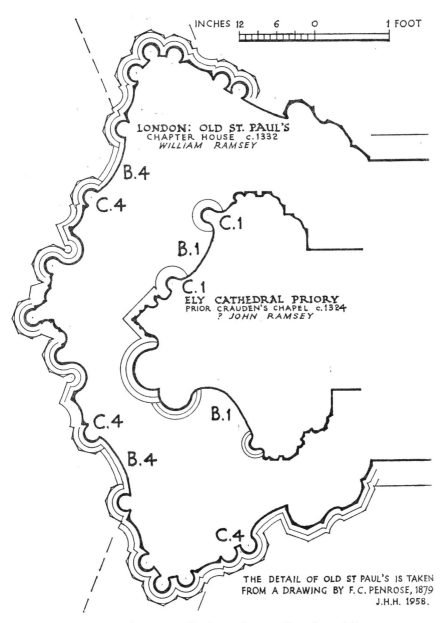

INCHES 12 6 0 1 FOOT

LONDON: OLD ST. PAUL'S
CHAPTER HOUSE c.1332
WILLIAM RAMSEY

B.4

C.4

C.1

B.1

C.1
ELY CATHEDRAL PRIORY
PRIOR CRAUDEN'S CHAPEL c.1324
? JOHN RAMSEY

B.1

C.4

B.4

C.4

THE DETAIL OF OLD ST PAUL'S IS TAKEN
FROM A DRAWING BY F.C. PENROSE, 1879
J.H.H. 1958.

Origin of the Perpendicular style: profiles of mouldings.

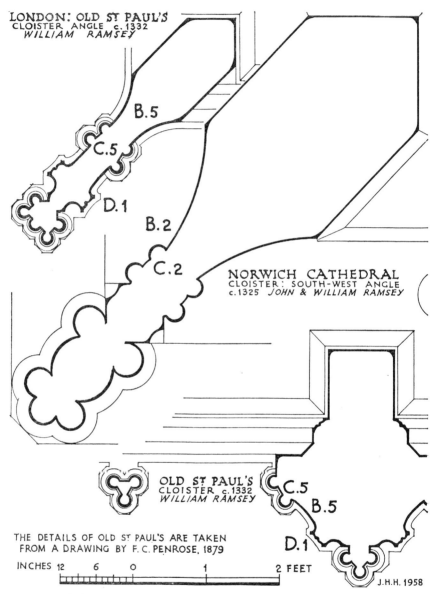

LONDON: OLD ST PAUL'S
CLOISTER ANGLE c.1332
WILLIAM RAMSEY

B.5

C.5

D.1

B.2

C.2

NORWICH CATHEDRAL
CLOISTER: SOUTH-WEST ANGLE
c.1325 *JOHN & WILLIAM RAMSEY*

OLD ST PAUL'S
CLOISTER c.1332
WILLIAM RAMSEY

C.5

B.5

D.1

THE DETAILS OF OLD ST PAUL'S ARE TAKEN
FROM A DRAWING BY F. C. PENROSE, 1879

INCHES 12   6   0   1   2 FEET

J.H.H. 1958

Origin of the Perpendicular style: profiles of mouldings.

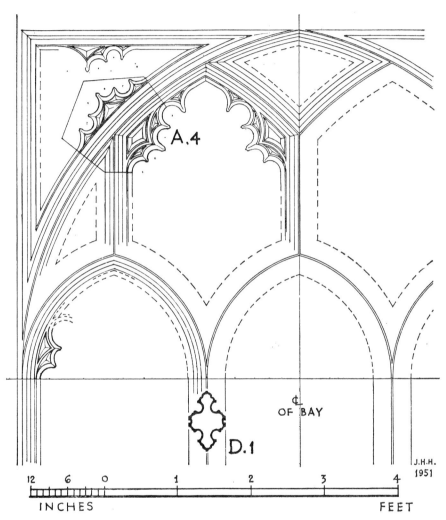

London: Old St. Paul's, cloister tracery designed in 1332 by William Ramsey.

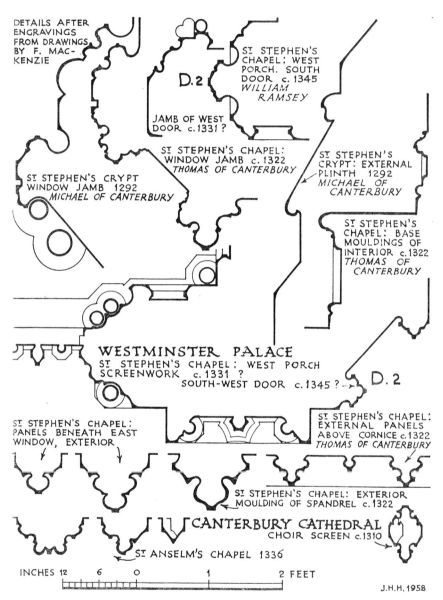

DETAILS AFTER
ENGRAVINGS
FROM DRAWINGS
BY F. MAC-
KENZIE

D.2

ST STEPHEN'S
CHAPEL: WEST
PORCH. SOUTH
DOOR c. 1345
*WILLIAM
RAMSEY*

JAMB OF WEST
DOOR c.1331 ?

ST STEPHEN'S CHAPEL:
WINDOW JAMB c. 1322
THOMAS OF CANTERBURY

ST STEPHEN'S CRYPT
WINDOW JAMB 1292
MICHAEL OF CANTERBURY

ST STEPHEN'S
CRYPT: EXTERNAL
PLINTH 1292
*MICHAEL OF
CANTERBURY*

ST STEPHEN'S
CHAPEL: BASE
MOULDINGS OF
INTERIOR c.1322
*THOMAS OF
CANTERBURY*

WESTMINSTER PALACE
ST STEPHEN'S CHAPEL : WEST PORCH
SCREENWORK   c.1331 ?
SOUTH-WEST DOOR c.1345 ?

D.2

ST STEPHEN'S CHAPEL:
PANELS BENEATH EAST
WINDOW, EXTERIOR

ST STEPHEN'S CHAPEL:
EXTERNAL PANELS
ABOVE CORNICE c.1322
THOMAS OF CANTERBURY

ST STEPHEN'S CHAPEL: EXTERIOR
MOULDING OF SPANDREL c.1322

CANTERBURY CATHEDRAL
CHOIR SCREEN c.1310

ST ANSELM'S CHAPEL 1336

INCHES 12   6   O   1   2 FEET

J.H.H.1958

Origin of the Perpendicular style: profiles of mouldings.

SOUTH-EAST
ANGLE OF
WESTMINSTER
HALL

? VESTRY
HERE

WESTMINSTER PALACE:
ST STEPHEN'S CRYPT 1292
MICHAEL OF CANTERBURY

SCREEN
OF PORCH

ST STEPHEN'S CHAPEL c. 1322
THOMAS OF CANTERBURY

10 5 0   10   20   30   40   50 FEET

EXTERIOR   INTERIOR

ST STEPHEN'S CHAPEL c.1322
THOMAS OF CANTERBURY

EAST FRONT c.1331
THOMAS OF CANTERBURY

CHOIR SCREEN c.1310?   ST ANSELM'S CHAPEL 1336

CHAPTER HOUSE
1304

CANTERBURY CATHEDRAL   J.H.H. 1958.

Origin of the Perpendicular style: details and tracery.

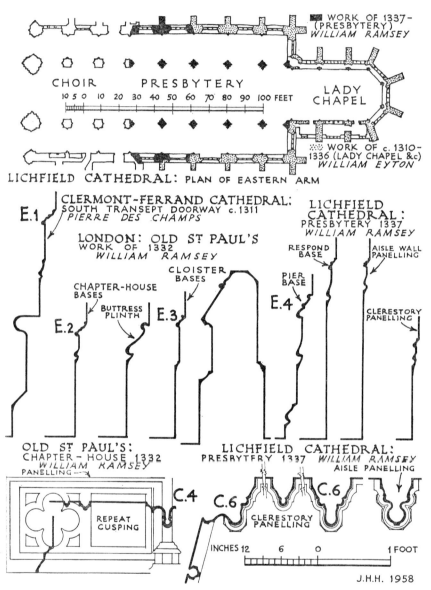

Origin of the Perpendicular style: details and profiles of mouldings.

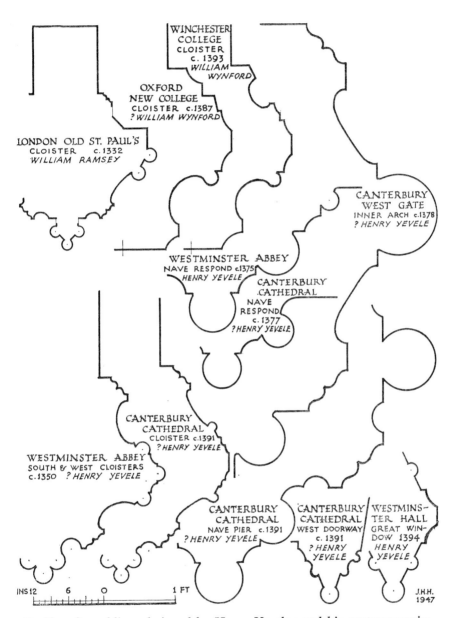

Profiles of mouldings designed by Henry Yeveley and his contemporaries.

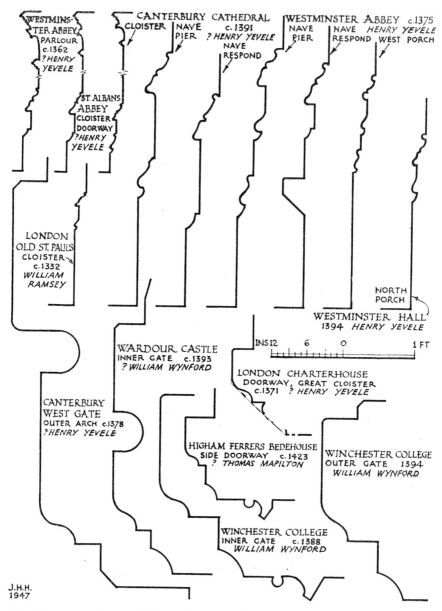

Profiles of mouldings designed by Henry Yeveley and his contemporaries.

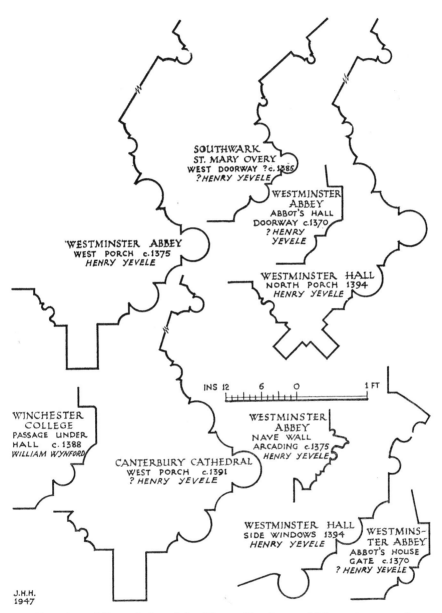

Profiles of mouldings designed by Henry Yeveley and his contemporaries.

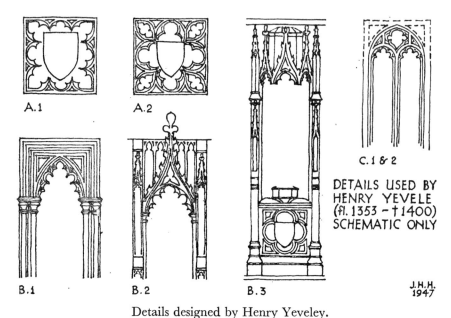

A.1

A.2

C.1 & 2

DETAILS USED BY
HENRY YEVELE
(fl. 1353 – †1400)
SCHEMATIC ONLY

B.1

B.2

B.3

J.H.H.
1947

Details designed by Henry Yeveley.

A.1   Panel used by Yeveley on the porches at Westminster Abbey, Westminster Hall, and Canterbury Cathedral; also found on the Black Prince's tomb at Canterbury.

A.2   Panel used by Yeveley on tombs in Westminster Abbey; also found on tombs at St. Bartholomew-the-Great, London, and at Layer Marney, Essex; as well as later examples.

B.1   Niche-head or archway used by Yeveley at Westminster Abbey, and on the tomb of Sir Walter Manny at the London Chaterhouse; also found at St. Albans, and later at York Minster.

B.2   Niche-head or canopy used by Yeveley at Westminster Abbey, Canterbury Cathedral, and on tomb of Sir Simon Burley in Old St. Paul's; also at Arundel; Cobham, Kent; and Maidstone.

B.3   Niche with projecting canopied head, used by Yeveley on the tombs of Edward III, Richard II, and Sir Simon Burley.

C.1 and C.2   Two-light window or blind-traceried design, used by Yeveley at Westminster, Canterbury and elsewhere; on the Neville Screen made in London for Durham Cathedral; also found at New College, Oxford; and later at York Minster.

APPENDIX OF SOURCES

A

Historical Texts on the Architect

*T*HE *first text given may be regarded as literary rather than strictly historical, since it comes from the New Testament Apocrypha, but the assumptions in regard to what was understood about building in the early Christian period (the Acts of Thomas go back to the third century A.D.) cannot be challenged.*

ACTS OF THE HOLY APOSTLE THOMAS (from *The Apocryphal New Testament,* translated by M. R. James, Oxford, Clarendon Press, 1924, 365–6, 371–2).

"There was there [Jerusalem] a certain merchant come from India whose name was Abbanes, sent from the King Gundaphorus [Gondophares or Hyndopheres, a historical king of Kabul and the Punjab who reigned *c.* A.D. 21–50], and having commandment from him to buy a carpenter and bring him unto him.

"Now the Lord seeing him walking in the market-place at noon said unto him: Wouldest thou buy a carpenter? And he said to him: Yea. And the Lord said to him: I have a slave that is a carpenter and I desire to sell him. And so saying he showed him Thomas afar off, and agreed with him for three litræ [roughly pounds] of silver unstamped, and wrote a deed of sale, saying: I, Jesus, the son of Joseph the carpenter, acknowledge that I have sold my slave, Judas by name, unto thee Abbanes, a merchant of Gundaphorus, king of the Indians. And when the deed was finished, the Saviour took Judas Thomas and led him away to Abbanes the merchant ...

"... when they were embarked in the ship and set down, Abbanes questioned the apostle, saying: What craftsmanship knowest thou? And he said: In wood I can make ploughs and yokes and ox-goads, and boats and oars for boats and masts and pulleys; and in stone, pillars and temples and court-houses for kings. And Abbanes the

merchant said to him: Yea, it is of such a workman that we have
need ...

"Now when the apostle was come into the cities of India with
Abbanes the merchant, Abbanes went to salute the king
Gundaphorus, and reported to him of the carpenter whom he had
brought with him. And the king was glad, and commanded him to
come in to him. So when he was come in the king said unto him:
What craft understandest thou? The apostle said unto him: The
craft of carpentering and of building. The king saith unto him:
What craftsmanship, then, knowest thou in wood, and what in
stone? The apostle saith: In wood, ploughs, yokes, goads, pulleys,
and boats and oars and masts; and in stone: pillars, temples and
court-houses for kings. And the king said: Canst thou build me a
palace? And he answered: Yea, I can both build and furnish it;
for to this end am I come, to build and to do the work of a
carpenter.

"And the king took him and went out of the city gates and
began to speak with him on the way concerning the building of
the court-house, and of the foundations, how they should be laid,
until they came to the place wherein he desired that the building
should be; and he said: Here will I that the building should be.
And the apostle said: Yea, for this place is suitable for the
building ... And the king said: If, then, this seem good to thee,
draw me a plan, how the work shall be, because I shall return
hither after some long time. And the apostle took a reed and drew,
measuring the place; and the doors he set toward the sunrising to
look toward the light, and the windows toward the west to the
breezes, and the bakehouse he appointed to be toward the south,
and the aqueduct for the service toward the north. And the king
saw it and said to the apostle: Verily thou art a craftsman, and it
befitteth thee to be a servant of kings. And he left much money
with him and departed from him. And from time to time he sent
money and provision, and victual for him and the rest of the
workmen. But Thomas receiving it all dispensed it, going about the
cities and the villages round about, distributing and giving alms to
the poor and afflicted ..."

*It is hardly surprising that when Thomas later explained to the
king that he could not see the palace until after he had departed
this life, Gundaphorus was "exceeding wroth, and commanded both
the merchant and Judas which is called Thomas to be put in
bonds and cast into prison", or that Thomas should ultimately have
won a martyr's crown. The interest of the story to us lies particularly in the three fundamental points, that a builder was skilled*

in both wood and stone; that he drew a plan (design) to scale, and with a reed pen; and that his skill included accepted views on orientation of the parts of the building. These points are fully in agreement with what we know of the architects of Greece and Rome, and with the information given by Vitruvius. The unity of classical western architecture with that of the early Christian Near East and India is thus demonstrated: however styles and fashions might vary, the basic facts of design and building technique remained constant.

It is of considerable interest that closely similar methods of ordering building works occur in the letter of a much later Indian monarch, Babur, written in A.D. 1529 to his governor of Kabul, Khwaja Kalan. (The Babur-Nama in English, *translated by A. S. Beveridge, London: Luzac, 1922/1969, 646–7*):

"The things that must be done are specified below; for some of them orders have gone already, one of these being, 'Let treasure accumulate'. The things which must be done are these: First, the repair of the fort; again: the provision of stores; again: the daily allowance and lodging of envoys going backwards and forwards; again: let money, taken legally from revenue, be spent for building the Congregational Mosque; again: the repairs of the Caravan-sarai and the Hot-baths; again: the completion of the unfinished building made of burnt brick which Ustad (Master) Hasan Ali was constructing in the citadel. Let this work be ordered after taking counsel with Ustad Sultan Muhammad; if a design exist, drawn earlier by Ustad Hasan Ali, let Ustad Sultan Muhammad finish the building precisely according to it; if not, let him do so, after making a gracious and harmonious design, and in such a way that its floor shall be level with that of the Audience-hall . . ."

THE CONSTITUTIONS OF MASONRY (from the Cooke MS., B.M. Add. 23198).

The following is a complete text, with spelling modernized, of what is believed to represent the earliest surviving form of the English "Constitutions of the art of Geometry according to Euclid", dating in its essentials from the middle of the fourteenth century. The existing manuscript was written about 1400, but is thought to represent an earlier version of the constitutions than the poem by a cleric known as the Regius MS. (B.M. Royal 17 A1), itself written c. 1390; of this poem an extract is given in modernized form, to include a small amount of additional matter not represented in the Cooke MS. prose version. For definitive parallel texts of the two manuscripts and for a full discussion and notes, see Douglas Knoop, G. P. Jones and Douglas Hamer, The Two earliest Masonic MSS.,

Manchester University Press, 1938. The opening lines are translated from the Latin heading of the Regius MS., since the Cooke MS. has no title.

Here begin the Constitutions of the art of Geometry according to Euclid.

Thanked be God our glorious Father and founder and former of heaven and of earth and of all things that in them is that he would vouchsafe of his glorious Godhead for to make so many things of divers virtue for mankind. For he made all things for to be obedient and subject to man. For all things that be comestible of wholesome nature he ordained it for man's sustenance. And also he hath given to man wits and cunning of divers things and crafts by the which we may travail in this world to get with our living to make divers things to God's pleasance and also for our ease and profit. The which things if I should rehearse them it were too long to tell and to write, wherefore I will leave them. But I shall show you some, that is to say how and in what wise the science of Geometry first began and who were the founders thereof, and of other crafts more, as it is noted in the Bible and in other stories.

How and in what manner that this worthy science of Geometry began I will tell you as I said before. Ye shall understand that there be seven liberal sciences by the which seven all sciences and crafts in the world were first found; and in especial, for he is causer of all, that is to say the science of Geometry of all other that be. The which seven sciences be called thus: as for the first, that is called fundament of science, his name is Grammar: he teacheth a man rightfully to speak and to write truly. The second is Rhetoric, and he teacheth a man to speak formably and fair. The third is Dialectic, and that science teacheth a man to discern the truth from the false and commonly it is telled the art of sophistry. The fourth is called Arithmetic, the which teacheth a man the craft of numbers for to reckon and to make accounts of all things. The fifth is Geometry the which teacheth a man all the metes and measures and ponderation of weights of all manner crafts. The sixth is Music that teacheth a man the craft of song in notes of voice and organ and trump and harp and of all other pertaining to them. The seventh is Astronomy that teacheth man the course of the sun and of the moon and of other stars and planets of heaven.

Our intent is principally to treat of the first foundation of the worthy science of Geometry and who were the founders thereof, as I said before there be seven liberal sciences that is to say seven sciences or crafts that be free in themselves the which seven live only by Geometry. And Geometry is as much as to say the measure of the earth. *Et sic dicitur a* "geo", *grœce quod redditur* "terra" *latine et metrona quod est mensura. Unde Geometria, id est, mensura terræ vel terrarum*; that is to say in English that Geometria is said of *geo* that is in Greek "earth" and *metrona* that is to say "measure". And thus is this name of Geometria compounded and is said "the measure of the earth".*

Marvel ye not that I said that all sciences live only by the science of Geometry. For there is no artificial nor handicraft that is wrought by man's hand but it is wrought by Geometry; and a notable cause. For if a man work with his hands he worketh with some manner tool and there is no instrument of material things in this world but it come of the kind of earth, and to earth it will turn again. And there is no instrument, that is to say a tool to work with, but it hath some proportion more or less. And proportion is measure and the tool or the instrument is earth. And Geometry is said the measure of earth wherefore I may say that men live all by Geometry. For all men here in this world live by the labour of their hands.

Many more probations I will tell you why that Geometry is the science that all reasonable men live by, but I leave it at this time for the long process of writing. And now I will proceed further on my matter. Ye shall understand that among all the crafts of the world of man's craft masonry hath the most notability and most part of this science of Geometry as it is noted and said in history as in the Bible and in the Master of Stories (Peter Comestor, *Historia Scholastica*), and in *Polychronicon*, a chronicle proved, and in the stories that is named Bede, (Honorius of Autun) *De Imagine Mundi*, and Isidore *Etymologiarum*, Methodius bishop and martyr (*Revelationes*); and other many more said that masonry is principally of Geometry as me thinketh it may well be said, for it was the first that was founded as it is noted in the Bible in the first book of Genesis in the fourth chapter. And also all the doctors aforesaid accordeth thereto : and some of them saith it more openly and plainly right as it saith in the Bible Genesis.

(From) Adam is line lineal, sons descending down the seven ages : of Adam before Noah's flood there was a man that was clept Lamech the which had two wives, the one hight Adah and another Zillah; by the first wife that hight Adah he begat two sons, the one hight Jabal and the other hight Jubal. The elder son Jabal he was the first man that ever found Geometry and masonry, and he made houses and is named in the Bible : *Pater habitancium in tentoriis atque pastorum*, that is to say Father of men dwelling in tents, that is dwelling houses

---

*These statements also appear in a contemporary Treatise of Geometry "whereby you may know the height, deepness, and breadth of mostwhat earthly things".

("and of such as have cattle"). And he was Cain's master mason and governor of all his works when he made the city of Enoch that was the first city that ever was made, and that made Cain, Adam's son; and gave to his own son Enoch, and gave the city the name of his son and called it Enoch. And now it is called Ephraim, and there was the science of Geometry and masonry first occupied and contrived for a science and for a craft, and so we may say that it was cause and foundation of all crafts and sciences. And also this man Jabal was called *Pater Pastorum* (father of such as have cattle).

The Master of Stories saith, and Bede, *De Imagine Mundi*, *Polychronicon*, and others more say that he was the first that made partition of land that every man might know his own ground, and labour thereon as for his own. And also he parted flocks of sheep that every man might know his own sheep and so we may say that he was the first founder of that science. And his brother Jubal, or Tubal, was founder of Music and song as Pythagoras saith in *Polychronicon* and the same saith Isidore in his Etymologies in the sixth book: there he saith that he was the first founder of Music and song and of organ and trump and he found that science by the sound of ponderation of his brother's hammers, that was Tubalcain. Soothly as the Bible saith in the chapter, that is to say the fourth of Genesis, that he saith Lamech gat upon his other wife that hight Zillah a son and a daughter the names of them were clept Tubalcain, that was the son; and his daughter hight Naamah, and as the *Polychronicon* saith that some men say that she was Noah's wife—whether it be so other no we affirm it not.

Ye shall understand that this son Tubalcain was founder of smith's craft and of other crafts of metal, that is to say of iron, of brass, of gold and of silver, as some doctors say. And his sister Naamah was finder of weaver's craft; for before that time was no cloth woven but they did spin yarn and knit it and made them such clothing as they could, but as that woman Naamah found that craft of weaving and therefore it was called women's craft:* And these three brethren aforesaid had knowledge that God would take vengeance for sin either by fire or water and they had great care how they might do to save the sciences that they had found and they took their counsel together and by all their wit they said that there were two manner of stone of such virtue that the one would never burn and that stone is called marble. And that other stone that will not sink in water, and that stone is named "lacerus".† And so they devised to write all the science that

*The compiler must have presumed a common etymology for "weave" and "wife".

†"Lacerus", misunderstood corruption of *lateres*, *i.e.* clay bricks or tiles; the confusion between the materials proves that the MS. is derived from an earlier source, presumably in Latin.

they had found in these two stones if that God would take vengeance by fire that the marble (*sic*) should not burn; and if God sent vengeance by water that the other should not drown. And so they prayed their elder brother Jabal that he would make two pillars of these two stones, that is to say of marble and of "lacerus", and that he would write in the two pillars all the sciences and crafts that all they had found. And so he did; and therefore we may say that he was the most cunning in science, for he first began and performed the end before Noah's flood.

Kindly (*i.e.* of what kind) knowing of that vengeance that God would send, whether it should be by fire or by water, the brethren had it not; by a manner of a prophecy they wist that God would send one thereof. And therefore they wrote their science in the two pillars of stone. And some men say that they wrote in the stones all the seven sciences, but as they had in their mind that a vengeance should come. And so it was that God sent vengeance, so that there came such a flood that all the world was drowned. And all men were dead therein save eight persons, and that was Noah and his wife, and his three sons and their wives, of which three sons all the world came of, and their names were named in this manner: Shem, Ham, and Japhet. And the flood was called Noah's flood, for he and his children were saved therein. And after this flood many years as the chronicler telleth, these two pillars were found, and as the *Polychronicon* saith that a great clerk that men called Pythagoras found that one and Hermes the philosopher found that other; and they taught forth the sciences that they found there written.

Every chronicle and history and many other clerks, and the Bible in principal, witness of the making of the Tower of Babylon, and it is written in the Bible, Genesis chapter ten, how that Ham, Noah's son, gat Nimrod and he waxed a mighty man upon the earth and he waxed a strong man like a giant, and he was a great king. And the beginning of his kingdom was the true kingdom of Babylon, and Erech, and Accad, and Calneh, and the land of Shinar. And this same Ham began the Tower of Babylon and he taught to his workmen the craft of masonry and he had with him many masons, more than forty thousand. And he loved and cherished them well, and it is written in *Polychronicon* and in the Master of Stories, and in other stories more; and this apart, witness the Bible in the same tenth chapter where he saith that Asshur that was nigh kin to Nimrod goed ("yede"; *i.e.* went) out of the land of Shinar, and he built the city of Nineveh and "plateas"* and other more, thus he

---

*The writer of the Cooke MS., as above (p. 194 and note †), has failed to understand the Latin Bible, where "plateas civitatis" means the plots, squares or streets of the city.

saith: *De terra illa id est de Sennare egressus est Asure et edificavit Niniven et plateas civitatis et Cale et Jesen quoque inter Niniven et haec est Civitas magna* ("Out of that land went forth Asshur, and builded Niniveh, and *the city Rehoboth*"—or "the streets of the city"—"and Calah, and Resen between Niniveh and Calah: the same is a great city").

Reason would that we should tell openly how and in what manner that the charges of masoncraft was first founded and who gave first the name to it of masonry. And ye shall know well that it is told and written in *Polychronicon* and in Methodius bishop and martyr, that Asshur that was a worthy lord of Shinar sent to Nimrod the King to send him masons and workmen of craft that might help him to make his city that he was in will to make. And Nimrod sent him thirty hundred of masons. And when they should go and send them forth, he called them before him and said to them: Ye must go to my cousin Asshur to help him to build a city, but look that ye be well governed and I shall give you a charge profitable for you and me.

When ye come to that lord, look that ye be true to him like as ye would be to me; and truly do your labour and craft and take reasonably your need therefor as ye may deserve, and also that ye love together as ye were brethren and hold together truly. And he that hath most cunning teach it to his fellow and look ye govern you against (*i.e.* towards) your lord and among yourselves, that I may have worship and thanks for me sending and teaching you the craft. And they received the charge of him that was their master and their lord, and went forth to Asshur, and built the city of Niniveh in the country of "plateas" and other cities more that men call Caleh and "Jesen" (Resen) that is a great city between Caleh and Niniveh. And in this manner the craft of masonry was first proffered and charged it for a science.

Elders that were before us of masons had these charges written to them as we have now in our charges of the story of Euclid, as we have seen them written in Latin and in French both; but how that Euclid came to Geometry reason would we should tell you as it is noted in the Bible and in other stories. In the twelfth chapter of Genesis he telleth how that Abraham came to the land of Canaan and Our Lord appeared to him and said: I shall give this land to thy seed. But there fell a great hunger in that land, and Abraham took Sarah his wife with him and goed in to Egypt in pilgrimage while the hunger endured he would bide there. And Abraham, as the chronicle saith, he was a wise man and a great clerk, and "cowthe" (knew) all the seven sciences and taught the Egyptians the science of Geometry. And this worthy clerk Euclid was his scholar and learned of him. And he gave the first name of Geometry albeit that it was occupied before it had no name of Geometry. But it is said of Isidore, *Etymologiarum* in the fifth book. *Etymologiarum*, chapter first, saith that Euclid was one of the first founders of Geometry and he gave it name. For in his time there was a water in that land of Egypt that is called Nile, and it flowed so far into the land that men might not dwell therein.

Then this worthy clerk Euclid taught them to make great walls and ditches to hold out the water, and he by Geometry measured the land and parted it in divers parts, and made every man to close his own part with walls and ditches, and then it became a plenteous country of all manner of fruit and of young people of men and women that there was so much people of young fruit that they could not well live. And the lords of the country drew them together and made a council how they might help their children that had no livelihood competent and able for to find themselves and their children for they had so many; and among them all in council was this worthy clerk Euclid, and when he saw that all they could not bring about this matter, he said to them : will ye take your sons in governance and I shall teach them such a science that they shall live thereby gentlemanly, under condition that ye will be sworn to me to perform the governance that I shall set you to, and them both; and the king of the land and all the lords by one assent granted thereto.

Reason would that every man would grant to that thing that were profitable to himself; and they took their sons to Euclid to govern them at his own will and he taught to them the craft of masonry and gave it the name of Geometry because of the parting of the ground that he had taught to the people in the time of the making of the walls and ditches aforesaid to close out the water; and Isidore saith in his Etymologies that Euclid calleth the craft *Geometria*. And thus this worthy clerk gave it name and taught it the lords' sons of the land that he had in his teaching. And he gave them a charge that they should call them each other "fellow" and no otherwise, because that they were all of one craft and of one gentle birth born and lords' sons. And also he that were most of cunning should be governor of the work and should be called Master; and other charges more that be written in the Book of Charges. And so they wrought with lords of the land and made cities and towns, castles and temples and lords' places.

What time that the children of Israel dwelt in Egypt they learned the craft of masonry. And afterward they were driven out of Egypt they came into the land of behest and is now called Jerusalem, and it was occupied (*i.e.* employed) and charges held, at the making of Solomon's Temple that King David began. King David loved well masons and he gave them charges right nigh as they be now. And at the making of the Temple in Solomon's time, as it is said in the Bible in the third book of Kings *in tercio Regum, capitulo quinto (i.e.* I Kings, chapter 5), that Solomon had four score thousand masons at his work, and the king's son of Tyre was his master mason. And in other chroniclers it is said, and in old books of masonry, that Solomon confirmed the charges that David his father had given to masons. And Solomon himself taught them their manners;* but little different from the manners that now be used. And from thence this worthy science was brought into France and into many other regions.

Sometime there was a worthy king in France that was clept *Carolus secundus* that is to say, Charles the second. And this Charles was elected king of France by the grace of God and by lineage also. And some men say that he was elected by fortune, the which is false, as by chronicle he was of the king's Blood Royal. And this same king Charles was a mason before that he was king. And after that he was king he loved masons and cherished them and gave them charges and manners of his device, of the which some be yet used in France, and he ordained that they should have an assembly once in the year and come and speak together and for to be ruled by masters and fellows of all things amiss.

And soon after that came Saint Amphibalus into England and he converted Saint Alban to christendom. And Saint Alban loved well masons and he gave them first their charges and manners first in England. And he ordained convenient wages to pay for their travail. And after that was a worthy king in England that was called Athelstan and his youngest son loved well the science of Geometry. And he wist well that no handicraft had the practice of the science of Geometry so well as masons, wherefore he drew him to counsel and learned practice of that science to his speculative. For of speculative† he was a master, and he loved well masonry and masons; and he became a mason himself. And he gave them charges and manners as it is now used in England and in other countries. And he ordained that they should have reasonable pay, and purchased a free patent of the king that they should make an assembly when they saw reasonably time to come together to their counsel, of the which charges, manners and assembly as is written and taught in the book of our charges wherefore I leave it at this time.

*"Manners" here means the usages and methods *taught* (not "fine manners")— this is precisely the sense of the contemporary phrase used by William of Wykeham: "Manners makyth Man."

†Not "speculative freemasonry" in the modern sense, but the theoretical side of geometry, the design and proportion of buildings and other architectural functions as distinct from stonecutting.

(The Old Book of Charges)*

Good men, for this cause and this manner masonry took first beginning. It befell sometime that great lords had not so great possessions that they might not advance their free begotten children for they had so many. Therefore they took counsel how they might their children advance and ordain them honestly to live; and sent after wise masters of the worthy science of Geometry that they through their wisdom should ordain them some honest living.

Then one of them that had the name which was called Euclid, that was most subtle and wise founder, ordained an art and called it masonry. And so with his art honestly he taught the children of great lords by the prayer of the fathers and the free will of their children, the which when they taught with high care by a certain time they were not all alike able for to take of the foresaid art; wherefore the foresaid master Euclid ordained they that were passing of cunning should be passing honoured. And commanded to call the cunning master for to inform the less of cunning; masters of the which were called "masters" of nobility of wit and cunning of that art. Nevertheless he commanded that they that were less of wit should not be called servant nor subject, but fellows, for nobility of their gentle blood. In this manner was the foresaid art begun, in the land of Egypt by the foresaid master Euclid, and so it went from land to land and from kingdom to kingdom, after that many years in the time of King Athelstan, which was sometime king of England, by his council and other great lords of the land, by common assent, for great default found among masons they ordained a certain rule amongst them one time of the year or in three years as need were to the king and great lords of the land and all the commonalty, from province to province and from country to country congregations should be made by masters, of all master masons and fellows in the foresaid art. And so at such congregations they that be made masters should be examined of the articles after written, and be ransacked whether they be able and cunning to the profit of the lords them to serve, and to the honour of the foresaid art, and moreover they should receive their charge that they should well and truly spend the goods of their lords and that as well the lowest as the highest, for they be their lords for the time, of whom they take their pay for their service and for their travail.

The first Article is this: that every Master of this art should be wise and true to the lord that he serveth, spending his goods truly

* From this point the Cooke MS. seems to incorporate a copy of an older book from which the "Charges" were read to the assembly.

as he would his own were spent; and not give more pay to no mason than he wot he may deserve, after the dearth of corn and victual in the country, no favour withstanding for every man to be rewarded after his travail.

The second Article is this: that every master of this art should be warned before to come to his congregation that they come duly but if they may be excused by some manner cause. But nevertheless if they be found rebel at such congregations or faulty in any manner harm of their lords and reproof of this art, they should not be excused in no manner, out take peril of death, and though they be in peril of death they shall warn the master that is principal of the gathering of his disease.

The third Article is this: that no master take no prentice for less term than seven year at the least, because why such as be within less term may not perfectly come to his art, nor able to serve truly his lord to take as a mason should take.

The fourth Article is this: that no master for no profit take no prentice for to be learned that is born of bond blood, for because of his lord to whom he is bond will take him as he well may from his art and lead him with him out of his lodge or out of his place that he worketh in, for his fellows peradventure would help him and debate for him; and (since) thereof manslaughter might rise it is forbid. And also for another cause of his art, it took beginning of great lords' children freely begotten as it is said before.

The fifth Article is this: that no master give more to his prentice in time of his prenticehood for no profit to be taken than he wot well he may deserve of the lord that he serveth nor not so much that the lord of the place that he is taught in may have some profit by his teaching.

The sixth Article is this: that no master for no covetousness nor profit take no prentice to teach that is imperfect: that is to say having any maim for the which he may not truly work as him ought for to do.

The seventh Article is this: that no master be found wittingly, or help or procure to be maintainer and sustainer, any common nightwalker to rob, by the which manner of nightwalking they may not fulfil their day's work and travail through the condition (that) their fellows might be made wroth.

The eighth Article is this: that if it befall that any mason that be perfect and cunning come for to seek work and find any imperfect and uncunning working, the master of the place shall receive the perfect and do away the imperfect to the profit of his lord.

The ninth Article is this: that no master shall supplant another, for it is said in the art of masonry that no man should make end so well of work begun by another to the profit of his lord, as he began it for to end it by his matters (ideas), or to whom he showeth his matters.

(The Points of Masonry, instructing the subordinate masons):

This counsel is made by divers lords and masters of divers provinces and divers congregations of masonry. And it is to wit that who that coveteth for to come to the state of the foresaid art it behoveth him first principally to love God and Holy Church and All Hallows, and his master and his fellows as his own brethren.

The second Point: he must fulfil his day's work truly that he taketh for his pay.

The third Point: that he can hele (conceal) the counsel of his fellows in lodge and in chamber and in every place thereas masons be.

The fourth Point: that he be no deceiver of the foresaid art nor do no prejudice nor sustain no articles against the art nor against none of the art, but he shall sustain it in all honour in as much as he may.

The fifth Point: when he shall take his pay that he take it meekly as the time is ordained by the master to be done, and that he fulfil the acceptions (conditions) of travail and of his rest ordained and set by the master.

The sixth Point: if any discord shall be between him and his fellows he shall obey him meekly and be still at the bidding of his master or of the warden of his master in his master's absence to the holiday following, and that he accord then at the disposition of his fellows, and not upon the workday for letting (hindering) of their work and profit of his lord.

The seventh Point: that he covet not the wife nor the daughter of his masters nor of his fellows, but if it be in marriage, nor hold concubines, for discord that might fall amongst them.

The eighth Point: if it befall him for to be warden under his master that he be true mean between his master and his fellows and that he be busy in the absence of his master to the honour of his master and profit to the lord that he serveth.

The ninth Point: if he be wiser and subtler than his fellow working with him in his lodge or in any other place, and he perceive it that he should lose the stone that he worked upon for default of cunning, and can teach him and amend the stone, he shall inform him and help him, that the more love may increase among them and that the work of the lord be not lost.

(The Assemblies or Congregations of the Masons):

When the master and the fellows before warned be come to such congregations, if need be the Sheriff of the country (*i.e.* county) or the Mayor of the city or Alderman of the town in which the congregations is held shall be fellow and associate to the master of the congregation, in help of him against rebels and upbearing the right of the realm.

At the first beginning, new men that never were charged before be charged in this manner, that they should never be thieves nor thieves' maintainers, and that they should truly fulfil their day's work and travail for their pay that they shall take of their lord, and true accounts give to their fellows in things that be to be accounted of them, and to hear and them love as themselves. And they shall be true to the King of England and to the realm and that they keep with all their might and all the articles aforesaid.

After that it shall be enquired if any master or fellow that is warned have broken any article before said, the which if they have done it shall be determined there. Therefore it is to wit if any master or fellow that is warned before to come to such congregations, and be rebel and will not come, or else have trespassed against any article before said, if it may be proved he shall forswear his masonry and shall no more use his craft. The which if he presume for to do the Sheriff of the country in the which he may be found working he shall prison him and take all his goods into the King's hand till his grace be granted him and showed, for this cause principally, where these congregations be ordained, that as well the lowest as the highest should be well and truly served in this art before said, throughout all the kingdom of England. Amen, so mote it be.

The Regius Poem
Apart from the fact that it is in verse, the Regius poem differs considerably in arrangement from the Cooke MS. The cleric who produced it, perhaps at the suggestion and with the concurrence of a master mason very likely his brother, undoubtedly had access to manuscript sources including closely similar versions of some of those used as a basis for the other compilation. The poem lacks the "New Long History"—all the preliminary matter prefixed in the Cooke MS. to the "Old Book of Charges"—but has a longer series of Articles and Points (fifteen of each instead of nine of each), includes the masonic legend of the Four Crowned Martyrs, the "Ars Quatuor Coronatorum", and adds long sections taken from John Mirk's Instructions for Parish Priests *and the poem* Urbanitatis *in its entirety. These latter instructions as to behaviour and moral exhortations are not relevant to the architectural content, but a modernized extract is given below of the additional matter which directly*

supplements the account of the Assemblies and the charges given in them.

The first eighty-six lines of the Regius poem closely parallel the "Old Short History" prefixed in the Cooke MS. to the Charges. The first four Articles are essentially identical in both versions; Regius Article V corresponds to Cooke Article VI and vice versa; the purport of Articles VII and VIII is again identical; and Regius Article X gives an amplified version of Cooke Article IX. The following extract includes the whole of Regius Articles IX–XV; considerably more liberties have had to be taken with the original than are necessary in the case of the straightforward prose of the Cooke MS.

Article IX

The ninth article showeth full well
That the master be both wise and fell (shrewd),
That no work he undertake
But he can both it end and make,
And that it be to the lord's profit also
And to his craft wheresoever he go;
And that the ground be well taken
That it neither flaw nor crack.

Article X

The tenth article is for to know
Among the craft, to high and low,
There shall no master supplant other,
But be together as sister and brother,
In this curious craft all and some
That belongeth to a master mason.
Nor he shall not supplant no other man
That hath taken a work him upon
In pain (penalty) thereof that is so strong
That amounteth no less than ten pound (£10),
But if he be guilty found
That took first the work in hand.
For no man in masonry
Shall not supplant other surely
But if that it be so wrought
That it turn the work to nought.
Then may a mason that work crave,
To the lord's profit it for to save.
In such a case but it do fall,
There shall no mason meddle withal,
For sooth he that beginneth the ground,

An he be a mason good and sound,
He hath it surely in his mind
To bring the work to full good end.

Article XI

The eleventh article I tell thee
That he is both fair and free,
For he teacheth by his might
That no mason should work by night
But if it be in practising of wit,
If that he could amend it.

Article XII

The twelfth article is of high honesty
To every mason wheresoever he be :
He shall not his fellow's work deprave (disparage)
If that he will his honesty save.
With honest words he it commend
By the wit that God thee did send,
But it amend by all that thou may
Between you both without nay.

Article XIII

The thirteenth article, so God me save,
Is if that the master a prentice have,
Entirely then that he him teach,
And measurable points that he him reach (promote)
That he the craft ably may con
Wheresoever he go under the sun.

Article XIV

The fourteenth article by good reason
Showeth the master how he shall do :
He shall no prentice to him take
But divers cares he have to make
That he may within his term
Of him divers points may learn.

Article XV

The fifteenth article maketh an end
For to the master he is a friend,
To teach him so that for no man
No false maintenance he take him upon,
Nor maintain his fellows in their sin

For no good that he might win;
Nor no false swearing suffer them to make
For dread of their souls' sake,
Lest it would turn the craft to shame
And himself to much blame.

The first eight of the Points of Masonry are closely similar in the two versions, Regius Point XI is Cooke Point IX, and Regius Points XII–XV cover similar matter to that of the conclusion of the Cooke MS. Below are given modernized texts of Regius Points IX and X, not directly paralleled in Cooke; and also of the additional ordinance which in the Regius poem follows Point XV.

Point IX

The ninth point : we shall him call
That he be steward of our hall;
If that ye be in chamber together
Each one serve other with mild cheer.
Gentle fellows, ye must it know
For to be stewards all arow,
Week after week without doubt,
Stewards to be so, all about;
Lowly to serve each one other
As though they were sister and brother.
There shall never one (at) another's expense
Free himself to no advantage,
But every man shall be alike free
In that expense, so must it be.
Look that thou pay well every man always
That thou has bought any victuals eaten,
That no demands be made to thee
Nor to thy fellows in no degree.
To man or to woman, whether he be,
Pay them well and truly, for that will we.
Thereof on thy fellow true record thou take
For that good pay as thou dost make,
Lest it would thy fellows shame
And bring thyself into great blame.
Yet good accounts he must make
Of such goods as he hath taken;
Of thy fellow's goods that thou hast spent,
Where and how and to what end,
Such accounts thou must come to
When thy fellows will that thou do.

Point X

  The tenth point presenteth well good life,
  To live without care and strife;
  For an the mason live amiss
  And in his work be false ywis (surely),
  And through such a false excusation
  May slander his fellows without reason;
  Through false slander of such fame
  May make the craft catch blame.
  If he do the craft such villainy
  Do him no favour then surely,
  Nor maintain not him in wicked life
  Lest it would turn to care and strife;
  But yet him ye shall not delay,
  But that ye shall him constrain
  For to appear wheresoever ye will,
  Where that ye will, loud or still.
  To the next assembly ye shall him call
  To appear before his fellows all;
  And but if he will before them appear
  The craft he must needs forswear;
  He shall then be chastised after the law
  That was founded by old days.

Another Ordinance of the Art of Geometry

  They ordained there an assembly to be held
  Every year wheresoever they would,
  To amend the defaults, if any were found
  Among the craft within the land.
  Each year or third year it should be held
  In every place wheresoever they would :
  Time and place must be ordained also
  In what place they shall assemble to
  All the men of craft, there they must be,
  And other great lords, as ye may see,
  To mend the faults that be there spoken
  If that any of them be then broken.
  There they shall be all sworn,
  That belong to this craft's lore,
  To keep these statutes every one
  That be ordained by King Athelstan.
  (*here follow the words of King Athelstan*):

These statutes that I have here found
I command they be held through my land
For the worship of my royalty
That I have by my dignity.
Also at every assembly that ye hold
That ye come to your liege king bold
Beseeking him of his high grace
To stand with you in every place,
To confirm the statutes of King Athelstan
That he ordained to this craft by good reason.

It is a curious fact that both the Cooke MS. and the Regius poem seem to have come from the same part of England, as shown by their dialect being that spoken in the South-West Midland area (Gloucestershire and West Oxfordshire) in the later part of the fourteenth century. More Southern forms are, however, found in the Cooke MS. The Regius poem belonged to John Theyer (1597–1673), born at Brockworth, Gloucestershire, a manor of which Richard Hart, last prior of Lanthony Priory near Gloucester, had been lord. Hart's sister Ann was grandmother of Theyer's father, John Theyer the elder, who died in 1631. There is thus a series of tenuous links possibly implying that the poem came from the mason's lodge of Lanthony by Gloucester or at any rate from Gloucester. It is known too that the Cooke MS. had been "got in the West of England" before 1721 by George Payne, Grand Master of Grand Lodge of Freemasons. There is some likelihood, hinted at by the stress laid on the legendary connection of King Athelstan with masonry, that the Constitutions or their source came from Malmesbury, Wiltshire. Athelstan, who died at Gloucester in 940, was buried at Malmesbury, and traditions of him were still alive there in the fourteenth century (see Knoop, Jones and Hamer, op cit., pp. 7, 17, 51–7, 62–3).

LOUIS DE BOURBOURG BUILDS A HOUSE IN THE CASTLE OF ARDRES FOR ARNOLD, STEWARD OF EUSTACE COUNT OF BOULOGNE (from *Chronique de Lambert d'Ardres*, ed. Heller, in *Monumenta Germaniæ historica, Scriptores*, XXIV, 1879, 624; Mortet 1911, 183–5).

This chronicle, notable for its lively detail, was written 1194–98.
(c. 1120) After peace had been made and ratified between Manasseh the count of Guines and Arnold, lord of Ardres, Arnold built a timber house at Ardres which through the extraordinary skill of the carpenters outdid any building of its time in the whole of Flanders. A certain craftsman or carpenter of Bourbourg (near Dunkirk), Louis

by name, not much inferior to Dædalus in his skill in this art, fashioned and wrought it. He provided it with a labyrinthine entrance hardly to be penetrated, and devised means of partitioning off the provision stores, the various rooms and lodgings, set the granary next the cellars; and built a chapel above in the upper part of the house on the east side in the most convenient place. He made the building of three stories and suspended the floors, distant from each other, as if they hung in the air. The first was on the surface of the ground, where the cellars and granaries were, with great chests, barrels and tubs, and other household utensils. On the second floor were the living rooms and common dwelling for the inhabitants, with the stores—here the pantry, there the buttery—and the great chamber of the lord and his wife, in which they slept, close to the garderobe, and the chamber or dormitory of the attendants and pages. In the inner part of the great chamber there was a private room partitioned off where they could light a fire at dawn or dusk, or in case of sickness or at times of blood-letting or to warm the attendants or weaned children. On this floor too was the kitchen, adjoining the house, with two floors. On the lower floor pigs were put to fatten, geese to feed, and capons and other birds for killing, always ready for eating. On the other floor of the kitchen the cooks and the purveyors of foodstuffs carried on their work, preparing exquisite meals there for the lord and lady, concocted and prepared for the table with every sort of cooking utensil—and with hard work. There too the daily messes for the household and staff were made ready. On the top floor of the building were made sets of rooms in which the boys and girls separately, as was fitting, and the masters of the house slept; elsewhere the watchmen and servants set as guardians, ever ready to defend the house, could take their slumbers. Staircases and passages led from floor to floor, from house to kitchen and room to room, as well as from the house to the lodge, which gets its name for a good and sensible reason—for they were wont to sit there taking pleasure in conversation—derived from *logos,* meaning speech;* and from the lodge into the oratory or chapel, like to the tabernacle of Solomon in its carvings and paintings.

GEOFFREY PLANTAGENET AS MILITARY ENGINEER

(Chroniques des comtes d'Anjou et des seigneurs d'Amboise, ed. L. Halphen and R. Poupardin, 1913, 217–19; Mortet 1929, 81–2).

---

*Though *logia,* lodge, is thought to be from a Germanic root cognate with *Laube,* an arbour, Lambert's derivation is good evidence of the mediæval sense of a lodge as a place for discussion, and where meetings could take place.

The siege of Montreuil-Bellay in the Saumurois, 1151.

That castle made its besiegers despair of taking it owing to the difficulty of its position. For it was surrounded by a double curtain of wall and fore wall (*duplici . . . muro et antemuro cingebatur*) and had a tower of amazing strength stretching towards the stars. It held off the shots of siege-engines, which had to be placed far from the walls and the tower, by an unusual rugged chasm called the Valley of Judas. Geoffrey (the Handsome, or Plantagenet, count of Anjou) . . . turned to more subtle methods . . . On the count's orders and following his instructions—for he was highly skilled in engineering and carpentry—they made wooden towers of such a height that they looked down on the walls and tower; set on wheels, these were dragged towards the walls. The count's men, first destroying the fore-wall, undermined the inner curtain. . . . But the damage and fractures caused by oak timbers, brought in from beneath during the day, were repaired by hard work at night. At this stage the well-read count (*litteratus consul*) studied the work of Vegetius Renatus who wrote (the standard book) on military affairs (*De re militari*).

In the meantime some monks of Marmoutier arrived, bringing the count a reply from their monastery. The count, out of respect for the monks, put aside the book which he had in his hands, to pay attention to them. One of the monks, called G., a man of distinction, of good reputation and even better life, with a sharp intellect and a penetrating knowledge of written matter, took up the book and began to read. He came on the section where Vegetius Renatus gives detailed instructions as to how, by means of oak timbers bound together, the work made good may be speedily exposed to capture. The count, discerning how keen and serious the monk was in understanding what he was reading, said: "My dear Brother G., exactly what you are finding in that text, you shall see demonstrated in effect tomorrow." He ordered an iron chaldron, strengthened with iron bands and hanging from a strong chain, to be filled with oil of nuts, hempseed and linseed, and then to be sealed with a strong iron lid firmly wedged. He then had it set in a furnace until it glowed with the great heat, and the oil within was boiling. It was taken out, and after cooling the chain by throwing water on it, it was hooked to the pole of a mangonel and shot, in its fiery state, with careful aim and with all the force of the slings, straight at the oak timber in the mine-shaft. It burst on the target, setting alight the timber in the mine; the oil poured out, providing fuel for the flames, and ran in balls of fire . . . Gerald . . . offered surrender . . . and peace was made, the count restoring to Gerald all his lands, but on condition that neither he nor his heirs should ever rebuild the tower of Montreuil or any other fortifications.

REBUILDING THE CHOIR OF CANTERBURY CATHEDRAL

(*Historical Works of Gervase of Canterbury,* ed. W. Stubbs, Rolls Series 73, **i,** 1879, 3 ff.)

Though this famous account has been printed and translated several times, it cannot be omitted, for it gives a more detailed picture of mediæval building operations than any other contemporary record. It has also the special interest that it refers to one of the two earliest works in England that can strictly be termed "Gothic" in style—the other being the choir, now mostly destroyed, of Wells Cathedral— and that it proves that the Canterbury (though not the contemporary Wells) style was due to a French architect from Sens (see plan, page 145).

The burning of Prior Conrad's choir, 1174.

In the year 1174, by the . . . judgment of God, Christ Church at Canterbury was burned, that is to say that glorious choir which had been splendidly completed by the diligence and care of Prior Conrad, in the forty-fourth year from its dedication. . . . Not only was the choir destroyed by this fire, but also the Infirmary with St. Mary's Chapel, and some other buildings in the courtyard. . . . [The monks gathered the relics of the saints from their tombs in the ruined choir and placed them in the nave at the altar of the Holy Cross]; for five years they remained in the nave of the church, in grief and sadness, divided from the layfolk by a low wall.

In the meantime the brothers sought counsel how and by what means the burnt church might be repaired, but they were unsuccessful. The columns of the church, ordinarily termed the pillars, were so weakened by the great heat of the fire, with pieces falling off and hardly able to stand, that they put it beyond even the wisest to make any useful suggestions. So they called together both French and English architects (*artifices*), but they disagreed among themselves. Some said that they could repair these columns without risk to the upper part of the building; others, contradicting their arguments, said that the whole church must be pulled down if the monks wished to live in safety. It was not surprising that this view, though correct, shocked the monks, for they could hardly hope that in their days so great an undertaking might be completed by any ingenuity of man.

Among the other architects had come one from Sens, named William, a most clever artist in wood and stone, and extremely active. The monks let the rest go and, impressed by his vigour and ability, engaged him for their work. Under God's providence, the conduct of the job was entrusted to him. He spent many days with the monks in a careful survey of the burnt walls, above and below, inside and out, but for the time being avoided saying what would have to be done, in order not to shock them too severely in their enfeebled state of mind. But he kept on getting ready what was needed for the work, either personally or through agents. When he saw that the monks were somewhat more cheerful he admitted that the pillars damaged by the fire, with everything above them, would have to be taken down if they wished to have a safe and seemly building. In the end, after hearing his arguments, they agreed to the scheme he proposed, anxious to obtain a safe result. So, even if not willingly, at least with resignation, they consented to have the burnt choir demolished.

Arrangements were made for buying stone overseas [from Caen in Normandy], and (William of Sens) designed ingenious machinery (*tornamenta*) for loading and unloading the ships and for the transport of mortar and stones. He handed templates for shaping the stones to the carvers (*sculptoribus*) who had been taken on, and made other careful preparations of this kind. And so the choir, condemned to destruction, was demolished and nothing else was done that year (1174–75). . . .

Let us see what our Master William (of Sens) has been doing in the meantime. As I said before, he began to make ready what was needed for the new work and for the destruction of the old. The first year was taken up with these arrangements. In the next year—that is, starting from the feast of St. Bertin (5th September), he built four pillars before winter, that is two on each side; and after winter was over two more, so that there was a row of three on each side; on these and on the outer walls of the aisles he set arches and vaults in a proper manner, namely three keystones on each side. I put "keystone" for the whole bay, in that the keystone set in the middle seems to bind together and lock the parts that come towards it from all sides. The second year (1175–6) was taken up with these operations.

In the third year (1176–77) he built two pillars on each side, the two last being adorned with marble shafts set around them; these were made into main piers because upon them the choir and the (eastern) transepts join together. After setting on these pillars their keystones and vault, he inserted many marble shafts into the lower triforium from the great (crossing) tower to the piers aforesaid, that is to the (eastern) transept. Above that triforium he formed another (clerestory) stage of different materials, with the upper windows; then he set three bays of the great vault, from the tower to the transepts. All these works seemed to us, and to all who saw them, unequalled and most worthy of praise. Gladdened by so glorious a start, and becoming really hopeful of completion, we set out with all our powers to speed the work. So in these tasks the third year was employed and the beginning of the fourth (*i.e.* to the end of 1177).

In the summer of (1178), beginning from the (eastern) crossing, he built ten pillars, five on each side. The first two of these he enriched with marble shafts to match the other two main piers. Above these he set the ten arches and vaults. Then, after he had completed the triforia and clerestory windows on each side, and as he was erecting the centerings (*machinas*) for turning the great vault, at the beginning of the fifth year (September 1178), the scaffolding suddenly broke beneath his feet and he fell to the ground amid stones and timbers. His fall, from the level of the capitals of the high vault, was about fifty feet. Seriously injured by the blows of the timbers and stones, he was rendered helpless as regarded himself and the work. Nobody else was in any way hurt; only the master was injured, by the vengeance of God or the Devil's ill-will.

Thus the crippled master stayed in bed for some time in the hands of physicians, hoping to recover; but his hopes were vain and he got no better. Since winter was coming on and it was essential to finish the high vault, he handed over the completion of the work to one of the monks, both hard-working and clever, who acted as warden of the masons (*qui cementariis præfuit*). Since he was a young man, and might seem to be more highly skilled than others more powerful and influential, a great deal of envy and backbiting arose from this. The master, however, ordained what was to be done first, and what next, from his bed. So the bay between the four main piers, at whose keystone the choir and transepts seem to meet, was finished. Before winter two other vaults on each side (*i.e.* those of the eastern transepts) were completed before heavy rainstorms stopped the work. On this the fourth year was occupied and the start of the fifth. In that same fourth year there was an eclipse of the sun on the [13th] September about the sixth hour (12–2 p.m.), before the master's fall.

Since the master found that he was getting no better for the skill and treatment of his doctors, he resigned his commission, crossed the Channel, and returned to his home in France. There succeeded him in charge of the job another named William, English by birth, short in stature but honest and highly skilled in several crafts. He brought to completion in the summer of the fifth year (1179) the transepts on each side, north and south, and turned the vault above the High Altar, unable to be made the previous year because of the rains, though all had been prepared for it. He also laid the foundations for the extension of the church at the east end, where a new chapel of St. Thomas was to be built. For here was assigned to him (Becket) the place where he celebrated his first mass, in the chapel of the Holy Trinity; where he used to prostrate himself with tears and prayers, and beneath whose crypt he was buried for so many years. There God through his merits performed many miracles, and there rich and poor, kings and princes, worshipped him, so that the sound of his praise went forth from it all over the world.

In digging these foundations Master William (the Englishman) began to disturb the bones of monks (buried in their cemetery). These bones were carefully collected and reburied in a large pit on the south side, in the corner between the chapel and the Infirmary. After making a very strong foundation of stone and mortar for the outer wall, he built the wall of the crypt up to the sills of the windows. So the fifth year was spent on these works, and the sixth began. In the spring, that is of the sixth year after the fire (1180) and at the season when work began again, the monks became very anxious to prepare the choir so as to be able to enter it at Easter. The master, seeing how keen the monks were on this, set himself manfully to work to satisfy their wishes. He therefore made the utmost haste to build the wall which surrounds the choir and the presbytery, set up the three altars in the presbytery, and prepared a suitable resting-place for St. Dunstan and St. Ælfege. A timber partition containing three glass windows was also set up on the east, between the last pair of pillars but one, to keep out the weather. . . .

The convent was ejected from the choir by the fire, like Adam from Paradise, on 5th September, 1174, about the ninth hour (3 p.m.), and remained in the nave of the church for five years seven months and thirteen days. It returned to the new choir in the year 1180, in the month of April, the nineteenth day of the month, about the ninth hour (3 p.m.) on the eve of Easter . . .

Our architect (*artifex*) had built outside the choir four altars where the bodies of the holy archbishops were placed as they had formerly been, as above stated . . . Moreover, in the same summer of the sixth year the outer wall around St. Thomas's chapel, begun before the preceding winter, was raised to the level of turning the vault. The master had begun a tower at the east end, outside the ambulatory wall, and its lower vault had been finished before the winter. The chapel of the Holy Trinity, mentioned above, was demolished to ground level; it had hitherto been left standing out of reverence for St. Thomas who lay beneath its crypt. The bodies of the saints buried in the upper part were translated elsewhere, and lest the memory of what occurred in their translation should be lost, a few words must be said. On the 8th of July the altar of the Holy Trinity was broken up and of it the altar of St. John the Apostle was made; I say this, that the record be not lost of this holy stone, since St. Thomas celebrated his first mass upon it and in course of time frequently performed the office there. [Account of the translation of various saints.]

After the translation of these fathers had thus been carried out, that chapel with its crypt was pulled down to the ground; only the translation of St. Thomas himself was held back for the completion of his chapel. For it is fitting and reasonable that a translation of such importance should be most solemn and in public. A timber chapel, adequate enough for the place and circumstances, was built above and around his tomb. Outside its walls a foundation was laid of stone and mortar, and on this eight pillars of the new crypt, with their capitals, were erected. The master wisely (*prudenter*) opened a passage from the old to the new crypt. The sixth year was completed and the seventh begun in these matters, but before going on with the works of the seventh year (1181) it may not be amiss to go over some of the earlier works which have either been overlooked or deliberately left out for the sake of brevity.

It has been said above that after the fire almost all of the old choir was pulled down, and changed to a new and more majestic design (*augustioris formæ*). It should now be stated what the differences were between the old and new builds. The pillars of both old and new are alike in shape and diameter, but vary in height, for the new were made taller by almost twelve feet. In the old capitals the work was plain, while the new ones had fine carving. Around the choir there used to be 22 pillars, but now 28; there all the arches and every part of the work were plain, or cut with an axe, not a chisel; here is proper carving everywhere. There used to be no marble shafts, while here they are numberless. There, around the choir, were plain vaults, here they have arch-ribs and bosses. There a wall raised on pillars separated the transepts from the choir; here they are not divided by any partition but appear to come together at a single keystone set in the midst of the great vault, carried on the four main piers. There, the wooden ceiling was adorned with uncommon paintings; here, the vaulting is well built of stone and light tufa. There was a single triforium gallery; here are two in the choir, and a third in the aisle of the church. All this can be better understood on sight than by description.

Here it must be recorded that the new work is higher than the old by as much as the clerestory windows of the choir, and those of its side-aisles, rise above the marble string-course. And should anyone in time to come wonder why the choir was given such a breadth near the tower, yet was narrowed in so at the head of the church, it may not be pointless to give the reasons. One of them is that the two towers placed on either side of the old church, those of St. Anselm and St. Andrew, would not allow the width of the choir to continue in a straight line. Another reason is that it was decided to set the chapel of St. Thomas at the head of the church, where stood the chapel of the Holy Trinity, much narrower than the choir. Thus the master, not wishing to pull down the aforesaid towers and not being able to move them wholesale, designed the width of the choir in a straight line as far as the junction with the towers. From there onwards, slanting slightly away from the towers, yet keeping as much space as he could outside the choir for the processions which frequently have to pass there, he drew in the work gradually, so that opposite the altar at the third pillar it might be contracted to fit the width of the chapel of the Holy Trinity.

Beyond are built four pillars on each side, at the same span as before, but of a different design, and after these four more arranged in a circle, the work above being brought round to end (in an apse)—such is the arrangement of the pillars. The outer wall, which runs from the towers already mentioned, first goes in a straight line and then curves inwards as an ambulatory (*girum*), so that the building is there ended by the walls of either side joining as one. All this can be more clearly, as well as pleasantly, seen by the eyes than told or written; but this much has been said to explain the difference between the old and the new work.

Now let us see more precisely what our masons finished in this seventh year after the fire (1181): in short, the new crypt of a sufficiently handsome design, and above the crypt the outer walls of the aisles up to the marble capitals. The master could not or thought better not to build the windows, or the internal pillars, on account of rainy weather setting in; so the seventh year was completed and the eighth begun.

In this eighth year (1182) the master erected the eight pillars within, and turned the arches, vault and windows of the ambulatory. He also raised the tower (*i.e.* the Corona, or Becket's Crown) to the sills of the clerestory windows below the vault. In the ninth year (1183) the work was stood off for lack of funds. In the tenth year (1184) the upper windows of the tower, with the vault, were finished. Above the pillars were built a lower triforium and an upper (clerestory), with its windows, and the high vault; and the outer roof where the cross stands on the summit, and the aisle roof ready for laying the lead. The tower (Corona) too was roofed, and much else was done this year. On the 15th December (1184) Baldwin, bishop of Worcester, was elected (as archbishop of Canterbury) to rule the church of Canterbury, and was enthroned at Canterbury on the feast of St. Dunstan following, the 19th May (1185).

A BISHOP AMONG THE GENERALS (Mortet 1911, 96–8).

Hugh de Noyers (Bishop of Auxerre, 1183–1206) was endowed with knowledge, energetic in getting things done, among the skilful yet more skilled than they, ... with the powers of a most fluent orator, of so lively a capacity in letters that in any of the liberal or mechanic arts he had ready words suited to the matter in hand, as if he had acquired complete mastery of the subject.... He delighted in the company of knights and was glad to debate with them on military affairs; to this purpose he used to read again and again the book (*De re militari*) of

Vegetius Renatus, which treats of these subjects, and from which he drew many theories to put before the soldiers.*

AN ARCHITECT-CONTRACTOR (P.R.O., Exch. T.R., Misc. Books 279, f. 197, printed in L. F. Salzman, *Building in England down to 1540*, 439–41).

*This contract, here translated from the French, is an outstanding proof of the combination of the two functions, of building contractor and architect, in a single person. The mason involved, William of Helpeston (Helpston, Northamptonshire), had a distinguished career as Master Mason for Chester, Flint and North Wales from 1361 and was surveyor of murage for the city of Chester; his status was certainly that of a professional man of high standing. The contract for his building of the eastern chapels at Vale Royal Abbey is noteworthy for another reason: that the chapels to be undertaken, together with one already built by him, are on a most unusual plan. This plan, of polygonal and square chapels alternating, is in fact unique in England, but is closely based upon that of the eastern chapels of Toledo Cathedral, the metropolitan church of Castile, built between 1226 and 1238. It can hardly be a coincidence that it was precisely during the eighteen months preceding this contract that there had been intense diplomatic activity leading to a treaty of alliance between England and Castile (**P. E. Russell**, The English Intervention in Spain and Portugal . . . , 1955, pp. 1–2). The contract, with the plan recovered by excavation (F. H. Thompson in The Antiquaries Journal, XXII, 1962, pp. 183–207), thus demonstrates one of the means by which elements of architectural design passed from one country to another* (see plans, page 161).

The building of the eastern chapels of Vale Royal Abbey, 1359.
This indenture made between the noble Lord Edward Prince of Wales, his chaplains the Abbot and convent of his of Vale Royal of the one part, and Master William de Helpeston, mason, of the other part witnesseth that the said William has undertaken the work of masonry of twelve chapels around the choir of the church aforesaid to be made towards the east and to perform them with the help of God in good and suitable manner, changing and ordaining his moulds at his will and stopping the blind tracerywork (*le orbe oeuereigne*) of the abovesaid chapels without challenge from anyone, beginning the said work of the chapels aforesaid at the plinth-course above ground level, in height to the crest of the parapet of the chapel next to the said choir already new built by the said William. And also the said William shall name and choose all the masons and other workmen when he has need for the said chapels: that is to say masons, porters, mortar-makers, winders-up of stones, for whom the said Abbot and convent shall purchase a

*Vegetius wrote under Valentinian II, 375–92.

commission from our said lord the Prince to cause the said workmen to come when found within his lordship by the said William; and when they are not profitable for the said work they shall be removed by the said William at his will. So that there be not delay nor damage to the said work, and for this the said William shall find iron and steel to make and amend the tools of the masons aforesaid, that is to say axes and chisels, without being charged with any other tools. And for this the said William shall pay the said masons, porters, mortar-makers and winders of stone their wages and the Smith for his work on the said axes and chisels, without any other charges to be found touching the work of the chapels aforesaid, apart from the work of a tracing-house in the same church in a certain place settled between them that is to say in the North Transept, taking from the said Abbot and convent for the said tracing-house 10 marks of silver (£6 13s. 4d.) in hand. And for this the said Abbot and convent shall find all manner of workmen and all other things to hand on the site (prestz sur la place) touching the work aforesaid for the provision (garmissement) of the said William. And also the said Abbot and convent shall find for the said masons and workmen houses, fuel and bedding (liter), and in case the said work should be delayed or the said William damaged by the said Abbot and convent, that then amends shall be made to the said things to hand on the site (prestz sur la place) touching the work William by the said Abbot and convent according to the assessment of good men of the country and masons, for which work of the chapels aforesaid our said lord the Prince will pay yearly to the said William in the said Abbey by the hands of the said Abbot 200 gold or silver marks (£133 6s. 8d.) at the feasts of Michaelmas and Easter by equal portions until the sum of £860 in gold or silver has been fully paid, the first term of payment beginning at the feast of Michaelmas next following the making of these presents. And in case our said lord the Prince ceases to make his payment to the said William after the third part of the said work have been made that then the third part of a corrody and of a pension of 40s. granted to the said William for term of his life by the said Abbot and convent according to the purport of the deed of the same Abbot and convent shall remain to the said William for term of his life according to the same deed, and the remainder of the said corrody and pension shall stop altogether in case no fault be found in the said Abbot and convent of the things abovesaid or any of them, and otherwise the said William shall be free to make his profit elsewhere without challenge from our said lord the Prince or of the said Abbot and convent or any other. And in case our said lord the Prince ceases to make his payment to the said William before the third part of the said work be made and no default be found in the said Abbot and convent of the things abovesaid or of any of them, that then the said William shall be free to make his profit without challenge from anyone, and the said corrody and pension shall cease altogether. And after the completion of the said third part of the said work, until the accomplishment of three parts of the same work divided into four, the said corrody and pension shall be increased proportionately according to the amount of work of the said William towards the third part of it as above is said. And after the accomplishment of the said three parts of the said work, in case our said lord the Prince cease to make his payment to the said William, that then the said William shall be free to make his profit without challenge from anyone and the said corrody and pension shall remain entirely to the said William according to the purport of the deed abovesaid. So always that the said Abbot and convent be found in any default during the said work by which the said work be delayed or disturbed, that then the foresaid corrody and pension remain entirely to the said William for the term of his life according to the purport of the deed abovesaid. In witness of which thing the parties aforesaid to these indentures have put their seals. Given etc. at Chester the 20th day of August the year etc. of England the 33rd and of France the 20th hand 12 *l.**

A COMMISSION OF CONSULTANTS (B.M., Additional MS. 15803, f. 116).

Throughout the later centuries of the Middle Ages it was common for the administration of greater building works to consult commissions of leading architects brought from a distance. In some cases the members of the commission differed among themselves and a decision was taken by, for example, the chapter of a cathedral or monastic church. In the present example the commissioners were led by a single architect, nominated by the famous Master Raymond du Temple, and his advice was apparently accepted without further ado.

Expenses of consultants at Troyes Cathedral, 1401.

For the expenses of M. Jean Gaillart who was sent by my said lords to Paris to speak to Master Raymond (du Temple), master of the King's works, and to know if he could come here to survey the church: who excused himself in the presence of M. d'Auxerre (? the bishop of Auxerre) and recommended to the said M. Jean Gaillart Master Jean Aubelet and Master Jean Prevost his nephew for that survey. The said M. Jean Gaillart left Troyes to go on the said journey the 29th October, 1401 and remained until the 17th November following inclusive, and spent as appears by the accounts written by his hand 12 *l.**

*The French *livre* (divided into 20 *sous*, each of 12 *deniers*) had depreciated by the mid-fourteenth century to one-quarter of the value of English money; by the mid-fifteenth century to about one-eighth.

The said Master Jean Aubelet and his nephew and their servant, with three horses, arrived at Troyes the Thursday after St. Andrew (30th November) about prime (6–9 a.m.) and immediately set themselves to survey the church from top to bottom in the presence of our lord the Bishop, there being summoned to accompany them Thomas Michelin, Colin Guignon, Jean Gilot, masons; Jean de Nantes and Raymond, carpenters; and the other craftsmen of the church, who were always with the aforesaid Aubelet and Prevost. And the said Master Jean Aubelet had (the report of) the survey written, and devised concerning certain piers and arches to be made above the vaults and elsewhere, and this was brought and read in full chapter. And they were lodged in the hostel of the Swan.

For the expenses of the said Master Jean and his nephew the said Thursday for dinner—Nothing, because he dined with my lord the Bishop—but the other craftsmen were all at dinner at the said hostel of the Swan and spent   16s. 8d.

For supper that day at the said hostel, with M. Jean Gaillart and the Master of the Work and the craftsmen, with bread and wine and other things taken at the said hostel of which mention will hereafter be made, spent for commons   6s. 8d.

Also the Friday following for fish at dinner and at supper, for the company as before   17s. 6d.

And for herrings and for tarts   2s. 6d.

The Saturday following at dinner for fish   15s.

And in herrings and tarts that day   2s. 6d.

Also for bread, wine, meat and fine peas and other things taken at the said hostel the said Thursday and Friday for dinner and supper and the said Saturday for dinner by account made with the hostess (*la capitaine*)   77s. 6d.

Also for the expenses of their three horses for the said whole Thursday and Friday and for the said Saturday to dinner time, foddered at 6 bl.* for each horse a day, making   17s. 6d.

To the said Master Jean Aubelet as a gift made to him at the commandment of the lords for his trouble in having made the said survey and for his return etc.   20 écus   22 *l.* 10s.

To his clerk for his pains in writing the said survey (report)   22s. 6d.

To Jean de Nantes, carpenter, who was for 3 days with

---

*"bl." presumably stands for *blanc*, a coin of 5 *deniers*; this would amount to 18s. 9d., but there must have been a difference in exchange value with the local currency at Troyes.

the said masters Jean Aubelet and Jean Prevost, 3s. 9d. a
day, making   11s. 3d.
 To Raymond, carpenter, who was with the said Jean de
Nantes for the said 3 days   10s.
 To Thomas Michelin, mason, for the like reason, for the
said 3 days   11s. 3d.
  To Jean Gilot, mason, for the said 3 days   10s.
  To Felisot le Couvreur for the said 3 days   10s.
  To Simon Daubetriz for the like reason   10s.
  To Nicholas Matan, servant of Jean de Nantes, for 3
days   10s.
  To Colin Guignon who was summoned there for 2 days   6s. 8d.
  To Jean Dosse, mason, for 3 days   10s.
    Total   47 l. 17s. 6d.

*The method of sending experts was used also by central admin-
istrations responsible for the maintenance of relatively distant buildings,
and among many instances is seen at work in France during the English
ascendancy under Henry VI. The accounts of the Receiver-General of
Normandy for 1428–92 (Paris, Bibliothèque Nationale, MS. fr. 4488,
p. 646) include a payment of 14 l. tournois (then at approximately 8 l.
to £1 sterling) "to Master Jacques de Soteville, master of the works of
carpentry of our lord the King at Rouen, and Master Jenson Salvart,
master of the works of masonry at the same place", with their servant,
"for a journey made by them by the orders of the lord Cardinal of
England (Cardinal Beaufort) and of the corporation of the city of
Rouen, to the town of Harfleur, with Master Jean Dole, Councillor of
our said lord the King to see visit and draw up in writing (a report on)
the repairs, fortifications and defects, necessary to be done (or made
good) in haste on the walls, towers and gates of Harfleur, spending
7 days from 25th August, 1429."*

*(For details of the works done in Normandy for the English Kings
between 1415 and 1449, see* The History of the King's Works, I, 1963,
457–63).

A BISHOP AND HIS ARCHITECTS (Westminster Abbey
Muniments, 16040, 16046; printed by J. Armitage Robinson in
Proceedings of the Somerset Archæological and Natural History Society,
LX for 1914, 1915, pt. ii, pp. 1–10).

*Bishop Oliver King of Bath and Wells decided, as a result of a
remarkable dream, to rebuild the Norman priory church of Bath. As
architects for the new church he employed the brothers Robert and
William Vertue. Robert, the elder brother, had worked at Westminster
Abbey with his father Adam Vertue in 1475–80, and after an absence of*

three years, during which he was probably travelling as an "improver" aged about 21–24, returned as a fully paid mason, from 1483 to 1490. By 1499, if not earlier, he was in charge of royal works at Greenwich for Henry VII. The boast recorded in the first of the two letters here reproduced probably implies that some part of Robert's wanderyears had been spent in working his way around France and inspecting its major churches. Spelling has been modernized, but the letters are in English.

The new design for the church of Bath cathedral priory, c. 1502 (Fig. 5). (Bishop Oliver King to Sir Reginald Bray) Robert and William Virtue have been here with me, that can make unto you report of the state and forwardness of this our church of Bath, and also of the vault devised for the chancel of the said church—whereunto as they say now there shall be none so goodly, neither in England nor in France—and thereof they make them fast and sure. They have with them a writing of recess [French *recez*, an abstract or minute of proceedings] upon the communication between them and me had in all things, for to show the same to you; wherefore I am the shorter in that behalf.

I beseech you to remember Cunesby, one of the king's serjeants-at-the-law, for the writing the prior here should make unto us two for our chantries and other suffrages (prayers) to be had in this monastery for ever.*

Item, that I may have knowledge from my fellow Dawtry of Hampton what bargain he hath made for the hundred cases of glasses to be had out of Normandy,† with the price of every hundred cases both of coloured glasses and others.

This church as far as I can see shall be thoroughly covered (roofed) far before Allhallow tide (1st November) next coming, with the leave of Our Lord, Who send unto you the accomplishment of your goodly desires. At my monastery of Bath foresaid the 18th day of January with the scribbling hand of him that is

all your own
Oliver Bath

To Master Sir Reginald Bray

Sir,

I beseech you to be good loving father in mine absence to my niece Dame Elizabeth Philpot in all her causes; and that ye give no licence to any freemason to absent him from this building. Divers masons

---

*Perpetual chantries were to be established in Bath Priory for Bishop Oliver King and for Prior William Bird.

†Normandy was one of the chief places of supply of coloured glass for stained glass windows.

there be that will not come till after Candlemas (2nd February), trusting that in the mean season they will cause you to be entreated to write unto me for to suffer them to work in other men's businesses. One there is called Thomas Lynn, one the most necessary mason for me that I can have, and one of them that is appointed by Robert Vertue.

It shall please you to remember Mr. Dawtry for the Normandy glass, and Mr. Cunesby for our book for our chantries and other suffrages. And thus I recommend me unto you with all mine heart. At my monastery of Bath the 25th day of January where is mine hab. . . (*8 letters lost*) harm, I perceive it well.

all your
Oliver Bath

To Master Sir Reginald Bray

(*The Vertues, and particularly Robert, were deeply involved in the many royal works being carried out for Henry VII, at Greenwich Palace, the Tower of London, and especially with the plans for the intended memorial chapel for Henry VI at Westminster Abbey, which became Henry VII's own Chapel. Thomas Lynn had evidently been recommended by Robert Vertue as a trustworthy deputy to carry out the works at Bath in accordance with the designs.*)

B

Texts on Æsthetics
and Symbolism

*A*LTHOUGH *philosophers of the Middle Ages, especially in the thirteenth century, were deeply concerned with æsthetics, their treatment was primarily theoretical and had little effect upon the "applied æsthetics" of architectural style. What can be discerned is an alternation of waves of keen interest in decorative enrichment with corresponding revulsions of taste in favour of what is often described as puritanism in art: the cult of simplicity. Practical factors such as economy clearly played a part in this ebb-and-flow, but it is probable that it fundamentally corresponded to a deeper awareness of modes of religious thought. Put in its simplest form the antithesis is between the spending of wealth upon enrichments for the glory of God, and the view that God is a Spirit not to be delighted with any material pomps of this world. Scriptural texts could be found, and were bandied to and fro, in support of each extreme view—the Old Testament, with its description of the Temple of Solomon and its underlying devotion to the material house of God in the earthly Jerusalem, providing most of the ammunition for the proponents of costly architecture and its enrichment; the Gospels supporting the negative view of the total unimportance of artistic show. Most of the sources directly applicable to architecture are short, and appear in the text, but two longer extracts must be given here. Both were written in the decade 1120–30 and exactly coincide with the first appearance of Gothic architecture: they remained fundamental to the understanding of all subsequent church art.*

THE CISTERCIAN VIEW (*Apologia ad Guillelmum, Sancti Theodorici Remensis abbatem*, in *Sancti Bernardi opera*, ed. Mabillon, 1690, col. 538–40; 1839, I, i, col. 1242–44; Migne, *Patrologia latina*, CLXXXII, col. 914–16; Mortet 1911, 366–70).

Saint Bernard and the church art of his time, c. 1124.
... But these are small matters: I come to greater things which seem less important than they are because they are so familiar. I pass over

the tricks of preachers ... which for me in some way recall the ancient rites of the Jews. But let it be, these things may be done in honour of God. Yet I as a monk put to monks the question which a pagan put to pagans; said he (Persius, *Satires*, II, v. 69): "Tell, pontiffs, what has gold to do with holiness?" I say: Tell, ye poor (for I am not concerned with the verse, but the sense), tell, I say, ye poor, if ye be really poor, what has gold to do with holiness? Indeed it is one thing for bishops, another for monks. For we know that the former, having to provide as they do for both the learned and the ignorant, arouse the devotion of fleshly people with material adornments, seeing that they cannot do so with things of the spirit. But we who have already left our people, who have abandoned whatever is lovely and precious on this earth for Christ, who have regarded as dung all things shining with beauty, delightful in sound, sweetly smelling, exquisite in taste, pleasant to touch, in fact every kind of bodily amusement, in order to win Christ—how, I insist, do we mean to arouse such men's devotion? What fruits of these, I say, do we look for, the wonder of fools or the delight of the simple? Since we mingle among men, have we perhaps learned their works, and kept even now their graven images?

To speak frankly, is it not avarice which is the cause of all this, the very service of idols? We do not look for the fruit, but for the gift. If you ask in what manner, I reply, in a remarkable manner: for by a certain art of this kind money is cast out to multiply; with it one speculates to accumulate (*expenditur ut augeatur*), and casting forth reaps abundance. For certainly men are provoked, by the mere sight of rich vanities intended to be seen, more towards offerings than towards prayers. So riches are drawn by riches, so money brings money; for I know not how, but where most riches are seen, there offerings flow most liberally. The eyes are feasted upon relics covered with gold, and coffers are opened. The reliquary of a male or female saint takes on a lovely form, and the gaudier the casket the greater is the attributed holiness. Men run to kiss the relic, they are induced to give; and beauty is more admired than sanctity is revered. So in church are placed, not just jewelled crowns, but wheels encircled about with lamps, no less shining than the gems with which they are set. We see also candlesticks like standing trees made by wondrous craftsmanship of the artist from a great weight of metal, and sparkling with jewels as much as with the lamps they carry. What, you may wonder, is sought in all this, the remorse of the penitent, or the admiration of beholders? O vanity of vanities, yet not more vain than insane! The church glitters upon its walls, and its poor are destitute. It clothes its stone with gold and leaves its children naked. The eyes of the rich are gladdened at the expense of the needy. The curious find matter for pleasure where the wretched do not even find sustenance; and how may we revere the images of the saints with which the very pavement, trodden by the feet, abounds? Often someone spits on an angel's face, and often the countenance of one of the saints is stamped on by the feet of the passers-by. And if these images are not sacred, why not omit the fine colours? Why adorn what will soon be made filthy? Why paint what needs must be trodden upon? Of what worth are beautiful shapes where they must be dirtied by constant dust? In fine, what have these to do with the poor, with monks, with spiritual men? Yet against the verse of the poet above mentioned, this reply may be made in the words of the prophet: "Lord, I have loved the splendour (*decorem*) of thy house and the place of habitation of thy glory."* Agreed: let us permit even these things to be done in the church since, though they be harmful to the vain and miserly, yet are not so to the simple and devout.

But in the cloisters, among the brothers reading, what are they doing, this laughable monstrosity, a certain strange deformed beauty and beautiful deformity? What are they doing there, filthy monkeys? savage lions? monstrous centaurs? half-men? spotted tigers? (*maculosæ tigrides*) soldiers fighting? huntsmen sounding their horns? You see under a single head many bodies, and again one body with many heads. Here on a four-footed beast is the tail of a serpent, there on a fish an animal's head. There a beast puts forth a horse's head, but drags the hinder half of a goat; here a horned creature bears a horse behind it. Such a multitude in fact, and so strange a variety of divers forms appears, that it can better be read in marbles than in books, and easier to spend the whole day in looking at all this than in meditating on the law of God. In the name of God! if one is not ashamed at these absurdities, why not feel sorrow at the cost?

A MANUAL OF SYMBOLISM (Honorius of Autun, *De gemma animle*, in Migne, *Patrologia latina*, CLXXII, col. 586 ff.; Mortet 1929, 14–18).

Written before 1130, the famous treatise of Honorius of Autun provided for the Gothic period a programme of symbolism, at the same time a justification and an outline specification for church architecture. Only a selection is given here of the more strictly architectural sections of the work, sufficient for the interpretation of what the patrons of church building meant to achieve. The actual

---

*Psalm XXVI 8, literally translated from the Vulgate Latin; the Douai version has: "I have loved, O lord, the beauty of thy house; and the place where thy glory dwelleth." Most versions avoid the meaning accepted in the Middle Ages, even by Saint Bernard, and in fact supported by both by the Hebrew and LXX Greek (see *The Jerusalem Bible*, 1966, 807, notes *in loc.*).

8—TMA * *

achievements, translated into practical terms, remained always within the competence of architect and artist.

The church, its symbolism and meaning; before c. 1130.

Chapter XXIX. The position of the Church. Churches are directed to the East, where the sun rises, because in them the Sun of justice is worshipped and it is foretold that it is in the East that Paradise our home is set. In the (material) church the (living) Church is symbolized, congregated in it for the service of God. This House is set upon a stone foundation, and the Church is founded on the sure rock of Christ. The one rises on high between four walls, while the Church grows to a height of virtues through the four Gospels. This house is built of hard stones, the Church put together of those strong in faith and works. The stones are held together with mortar, and the faithful linked by the bond of love. The sanctuary is the first fruits of the Church gathered from the Jews; the outer house (*i.e.* the nave), those who serve God in active life.

Chapter XXX. The church windows. The transparent windows, which keep out the weather and let in the light, are the Doctors who resist the storm of heresies and pour in the light of the Church's teaching. The glass in the windows, through which pass the rays of light, is the mind of the Doctors, seeing heavenly things as in a glass darkly.

Chapter XXXI. The columns of the church. The columns which support the house are the bishops, who bear up the organization (*machinam*) of the Church by their righteous life. The beams which hold the fabric together are the princes of this world, who provide the Church with protection. The tiles of the roof, keeping off the wet from the house, were soldiers who protect Church from heathens and foes.

Chapter XXXII. Paintings. The paintings on the ceilings (*laquearium*) are examples of the just, representing for the Church the adornment of good behaviour. For three reasons is the painting made : first, because it is reading matter for laymen; secondly, for the adornment of the building; thirdly, as a memorial of our predecessors in life.

C. XXXIII. The crown (nimbus) in the church. The lights (haloes) painted in circular form round the heads of saints in the church indicate that they enjoy the light of eternal glory. They are depicted in the form of a round shield because they are now safeguarded by the divine protection as if with a shield. Hence they sing joyfully : "O Lord, thou hast crowned us, as with a shield of thy good will."*
The tradition of carving images began in the Law, when Moses

*Psalm V.13 (Douai version).

made two cherubim of gold at the Lord's command. The painting of churches took its rise from Solomon, who caused divers paintings to be made in the Temple of the Lord. The use too of candlestick and censer began under the Law.

C. XXXIV. The pavement. The pavement trodden by feet is the common folk by whose work the Church is maintained. The crypts made beneath the ground are the cultivators of the inner life. The altar on which sacrifice is offered is Christ, upon whom the Church's sacrifice is accepted. Thus the body of Christ is made upon the altar that the people believing in him may by him be re-made, and made one with Christ, as many stones form one altar. Relics are hidden in the altar because all the treasures of wisdom and knowledge are concealed in Christ. Upon the altar are placed reliquaries; they are the apostles and martyrs who are recorded to have suffered for Christ. The palls and altar-cloths with which the altar is enriched are the confessors and virgins by whose works Christ is adorned.

C. XLI. The crown (of lights). The crown is hung in the temple for three reasons: firstly, that the church may be decorated by it, illumined by its lights; secondly, that in seeing it we may be reminded that those who here serve God devoutly receive the crown of life and the light of rejoicing; and thirdly, that the heavenly Jerusalem, after whose shape it is made, may be brought to our minds. For it is made of gold, silver, brass and iron ... The turrets of the crown are protecting the Church with writings: the lamps shine with its good acts. The jewels sparkling in the crown are those who shine in virtue ... The chain that holds the crown up is hope, by which the Church is held up to the heavens above earthly affairs. The ring above, from which it hangs, is God on whom all things depend.

C. XLIV. The belfry. The belfry placed on high is lofty preaching which speaks of heavenly matters. Nor is the cock placed above the belfry without reason, for the cock arouses sleepers, and in this way the priest, the cock of God, is warned to arouse the sleepers to matins by the bell.

C. XLVII. (Church plans). .... Churches made in the form of a cross show how the people of the Church are crucified by this world; those made round in the form of a circle show that the Church is built throughout the circuit of the globe to become the circle of the crown of eternity through love.

C

Texts on Style
and Fashion

*T*HE *leaders of mediæval thought concerned themselves with the general problem of whether material beauty should be attempted in the building and adornment of churches, but they were not so actively interested in the style of what was designed. This has led to the false assumption that educated men of the period simply accepted style and changing fashion heedlessly. Many texts prove the contrary: changes were keenly observed, and in particular the great change from Romanesque to Gothic form.*

THE STYLE OF TENTH-CENTURY ANTIQUITY (*Chronicon Abbatiæ Rameseiensis,* ed. W. D. Macray, Rolls Series 83, 1886, 41, 85).

Ramsey Abbey: a stone church with two towers built, 968–9.
Then having agreed on a plan they prepared during the whole of the winter that followed all that seemed needful for the future building, and sought out whatever the skill of the masons might foresee was required in the way of iron or wooden instruments. So when winter was at length past and spring raised her head sown with flowers, amassed treasures were dispersed, excellent craftsmen were hired, the length and breadth of the church to be built were measured out, the foundations dug more deeply on account of the wet neighbourhood all around, and by repeated blows of rams beaten down to provide a yet stronger basis for the load to be set upon them.

The workmen carried on their labours as much by the keenness of their devotion as by desire for their wages, and while some brought stones others mixed mortar, and yet others raised both to the top of the work by a hoisting wheel (*rotali machina*); God gave increase and the job rose higher day by day. Two towers rose above the ridges of the roofs, the lesser at the west end offered a fine sight from afar to those entering the nave at the main front* of the church, while the larger stood on four

*Turres . . . quarum minor versus occidentem in fronte basilicæ pulchrum intrantibus insulam a longe spectaculum præbebat . . . It has been usual to understand

piers placed at the crossing and linked with one another by arches to prevent them from spreading (!). Judged by the style of building used in that early period (*qua vetus illa antiquitas utebatur*), the work was handsome enough.

How and why the church of Ramsey was pulled down to the ground and then rebuilt in better form, c. 985.
One day when they had got up early, lo and behold! they could see a crack in the wall of the taller tower, gaping open from top to bottom, seeming to threaten all the rest of the church adjoining it with collapse. Whether this occurred from the weakness of work that had been hurried or from mistakenly inadequate foundations, it was certainly due to the masons' lack of foresight. . . . The leaning side struck the beholders with terror. Masons were asked for their views, and all agreed that the reason for the mishap was a defect of weak foundations, and that this could not be consolidated by itself without taking down the whole of the damaged building. . . . The brethren, after getting leave, hired workmen and attacked the tower from the roof; a certain obstinacy giving strength to their labours, they did not leave one stone upon another, down to ground level. Seeking the cause of the trouble they dug down more deeply and found the inadequacy of the foundations. So they filled up the space afresh with stronger masonry of stones rammed hard together, and building upon this rejoiced in the outcome of their daily labours.

IMPROVEMENT IN ASHLAR MASONRY (William of Malmesbury, *De gestis regum Anglorum,* ed. W. Stubbs, Rolls Series 52, ii, 1889, 484; Migne, *Patrologia latina,* CLXXIX, col. 1364; Mortet 1911, 338–9).

The works of Roger "the Great", bishop of Salisbury 1107–1139
A noble prelate, never sparing expense on what he meant to do, he was especially accomplished in building, as can be seen among others particularly at Salisbury* and Malmesbury.† For he erected there buildings on a spacious plan, with liberal expenditure of money, in exquisite form, and with so well ordered a type of stonework that the joints deceive the eye and the whole mass of

---

insulam as the topographical island of higher ground upon which Ramsey Abbey stood, rising out of the fens. In that case it would hardly be the smaller western tower that was noticed, as it would have been overtopped by the central lantern. *Insula* in the sense of an aisle of a church, including the central "aisle", is evidenced from the period when the chronicle was written, and seems to yield better sense.

*i.e. Old Sarum.

†Probably the castle, as no work of this period is recorded at Malmesbury Abbey.

masonry might be thought a single stone. He made anew the
church of Sarum and enriched it with ornaments so that it yielded
to none in England but excelled many, and he could truthfully say
to his God : "Lord, I have loved the splendour of thy house."

THE   NEED   TO   GO   GOTHIC   (*Gesta   pontificum*
Autissiodorensium, in Labbe, *Nova Bibliotheca manuscripta,* I, Paris
1657, 487 ff.; Mortet 1929, 203).

How bishop Guillaume de Seignelay had the old building of
Auxerre Cathedral demolished, to build it anew, 1215.
At that time popular devotion was eager for the building of new
churches. The bishop saw that his cathedral at Auxerre was an old
building and very small, suffering from decay and age, while others
in every direction round about were raising their heads in a
wonderfully beautiful style (*mira specie venustatis*). So he determined on a new building and that it should be designed by those
skilled in the art of masonry, lest it might be in any way unequal
to others. He had it pulled down to the ground . . . that, putting off
the decrepitude of antiquity, it might grow young in a more
elegant style of novelty.

THE SPREAD OF GOTHIC STYLE (J. F. Schannat, *Vindemiæ*
literariæ, Fulda and Leipzig 1724, II, 59; Mortet 1929, 296).

This famous text has been much commented, mainly by chauvinistic
French scholars anxious to prove—what was not in doubt—that
France had priority over Germany in Gothic style. The point may
still be made that the adjective Francigenus *means not merely*
French, but also Frankish, referring to the western Crusaders and to
the Latins who had overrun Byzantium in 1204. Though no stress
can be laid upon this, it is quite possible that in the thirteenth
century there was some realization of the link between the Crusades
and Gothic (see Fig. 4).

The collegiate church of St. Peter of Wimpfen-im-Thal, near
Heidelberg, built by a French architect, 1268–1278.
Dean Richard of Ditensheim pulled down the monastery built by
the reverend father Crudolf, so ruinous from its great age that it
was regarded as threatening to fall at any moment. He summoned
a mason highly skilled in architectural design (*architectoriæ artis*),
who came straight from France from the city of Paris, and ordered
him to build the church of hewn ashlar (*ex sectis lapidibus*) in the
French style (*opere Francigeno*). This architect (*artifex*) made the
church with much effort and at great expense just as it can be

seen to the present day, of wondrous design (*mirabilis architecturæ*), adorned with images of the saints inside and out, with windows and columns of carved work. People flocking from all sides admire the uncommon work, praise its architect, venerate God's servant Richard (the dean), rejoice to have seen him, and spread his renown far and wide.

D

Contemporary Descriptions of Architecture

*I*N *Appendix (A) the account by the monk Gervase of the rebuilding of the choir at Canterbury was largely descriptive, but its main importance is for the detail given of the successive architects and their methods. Other lengthy accounts of buildings are given here, as evincing an interest in the details and scale and proportion of architecture by those who were contemporary with the work, or who wrote within a few years after erection.*

THE CHURCH OF SANTIAGO DE COMPOSTELA (*Liber de miraculis sancti Jacobi*, lib. iv, ed. P. Fita and J. Vinson, 1882, 46 ff.; A. López Ferreiro, *Historia de la santa iglesia de Santiago de Compostela*, III, 1900, App., 9ff.; Mortet 1911, 397–407).

The measurement of the church (built *c.* 1074–1122).
The basilica of St. James has in length 53 times a man's stature, that is from the west door to the altar of the Blessed Saviour; in width it has 40 less one, from the door called "of the Franks" (*Francigena*) to the south door; the height within is 14 statures. What is beyond its length and height cannot be described by anybody.*

The same church has nine naves below and six above, and one head, that is the great apse in which the altar of the Blessed Saviour stands; and one presbytery (*laurea*) and one body and two limbs, and eight other little apses (*capita*). In each of these is a single altar. We may say that six of the naves are of moderate size, and three are large. The first is the chief nave from the west door to the four crossing piers which govern the whole church, with one aisle (*naviculam*) to right and another to left. The two other large naves are the two sections from the Franks' door to the four piers of the crossing of the church; and from the same piers to the south door; and both these naves (*i.e.* the transepts) have pairs of side aisles. These three chief naves extend to the ceiling of the church; and the six little aisles rise to the middle arcades

*In other words, the impression made by the church is ineffable.

(*ad medias cindrias*). Each of the great naves has 11½ statures of a man in width. We say that the stature of a man correctly consists of 8 palms.* In the great nave the piers have 30 less one; 14 to right and as many to left, and one is between the two portals, within towards the north, separating the bays. In the naves of the transept of the church, that is from the Franks' door to the south door, there are 26 piers, 12 to right and as many to left, and two placed within, before the doors, separate the bays and the portals. In the crown of the church are eight single columns about the altar of St. James. The six aisles which are above in the galleries of the church are in length and width like the other aisles beneath : on one side they have walls and on the other piers which from beneath rise up above from the great nave; and double piers called by the stonemasons (*lapicidibus*) middle arcades (*cindræ*). As many piers as there are below in the church, so many are above in the naves; and as many cross-arches (*cingulæ*) as there are below, so many are in the gallery above; but in the galleries, between the single piers there are always two columns at once, called by the stonemasons arcade columns (*columnæ cindriæ*). In this church no rent or break is found; it is wonderfully wrought, large, spacious, light, of proper size with width, length and height suitably proportioned, in marvellous and indescribable craftsmanship, which is even worked twice over (*dupliciter*) as if it were a royal palace. Whoever goes above, through the galleries, though he climb up sorrowful, is made happy and joyous by the sight of the exquisite beauty of this church (Fig. 1a).

The windows. The glass windows in the same basilica are 63 in number. There are three for each altar in the crown; five windows in the vault (*cælum*—sic) of the basilica, about the altar of St. James, by which the apostolic altar is well illuminated; in the gallery above are forty-three windows.

The portals. The same church has three main portals and seven little ones. There is one portal, the chief one, facing west, and one to the south and one to the north; and there are two doorways in each of the main portals, each with two doors. The first of the seven portals is that of Santa Maria, the second of the Via Sacra, the third of San Pelayo (*i.e.* the Puerta Santa), the fourth of the Canonry, the fifth of the Stoneyard, the sixth likewise of the Stoneyard, the seventh of the Grammar School, which is also the way to the Archbishop's Palace . . .

The north door. The north door, "of the Franks", of the same church of St. James comes next after the parvis, with two doorways finely carved with these works. Outside each doorway are six columns, some of marble and others of stone, three to the right and three to the

---

*The Spanish *estado*, stature or fathom, was equal to 1.670 metre (5 feet 5¾ inches), and was divided into 2 *varas* or 6 feet or 8 *palmos* or 72 *pulgadas* (inches). The palm was 208.75 mm or 8.219 statute inches.

left. That is to say there are six columns to each doorway and so twelve in all. Seated above the column outside between the two doorways is the Lord enthroned in majesty, giving a blessing with the right hand and in the left holding a book. Around his throne are the four Evangelists, as if supporting the throne, and Paradise is carved at his right hand. There is the Lord in another sculpture, rebuking Adam and Eve for their sin, and on the left likewise in another figure casting them out of Paradise. Thereabout are many carved figures of saints, of beasts, men, angels, women, flowers and other creatures, which we cannot describe because of their great number. But over the left-hand door as we enter the church, in the vault, (*ciborio*), is carved the Annunciation of the Blessed Virgin Mary with the Angel Gabriel speaking to her. On the left, above the doors in the side entrance, are carved the months of the year and other beautiful things. There are two large fierce lions on the walls outside, always watching the doors, one on the right, the other on the left. On the lintels above are four apostles each holding a book in the left hand and with right hands raised, blessing those who enter the church. Peter is on the right in the left-hand entrance and St. James on the left. Over each of the apostles' heads are the heads of oxen, carved starting forward from the lintels.

The south door. In the south portal of the apostolic church there are two doorways, as we have said, and four doors. On the right-hand doorway, outside in the first range the Betrayal of our Lord is carved with wonderful skill. There the Lord is tied to a pillar by the Jews, there he is flogged with whips, there sits Pilate on his throne as if in judgment on him. Above in the upper range is carved the Blessed Mary, the mother of the Lord, with her Son at Bethlehem; with the Three Kings who come to visit the Child with his mother, offering their threefold gifts; and the star, and the angel warning them not to return to Herod. On the lintels of the same doorway are two apostles as keepers of the doors, one on the right and the other on the left. Likewise on the other, left-hand, doorway on the lintel are two other apostles. In the first range of this doorway, above the doors, is carved the Temptation of the Lord: before the Lord are angels of darkness like scarecrows, setting Him on the pinnacle of the Temple; others offer Him stones, telling Him to turn them into bread; yet others show Him the kingdoms of the world, pretending that they will give them to Him if He will fall down and worship them—God forbid. But there are other angels of light, that is good ones, behind His back, and others above with censers. There are four lions in this portal, one on the right of each doorway and another opposite. Between the two doorways, on the pillar above, are two more fierce lions back to back. There are eleven columns in this portal: five to the right-hand doorway, on the right; as many to the left-hand doorway, on the left; and the eleventh between the two doorways, separating the bays. These columns, some of marble and others of stone, are marvellously carved with images, flowers, men, birds and animals; and these columns are of white marble. Nor must one forget that a certain woman stands next to the Lord's Temptation, holding in her hands the rotting head of her lover, cut off by her husband, and forced by her husband to kiss it twice a day. Oh! how great and wonderful is the justice displayed to all by the adulterous woman! In the upper range above the four doors towards the palace of the church there is a scene shining in stones of white marble, wonderfully cut. The Lord stands upright, with St. Peter on the left holding his keys, and St. James on the right between two cypress trees, and St. John his brother next him; to right and left are the rest of the apostles. The wall above and below, to right and left, is carved very finely with flowers, holy men, beasts, birds, fishes, and other work which we cannot include in our account. There are four angels above the bays, each holding a horn, to announce the Day of Judgment.

The west door. The west portal has two doorways which in beauty, size and artistry outdo the rest. It is larger and finer than they, and wonderfully wrought. It has many steps without, and is adorned with numerous marble columns and carved with various sorts of figures in different ways: of men, women, animals, birds, saints, angels, and flowers and different kinds of ornament. There are so many details that they cannot be stated in our account. Above is the Lord's Transfiguration upon Mount Tabor, marvellously carved: the Lord stands on a white cloud, His face glowing as the sun and His garment shining like snow; the Father stands above, speaking to Him. Moses and Elias, who appeared with Him, tell Him of His death to be fulfilled in Jerusalem. There are St. James and Peter and John, to whom the Lord revealed His Transfiguration.

The towers of the church. There are to be nine towers in the church: two above the south portal and two above the west portal; two above each of the spiral staircases, and another larger one over the crossing in the midst of the church* The basilica of St. James is glorified by these and by other most lovely works; and it is entirely built of very strong natural stones, brown and extremely hard, like marble. Within it is painted in various ways and without it is very well covered with tiles and with lead. Of the works we have described some are altogether complete, and others are yet to be finished. . . .

The masons of the church, and the beginning and end of its building. The masters of masonry (*didascali lapicidæ*) who first built the church of

---

*There must be some confusion in the text, as it is obvious that the intended towers included two above the north front. The spiral staircases were those to west of the transepts in the angles of the nave. The large tower above the crossing implies Norman influence.

St. James were called Master Bernard the old (*senex*), the wonderful master (*mirabilis magister*), and Robert, with about fifty other masons who worked there diligently under the management of the most religious lords Wicart and the reverend canon Segered, and abbot Gundesund.* This was done in the reign of Alfonso (VI) king of Spain (1072–1109) under bishop Diego (Gelmirez; 1101–39) ... The church was begun in the year of the Era 1116 (A.D. 1078). From the year it was begun to the death of Alfonso (I), king of Aragon (1134), were fifty-nine years; to the death of Henry (I), king of the English (1135), sixty-two years; and to the death of Louis (VI) the Fat, king of the Franks (1137), sixty-three years. From the year the first stone was placed on the foundations to that in which the last is set is forty-four years. ...†

THE POETRY OF ARCHITECTURE (*Metrical Life of St. Hugh, bishop of Lincoln*, ed. J. F. Dimock, Lincoln 1860, 32–7, lines 833–965; written *c. 1225*).

The Latin original is one of the few outstanding poems devoted to the subject of architecture, and it is regrettable that no prose translation can do justice to—or even approach—its literary felicity. What is here attempted is to reproduce, as closely as possible, the train of thought of the text, because of its unusual preoccupation with architectural forms and design.

How St. Hugh built the cathedral church of Lincoln, 1192–1200.
Prudent religion, a religious foresight, indeed builds the bishop's‡ bridge to Paradise: to build Sion working in purity, not in blood. And with wondrous art he built the work of the cathedral church: for in its erection he not merely granted money and the labour of his servants, but the aid of his own sweat; for often he carries the hewn stones in a hod, and the lime-mortar too. Believing in the virtue of that hod a cripple, propped on two sticks, obtained its use for the sake of his infirmity; and thereafter spurned the aid of his two crutches. So his day's work, which used to make the straight crooked, set his crookedness straight.

O uncommon shepherd of the flock, by no means a hireling! Thus

---

*Wicart, Segered and Gundesund formed the clerical building committee with administrative powers; Bernard was the architect; Robert (by his name probably Norman) was probably warden of the masons or deputy to the master.

†The chronology is oddly confused and the backward reckoning from the deaths of kings—probably later than the original compilation of the descriptive text—puts the start variously between 1073 and 1075. This must have been the date of setting out or of design, while 1078 will have been the year of laying the ceremonial foundation stone. This gives a date of completion in 1122. An inscription in the central chapel of the ambulatory (Capilla del Salvador or Capilla del Rey de Francia) gives the date of foundation as 1075; an independent document proves that works at the east end were in progress in 1077.

‡*Pontificis*, of the pontiff, literally "bridge-builder", *i.e.* between this world and the next.

the fresh structure of the church appears: for truly mother Sion lay low and narrow, straying, ignorant, ailing, aged, bitter, destitute, mean, ugly. Hugh raised her when down, widened her narrowness, steered her when astray, taught her ignorance, healed her sickness, gave her new youth for age, sweetened her bitterness, enriched her need, made fair what was mean and ugly. The ancient pile is pulled down to the ground and a new church grows, portraying by its plan the apt shape of a rising cross. Hard work makes a unity of three separate parts, for the solid bulk of the foundation rises from the centre, the wall supports the roof, hanging in air. Thus the foundation is buried in the womb of earth but walls and roof appear, and with proud daring the wall rushes towards the clouds, the roof towards the stars. The skill of the craftsmen fitly matches the cost of the materials, for the vault spreading wide its wings* like the feathered birds and as if in flight, strikes the clouds, though resting on its solid columns. The gripping mortar holds together the white stones, all cut true to the mark by the craftsman's hand. The wall, built by their heaping together, seems to disdain this, appearing as though its close-laid parts were all one piece; it looks not artificial but a work of nature, not a thing united, but one. Another precious material, black stones (of Purbeck marble), supports the work, not content with a single colour; instead of having a rough grain, these shine with a high polish, strongly built in stiff positions, by no means deigning to be tamed by iron (tools), were it not softened by special skill: when the surface is ground down by the manifold rubbing of sand, and the solid marble permeated with strong vinegar. On examining the (texture of the) stone, the mind might doubt whether it were of jade or marble; if of jade, then a dull jade; but if marble, one exceptionally fine. As for the slender shafts themselves, which thus surround the columns, they look like (maidens) in a round dance. Their outer surface, more polished than the growing fingernail, reflects a sparkling brilliance to the view: for nature has there painted so many different forms that, if art by long persistence laboured to get the likeness exact, it could hardly equal the reality. Thus precise jointing together sets there in becoming rank a thousand shafts which, stiff, precious and shining, enduringly maintain the whole structure of the church, endow it with riches, make it bright with their gleam. Although their posture is tall and lofty, their appearance is pure and brilliant, their ranks beautiful and geometrical, their elegance fitting and serviceable, their utility pleasing and excellent, their firmness undaunted and brave.

The glass windows. The twin display of the windows (on both sides) offers to the eyes glowing obscurities; above are inscriptions denoting dwellers in the Heavenly City and the weapons with which they

*Alas, meaning both "wings" and "aisles".

overcame the Stygian tyrant.* The two great windows (of the transepts) are like two heavenly bodies; and their circular display, facing the north and south, outshines all the rest with its twofold light. The others may be likened to the common stars; these two resemble, the one the sun, the other the moon. So two candelabra shine on the head (chevet) of the church, their burning and varied colours like the rainbow; nor are they merely like, but they excel: for the sun, reflected on the clouds, produces the rainbow; while these two flash without the sun, and gleam without the clouds.

The significance of the separate parts. Though described as by a child, these allegories have meaning. Without it seems a shell, yet within is a kernel; without like wax, as honeycomb within; as in the shade a fire more gaily shines. For the foundations, walls and roof, the hewn white stone, the marble smooth and black and fair to see, the double range of windows, the twin windows which, as it were, gaze down from ends both north and south, are truly great in size, yet appear greater still.

The parts of the whole church. The foundation is the body, the wall the man, the roof the spirit; a threefold division of the church. The body belongs to the earth, man to the clouds, the spirit to the stars.

The white stones. The hewn white stone stands for the chaste and wise : whiteness is decency and its shaping, doctrine.

The marble stones. In the guise of marble, smooth, shining, dark, is signified the Bride, frank, virtuous, afflicted. Its smoothness truly exemplifies her utter candour, the polish her virtues, and the darkness her distress.

The glass windows. Illuminating the world with divine light is the noble body of the clergy, expressed by the clear windows. Their subordinate hierarchy may be seen on either side : the canons stand ranked above [in the clerestory windows], the vicars below [in the aisles]. And since, while the canons are dealing with the world's affairs, the vicars perpetually and unremittingly carry on the divine offices, the upper row of windows shines as the lovely petals of flowers, signifying the changing show of the world; the lower range displays the names of the holy fathers.

The two round windows. The twin windows which display a circular splendour are the two eyes of the church : rightly the greater is the bishop, the lesser the dean. For on the North is the devil, to South the Holy Ghost; towards these the two eyes look. For the bishop faces South, that he may receive the one; the dean North, that he may avoid the other; one looks to be saved, the other, lest he perish. The front of the church is the lantern of heaven, and with these eyes surveys the gloom of Lethe.

*i.e. Saints with their symbols, notably those of martyrdom.

The consummation of the whole allegory. Thus the insentient stones conceal the mysteries of stones that live; the fabric made with hands displays that of the spirit; the outward appearance of the church shines doubly, enriched with twofold array.

The crucifix, and the golden table at the entry of the choir. A golden majesty is painted at the entry of the choir: and fitly is Christ crucified displayed in his own image; the course of His life is there precisely shown. Not alone the cross or image, but the wide surface of six columns and of two timber beams, shines with burnished gold.

The chapter house. Beside the church stands the chapter house, the like of whose pointed roof never Roman possessed; the coined money of a Crœsus might hardly begin its admirable work. Its entrance is like a square porch; within, its space is round, vying with Solomon's Temple in material and craftsmanship. If something of this remains to be perfected, let the work of Hugh the first be finished under Hugh the second [Bishop Hugh de Wells, 1209–1235]. Lincoln may therefore boast so great a father, who blessed her in all ways with such marks of favour.*

A TRAVELLER'S NOTES ON ART (*Itinerarium Symonis Semeonis,* ed. M. Esposito, *Scriptores Latini Hiberniæ,* IV, Dublin 1960, 24–6).

Throughout the Middle Ages topographical literature was produced, but most of it was limited to accounts of the great centres of pilgrimage. In some cases, however, buildings seen incidentally in the course of pilgrimage are mentioned, and this is the case in the valuable account of the journey of two Irish Franciscan friars who in 1323 set out from Dublin for the Holy Land.

Simon Simeon and Hugh the Illuminator journey through England, 1323 (see Fig. 13).
We arrived on Holy Thursday (24th March, 1323) at the city called Chester in England, the chief port constantly frequented by ships from Ireland. After keeping Easter there we went through Stafford to the city of Lichfield, where there is a most lovely church dedicated to St. Chad, bishop and confessor. It is of wondrous beauty, having very high stone steeples or belfries, and is finely adorned and enriched with paintings, carvings, and other church fittings. Passing on through Coventry, beloved by merchants who prosper there, Dunstable, and

*The reference to work not yet completed seems, from its context, to refer to the chapter house; and as its pointed roof was already up, what was still to be done can only have been the stone vault and/or the glass windows. The poem refers elsewhere (line 1253) to St. Hugh's canonization in 1220, and is likely to have been written soon afterwards—in any case before 1235, the end of the episcopate of the second Bishop Hugh. The poem provides uniquely important dating evidence that the detail of the chapter house is pre-1235.

St. Albans with an abbey of Benedictine monks dedicated to that saint, we reached London, the most noble and the richest city under the sun.

To London there continually ebb and flow the tidal waters of the sea, by that famous river called the Thames, over which is the bridge, filled with dwellings and with riches. In the midst of the bridge is the Chapel of St. Thomas, archbishop and martyr, with frequent services. Near the centre of the city is the church of St. Paul, of amazing size, with that most famous and unequalled steeple in the middle, with a spire reaching, it is said, 500 feet in height. In that same church at the east end is the most noble chapel of the Blessed Virgin, enriched with stories from the Bible, where at daily masses the English, say rather the angelic, sing joyfully to Mary with the harmony of nightingales and cherubim, far removed from the yells of Lombards or the howling of Germans. At the seaward end of the city is a most famous and impregnable castle, surrounded by a double wall with wide ditches, moats of water, and other warlike array. In its midst is that most famous tower called the Tower of London, built with the utmost sturdiness of hewn ashlar stones to a great height. Outside the walls at the other end of the city is the abbey of Benedictine monks called Westminster, where all the kings of England are buried. Among them lies the body of the lord Edward (I) of notable memory, king of the English, most like to a hammer; he, along with Louis the most Christian king of the French, sailed across the seas with an army to the land of the Saracens. In the church are two bells, surpassing all other bells in the world in size and in sweetness of tone. Almost joined on to this abbey is the far-famed palace of the kings of England with the renowned Painted Chamber, wonderfully displaying on its walls all the warlike stories of the whole Bible. These are fully and in the most complete manner described in inscriptions in French, to the no little wonder of beholders and with the most royal splendour.

E

Texts describing Programme and Intention

*A*LTHOUGH *plans and drawings were made—indeed, for all large and complex buildings, had to be made—at all periods from remote antiquity, few have survived. The reasons for their disappearance are discussed in the text. In spite of the small number of actual drawings, the evidence for their former existence is voluminous, and many written contracts and similar documents concerned with buildings to be erected either contain specific mention of drawings, designs, or templates, or show by the detailed measurements given that plans or designs must have been drawn out beforehand, and were available when the document was drawn up. The first document, the so-called Customs of Cluny, or of Farfa (an Italian daughter-house), represents in detail the plan of Cluny II as it was about 1032, together with the layout and dimensions—evidently taken from the plan—of parts of the buildings not yet completed. This document has been much commented, but for a definitive study see Kenneth J. Conant,* Cluny *(Maçon, 1968), 42–5.*

A MODEL MONASTERY (*Consuetudines monasticæ*, I, *Consuetudines Farfenses*, ed. B. Albers, 1900, lib. II cap. i, 137–9; cap. xliii, 176; Mortet 1911, 132–9; Conant, *Cluny*, 43).

The position and measurements of the buildings.
The Church is 140 feet in length and 43 in height; and has 160 glass windows. The Chapter-house is 45 feet in length, 34 in width, with 4 windows at the east end and 3 towards the north; to the west 12 arches with 2 columns in each. The Parlour 30 feet in length, and the Chamber 90 feet in length. The Dormitory 160 feet in length, in width 34 feet; the glass windows in it are 97 in all and all have in height the stature of a man as high as he can stretch to his finger-tip, and $2\frac{1}{2}$ feet wide; the height of the walls 23 feet. The Reredorter 70 feet in length, in width 23; 45 privies are arranged in this building and each has a little window in the wall 2 feet high and in width half a foot; and upon

the privies are set wooden seats, and above the timber construction are 17 windows 3 feet in height and in width 1½ feet. The Warming House 25 feet in width and the same in length; from the door of the Church to the door of the Warming House 75 feet. The Refectory 90 feet in length, in width 25; the height of its walls 23 feet; eight glass windows in it on each side, all of 5 feet in height and 3 feet in width. The Monks' Kitchen 30 feet in length and 25 feet in width; the Laybrothers' Kitchen of the same measurements. The Cellars are in length 70 feet and in width 60 feet.

The cell of the Almonry is 10 feet wide and 60 feet long, like the width of the Cellars. The Galilee is 65 feet long and with two towers set on the front of the Galilee; and beneath them is an Atrium where the laity stand in order not to get in the way of the procession. From the south gate to the north gate 280 feet. The Sacristy 58 feet long with a tower set at its head. The Oratory of St. Mary 45 feet long, 20 feet wide, its walls 23 feet high. Six little cells are to be set apart for the sick. The first cell of the Infirmary is 27 feet wide and 23 feet long, with 8 beds and as many cubicles; in the porch next to the wall outside the cell and the partition of the said cell it is 12 feet wide. The second cell is alike in all respects and the third and fourth too. The fifth should be smaller, where the sick can wash their feet on Saturdays, or those brothers who have stripped to change. The sixth cell should be provided for the household servants to wash their dishes and all utensils. Next the Galilee there should be built a Guesthouse (*palatium*) 135 feet long, 35 feet wide, to receive all men who arrive at the monastery attended by mounted servants (*omnes supervenientes homines qui cum equitibus adventaverint monasterio*). On one side of this house 40 beds are to be prepared, with as many pillows of cloth where that number of men may rest, and with 40 privies. On the other side there are to be 30 single beds where countesses or other noble women may stay, with 30 privies which they alone may use. In the midst of this hall are to be fixed tables like the tables of the Refectory, where both men and women may eat.

At great feasts this house is to be adorned with curtains and cloths and bankers over the seats. In front of it is to be another house 45 feet long and 30 feet wide. Its length should reach the Sacristy, and there are to sit all the tailors and cobblers to sew all that the Chamberlain bids them; and they are to have a table prepared there, 30 feet long, and another fixed table with it, so that the width of the two together is to be 7 feet. Between that dwelling and the Sacristy, the Church and the Galilee is to be the Cemetery, where laymen are to be buried. From the south door to the north door on the west is to be built a house 280 feet long by 25 feet wide; and there are to be made stables for horses divided into stalls, and above a loft, where the menials may eat and sleep, and they should have tables set up 80 feet long and 4 feet wide. And as many of those who come as cannot be fed in that dwelling we have described above, are to take their meals here. At the end of the same dwelling is to be a place made suitable for those who come without horses and there receive from the brother almoner alms of food and drink as much as they require. Outside the Refectory of the brothers, taking up 60 feet at the end of the privy are 12 vaults with as many tubs provided, where at the appointed times baths may be prepared for the brothers. Behind that place let the cell for the novices be built, and let it be (partitioned off in compartments at the) four corners, with the first corner for meditation, the second for meals, the third to sleep in, and the fourth with the privy at the side. Next to this let there be made another cell where the goldsmiths or enamellers or master glaziers may exercise their crafts. Between the vaults and the cells of the novices and the goldsmiths they are to have a building 125 feet long and 25 feet wide, its length stretching to the Bakehouse, which is to be 70 feet long with the tower built at its end, and 20 feet wide.

THE LOMBARD MASTERS IN SPAIN (J. Villanueva, *Viage literario a las iglesias de España*, IX, 1821, app. xxix, 298–300; Mortet 1929, 129–31).

(Arnaud de Perexens, bishop of Urgel 1167–1195, contracts with Raymond the Lombard to vault the cathedral of La Seo de Urgel in 7 years from Easter 1175).
In the name of Jesus Christ the everlasting Saviour I Arnold, by the grace of God bishop of Urgel, with the counsel and common assent of all the canons of the church of Urgel, entrust to Raymond the Lombard the work of the Blessed Mary, with all its estate moveable and immoveable, namely houses, lands, vineyards, rents and fines for violence and penances, and with the alms of the faithful and with the payments of the clergy, and with all that now or formerly by any title seems to have belonged or belong to the aforesaid work of the Blessed Mary. And moreover we give thee the board of a canon (*cibum canonicalem*) for thy whole life on this condition, that thou shalt faithfully and without any trickery vault (*claudas*) the whole church for us, and shalt raise the stair-turrets or towers (*coclearia sive campanilia*) one course above all the vaults, and shalt make the lantern (*cugul*) well and properly with all that belongs to them.

And I R(aymond) the Lombard covenant with the Lord God and the Blessed Mary and the lord bishop and all the clerks of the church of Urgel, who now are there or in future shall be, that all this as is above written, while I have life, I shall perform from this present Easter (13th April) kept in the year of the Lord's Incarnation 1175 faithfully for 7 years, and without any trickery. So that every year I shall have and keep in the service of the Blessed Mary myself the fifth of the Lombards —that is four Lombards and me—and that continually both in winter and in summer. And if with these I can complete it, I shall; and if I cannot, I shall add so many masons (*cementarios*) that the aforesaid work shall be finished within the foresaid term. But after the 7 years, when with the help of the divine mercy I shall have completed the said work, I shall have freely and quietly my board while I live, and of the fee and goods of the Work I shall stand at the will and order of the Chapter afterwards.

Moreover we, both bishop and canons, altogether forbid thee, Raymond the Lombard, thyself or by any agent, to alienate or pledge on any account anything of the fee of the Work which it now has or shall have henceforward. Of thy own fee, which thou hast gained in thine own name, and of thy goods, do in life and in death what shall please thee after that seven years. If there should happen—which God forbid—that there should be such dearth in the land that we see thee too much burdened, it shall be lawful for us to prolong the foresaid term at our discretion, lest thou shouldst incur the brand of perjury. But no one or more of us may grant for thee the aforesaid relaxation of thine oath except in full chapter by common deliberation and the consent of all. And whatever improvement thou shalt have made in the fee of the Work shall remain to the said Work. But if for the improvement of the fee of the Work thou shouldst have to pledge or exchange anything, thou canst not do this without the counsel and concurrence of the Chapter.

I, R. Lambardus, swear that I will perform all this as is above written, and fealty and immunity to the canonical church of the blessed Mary of Urgel, to the best of my ability, by God and these holy Gospels.

Marks of R. Lombard, who swears, conclude and confirm this; of lord Arnold, bishop of Urgel; of William, prior; of W. the sacrist; of B. the archdeacon; of R. de Adantes, archdeacon; of B. de Sancta Fide, archdeacon; of B. the chanter; of Bernard Anascensis, writer, who have written this at the request of Arnold, chaplain of Iel, on the day and year as above.

(*Note: the above arrangements are unusual in that Master Raymond was not merely made an administrator of the fabric fund—"the Work of the blessed Mary"—but was actually made sole legal trustee of the fund during the seven years within which it was expected his work could be completed. Even admitting the oath which Raymond swore, the degree of confidence placed in him, and the implied importance of his position, are very great. This is further confirmed, in regard to his social status, by the fact that part of his remuneration was to consist of a corrody or life-pension of board equivalent to that of one of the canons.)*

ARCHITECT AND MASON-CONTRACTORS (P.R.O., Pleas of Exchequer, 10 Edward II, m. 16, printed in L. F. Salzman, *Building in England*, 422–4).

Until the thirteenth century it was usual, though not universal, for masters of architectural standing to undertake contracts themselves, so that the two distinct functions of architect and builder became confused in the same man. This became less common in the last three hundred years of the Middle Ages, and documents more and more frequently refer to a master of architectural status as responsible for design, for supervision, and for measurement of work carried out by contract by other masons.

Building a wall round Eltham Palace, 1315.
Memorandum that on Monday the morrow (12th May) of the feast of Whitsun in the 8th year of the reign of King Edward son of King Edward (1315) at Eltham it is covenanted by Sir William Inge, Sir John Fillol, Sir John Launge, knights, John Vanne merchant of London and William de Boudon clerk on behalf of our lady the Queen (Isabella of France) of the one part, and Masters William de Hoo, John de Offynton, John de Hardynggesham and John de Seint Omer, masons, of the other part. That the foresaid masons William John John and John have undertaken to make a wall around the moat of the manor of the said lady at Eltham of stone and lime in the manner following that is to say: that the foresaid masons at their own costs shall seek for a certain and sure foundation as soon as it may be agreed by view of Master Michael of Canterbury* or another whom our lady shall assign. And if by chance it happen that one cannot find a foundation upon firm ground on which account it is necessary to drive piles to make a good foundation, then our said lady the Queen will have the timber found for the piles and the said masons shall have them worked and set at their own costs; and the wall beneath at the foundation shall be 5 feet thick and above at the wall-top 4 feet thick, and it shall be from the foundation to the wall-top 12 feet in height, the wall battering on the outside to the top to the thickness abovesaid by the advice of the said Master Michael, and if need be to make the wall higher in places by default of good foundation they shall make it, taking for what it shall measure by the perch by agreement, and the foresaid masons shall find stone and lime and all things that may be needful for the wall at their own costs; and the foundation of the said wall shall be laid of good hard stone, one course through without

*The king's chief mason from *c.* 1292 to 1321 or later.

putting chalk or rubble stone, and then rising up the whole of the side towards the water up to the top, for half the thickness of the said wall it shall be laid of good hard stone well and closely, and the foresaid masons may well place (on the side) towards the earth in the said wall, if in front it will be covered with earth, good chalk stone or good lime mortar, and where the wall stands above the ground it shall be laid for half (its thickness) of good hard stone; and the said masons shall make at each perch length, which shall be of 18 feet, within towards the earth an arch buttress of good hard stone by the advice of the said Master Michael, which shall be at the foundations 5 feet in depth and in thickness, and above of 4 feet, and the said arch shall rise from the foundation of the said wall and shall rise to the old work above the ground to sustain the said foundation of the old work, and so all round as the place is marked out they shall make the buttresses in the manner aforesaid, save around two turrets towards the East, where there was formerly a lodging, where the place is not now set to be a lodging, and shall make the wall level throughout by the advice of Master Michael, and at each of the corners there shall be two buttresses the better to sustain the turrets, and the aforesaid masons shall cause the earth to be filled in against the wall and placed closely to the wall without, level to the earth within, at their own costs; and the said masons shall have for each perch of 18 feet to be made in the form aforesaid with the arches 100s. sterling.

And they shall find stone and lime and shall carry them at their own costs, and workmen and whatever is needed for the work aforesaid. And if it happen, which God forefend, that any of the foresaid masons by sickness or by reasonable excuse be prevented from being able to carry out the said work, the others undertake to perform it, and bind themselves to do this, each for all. And the said masons shall begin to work on the said work the Monday after this fortnight of Trinity next (*i.e.* on Monday 2nd June) and shall work from then on with such men and at such speed that they shall have completed half the said work before the feast of All Saints next to come (1st November, 1315). And for the rest they shall begin at the fortnight after Easter next to come, and sooner if it please our said lady, and shall have finished it before Michaelmas next following (29th September, 1316). In witness of which thing this indenture is made, of which one part remains with the foresaid masons sealed on behalf of our said lady with the seals of the foresaid Sir John Fillol, John Vanne and William de Boudon. And the other part remains for our said lady in the hands of the said John Vanne sealed with the seals of the foresaid masons. Given at London the year and day aforesaid.

(*Note: the above contract owes its preservation to the fact that proceedings had to be taken under it in the following year to prosecute the three masons William de Hoo, John de Hardingham and John de St. Omer for the fraudulent breach of their undertaking. The jury in the case found that the wall had been built 1½ feet too thin at the base and a foot and upwards elsewhere, and that there were other defects in the materials used and in the workmanship, so that the whole of the work would have to be taken down and rebuilt. The overall length of the wall was stated to be 79 perches and 12 feet (1434 feet), and damages were set at 4 marks for each perch and 2½ marks for each of the 56 defective buttresses. The masons were imprisoned but later released on giving fresh undertakings to carry out the work in the proper way. Their sureties for good behaviour were headed by the architect, Master Michael of Canterbury. For the full details see L. F. Salzman,* Building in England, *27–8.*

HENRY YEVELEY AS ARCHITECT

The group of documents which follow is concerned with the functions of Master Henry Yeveley as an architect, in regard to works at Cowling Castle in Kent, and the church of St. Dunstan-in-the-East, London, where his client was John lord Cobham; and at Tower Wharf and Westminster Hall, where he was responsible to the Crown in the person of King Richard II.

Documents concerning work at Cowling Castle, Kent, 1381. (D. Knoop and G. P. Jones in *Transactions Quatuor Coronati,* XLV; L. F. Salzman, *Building in England, 461–2).*
This indenture witnesseth that the 26th day of September the year of the reign of king Richard II after the Conquest the 5th Sir John de Cobham lord of Cobham has accounted with Thomas Crump mason of Maidstone for the great gatehouse of Cowling. That is to say according to his account the one tower contains 7½ perches and ¾ of a perch, the other tower 7½ perches and ¼ of a perch; and one perch is by his account between the two towers; the total of perches amounts in all to 17 perches. And the said Thomas shall take for the perch 40s. as is set down in his old indentures; and the said Thomas has received of this before the day of the making of these £46 16s. 7d., so that the said Thomas has deserved, with the £10 received for freestone, £44. And thus the said Thomas owes to the said Sir John the day of making these by his own account 56s. 7d. And beyond that the said Thomas will pay for all the quoins in the said gatehouse and towers as appears by his indentures aforesaid. In witness of which to these indentures the parties aforesaid have interchangeably set their seals. Given at Cowling the day and year abovesaid.

Memorandum that the said Crump owes to the lord beyond the parcels abovesaid 366 feet of quoins, price 5d. a foot. Also he owes the lord a postern by his first indenture.

Memorandum that Crump has accounted for more than he should

2 perches and a half foot and quarter, which amounts to 100s. that he is
bound to restore to the lord according to the account of Master Henry
Yeveley made at Cowling before Ascension Day of the 5th year of king
Richard II (15th May, 1382).

This indenture made between Sir John de Cobham lord of Cobham of
the one part and Thomas Crump mason of the other part witnesseth
that the said Thomas has undertaken of the said Sir John to make, that
is to say: 10 loopholes of 3 feet long in all without cross-slit with the
apparel within and without, 7 little doorways each of 2½ feet wide, with
the height of the said doorways as is suitable, with the apparel within
and without, and 54 newel-steps each 4½ feet long and 7 inches in
height and 30 other newel-steps each 3 feet long and 7 inches in height,
and 53 corbels one foot square and of good and convenient length for
machicolations, and 43 stones for half-arches, the which arches and
corbels shall be neatly chamfered. And the said Thomas shall have, for
all the stones and for all the work and carriage as far as Maidstone,
and for setting the said stones in the said work in seasonable time next
season £20, which will be paid him as he does his work. To keep which
covenants well and loyally the said parties bind themselves by these
indentures. In witness of which thing they have interchangeably set
their seals. Given at London the day of St. Luke Evangelist (18th
October) the year of our lord the king Richard the second since the
Conquest the 5th (1381).

(*Endorsed*:) The latter indenture of Thomas Crump. To be
examined if the said Thomas has brought all his newels to Cowling
according to the purport of his indenture or not.

The south aisle of St. Dunstan-in-the-East designed by Yeveley
(L. F. Salzman, *Building in England, 462–3*).

This indenture made between Sir John de Cobham lord of Cobham
of the one part and Nicholas Typerton mason of the other part
witnesseth that the said Nicholas shall perform the foundations of the
south aisle of St. Dunstan's in Tower Street, London, of the length
of the church well and sufficiently with the foundation of a porch
according to the design (*solom la deuyse*) of Master Henry Yeveley
and also the foundations of the buttresses and with a plinth
(*watertable*) well and sufficiently made of hard stone according to the
design of the said Master Henry, and shall have for digging the said
foundation and finding stone, chalk, lime and sand and the moulding
(*tablement*), carriage and all things belonging to the said work 25 marks
as he shall do his work, 5 marks at the beginning—which the said
Nicholas has received from the aforesaid Sir John—and so from time to
time 5 marks until the said 25 marks (£16 13s. 4d.) be fully paid. And
the said work shall be performed well and sufficiently between the

making of these presents and the next month after the feast of Easter
(6th April, 1382) according to the design of the said Master Henry. To
the good and loyal performance of this the aforesaid Nicholas binds
himself by these presents. In witness whereof the parties abovesaid have
interchangeably set their seals to these. Given at London the Eve of
Christmas in the year of the reign of king Richard the second after the
Conquest the 5th (24th December 1381).

Building Tower Wharf, London (L. F. Salzman, *Building in England,
469–70*).
This indenture made between our lord the king Richard the second of
the one part and John Westcote of London, William Jancook of
Maidstone and Thomas Crump of Otham masons of the other part,
witnesseth that the said masons have undertaken to make the following
works that is to say : a Wharf with two returns stretching in length
from the corner of the wall of the east end of the Tower of London
towards St. Katherine's as far as the turret of the Watergate of the said
Tower and in width shall contain, that is to say the one return towards
the water of Thames of the said wall at the east end 30 feet of assize,
and the other return shall be suent and according to this reasonably
and conveniently, and the said masons shall cause to be dug the ground
where the said wharf shall be made in depth 3 or 4 feet if need be, and
if the foundation will not be adequate at 4 feet then our lord the King
will cause it to be dug or piled and placed ready to the hand of the said
masons to work upon. And the walls of the said Wharf shall be within
the ground 8 feet in thickness the which shall be of ragstone and chalk
and shall rise in height, from the first stone set in the ground to the top
$16\frac{1}{2}$ feet of assize, and shall be in the middle of the thickness of 6 feet of
assize, and above in thickness 5 feet, and the said walls on the outer
face towards the water shall be made of Kentish ashlar good and
suitable and well laid and jointed and filled within with rag for the
thickness of 3 feet and the rest with chalk. And at the end of each 10
feet they shall cause to be set stones called endstones in length good and
suitable in each course. And while the work is in progress our lord the
King at his costs will have it filled with earth and rubble to keep the
work safe. To which works abovesaid the said masons shall find all
manner of stone, lime, sand and all other things belonging to masonry
with the carriage. And the said works shall be well and suitably
performed as far as pertains to the said masons according to the advice
and survey of the Treasurer of our lord the King, Sir John
Hermesthorpe, and the clerk of the works of our said lord the King,
and Henry Yeveley, and shall all be ready within two years next
following the date of these in case they be not delayed by default of
payments. And the said masons shall take for each perch of $16\frac{1}{2}$ feet

square of the said work £9 13s. 4d. Of which they shall be paid in hand at the making of these £50, and of the rest they shall be paid by divers times as the said work continues and as they shall have need. And in case that the said walls shall extend in height higher than 16½ feet before specified our said lord the King will pay for the extra as much as will amount to what is suitable and according to the price per perch above laid down. And if they be less then they shall be abated reasonably according to the amount. And our lord the King will find for the said masons a (lodge) during the time of their work to work in. In witness of which thing to these indentures the parties aforesaid interchangeably have set their seals. Given the morrow (25th June) of St. John Baptist the year of the reign of our said lord the King the 13th (1389).

New masonry details for Westminster Hall (Salzman, *Building in England, 472-3* (see Fig. 36).
This indenture made between our lord the King of the one part and Richard Washbourne and John Swallow masons of the other part witnesseth that the said masons have undertaken to make well and truly all the table (cornice) of the walls of the great Hall in the Palace of Westminster on the one side and on the other, the which table shall rise above the old wall 2 feet of assize at the midst of the said wall with sawn Reigate stones, and where needs be to set Marr stone to secure the said table, and the topmost course of the same table they shall well and conveniently lay level the one side and the other, and they shall make the said table according to the purport of a design and template *(forme et molde)* made by the advice of Master Henry Yeveley and delivered to the said masons by Watkin Walton his warden. And the said masons shall take for each foot of assize length of the said wall so made 12d. And the said masons have also undertaken to make 26 corbels in the said Hall of Marr stone and shall cut out the wall for the said corbels there to be set at their own costs and the said corbels they shall well and conveniently set each in its place and they shall have each corbel carved according to a pattern shown to them by the Treasurer of England and they shall fill each spandrel (of wall) with sawn stone of Reigate from each corbel beneath up to the arch above, taking for each corbel so made by survey of the said Master Henry and Watkin his warden 20s. And our lord the King will find all manner necessaries and material for the said works that is to say stone, lime, sand, scaffold, (hoisting) engines and other materials whatsoever apart from handiwork and tools for masons to work with in their craft. And if any pillar be taken down it shall be at the costs of our lord the King. And our said lord the King will find lodging for the said masons and their fellows for all the time they shall be occupied about the said works. And the

foresaid masons shall make and perform the half of the said table and corbels in manner as aforesaid between now and the feast of St. John the Baptist (24th June) next to come and the other half between the said feast of St. John and the feast of Candlemas (2nd February) then next following. In witness of which thing to the part of this indenture remaining with our said lord the King the foresaid masons have put their seals. Given at Westminster the 18th day of March the year of the reign of our said lord the King the 18th (1394/95).

ARCHITECTURAL SUPERVISION (*The Talbot Deeds 1200–1682*, ed. E. E. Barker, Lancashire and Cheshire Record Society, CIII for 1948, 1953, 48, no. 164).

Contract to build a chapel at St. Mary-on-the-Hill, Chester, 1433.
This indenture made between William Troutbeck, esquire, on the one part and Thomas Bates, mason, on the other part, bears witness that the foresaid Thomas has made covenant and grants to the said William that he shall make a chapel in the churchyard of St. Mary of the Hill on the south side of the chancel of the church there, that is to wit the east end, the south side and the west end, containing the length of the chancel there and 18 feet wide within the walls, and as high as it needs reasonably to be : with 5 fair and cleanly wrought windows full of light that is to say : one gable window in the east end with 4 lights and 3 windows on the south side each one of 3 lights, and one in the west end in the best wise to be devised; and 4 buttresses on the south side, with a great arch in the west end; and the chapel to be (em)battled above, like to the little closet within the castle of Chester, with a corbel table (be)longing thereto; and at either end 3 honest finials.

And the foresaid William shall pay to the foresaid Thomas £20 like as the work goes forward, and also give him a gown, and also the foresaid William shall find freestone, lime, sand, water, windlass and stuff for to scaffold with, and such manner necessaries as the foresaid Thomas needs. And all manner of carriages that (be)long thereto. And the foresaid Thomas shall, by the oversight of Master John Asser,*

*John Asser the younger, who on the previous 1st March had succeeded his father, John Asser the elder, in the office of Master Mason of the counties of Chester and Flint, with North Wales, an appointment within the Palatine Earldom of Chester. On 10th June, 1439, Asser had a grant of the office of surveyor of the walls of the city of Chester, and he died on 16th June, 1446. The precise extent of Asser's "oversight" of Bates is left uncertain : the height of the walls of the chapel still had to be determined, as well as the design of the western window, which had somehow to be fitted in above (?) the great arch. The battlementing of the chapel was to be directly copied from that of an existing building in Chester Castle, officially in Asser's charge. It seems likely that Bates would have consulted Asser on any details about which he felt uncertain, or for which he was not provided with drawings or templates by Asser as the work proceeded.

make the chapel and all things that (be)long there to masoncraft honestly. In witness of the which thing to these presents indentures the parties aforesaid either against other have set to their seals.

Given at Chester the Monday next before the feast of the nativity of St. John the Baptist in the year of the reign of King Henry the sixth after the Conquest 11 (22nd June, 1433).

ACCORDING TO THE WORKING DRAWING (Winchester College Muniments no. 1011, printed in L. F. Salzman, *Building in England, 583–4*).

The contract which follows is less detailed than many others, and this is explained by the clause that the work was to be done as shown in a drawing on a skin of parchment.

A house in St. Pancras Street, Winchester, 1436.

This indenture witnesseth that these be the covenants between the Warden of the New College of Winchester in that one part and John Berewik of Romsey carpenter of that other part. Witnessing that the said John shall make a house to the foresaid Warden of 28 feet in length and 24 foot of width by the ground, with a jetty above of 22 inches; the house shall be set in the street of St. Pancras there as the bounds of the ground openly show. The same John to begin the work the Monday next after Easter (8th April) week, the year of King Henry the VI the 14th year reigning (1436) in that the same John have no default of timber neither of carriage for the same timber when it is wrought to carry it to Winchester to the ground aforesaid. Also the foresaid Warden to pay to the said John for the making and workmanship of the house that toucheth his craft 11 mark and a half that is to say, 4 mark the Monday (16th April) next after the Easter week when he beginneth his work; also 4 mark at Whitsunstide (27th May) next following; and when this said John hath reared the house to receive of the same Warden for the last payment that is (to) say at Lammas (1st August) next after following 3 mark and half. Also the foresaid Warden shall do rid the ground that it be void there as the house shall stand that the said John Carpenter have no let (hindrance) in rearing of the house. The work to be made as the tracing showeth drawn in a parchment skin between them made. And the same John to do to the house all that (be)longeth to his craft. In witness of these covenants above written either party have set to their seals.

ÆSTHETIC PURITANISM

The last two documents, though well known, are of unusual value as they mark the expression of a cultured taste which deplored the fussy repetitive detail which, in the first third of the fifteenth century, had overlaid the noble simplicity of the English Perpendicular style. There was, then, a conscious reaction against florid detail in the period around 1440–50, and this reaction involved even if it was not originated by, the saintly king Henry VI. What may have had some psychological connection with a moral puritanism was for a time continued as a measure of financial economy; but it is striking that after the return of Edward IV from his exile in Flanders, in 1471, a new outburst of enriched style swept all before it. The sequence of the seventeenth century Interregnum and Restoration were exactly prefigured.

Continuing the Divinity Schools, Oxford, 1440. (Epistolæ Academicæ, Oxford Historical Society, i, 192; L. F. Salzman, Building in England, 513–14).

This indenture made between the University of Oxford of the one part and Thomas Elkyn, mason, of the other part, witnesseth that the said Thomas has undertaken the building of the new Schools of Divinity in the foresaid University as touches mason's work : and the said Thomas shall receive weekly in summer 4s. sterling and in winter 3s. 4d., when it shall happen that he shall work personally for the week. Also the said Thomas shall engage other masons, the best he knows, and at the best price he can to the profit of the said work. And the said Thomas shall receive from the University yearly during the said work one mark sterling (13s. 4d.) for his yearly fee.

And because numerous magnates of the realm and other knowledge-able (*sapientes*) men do not approve, but reprehend, the over curiosity of the said work already begun, therefore the said University wishes the said Thomas to continue, as he has already begun, to restrain the superfluous curiosity of the said work, as in niches for statues, bowtels, casements and fillets, and in other foolish curiosities, which do not concern the work but cause too great and extravagant expenses by the said University and the undue delay of the said work. And to the said undertakings on the part of the said Thomas to be faithfully kept and observed, he the same Thomas binds himself by these presents to the said University in £40 sterling. In witness of which thing as well the common seal of the said University as the seal of the said Thomas are affixed to these writings indented. Given at Oxford the 16th day of January in the year of the reign of king Henry the sixth after the Conquest the 18th (1439–40); Master Richard Rotherham, Doctor of Theology, Chancellor of the said University, William Orell and John Willey then being proctors of the same.

King Henry VI's intent for King's College, Cambridge, 1447–48. (R. Willis and J. W. Clark, The Architectural History of the University of Cambridge, I, 368–70; L. F. Salzman, Building in England, 520–22).

And as touching the dimensions of the Church of my said College of Our Lady and St. Nicholas of Cambridge, I have devised and appointed that the same church shall contain in length 188 feet of assize without any aisles and all of the wideness of 40 feet, and the length of the same church from the west end unto the Altars at the choir's door shall contain 120 feet. And from the Provost's stall unto the grece (step) called *gradus chori* 90 feet, for 36 stalls on either side of the same choir, answering unto 70 fellows and 10 priests conducts (*i.e.* hired) which must be *de prima forma* (of the best quality?); and from the said stalls unto the east end of the said church 62 feet of assize. Also a reredos bearing the roodloft departing (dividing) the choir and the body of the church, containing in length 40 feet, and in breadth 14 feet; the walls of the same church to be in height 90 feet, embattled vault and chare (wagon) roofed, sufficiently buttressed, and every buttress fined (finished) with finials.

And in the east end of the said church shall be a window of 11 days (lights), and in the west end of the same church a window of 9 days, and betwixt every buttress a window of 5 days. And betwixt every of the same buttresses in the body of the church, on both sides of the same church, a closet with an altar therein, containing in length 20 feet and in breadth 10 feet, vaulted and finished under the sill of the aisle windows; and the pavement of the church to be enhanced (raised) 4 feet above the ground without, and the height of the pavement of the choir $1\frac{1}{2}$ feet above the pavement of the church, and the pavement at the high altar 3 feet above that.

Item, on the north side of the choir a Vestry containing in length 50 feet and in breadth 22 feet, departed (divided) into two houses beneath and two houses above, which shall contain in height 22 feet in all with an entry from the choir vaulted.

Item, at the west end of the Church a Cloister square, the east pane (side) containing in length 175 feet, and the west pane as much; and the north pane 200 feet, and the south pane as much, of the which the deambulatory (walk) 13 feet wide, and in height 20 feet to the corbel table, with clerestories and buttressed with finials, vaulted and embattled, and the ground thereof 4 feet lower than the church ground (floor); and in the middle of the west pane of the cloister a strong Tower square, containing 24 feet within the walls, and in height 120 feet unto the corbel table, and 4 small turrets over that, fined with pinnacles, and a door into the said cloister-ward, and outward none (Fig 49).

And as touching the dimensions of the housing of the said College, I have devised and appointed in the south side of the said church a quadrant (quadrangle) closing unto both ends of the same church, the east pane whereof shall contain 230 feet in length, and in breadth within the walls 22 feet: in the midst of the same pane a Tower for a

Gatehouse, containing in length 30 feet and in breadth 22 feet, and in height 60 feet, with three chambers over the gate, every above other; and on either side of the same gate 4 chambers, every containing in length 25 feet, and in breadth 22 feet; and over every of those chambers two chambers above of the same measure or more, with two towers outward and two towers inward. The south pane shall contain in length 238 feet and in breadth 22 feet within, in which shall be 7 chambers, every containing in length 29 feet, and in breadth 22, with a chamber parcel of the Provost's lodging, containing in length 35 feet, and with a chamber in the east corner of the same pane, containing in length 25 feet and in breadth 22 feet; and over every of the same chambers two chambers, and with 5 towers outward, and three towers inward; the west pane shall contain in length 230 feet and in breadth withinforth (internally) 24 feet, in which at the end toward the church shall be a Library containing in length 110 feet and in breadth 24 feet, and under it a large house for reading and disputations, containing in length 40 feet, and two chambers under the same library, every containing 29 feet in length and in breadth 24 feet, and over the same library a house of the same largeness for diverse stuff of the College : in the other end of the same pane a Hall containing in length 100 feet upon a vault of 12 feet high ordained for the Cellar and Buttery, and the breadth of the hall 34 feet, on every (each) side thereof a bay window, and in the nether end of the same hall, toward the middle of the said pane a Pantry and Buttery, every of them in length 20 feet and in breadth 15, and over that two chambers for officers, and at the nether end of the hall toward the west a goodly Kitchen : and the same pane shall have two towers inward ordained for the ways into the Hall and Library. And in every corner of the said quadrant shall be two corner towers, one inward and one outward, more than (in addition to) the towers above rehearsed; and at the over end of the Hall the Provost's lodging, that is to wit more than the chambers above for him specified, a parlour on the ground containing 34 feet in length and 22 in breadth, two chambers above of the same quantity (size), and westward closing thereto a kitchen, larder, house, stable, and other necessary housing and grounds; and westward beyond these housings and the said kitchen ordained for the hall a Bakehouse and Brewhouse and other houses of offices between which there is left a ground, square of 80 feet in every pane for wood and such stuff. And in the middle of the said large quadrant shall be a Conduit goodly devised for the ease of the said College.

And I will that the edification of my same college proceed in large form, clean and substantial, setting apart superfluity of too great curious works of entail (carving) and busy moulding.

And I have devised and appointed that the precincts of my same

College of Our Lady and St. Nicholas, as well on both sides of the garden from the said College unto the water, as in all other places of the same precinct, be enclosed with a substantial wall of the height of 14 feet, with a large tower at the principal entry against the middle of the east pane out of the high street, and in the same tower a large gate, and another tower in the middle of the west end at the new bridge; and the said wall to be crested and embattled and fortified with towers, as many as shall be thought convenient thereto.

F

The Form of Holding Manorial Courts

THE Assemblies or Congregations of the mediæval masons seem, from the character of the Charges, to have been closely parallel to other customary courts held, from at least as early as the first half of the thirteenth century—and probably earlier—down to our own time. Although the Court Rolls form a written record of the outcome of court procedure, and there is a substantial literature on the legal jurisdiction of such Courts, the details of the precise procedure at such a court have rarely been written down and probably never published. For this reason the full transcript is given here of an account drawn up in 1948 by the late Herbert Chitty, F.S.A., Steward of the Manors of Winchester College, regarding the exact method he had used for holding courts from 1911 until the lapse of the system under the Law of Property Acts.

The Holding of a Court Leet and Court Baron

Precept to warn a Court, sent by the Steward :

To the Bailiff of the Manor of——in the County of——These are to will and require you on Receipt hereof to give Notice of Warning to all the Tenants of the Manor of——aforesaid that a Court Leet and a Court of the Manor will be there held at the usual place on ... day the ... day of ... next between the Hours of 10 and 11 of the Clock in the Forenoon and that they are required personally to be and appear at the said Court to do and perform their Suit and Service or in default thereof they will be amerced   Hereof fail not   Dated at Winton the ...Day of ... in the Year of our Lord. ...

The jury being assembled together in the Place where the Court is usually held the Bailiff opens the Court thus :

BAILIFF (says, or repeats after the Steward) :

"O yes   O yes   O yes   All Manner of Persons that were summoned to attend at this Time and Place draw near and answer to your names as you shall be called."

(hands List of Names of the Jury to the Steward)

STEWARD (calls over the Names of the Jury, the Jurors answering to them, and enters them in his Minute Book; then reads them over again, one by one, the Bailiff counting them after him).

Which being done the Jury among themselves choose a Foreman to whom the Steward administers the following oath :

"You as Foreman of this Jury shall inquire and true Presentment make of all such Matters and Things as shall be given you in charge you shall present the Truth and nothing but the Truth So help you God."

FOREMAN : "I swear by Almighty God that as Foreman of this Jury I will inquire and true Presentment make of all such Matters and Things as shall be given me in charge. I will present the truth the whole truth and nothing but the truth So help me God."

When the Foreman is thus sworn the Steward administers to each of the other jurymen the following Oath :

"The same Oath that your Foreman hath taken to observe and keep on his part you and each of you shall observe and keep on your parts So help you God."

JUROR : "I swear by Almighty God that the same Oath that our Foreman hath taken to observe and keep on his part I will observe and keep on my part So help me God."

The Jury being sworn the Steward gives the following Charge :
STEWARD "Gentlemen,

"The Design of our Meeting at this Time and Place is to hold a Court Leet and customary Court for the Lords of this Manor it is therefore incumbent on me as Steward to give you in charge such things as are proper and necessary for your Enquiry and Consideration and then it will become your duty as Jurymen in justice to yourselves and Neighbours and in discharge of the Oath you have just now taken to make due Presentment thereof.

"FIRST you are to enquire who those are that owe Suit and Service to this Court and whether they are here to do and perform the same—if not you are to present the Defaulters that they may be amerced unless essoined.

"ALSO you are to enquire if the Constables Tithingmen and other Officers within the Leet have been guilty of any neglect or misdemeanor in their respective Offices and present the Offenders.

"ALSO you are to enquire of all public nuisances such as are Offences against the Public by doing that which is an Annoyance to all the King's Subjects or by not doing what the Common Good requires : As all Defects or Decays of Bridges Obstructions or Encroachments on the Highways or by stopping up or diverting any ancient Way Stream or Watercourse out of its proper Channel.

"AS a Homage of the customary Court you are to enquire what Advantages have happened to the Lords since the last Court either by

Death Alienation or Forfeiture—If you find the Death of any Tenant it is your Duty to inquire what Lands he held of this Manor and who is the next Taker that he may come in and be admitted; also whether any Freeholder is dead since the last Court that his Heir may come and pay a Relief.

"ALSO if there have been any Alienations of the Estate held of this Manor who the Purchasers are that the Lords may know of whom to expect their Rents and Services. Forfeitures happen divers Ways the most material of which are : if any Tenant neglects or refuses to pay and perform his Rents and Services of which his Attendance at this Court is a material Part; Or if he suffers his copyhold Tenement to go to decay or to fall down or takes away the Buildings from one Estate to repair another or leases it for more than one Year without a License.

"ALSO you are to enquire if any Rents Customs or Services have been withheld or withdrawn from the Lords of this Manor what they are out of what Lands they issue and how long and by whom they have been so withheld.

"ALSO if any Persons enclose or encroach upon the Lords' Waste or Common or if any take Common who have no Right or having Right put in more Beasts than they ought or such as are not commonable.

"ALL these Things are inquirable and presentable by you; and if I have omitted any Thing which has fallen within your Knowledge and which at all concerns the Interest of the Lords or Tenants of this Manor you are bound by your Oaths to present it."

The Jury then adjourn to write their Presentments and afterwards bring them in to the Steward who reads them aloud for all the Jury to hear. When he has finished the Jury sign their Names to the Presentments and the Steward takes them to enter on the Court Rolls.

(The names being presented of the Constable, Tithingmen and Haywards etc. for the ensuing year, after each of these Officers has made his Presentment, the new Officers are sworn in after the following Oaths) :

The Constable "You shall well and truly serve our Sovereign Lord the King and the Lords of this Leet in the Office of Constable in and for the Hundred of B ... or Parish D ... until you be thereof discharged according to due Course of Law (or : for the Year ensuing and until another shall be sworn in your Room); you shall from Time to Time well and truly do and execute all Things belonging to the said Office according to the best of your Knowledge So help you God."

A Tithingman "You swear that you will faithfully serve our Sovereign Lord the King and the Lords of this Leet in the Office of Tithingman for the year ensuing and until you shall be from thence discharged by due course of Law So help you God."

A Hayward, etc. "You swear that you will faithfully execute the Office of Hayward for the year ensuing and until you shall be from thence discharged by due course of Law."

When a Copyhold Tenant surrenders his Tenement the form is:

STEWARD "You surrender into the Hands of the Lords of this Manor by the Acceptance of me their Steward One Messuage (etc.—giving description) To the Intent (etc.—whatever it is—as to the Use of the Tenant's last Will or for the Use of A. B.) are you content to make it?"

TENANT "Yes" (and delivers up a Rod or Pen or some other Symbol into the Steward's hands).

When a person is admitted to a Copyhold Tenement the Steward delivers him a Rod or Pen or other Symbol as the Custom is and says as follows:

STEWARD "The Lords of this Manor by me their Steward admit you to one Messuage etc. (description) which came into the Hands of the Lords on the Surrender (*or* Death *as the case may be*) of A.B. This is to hold to you for the Term of your Life (your Heirs for ever *as it happens to be*) by the yearly rent of 1*s.* (*or as it may be*) and by all other Rents Works burthens and Services before due and of Right accustomed."

This being done the Steward desires the Jury or Homage to take Notice of such Admission and that the person admitted gave a Fine to the Lords (*or not as the Case is*).

Upon his admission the Tenant takes the Oath of Fealty:

STEWARD "You swear that you will be faithful to the Lords of this Manor for the Lands and Tenements you hold of them and that you will pay and perform your Rents and Services therefore due and of Right accustomed So help you God."

The above Oath is not administered when the Person admitted is a Minor or a Feme Covert or when a Person is admitted by an Attorney—but in these Cases their Fealty is respited until etc. that is in the first place till the Minor is of Age—in the second till the Feme Covert is no longer so—and in the third until the Person that is admitted by Attorney appears in Court himself—at any of which periods they are obliged to take the Oath of Fealty if required.

(If the Death of a Copyholder has been presented the following Proclamation is made by the Bailiff for the Customary Heir to come into Court and be admitted in the presence of the Homage):

BAILIFF "The customary Heir of John Rice come into Court and be admitted to the customary (*or* Copyhold) Lands and Tenements descended to you on the Death of the said John Rice your late Father deceased."

(If the deceased Copyholder had surrendered the Premises to the use of his last Will the following Proclamation is made for the Devisee):

BAILIFF "William Budd come into Court and be admitted to the Copyhold or customary Lands and Tenements given and devised to you in and by the Will of John Budd your late Father deceased."

(If the customary Heir or Devisee is unknown the following Proclamation is made):

BAILIFF "Any person or Persons lawfully claiming an Estate in certain customary Premises within this Manor from by or under or by means of the Death of A. B. deceased come into Court and be admitted thereto or your Default will be recorded."

(This Proclamation, if no Taker comes, may be repeated at the next two Courts held; on the Third Proclamation the form is):

"... and be admitted thereto; or the same will be seized into the Hands of the Lords."

(For not attending the Court, and for the minor offences which came within its jurisdiction, the Suitors were said to be in the Lords' mercy; that is, they were amerced in small sums which had to be affeered, that is assessed, by the Jurors or by certain of them, known as Affeerers. The Steward first administered to the Affeerers the following Oath):

STEWARD "You shall well and truly affeer and affirm the several Amercements here made and now to you read over. You shall spare no one out of Love Fear or Affection nor raise or inhance any out of Hatred or Malice but impartially shall do your Duties herein. So help you God."

The Business of the Court being all finisht the Court is discharged by the Tythingman's saying by the Steward's direction as follows:

TITHINGMAN "All Manner of Persons that have made their Appearance here may for the present depart and attend again upon a new Summons. God save the King and the Lords of this Manor."

(In modern times the Court has been closed by the Steward's thanking the Jury for their attendance).

All the forms included above are taken from a manuscript handbook compiled by a former Steward of the College Manors (apparently Charles Knott, gent., Steward from 2nd November, 1774, until his death on 16th April, 1802) c. 1794, now Winchester College Muniments no. 6301, confirmed by printed forms used for some purposes in modern times.

Bibliography with Abbreviations

THIS bibliography includes all works quoted in the Notes to the text, with the abbreviations there used, as well as a few other titles for reference or further reading. For additional illustrations, see particularly my earlier books: *Gothic England* (1947, revised ed. 1948), *An Introduction to Tudor Architecture* (1949), *The Gothic World* (1950, paperback 1969), *The English Cathedrals* (1956, paperback 1961), *A Portrait of English Cathedrals* (photographs by Herbert Felton, 1957), *The Cathedrals of Spain* (1957) and *The Master Builders* (1971). *Gothic England* contains an extensive classified bibliography of English Mediæval Art, supplemented in my *Reader's Guide: English Cathedrals* (National Book League, 1951). In the Notes detailed references for lives of English architects and designers are given only where the information supplements my biographical dictionary *English Mediæval Architects* (1954).

A	*Archæologia* (Society of Antiquaries of London)
AB	*Art Bulletin* (The College Art Association of America)
Abbad Rios 1952	F. Abbad Rios, *Zaragoza* (Barcelona, Aries, Guías Artísticas de España), 1952
AC	*Archæologia Cantiana* (Kent Archæological Society)
AEA	*Archivo Español de Arte*
AHA	*Acta Historiæ Artium* (Budapest)
AJ	*Archæological Journal* (Royal Archæological Institute)
Amherst 1895	A. Amherst, *A History of Gardening in England*, 1895
Andrews 1925	F. B. Andrews, *The Mediæval Builder*, 1925 ——, "Further notes on the Mediæval Builder", in *Transactions* of the Birmingham Archæological Society, LV for 1931, 1933

ANJ   *The Antiquaries Journal* (Society of Antiquaries of London)

APS   Architectural Publication Society, *Dictionary of Architecture*, 7 vols., 1849–92, and *Detached Essays*, 1853

AR   *Architectural Review*

Arnold 1879   T. Arnold ed., *Henrici Archidiaconi Huntendunensis Historia Anglorum* (RS, 74), 1879

AS   *Acta Sanctorum* (Bollandists)

Atkinson 1933   T. D. Atkinson, *Architectural History of the Benedictine Monastery of St. Etheldreda at Ely*, 1933
——, *English Architecture* (12th ed.), 1946
——, *A Glossary of Terms used in English Architecture* (6th ed.), 1946

Aubert 1929   M. Aubert, *Notre-Dame de Paris* (Paris), 1929

Bannister 1968   T. C. Bannister, "The Constantinian Basilica of St. Peter at Rome", in JAH, XXVII, 1968, 3–32
C. Bauchal, *Nouveau Dictionnaire biographique et critique des Architectes français* (Abbeville), 1885

BEC   *Bibliothèque de l'École des Chartes*

Bergen 1906   H. Bergen ed., *Lydgate's Troy Book* (EETS, ExS, XCVII), **i**, 1906

Bergen 1918   —— ed., *Lydgate's The Fall of Princes*, 4 vols. (EETS, ExS, CXXI–CXXIV), 1918–19

Berthelson 1947   B. Berthelson, *Studier i Birgittinerordens Byggnadsskick*, I (KVH, Del 63), Lund 1947

Biddle 1961   M. Biddle, "A Thirteenth-century Architectural Sketch from the Hospital of St. John the Evangelist, Cambridge", in PCAS, LIV, 1961, 99–108

Blunt 1950   W. Blunt, *The Art of Botanical Illustration*, 1950

BM   British Museum, London

BMA   *The Burlington Magazine*

Bock 1961   H. Bock, "Der Beginn spätgotischer Architektur in Prag (Peter Parler) und die Beziehungen zu England", in WRJ, XXVII, 1961, 191–210

Bock 1962   H. Bock *Der Decorated Style* (Heidelberg), 1962

F. Bond, *Gothic Architecture in England*, 1906

——, *An Introduction to English Church Architecture*, 2 vols., 1913

Booz 1956   P. Booz, *Der Baumeister der Gotik* (Kunstwissenschaftlichen Studien 27, Munich), 1956

Branner 1958   R. Branner, "Drawings from a Thirteenth-century Architect's Shop: the Reims Palimpsest", in JAH, XVII, 1958, 9–22

Branner 1960   ——, "Villard de Honnecourt, Archimedes, and Chartres", in JAH, XIX, 1960, 91–6

Branner 1963   ——, "Villard de Honnecourt, Reims, and the Origin of Gothic Architectural Drawing", in GBA, March 1963, 129–46

Branner 1965   ——, *St. Louis and the Court Style in Gothic Architecture*, 1965

Brewer and Martin 1879   J. S. Brewer and C. T. Martin edd., *Registrum Malmesburiense* (RS, 72), 2 vols., 1879–80

M. S. Briggs, *A Short History of the Building Crafts*, 1925

Briggs 1927   M. S. Briggs, *The Architect in History*, 1927

Briggs 1929   ——, "Architectural Models", in BMA, LIV, 1929, 174 ff.

J. Britton, *Architectural Antiquities*, 5 vols., 1807–26

Brooke 1969   C. Brooke, *The Twelfth Century Renaissance*, 1969

Bucher 1968   F. Bucher, "Design in Gothic Architecture—a Preliminary Assessment", in JAH, XXVII, 1968, 49–71

Butler 1937   H. E. Butler, *The Autobiography of Giraldus Cambrensis*, 1937

C   *The Connoisseur*

Camón 1941(1)   J. Camón ed., *Simon García: Compendio de arquitectura y simetría de los templos* (Madrid), 1941

Camón 1941(2)   J. Camón in AEA, no. 45, 1941, 300–5

CCB   *The Connoisseur Coronation Book*, 1953

CCL   Canterbury Cathedral Library

CDN   *Codex Diplomaticus Neerlandicus* (Het Historisch Genootschap te Utrecht)

Chapman 1907   F. R. Chapman, *Sacrist Rolls of Ely*, 2 vols., 1907

Clapham 1952 A. W. Clapham, "The Survival of Gothic in Seventeenth-century England", in AJ, CVI for 1949, Supplement, 1952, 4–9

Clay 1944 C. T. Clay, "The Keepership of the Old Palace of Westminster", in EHR, LIX, 1944, 1–21

CMH *Cambridge Medieval History*

Cobb 1942 G. Cobb, *The Old Churches of London*, 1942

Cockerell 1846 C. R. Cockerell, "William of Wykeham", in *Proceedings of the Archæological Institute at Winchester in 1845*, 1846

Collins 1897 F. Collins, *Register of the Freemen of the City of York*, **i**, 1272–1558 (SS, XCVI for 1896), 1897

Colombier 1953 P. du Colombier, *Les Chantiers des Cathédrales* (Paris), 1953

Conant 1959 K. J. Conant, *Carolingian and Romanesque Architecture, 800 to 1200* (Pelican History of Art, Z 13), 1959

Conant 1963 ——, "Mediæval Academy Excavations at Cluny, ix: Systematic Dimensions in the Buildings", in S, XXXVIII, 1963, 1–45

Conant 1968 ——, "The After-life of Vitruvius in the Middle Ages", in JAH, XXVII, 1968, 33–8

Conant 1968(2) ——, *Cluny*—Les Églises et la Maison du Chef d'Ordre (Mâcon), 1968

Coulton 1928 G. G. Coulton, *Art and the Reformation*, 1928

CPL *Calendar of Papal Letters*

CPR *Calendar of Patent Rolls*

Creswell 1932 K. A. C. Creswell, *Early Muslim Architecture* (I, 1932), 2nd ed., I parts i and ii, 1969

Creswell 1952 ——, *The Muslim Architecture of Egypt*, 2 vols., 1952–60

Creswell 1958 ——, *A Short Account of Early Muslim Architecture*, 1958

CS Camden Society

Csemegi 1954 J. Csemegi, "Die Konstruktionsmethoden der mittelalterlichen Baukunst", in AHA, II, 1954, 15–50

CYS Canterbury and York Society
J. Dallaway, *Anecdotes of the Arts in England*, 1800
——, *Observations on English Architecture*, 1806
——, *A Series of Discourses upon Architecture in England*, 1833

Daras (1938) C. Daras, *L'Orientalisme dans l'art Roman en Angoumois* (reprint from *Bulletins et Mémoires de la Société Archeologique et Historique de la Charente*), 1938

Darlington 1969 C. D. Darlington, *The Evolution of Man and Society*, 1969

Davis 1939 R. H. C. Davis, "Masons' Marks in Oxfordshire and the Cotswolds", in OAS, 84th *Report* for 1938–39, 1939, 1–15

Davis 1947 ——, "The Chronology of Perpendicular Architecture in Oxford", in *Oxoniensia*, XI/XII, 1947, 75–89

Davis 1956 ——, "A Catalogue of Masons' Marks as an Aid to Architectural History", in JBAA, 3 S, XVII for 1954, 1956, 43–76

De Bruyne 1946 E. de Bruyne, *Études d'esthétique mediévale*, (Rijksuniv. te Gent. Werken, Afl. 97–99) 3 vols., (Bruges) 1946

Desimoni 1877 C. Desimoni (Accounts of Sir Geoffrey de Langley's embassy from Edward I to the Ilkhan Kaikhatu), in *Atti Liguri di Storia Patria* (Genoa), XIII, 1877–84, 537–698

Dimock 1860 J. F. Dimock, *Metrical Life of St. Hugh*, (Lincoln), 1860

Divald 1931 K. Divald, *Old Hungarian Art*, 1931

Dixon and Raine 1863 W. H. Dixon and J. Raine, *Fasti Eboracenses: Lives of the Archbishops of York*, I, 1863

Dodds 1926 M. H. Dodds ed., *A History of Northumberland*, vol. XII, 1926

Doursther 1840 H. Doursther, *Dictionnaire Universel des Poids et Mesures*, 1840 (reprint, Amsterdam, 1965)

Eden 1950 W. A. Eden, "St. Thomas Aquinas and Vitruvius", in MRS, II, 1950, 183–5

EETS Early English Text Society

EFR Exeter Cathedral, Fabric Rolls

Egli 1954 E. Egli, *Sinan: der Baumeister Osmanischer Glanzzeit* (Erlenbach-Zurich, Verlag für Architektur), 1954

EHR *English Historical Review*

Ellis 1838 H. Ellis, *Registrum vulgariter nuncupatum, the Record of Caernarvon* (Record Commission), 1838

Emery 1960 A. Emery, "Dartington Hall, Devonshire", in AJ, CXV for 1958, 1960, 184–202

Emery 1970 ——, *Dartington Hall*, 1970

Enlart 1902 C. Enlart, *Manuel d'Archéologie française*, I (Paris) 1902

Enlart 1906 ——, "Origine anglaise du style flamboyant", in *Bulletin Monumental*, LXX, 1906, 38–81; LXXIV, 1910, 125–47

Entz 1958 G. Entz, "La cathédrale de Gyulafehérvár", in AHA, V, 1958, 1–40

——, "Die Gotik in Ungarn", in AHA, VI, 1959, 217–32

——, "Die Baukunst Transsilvaniens im 11–13 Jahrhundert", in AHA, XIV, 1968, 1–48, 127–75

Esposito 1960 M. Esposito, *Itinerarium Symonis Semeonis ab Hybernia ad Terram Sanctam* (SLH, IV), 1960

Evans 1956 Joan Evans, *A History of the Society of Antiquaries*, 1956

—— ed., *The Flowering of the Middle Ages*, 1966

Ewald 1877 P. Ewald ed., *Andreas Floriacensis, Vita Gauzlini*, in NA III, 1877, 365–79

ExS Extra Series

Faral 1924 E. Faral, *Les Arts Poétiques du XIIe et du XIIIe Siècle*, 1924

Fitchen 1961 J. Fitchen, *The Construction of Gothic Cathedrals*: A study of Medieval Vault Erection, 1961

H. Focillon, *Art d'Occident*, 2nd ed., (Paris) 1947

Forster 1927 E. S. Forster tr., *The Turkish Letters of Ogier Ghiselin de Busbecq*, 1927 (1968)

Fowler 1882 J. T. Fowler ed., *Memorials of the Church of SS. Peter and Wilfrid, Ripon*, **i** (SS, LXXIV for 1881), 1882

Fowler 1911 R. C. Fowler ed., *Registrum Radulphi Baldock, Gilberti Segrave, Ricardi Newport et Stephani Gravesend, episcoporum Londoniensium* (CYS, VII), 1911

Frankl 1945 P. Frankl, "The Secret of the Mediæval Masons", in AB, XXVII, 1945

Frankl 1960 ——, *The Gothic: Literary Sources and Interpretations through Eight Centuries* (Princeton, N.J.), 1960

Funck-Hellet 1951 C. Funck-Hellet, *De la Proportion—L'Équerre des Maîtres d'Œuvre* (Paris), 1951

Furnivall 1868 F. J. Furnivall, *Early English Meals and Manners—The Babees Book* (EETS, OS, 32), 1868

GBA *Gazette des Beaux-Arts*

L. Gerevich, "Mitteleuropäische Bauhütten und die Spätgotik", in AHA, V, 1958, 241–82

GM *The Genealogist's Magazine* (Society of Genealogists)

Goodman 1927 A. W. Goodman, "The Choir Stalls, Winchester Cathedral", in AJ, LXXXIV for 1927, 1930, 125–26

Goodman 1927(2) ——, *Chartulary of Winchester Cathedral*, 1927

Graham 1925 T. H. B. Graham, "Vills of the Forest, Part ii", in TCW, NS, XXV, 1925, 290–310

Granger 1931 F. Granger ed., *Vitruvius on Architecture* (Greek text with English translation, Loeb Series), 2 vols., 1931, 1934

Grimschitz 1947 B. Grimschitz, *Hanns Puchspaum* (Vienna, Wolfrum), 1947

Grivot and Zarnecki 1961 D. Grivot and G. Zarnecki, *Gislebertus, Sculptor of Autun*, 1961

Guerrero Lovillo 1952 J. Guerrero Lovillo, *Sevilla* (Barcelona, Aries, Guías Artísticas de España), 1952

H *History* (Historical Association)

Hahnloser 1935 H. R. Hahnloser, *Villard de Honnecourt*, (Vienna) 1935

Hamilton 1870 N. E. S. A. Hamilton ed., *Willelmi Malmesbiriensis monachi de gestis pontificum Anglorum* (RS, 53), 1870

Harmer 1936 F. E. Harmer, "Three Westminster Writs of King Edward the Confessor", in EHR, LI, 1936, 97–103

Harmer 1952 ——, *Anglo-Saxon Writs*, 1952

Harrison 1968 K. Harrison, "Vitruvius and Acoustic Jars in England during the Middle Ages" in TAMS, NS, XV, 1968, 49–58

Harvey 1938 J. H. Harvey, "The Mediæval Carpenter and his Work as an Architect", in JRIBA, 3 S, XLV, 1938, 733–43

Harvey 1943 ——, "The Medieval Office of Works", in JBAA, 3 S, VI for 1941, 1943, 20–87

Harvey 1944 ——, "The Western Entrance of the Tower", in TLM, NS, IX, 1944, 20–35

Harvey 1944(2) ——, *Henry Yevele, c. 1320 to 1400*: The Life of an English Architect, 1944; rev. ed. 1946

Harvey 1944(3) ——, "Henry Yevele, Architect, and his Works in Kent", in AC, LVI for 1943, 1944, 48–53

Harvey 1945 ——, "Medieval Buildings", in J. Lees-Milne ed., *The National Trust*, 1945, 43–54

Harvey 1945(2) ——, "The Education of the Mediæval Architect", in JRIBA, 3 S, LII, 1945, 230–4

Harvey 1945(3) ——, "The Building Works and Architects of Cardinal Wolsey", in JBAA, 3 S, VIII for 1943, 1945, 50–9

Harvey 1946 ——, "Side-lights on Kenilworth Castle", in AJ, CI, 1946, 91–107

Harvey 1946(2) ——, "St. Stephens' Chapel and the Origin of the Perpendicular Style", in BMA, LXXXVIII, 1946, 192–9

Harvey 1947 ——, *Gothic England: A Survey of National Culture 1300–1550*, 1947; rev. ed. 1948

Harvey 1947(2) ——, "Some Details and Mouldings used by Yevele", in ANJ, XXVII, 51–60

Harvey 1948 ——, *The Plantagenets 1154–1485*, 1948; rev. ed. 1959; paperback 1967

Harvey 1948(2) ——, "The King's Chief Carpenters", in JBAA, 3 S, XI, 1948, 13–34

Harvey 1949 ——, "William Wynford, Architect", in WCR, No. 18, 1949, 4–7

Harvey 1950 ——, *The Gothic World 1100–1600: A Survey of Architecture and Art*, 1950; paperback 1969

Harvey 1950(2) ——, "The Architects of English Parish Churches", in AJ, CV, 1950, 14–26

Harvey 1951 ——, "Genealogical Problems of Mediæval Craftsmen", in GM, XI, 1951, 45–61

Harvey 1952 ——, "Four Fifteenth-century London Plans", in LTR, XX, 1952, 1–8

Harvey 1952(2) ——, "Henry Yevele Reconsidered", in AJ, CVIII, 1952, 100–8

Harvey 1953 ——, "Early Tudor Draughtsmen", in CCB, 1953, 97–102

Harvey 1954 ——, *English Mediæval Architects: A Biographical Dictionary down to 1550*, 1954

Harvey 1956 ——, *The English Cathedrals*, 1956; paperback 1961, rev. 1963

Harvey 1957 ——, "The Masons of Westminster Abbey", in AJ, CXIII, 1957, 82–101

Harvey 1958 ——, "Had Winchester Cathedral a central Spire", in WCR, No. 27, 1958, 9–13

Harvey 1959 ——, "Mediæval Design", in TAMS, NS, VI for 1958, 1959, 55–72

Harvey 1961 ——, "The Architects of St. George's Chapel", I. The Thirteenth and Fourteenth Centuries, in RSG, IV, No. 2, 1961, 48–55

Harvey 1961(2) ——, "The Wilton Diptych—a Re-examination", in A, XCVIII, 1961, 1–28

Harvey 1962 ——, "The Origin of the Perpendicular Style", in E. M. Jope ed., *Studies in Building History* ("1961"), 1962, 134–65

Harvey 1962(2) ——, "The Architects of St. George's Chapel", II. The Fifteenth and Sixteenth Centuries, in RSG, IV, No. 3, 1962, 85–95

Harvey 1965 ——, "Winchester College", in JBAA, 3 S, XXVIII, 1965, 107–28

Harvey 1966 ——, "The Mason's Skill—the Development of Architecture", in Joan Evans ed., *The Flowering of the Middle Ages*, 1966, 111–32

Harvey 1966(2) ——, "The Fire of York in 1137", in YAJ, XLI pt. 163 for 1965, 1966, 365–7

Harvey 1968 ——, "The Origins of Gothic Architecture: Some Further Thoughts", in ANJ, XLVIII, part i, 1968, 87–99

Harvey 1969 ——, "The Tracing Floor in York Minster", in RYM, XL for 1968, 1969, 9–13, Plate I and Fig. 1

Harvey 1969(2) ed., *William Worcestre: Itineraries* (Latin text with English translation, OMT), 1969

Harvey and Harvey 1936 W. Harvey and J. H. Harvey, "Master Hugh Herland, Chief Carpenter to King Richard II", in C, XCVII, 1936, 333–6

Harvey and Harvey 1938 ——, "Recent Discoveries at the Church of the Nativity, Bethlehem", in A, LXXXVII, 1938, 7–17

Haskins 1924 C. H. Haskins, *Studies in the History of Mediæval Science* (Harvard), 1924 etc.

Haug 1956 H. Haug, *Musee de l'Œuvre Notre-Dame, Strasbourg*, 1956

Hayter 1970 W. Hayter, *William of Wykeham: Patron of the Arts*, 1970

Heyman 1966 — J. Heyman, "The Stone Skeleton", in IJSS, II, 1966, 249–79

Heyman 1967 — ——, "Beauvais Cathedral" (preprint 1967); TNS, XL for 1967–68, 15–35

Heyman 1968 — ——, "On the Rubber Vaults of the Middle Ages, and other matters", in GBA, March 1968, 177–88

Hingeston-Randolph 1894 — F. C. Hingeston-Randolph ed., *The Register of John Grandisson, Bishop of Exeter*, 3 vols., 1894–99

Hitti 1927 — P. K. Hitti, *An Arab-Syrian Gentleman and Warrior in the period of the Crusades* (Columbia University Press), 1927; reprint (Beirut) 1964 (*Memoirs of an Arab-Syrian Gentleman . . . Usamah Ibn-Munkidh*)

HKW — *History of the King's Works*

W. H. St. J. Hope, *Windsor Castle*, 2 vols., 1913

F. E. Howard, "Fan Vaults", in AJ, LXVIII, 1911

——, "On the Construction of Medieval Roofs", in AJ, LXXI, 1914

HRS — Hampshire Record Society

Hughes 1955 — J. Q. Hughes, "The Timber Roofs of York Minster", in YAJ, XXXVIII pt. 152, 1955, 474–95

IJSS — *International Journal of Solids Structures*

C. F. Innocent, *The Development of English Building Construction*, 1916

Jackson 1913 — T. G. Jackson, *Byzantine and Romanesque Architecture*, 2 vols., 1913

——, *Gothic Architecture in France, England and Italy*, 2 vols., 1915

JAH — *Journal of the Society of Architectural Historians* (Philadelphia)

Janner 1876 — F. Janner, *Die Bauhütten des deutschen Mittelalters* (Leipzig), 1876

JBAA — *Journal of the British Archæological Association*

Jenkinson 1926 — H. Jenkinson, "The Teaching and Practice of Handwriting in England", in H, XI, 1926–27, 130, 211 ff.

JRIBA — *Journal of the Royal Institute of British Architects*

JSA   *Journal* of the Society of Archivists

JWC   *Journal* of the Warburg and Courtauld Institutes

Kidson 1967   P. Kidson, *The Medieval World*, 1967

Kitchin 1892   G. W. Kitchin, *Compotus Rolls of the Obedientiaries of St. Swithin's priory, Winchester*, (HRS, 7), 1892

Kletzl 1939   O. Kletzl, *Plan-Fragmente aus der deutschen Dombauhütte von Prag* (VAS, Heft 3, Stuttgart), 1939

Knoop and Jones 1933   D. Knoop and G. P. Jones, *The Mediæval Mason*, 1933; rev. ed. 1967

Knoop and Jones 1937   ——, *An Introduction to Freemasonry*, 1937

Knoop and Jones 1947   ——, *The Genesis of Freemasonry*, 1947

Knoop, Jones and Hamer 1938   D. Knoop, G. P. Jones and D. Hamer, *The Two Earliest Masonic MSS*, 1938

Knowles and Hadcock 1953   D. Knowles and R. N. Hadcock, *Medieval Religious Houses: England and Wales*, 1953

Krinsky 1967   C. H. Krinsky, "Seventy-eight Vitruvius Manuscripts", in JWC, XXX, 1967, 36–70

KVH   Kungl. Vitterhets Historie och Antikvitets Akademiens *Handlingar* (Stockholm)

Lampérez 1930   V. Lampérez y Romea, *Historia de la Arquitectura Cristiana Española en la Edad Media*, 2nd ed. (Madrid), 1930

       R. de Lasteyrie, *L'architecture religieuse en France à l'époque gothique*, 2 vols. (Paris), 1926

Latham 1965   R. E. Latham, *Revised Medieval Latin Word-List*, 1965

Lawrence 1936   T. E. Lawrence, *Crusader Castles*, 2 vols., 1936

Leask 1946   H. G. Leask, *Irish Castles and Castellated Houses* (Dundalk), 1946

       ——, *Irish Churches and Monastic Buildings*, 3 vols. (Dundalk), 1955–60

Lespinasse and Bonnardot 1879   R. De Lespinasse and F. Bonnardot, eds., *Le Livre des Métiers d'Étienne Boileau* (Paris), 1879

Lesser 1957   G. Lesser, *Gothic Cathedrals and Sacred Geometry*, 1957

Lethaby 1904   W. R. Lethaby, *Mediæval Art*, 1904

Lethaby 1906   ——, *Westminster Abbey and the Kings' Craftsmen*, 1906

Lethaby 1925   ——, *Westminster Abbey Re-examined*, 1925

Lévi-Provençal 1938   E. Lévi-Provençal, *La Civilisation Arabe en Espagne* (Paris), 1938; 3rd ed. 1961

López Ferreiro 1898   A. López Ferreiro, *Historia de la Santa A. M. Iglesia de Santiago de Compostela*, 11 vols. (Santiago), 1898–1909

Lowth 1758   R. Lowth, *The Life of William of Wykeham*, 1758; rev. edd. 1759, 1777

LTR   *London Topographical Record* (London Topographical Society)

Luard 1861   H. R. Luard ed., *Epistolæ Roberti Grosseteste episcopi Lincolniensis* (RS, 25), 1861

Luard 1872   —— ed., *Matthaei Parisiensis Chronica majora* (RS, 57), 7 vols., 1872–84

MacCracken 1934   H. N. MacCracken ed., *Lydgate's Minor Poems*, II Secular (EETS, OS, 192), 1934

Macpherson 1889   J. R. Macpherson tr., *Arculfus de Locis Sanctis* (PTS), 1889

Macray 1886   W. D. Macray ed., *Chronicon Abbatiae Rameseiensis* (RS, 83), 1886

Maere 1936   R. Maere, *Maquette des Tours de l'église de St.-Pierre à Louvain* (Brussels), 1936

MAF   *Mémoires de la Société Royale des Antiquaires de France*

Maritain 1930   J. Maritain, translated J. F. Scanlan, *Art and Scholasticism*, 1930

Menéndez Pidal 1941   R. Menéndez Pidal, *Poesía árabe y poesía europea* (Buenos Aires, Espasa-Calpe, Colección Austral), 1941

MGH   *Monumenta Germaniæ historica* (Scriptores)

Milne and Harvey 1945   J. G. Milne and J. H. Harvey, "The Building of Cardinal College, Oxford", in *Oxoniensia*, VIII/IX, 1945, 137–53

Mon 1817   *Monasticon Anglicanum*, ed. Caley, Ellis and Bandinel, 6 vols., 1817–30

Monro 1863   C. Monro ed., *Letters of Queen Margaret of Anjou, etc.* (CS, LXXXVI), 1863

Morgan 1961   B. G. Morgan, *Canonic Design in English Mediæval Architecture*, 1961

Mortet 1911   V. Mortet ed., *Recueil de Textes relatifs à l'Histoire de l'Architecture . . . XIe-XIIe siècles* (Paris), 1911

Mortet (and Deschamps) 1929   V. Mortet and P. Deschamps edd., *Recueil de Textes relatifs à l'Histoire de l'Architecture . . . XIIe-XIIIe siècles* (Paris), 1929

MPL   Migne, *Patrologia Latina*

MRS   *Mediæval and Renaissance Studies*

Mylne 1893   R. S. Mylne, *Master Masons to the Crown of Scotland*, 1893

NA   *Neues Archiv*

Neuwirth 1888   J. Neuwirth, *Die Satzungen des Regensburger Steinmetzentages im Jahre 1459* (Vienna), 1888

NHM   *New Oxford History of Music*, 1954 ff.

Nichols 1864   J. G. Nichols, "Henry de Yeveley, one of the Architects of Westminster Hall", in TLM, II, 1864, 259–66

C. A. Nicholson, "Construction and Design", in JRIBA, 3 S, XIX, 1912, 621 ff.

NS   New Series

OAS   Oxfordshire Archæological Society

OHS   Oxford Historical Society

O'Leary 1949   De L. O'Leary, *How Greek Science passed to the Arabs*, 1949

OMT   Oxford Medieval Texts (Clarendon Press)

OS   Original Series

E. G. Paley, *Gothic Mouldings*, 6th ed., 1902

Panofsky 1946   E. Panofsky ed., *Abbot Suger on the Abbey Church of St. Denis* (Princeton, N.J.), 1946

Papworth 1848   J. W. Papworth, "Roriczer on the Construction of Pinnacles", 1848; republished in *Dictionary of Architecture* (APS), *Detached Essays*, 1853

Parker 1929   J. Parker, "Lay Subsidy Rolls, 1 Edward III, N. R. Yorks. and the City of York" (YAR, LXXIV for 1929), 1929, 104–71

PHA   *Proceedings* of the Harrow Architectural Club

Prior 1900   E. S. Prior, *A History of Gothic Art in England*, 1900

Prior 1904   ——, "Masonry Dressing", in PHA, 1904

Prior 1905   ——, *The Cathedral Builders in England*, 1905

PRO   Public Record Office

PSA   *Proceedings* of the Somerset Archæological and Natural History Society

PTS   Palestine Pilgrim's Text Society

Quicherat 1859   J. Quicherat, *Facsimile of the Sketchbook of Villard d'Honnecourt*, 1859

Raine 1835   J. Raine ed., *Reginaldi monachi Dunelmensis libellus de Admirandis* (SS, I), 1835

Raine 1859   J. Raine ed., *The Fabric Rolls of York Minster* (SS, XXXV for 1858), 1859

Raine 1879   J. Raine ed., *The Historians of the Church of York and its Archbishops* (RS, 71), 3 vols., 1879–94

Read 1926   H. Read, *English Stained Glass*, 1926

Reichensperger 1845   A. Reichensperger ed., *M. Roriczer: Das Buchlein von der Fialengerechtigkeit* (Trier), 1845

Renn 1958   D. F. Renn, "The Decoration of Guildford Castle Keep", in SAC, LV, 1958, 4–6

T. Rickman and J. H. Parker, *Gothic Architecture*, 7th ed., 1881

Riley 1854   H. T. Riley ed., *Petri Blesensis Continuatio*, 1854

Riley 1867   —— ed., *Gesta Abbatum Monasterii Sancti Albani* (RS, 28.iv), 3 vols., 1867–69

Robinson 1915   J. Armitage Robinson, "Correspondence of Bishop Oliver King and Sir Reginald Bray", in PSA, LX for 1914, 1915, **ii**, 1–10

RS   Rolls Series (Rerum Britannicarum Medii Ævi Scriptores *or* Chronicles and Memorials of Great Britain and Ireland during the Middle Ages)

RSG   *Report* of the Society of the Friends of St. George's . . . Chapel, Windsor Castle

RWC   *Report* of the Friends of Wells Cathedral

RYM   *Report* of the Friends of York Minster

S   *Speculum*—A Journal of Mediæval Studies (Mediæval Academy of America)

SAC   *Surrey Archæological Collections* (Surrey Archæological Society)

SAL   Society of Antiquaries of London

Salter 1921   H. E. Salter, *Mediæval Archives of the University of Oxford*, II (OHS, LXXIII for 1919), 1921

Salzman 1952   L. F. Salzman, *Building in England down to 1540—A Documentary History*, 1952; rev. ed. 1969

Salzman 1968   ——, *Edward I*, 1968

Scheller 1963   R. W. Scheller, *A Survey of Medieval Model Books* (Haarlem), 1963

Sedding 1881   J. D. Sedding, "The Architecture of the Perpendicular Period", in TES I, 1881, 31–44

Shelby 1961   "Medieval Masons' Tools: The Level and Plumb Rule", in TAC, II, 1961, 127–30

Shelby 1964   L. R. Shelby, "The Role of the Master Mason in Mediæval English Building", in S, XXXIX, 1964, 387–403

Shelby 1965   ——, "Medieval Masons' Tools, ii: Compass and Square", in TAC, VI, 1965, 236–48

Shelby 1970   ——, "The Education of Medieval English Master Masons", in *Mediæval Studies* (Toronto), XXXII, 1970, 1–26

Skeat 1906   W. W. Skeat ed., *The Complete Works of Geoffrey Chaucer*, 1906 etc.

Skelton and Harvey 1969   R. A. Skelton and P. D. A. Harvey, "Local Maps and Plans before 1500", in JSA, III, 1969, 496–7

SLH   Scriptores Latini Hiberniae

    J. T. Smith, *The Antiquities of Westminster*, 1807

SS   Surtees Society

Stein (1909)   H. Stein, *Les Architectes des Cathédrales gothiques* (Paris, 1909)

Stenton 1943   F. M. Stenton, *Anglo-Saxon England*, 1943; rev. ed. 1947

Stow 1603   J. Stow, *Survey of London*, ed. C. L. Kingsford, 2 vols., 1908

Street 1865   G. E. Street, *Some Account of Gothic Architecture in Spain*, 1865 etc.

Stubbs 1864   W. Stubbs ed., *Chronicles and Memorials of Richard I* (RS, 38), 2 vols., 1864–65

Stubbs 1887   —— ed., *Willelmi Malmesbiriensis Monachi de Gestis Regum Anglorum* (RS, 90), 2 vols., 1887–89

Swartwout 1932   R. E. Swartwout, *The Monastic Craftsman*, 1932

TAC   *Technology and Culture* (University of Chicago)

TAMS   *Transactions* of the Ancient Monuments Society

Taylor 1950   A. J. Taylor, "Master James of St. George", in EHR, LXV, 1950, 433–57

Taylor 1955   ——, "The Date of Clifford's Tower, York", in AJ, CXI, 1955, 153–9

Taylor 1963   ——, "Some Notes on the Savoyards in North Wales, 1277–1300", in *Genava* (Geneva), NS, XI, 1963, 289–315

TBG	*Transactions* of the Bristol and Gloucestershire Archæological Society
TCW	*Transactions* of the Cumberland and Westmorland Antiquarian and Archæological Society
Thompson 1925	A. H. Thompson, *Cathedral Churches of England*, 1925
TLM	*Transactions* of the London and Middlesex Archæological Society
TNS	*Transactions* of the Newcomen Society
Toy 1939	S. Toy, *Castles: A Short History of Fortifications*, 1939
TRIBA	*Transactions* of the Royal Institute of British Architects
Turner 1851	T. H. Turner, *Some Account of Domestic Architecture in England*, 1851
VAS	Veröffentlichungen des Archivs der Stadt Stuttgart
Vöge 1914	W. Vöge, "Die Bahnbrecher des Naturstudiums", in ZBK, n.F., XXV, 1914, 193–216
WAM	Westminster Abbey Muniments
WCA	Winchester Cathedral Archives
WCM	Winchester College Muniments
WCR	*Winchester Cathedral Record* (Friends of Winchester Cathedral)
Wharton 1691	H. Wharton, *Anglia Sacra*, 1691
Whiffen 1948	M. Whiffen, *Stuart and Georgian Churches*, 1948
Willard 1926	J. F. Willard, "Inland Transportation in England during the Fourteenth Century", in S, I, 1926, 361 ff.
Willetts 1958	W. Willetts, *Chinese Art* (Pelican), 1958
Willis 1842	R. Willis, "On the Construction of the Vaults of the Middle Ages", in TRIBA, I.ii, 1842, 1–69
	——, *Architectural Nomenclature of the Middle Ages*, 1844
Willis 1845	——, *The Architectural History of Canterbury Cathedral*, 1845
Willis and Clark 1886	R. Willis and J. W. Clark, *The Architectural History of the University of Cambridge*, 4 vols., 1886
Wissell 1929	R. Wissell, *Des alten Handwerks Recht und Gewohnheit* (Berlin), 1929

Wood 1965	M. Wood, *The English Mediæval House*, 1965
Woolley 1953	L. Woolley, *A Forgotten Kingdom*, 1953
Wright 1857	T. Wright ed., *A Volume of vocabularies*, 1857
WRJ	*Wallraf-Richartz-Jahrbuch* (Cologne)
YAJ	*Yorkshire Archæological Journal* (Yorkshire Archæological Society)
YAR	Yorkshire Archæological Society, Record Series
YMA	York Minster Archives
ZBK	*Zeitschrift für bildende Kunst* (Leipzig)

Notes to the Text

Preface

p. 10 VÖGE—Vöge 1914, 194
p. 13 CIVILIZATION—largely based on the unpublished work of the late George F. Powell, *An Introduction to Cultural Heredity* (1932), which I was privileged to read soon after it was written. See also Darlington 1969
p. 14 ÆTHELBERT—Stenton 1943, 59, 105

Introduction

p. 18 ARCHITECT—cf. Harvey 1952(2), 104
p. 20 VITRUVIUS—Krinsky 1967; cf. Briggs 1927, 110; Granger 1931, xix; Atkinson 1933, 53; Eden 1950
p. 21 ACOUSTIC JARS—Harrison 1968, with list of MSS of Vitruvius, 50
       AUTUN—Grivot and Zarnecki 1961, 17–19
p. 22 DESIGN—Harvey 1959
       VINSAUF—Faral 1924, 198, quoting *Poetria Nova* of *c.* 1210, lines 43–8, 55–6
       CHAUCER—Skeat 1906, 221 (*Troilus*, Bk I, lines 1065–9); 442–3 (*Knightes Tale*, lines 1897–1901)
p. 23 GROSSETESTE—Luard 1861, 4–5
p. 24 LYDGATE—Bergen 1906, 158 (Bk II, lines 491–8)
       BRIGGS—Briggs 1927, 59
       QUARRYING—Knoop and Jones 1933, 67–70
p. 25 SHAKESPEARE—*King Henry IV Part II*, Act I, Sc. iii
p. 26 WORCESTRE—Harvey 1969(2), 288–91
       FLEURY—Ewald 1877, 365; Mortet 1911, 33–4
       SAINT-TROND—MGH, X, 1852, 384–5; MPL, CLXXIII, col. 317–19; Mortet 1911, 159–60
p. 27 NECKAM—Wright 1857, 103–4, 109–10; Mortet and Deschamps 1929, 181–3
p. 28 ST. BRIDGET—Berthelson 1947
p. 30 PROPORTION—Enlart 1902, 56–7
       CESARIANO—Cockerell 1846, 32–41; cf. Frankl 1945; Lesser 1957
       RORITZER—Papworth 1848; Kletzl 1939, 18; Reichensperger 1845
       HONTAÑÓN—Camón 1941, Camón 1941(2)
       LAMPÉREZ—Lampérez 1930, I, 81–99
p. 31 PATTERN-BOOKS—Kletzl 1939, 7; Harvey 1950, 34, 140

p. 31   CHINA—Willetts 1958, II, 513–20
p. 32   "RENAISSANCE"—Brooke 1969
         MUSIC—NHM, II, 16, 105, 241, 274–5, 285, 313
p. 33   "ANONYMITY"—Pevsner in AR, CXVIII (1955), 259; cf. CXIX
         (1956), 2; CMH, VIII (1936), 720; Pevsner in JWC, V (1942), 232;
         for the impossibility of this position see Street 1865 chap. xxi;
         Lampérez 1930, I, 36–8; and in general Harvey 1950
         "INSTINCT"—Prior 1905, 21–2
p. 34   CLERKS—Swartwout 1932
         COMPOSTELA—Lampérez 1930, I, 68; II, 157–66; López Ferreiro
         1898
p. 35   POITIERS—Mortet 1911, 141
         CANTERBURY—AS, t. vi maii, 414
         ST. ALBANS—Riley 1867, I, 63
         CROYLAND—Riley 1854, 250
         IVRY—Mortet 1911, 276
         DURHAM—Raine 1835, 112
         ARDRES—MGH, XXIV (1879), 640; Mortet and Deschamps 1929,
         189–91
p. 36   NOTRE-DAME—Aubert 1929, 138
         ST. ALBANS—Riley 1867, II, 124, 125
         DU TEMPLE—Stein (1909), 32
         BRAINE-LE-COMTE—Read 1926, 35
         BRISTOL—TBG, LXV, 152, quoting BM, Cotton Charter IV.58
         HONNECOURT—Quicherat 1859; Hahnloser 1935
p. 37   BONNEUIL—Mortet and Deschamps 1929, 305–6
         ST-DIÉ—Divald 1931, 35; Entz 1958, 27, 39
         WINCHESTER—Goodman 1927
         HUNT—Harvey 1954, 141, quoting WCM 22137
p. 38   AQUINAS—Maritain 1930, quoting Summa Theologiæ, I, q.5, a.4, ad 1
         ÆSTHETICS—De Bruyne 1946
         HEXHAM—Hamilton 1870, 255
         MALMESBURY, BRUTON—Ibid., 361, 374
         RAMSEY—Macray 1886, 39
         CANTERBURY—Willis 1845, 13–14
p. 39   BERMONDSEY—VCH, Surrey (1902), 296
         LETTER-WRITER—Mortet and Deschamps 1929, 135–6
         ANGERS—Mortet 1911, 84–5
         BEVERLEY—Raine 1879, I, 345
p. 40   RICHARD I—Stubbs 1864, I, 197
         LINCOLN—Dimock 1860, 33–4
         AUXERRE—Mortet and Deschamps 1929, 203
         REYNOLDS—CCL, Prior Eastry's Correspondence, V.27
p. 41   ST. PAUL'S—Fowler 1911, 217
         SPIRES—Harvey 1956, 44–5; paperback 1961, 35–6; Harvey 1958
         FRANCISCANS—Esposito 1960, 24–6
         YORK—CPL 1404–15, 137–8
         EXETER—Harvey 1969(2), 117

p. 41   ST. ALBANS—Sedding 1881, 42
        BATH—Robinson 1915, 4
p. 42   COCKERELL—Cockerell 1846, 32–3, 39

Chapter I

p. 45   WALPOLE—Evans 1956, 169
p. 48   ISLAM—Lethaby 1904, 7–8; Harvey 1968
p. 49   SYMBOLISM—Harvey 1950, 1–2
        GEOMETRY—Harvey 1968, 91–3
        EUCLID—O'Leary 1949, 29, 119, 157–8
p. 52   PROPORTIONS—Csemegi 1954; Conant 1968
p. 53   VITRUVIUS—Harvey 1950, 26; Harrison 1968
        SUGER—Panofsky 1946, 46–51; Harvey 1950, 88–9
p. 54   KUFA—Creswell 1932, I.i, 46
p. 55   SARAGOSSA—Abbad Rios 1952, 80
        ARCULF—Macpherson 1889
p. 56   MOUTIER—Mortet 1911, 107–8
        NEUVY—Mortet 1911, 123–4
        ANGERS—Mortet 1911, 18
        GLABER—MPL, CXLII, col. 710; Mortet 1911, 4
        RHEIMS—MPL, CXLII, col. 1417 ff.; Mortet 1911, 40–1
p. 57   SPANS—Conant 1959
p. 58   WESTMINSTER—Stubbs 1887, I, 280
        GRETSYD etc.—Harmer 1936, 98; Harmer 1952, 292, 353–5, 566,
        573; Harvey 1954, 89, 119, 261
p. 59   COUTANCES—Mortet 1911, 72–3
p. 60   NORMANS—Stubbs 1887, I, 306
        INDUSTRIALISM—Knoop and Jones 1933, 2–4
p. 61   WESTMINSTER—Clay 1944
p. 62   FÉCAMP—MPL, CLXVI, col. 1175 ff.; Mortet 1911, 343–6
p. 64   WOODSTOCK—Stubbs 1887, II, 485; Arnold 1879, 244
        DUNSTABLE—Mon 1817, VI.i, 239
        LE MANS—Mortet 1911, 165 ff.
p. 65   AUXERRE—Mortet 1911, 97–8
        CHEAPSIDE—Stow 1603, I, 257, 268; II, 329
        DARTINGTON—Emery 1960, 198–202; *PRO*, C.145/278 no. 37; cf.
        Emery 1970, 185–202
        KENILWORTH—Harvey 1946, 93, 98
p. 66   WINCHESTER—Extracts by C. W. Little from *WCM* 22078–22122
        (Bursars' Account Rolls 1394–1448) PEYVRE—Luard 1872, V, 242–3
p. 67   ROMSEY—Amherst 1895, 7
        MALMESBURY—Brewer and Martin 1879, II, 365–6

Chapter II

p. 69   SEVILLE—Guerrero Lovillo 1952, 39
        COLERIDGE—*Lectures on Shakespeare and Milton*
p. 70   APPRENTICIUS—Latham 1965, 26
p. 71   STAMFORDHAM—Dodds 1926, 311

p. 72   HARRISON—in R. Holinshed, *Chronicles*
      WESTMINSTER—*WAM* 17856

p. 73   LÉRINS—Mortet 1911, 231
      OUDENBOURG—MPL, CLXXIV, col. 1417; Mortet 1911, 174–5

p. 74   BARBASTRO—Menéndez Pidal 1941, 33–5

p. 75   HEREDITY—Darlington 1969, 120n, 624n
      JAPAN—Harvey 1954, 11
      SCOTLAND—Mylne 1893

p. 76   RUSSELL—Furnivall 1868, 187, 381
      MAGISTER—Latham 1965, 285

p. 77   STATUS—HKW, I, 201–3
      TOURNAI—MPL, CCXI, col. 493; Mortet and Deschamps 1929, 164–5
      SALISBURY—Luard 1872, III, 391

p. 78   BIARD—Mortet and Deschamps 1929, 290–1
      REWARDS—Harvey 1950, 44–5; cf. Harvey 1954, 327–32

p. 79   FAMILIES—Harvey 1951; Harvey 1952(2), 101
      CARNARVON—Ellis 1838, 220
      FELSTEDE—Salzman 1952, 436
      SAMPSON—Salter 1921, 21
      NEW COLLEGE—Harvey 1947(2), 56 note 2; Harvey 1952(2), 105–6
      BURY—Salzman 1952, 591–2
      RAGHTON—Dixon and Raine 1863, 432; Collins 1897, 17; Parker 1929, 166

p. 80   RAUGHTON—Graham 1925, 303–10
      MELTON'S WORKS—Dixon and Raine 1863, 414, 419, 432–3
      STOWELL—Harvey 1954, 254–5; information from *WAM* by L. E. Tanner (personal communication)
      CLERICAL ARCHITECTS—Harvey 1954, xi, 3–4, 324

p. 81   WAVERLEY—Harvey 1945, 49–50

p. 82   WALSINGHAM—Chapman 1907, I, 10 ff., 151–66
      WYKEHAM—Hayter 1970, 29–32

p. 83   WILL—Lowth 1758, 385, 386 ff.

p. 84   WYNFORD—Harvey 1949; *WCA*, Priory Register 1 (1345–1496), f. 8

p. 85   LESYNGHAM—*EFR*, 2640, 2641
      YEVELEY—Knoop and Jones 1937, 77; Harvey 1944(2); Harvey 1950, 28, 139; Harvey 1952(2), 101–2, 103

p. 86   DEVISOR—*Ordinances of the King's Household* (SAL), 1790

Chapter III

p. 88   SHELBY—Shelby 1970, 2
      HONNECOURT—Hahnloser 1935
      LITERACY—Jenkinson 1926, 134–6; Harvey 1950, 47, 142
      WESTMINSTER—*WAM*, 16000 (f), (g)
      PINKHILL—Monro 1863, 19–21; Harvey 1948, 115; paperback 1967, 176–7

p. 89   FRENCH—Harvey 1947, 6; Harvey 1945(2), 232

p. 91   VERTUES—Harvey 1957, 93–4

p. 92   GUILDS—*e.g.* at York, records deposited in City Archives
          RANKS—Harvey 1950, 7
p. 93   CARVERS—Harvey 1950, 37, 141; Harvey 1954, 324
          SIMON—Harvey 1945(2), 232, 233–4
p. 94   LYDGATE—Bergen 1918, Bk I, Lines 1199–1201; MacCracken 1934,
          801, *Everything to his Semblable*, lines 35–6
          SINAN—Egli 1954, 39
          ADELARD—Haskins 1924, 20–42; Harvey 1968, 91–4
p. 95   HOSPITALITY—Harvey 1950, 45–6
p. 96   RAOUL—Hitti 1927, 160
          "LALYS"—*Dictionary of Architecture* (APS); cf. Knowles and Hadcock
          1953, 112
p. 97   AUMERVAL—MGH, XXIV, 1879, 589–90; Mortet and Deschamps
          1929, 50–2
p. 98   DRAWINGS—Creswell 1932, I.i, 109–11
          CONANT—Conant 1959, 57
          MEASURES—Harvey 1950, 32, 140
p. 100   MARKS—Harvey 1966, 117–18

Chapter IV

p. 102   STUTTGART—Kletzl 1939
          WINCHESTER—Harvey 1965, 122
          BOARDS—Harvey 1938, 741
          GLAZE—Woolley 1953, 93–5
p. 103   CONRAD—*Kronijk van Arent te Bocop* in CDN, 2 S, V, 1860, 106–7;
          Annales Egmundani, NS, I, 1863, 21
          REGENSBURG—Neuwirth 1888; Harvey 1950, 21–2
          RORITZER—Reichensperger 1845; Papworth 1848
p. 104   3RD POINT—Knoop, Jones and Hamer 1938, 120
          SECRECY—Knoop and Jones 1937, 58; Harvey 1943, 32
p. 105   CONTRACTS—Salzman 1952, Appendix B
          VALENCIA—Street 1865, 265
          ADUARD—Mortet and Deschamps 1929, xviii
          COPYING—Harvey 1950(2), 14 ff.
          DIJON—Conant 1959, 96
p. 106   DURHAM—Prior 1900, 98, 107–9
          UNITY—Harvey 1962, 134–5
          VAULTS—Fitchen 1961
p. 107   TROYES—BEC, 5 S, III, 1862, 232–3; MAF, XIX, 1849, 61
          HURDLES—Leask 1946, 86–7 and Plate IV
          RAMSEY—Raine 1879, I, 434
p. 108   GERALD—Butler 1937, 89, quoting *De rebus a se gestis*, c. xii
          TOWER—Harvey 1944, 24
          SKENFRITH—Toy 1939, 100
          FORTINUS—Harvey 1945, 52
          SCALES—Harvey 1950, 32
          SURVEY—Harvey 1952, 4–5
          FEET—Doursther 1840, 402–19; Csemegi 1954, 45

p. 109 CLUNY—Conant 1959, 116; cf. Conant 1963
    DRAWING—Harvey 1950, 31–2; cf. Harvey 1953; Shelby 1965
    SETTING-OUT—Willis 1842
    PEN—Knoop and Jones 1933, 54 note 6
    TRACING-HOUSE—Harvey 1962, 164–5; Harvey 1966, 114–15; Harvey 1969
    REDMAN—Harvey 1945(3), 52
p. 110 EXETER—Thompson 1925, 141; *EFR*, 2641
    ETON—Willis and Clark 1886, I, 405; cf. HKW, I, 289
    LEBONS—Harvey 1945(3), 57; cf. Salzman 1952, 19
    DRAWINGS—Andrews 1925, 80 ff.; Briggs 1927, 86 ff.; Harvey 1950, 29–36; Biddle 1961; Harvey 1965, 122; Harvey 1966, 115–17; cf. Harvey 1944(2), ix, Figs. 7, 12, 14
    PLANS—Skelton and Harvey 1969
    CONTINENTAL DRAWINGS—Kletzl 1939; Bucher 1968
    HONNECOURT—Hahnloser 1935; Branner 1960; Branner 1963; cf. Scheller 1963
p. 112 RHEIMS—Branner 1958
    STRASSBURG—Haug 1956, 8–10
    BRANNER—Branner 1963, 146 note 40
    CENTRAL EUROPE—Csemegi 1954; Booz 1956
p. 113 PUCHSPAUM—Grimschitz 1947
    BUCHER—Bucher 1968, 49
p. 114 TRACING HOUSES—Harvey 1950, 30; Salzman 1952, 21–2; RWC 1954, 7; RWC 1957, 8–11; Harvey 1966, 114–15; Harvey 1969
    YORK—Raine 1859, 200
p. 116 WESTMINSTER—*WAM* 19633
    SCARBOROUGH—*PRO*, E.101/482/8
    HERLAND—CPR 1391–96, 707, 725
    MODELS—Briggs 1929; Maere 1936; Kletzl 1939, 13; Shelby 1964, 391–2
    CUTOUTS—Bucher 1968, 66–8; cf. Willis 1842, 39–40
p. 118 TEMPLATES—Salzman 1952, 20–1; cf. Harvey 1947(2)
    WESTMINSTER—BM, Add. Roll 27018
    YEVELEY—Nichols 1864; Harvey 1944(3), 50–3; Harvey 1947(2); Harvey 1952(2)

Chapter V

p. 120 SQUARING—Creswell 1932, I.i, 110
    BETHLEHEM—Harvey and Harvey 1938, 9–10
    CLUNY— Conant 1959, 116, 306–7; Conant 1968(2), 75–7
p. 122 SUGER—Panofsky 1946
p. 123 CALIXTUS II—Grivot and Zarnecki 1961, 18
p. 124 INSTRUMENTS—Panofsky 1946, 35
    KIDSON—Kidson 1967, 101
    NUMEROLOGY—Conant 1968; cf. Bannister 1968
    JERUSALEM—Creswell 1932, I.i, 73–5; cf. Creswell 1958, 19–21, 75–9
p. 125 OPTICAL ADJUSTMENTS—Creswell 1958, 270

p. 125 SYSTEMS—Frankl 1960, 702–34

CHAUCER—Skeat 1906, 101, *Parlement of Foules*, lines 22–5

WYKEHAM—Cockerell 1846

p. 126 ALBUMS—Scheller 1963

BOOKLETS—Frankl 1960, 144–54

CHAPTER HOUSES—Harvey 1956, 179; paperback 1961, 174

INSTRUMENTS—Harvey 1950, 15–16, 31–2; Salzman 1952, 342; Shelby 1961; Shelby 1965; Bucher 1968, 52

p. 127 SURFACES—Prior 1904

SQUARES—Funck-Hellet 1951, 111; Morgan 1961; Shelby 1965

p. 128 VAULTS—Harvey 1944(2), 65; Harvey 1947, 18–19, 52, 57, 120; Harvey 1950, 26; Harvey 1962, 135, 155 note 5

CLOISTERS—Harvey 1956, 179; paperback 1961, 174

QUADRANGLE—Harvey 1944(2), 30; Harvey 1945, 52–3; Milne and Harvey 1945, 149–51: Harvey 1954, 167; Harvey 1961, 55; Emery 1970, 117–36

p. 129 GALILEE—Harvey 1961, 51–2; Harvey 1962, 157 note 62

CORRECTIONS—Harvey 1965, 113 and note 2

NORMANS—Harvey 1966, 112–14

p. 130 WELLS—Harvey 1956, 72; paperback 1961, 57

LINCOLN—Harvey 1956, 74–82; paperback 1961, 59–61

p. 131 TOWERS—Harvey 1956

LANGLEY—Desimoni 1877; Harvey 1948, 71; paperback 1967, 117–18

PADUA—Harvey 1938, 741

DIAPERS—Harvey 1948, 71; paperback 1967, 117–18; Harvey 1950, 76–7

REDCLIFFE—Harvey 1966, 125

ELY—Harvey 1950, 77

p. 132 CANTERBURY—Harvey 1946(2); Harvey 1962, 161–2

REINFORCEMENT—JRIBA, 3 S, LIII, 199; Harvey 1950, 18, 139

p. 133 WITNEY—*PRO*, E.101/468/6, rot. 25–69, 106–18; Goodman 1927(2), 242; Harvey 1954, 298, 296, 264 (Thomas Mason V, VI); Hingeston-Randolph 1894, I, 218, 225; Kitchin 1892, 124, 235

p. 135 HAMMER BEAMS—Wood 1965, 313–21; cf. Emery 1970, 237–44

Chapter VI

p. 137 PARIS—Lespinasse and Bonnardot 1879; Colombier 1953, 37; cf. Harvey 1950, 22

p. 138 STRASSBURG—Frankl 1960, 117

p. 139 CONSTITUTIONS—Knoop, Jones and Hamer 1938

p. 141 REGENSBURG—Neuwirth 1888; cf. Janner 1876; Wissell 1929, II, 332–408, 685–722; Harvey 1950, 21–3; Frankl 1960, 126–34

p. 142 YORK—Taylor 1955, 156; cf. Harvey 1961, 51

MASTERS—CPR 1247–58, 538

HEREFORD—CPL 1305–42, 196

WINCHESTER—Wharton 1691, 271

p. 143 TRAVEL—Willard 1926; cf. Harvey 1947, 93–4, 152, 157, 173–8, 221, 224; Harvey 1950(2), 24; Harvey 1969(2), xiii–xv
FOTHERINGHAY—Knoop and Jones 1933, 220–23; Salzman 1952, 505–9
p. 144 LOMBARDY—Conant 1959, 53; Frankl 1960, 111–12
p. 145 JACKSON—Jackson 1913, I, 213
p. 146 ATHELSTAN—Fowler 1882, 33–5, 81, 89–93
LONDON—Turner 1851, 275–83
YORK—Harvey 1966(2)
p. 147 GERMANY—Frankl 1960, 122–34, 139–54
LONDON—Knoop and Jones 1933, 224–6
p. 148 EDUCATION—Frankl 1960, 132–4
p. 149 MASTERWORKS—Frankl 1960, 140–1
MASONS' MARKS—Coulton 1928, 242–64; Davis 1939; Csemegi 1954, 38–41; Davis 1956; cf. Harvey 1966, 117–18
p. 150 FREEMASONRY—Knoop and Jones 1947
YORK—*YMA*, Chapter Acts 1565–1634, f. 332v

Chapter VII

p. 151 CURVILINEAR—Enlart 1906; Bock 1961; Bock 1962
PERPENDICULAR—Sedding 1881; Harvey 1947; Harvey 1962
p. 152 ZIRYAB—Lévi-Provençal 1938, 69–74
PREJUDICE—Menéndez Pidal 1941, 35–7
p. 153 BUSBECQ—Forster 1927; Blunt 1950, 10–14
OGEE QUATREFOIL—Willetts 1958, 261
p. 154 POLYCHROMY—Renn 1958, 5–6
CUSPING—Daras (1938)
LICHFIELD—Lethaby 1925, 90; Harvey 1961, 52
TRAVEL—Harvey 1950, 21, endpapers
p. 155 ST. GEORGE—Taylor 1950; HKW, I, 203–5
ACRE—Harvey 1954, 100
LE MANS—MPL, CLVII, col. 124, 127–8, 131–2; Mortet 1911, 292–4
CRUSADERS—Lawrence 1936; Creswell 1952, II, 60
p. 156 AL-AZHAR—Creswell 1952, I, 256
TRACERY—Creswell 1952, plates 22, 27, 38, 40, 41, 56, 84, 85, 87, 92, 98, 101, 104, 115, 122; Harvey 1962, 158; Harvey 1966, 126–7
EDWARD I—Salzman 1968
p. 157 SAVOY—Taylor 1963
YORK—Harvey 1950, 78
p. 158 FRANCE—Branner 1965, 64–5, 128–33
CLERMONT—Branner 1965, 98, 141–2
p. 159 MOULDINGS—Harvey 1962, 150
RAMSEY—Harvey 1943, 40–1
p. 160 PERPENDICULAR—Harvey 1944(2), 69–74
WILTON DIPTYCH—Harvey 1961(2)
ROOFS—Harvey and Harvey 1936; Harvey 1938; Harvey 1948(2)
p. 162 YORK—Hughes 1955
GOTHIC—Heyman 1966, 250

p. 163 BEAUVAIS—Heyman 1967
    MODELS, MILAN—Heyman 1968, 185
p. 165 LICHFIELD—Heyman 1966, 263–4

Epilogue and Conclusions

p. 166 ENCYCLOPÆDISM—Harvey 1948, 70–1
p. 167 GOTHIC SURVIVAL—Harvey 1947, 145–8; Whiffen 1948, 9–13; Clapham 1952
    LETHABY—Lethaby 1906, 220
p. 168 GRIDIRON—Davis 1947, 79
p. 169 POLYGONAL TRANSEPT—Harvey 1962(2), 86
p. 170 ST. MARY ALDERMARY—Cobb 1942, 73 note

Appendices

p. 193 GEOMETRY—J. O. Halliwell, *Rara Mathematica* (1841), 56, quoting BM, Sloane MS. 213, f. 120

General Index

Mediæval architects, artists and craftsmen are listed separately after the main index. Numerals in italics refer to the figures on the photographic plates. The line illustrations on text pages are indexed in the four collected entries: Drawings, Maps, Mouldings *and* Plans.

Index of Architects

This index includes also artists and craftsmen, specified: the letter C indicates a carpenter. The names without addition are of masons.